HOLDING THE FORT

JOHN KENT

HOLDING THE FORT

Studies in
Victorian Revivalism

LONDON
EPWORTH PRESS

© John Kent 1978

First published 1978
by Epworth Press
All rights reserved
No part of this publication
may be reproduced, stored in a
retrieval system, or
transmitted, in any form or by
any means, electronic, mechanical,
photocopying, recording or
otherwise, without the prior
permission of Epworth Press

Enquiries should be addressed to
The Methodist Publishing House
Wellington Road
Wimbledon
London SW 19 8EU

7162 0303 0

Printed in Great Britain
by Ebenezer Baylis and Son Limited
The Trinity Press, Worcester, and London

To my wife

Acknowledgements

IN the past, revivalism has been more an American than an English subject, and it will be obvious that I have learned much from historians like W. R. Cross and W. G. McLoughlin. There seem to be no important manuscript sources surviving from Moody's visits to England, though printed sources, including newspapers, are plentiful. I am grateful to Lambeth Palace Library for access to the Tait Papers; to the Cowley Fathers for access to the papers of R. M. Benson; to the officials of the Salvation Army; to Hartley Victoria College (as it was then) where I saw Hugh Bourne's manuscripts; and to the trustees of Baillie Street Chapel, Rochdale, who enabled me to find Caughey's revival registers. Only those who remember Shude Hill, Manchester, can guess what I owed to its vanished bookstalls. On a personal level, I am indebted to the late G. Kitson Clark (and his nineteenth-century history group), to Professor Geoffrey Best, to Professor Owen Chadwick, and to Henry Rack, all of whom read parts of this book; they are not, of course, responsible for my interpretation of the material: I have also owed much to the advice and friendship of John Walsh, of Jesus College. Most of all I am indebted to my wife, who first suggested this subject to me.

J.K.

Contents

Contents

1

The American Revivalist Tradition

THIS book is a discussion of the part played by religious revivalism, and by the American professional religious revivalist, in the religious world of nineteenth-century England. It was during the Victorian period that popular Protestantism began to lose its grip on English society. This was true despite the strength of the denominations. It is therefore against a background of slowly changing popular religion that the role of the professional revivalist has to be studied. Of course, the religious crisis had its intellectual aspects, as for instance the increasing doubts about the validity of the claim that the Christian Bible was a unique direct revelation of the mind of God, or even a revelation at all; the parallel growth in the prestige of the sciences as sources of certain knowledge; and the revolution in the attitude to time and change which Darwinism and the philosophy of history fostered. More important, however, was the overall process of secularization which had been affecting Western culture before the Victorian era, but which developed rapidly in the nineteenth century.

The visible form of this secularizing process was the collapse of the old compact of Christendom, the assumption that Church and State fitted together to form a single, divinely-intended society, in which the Church was responsible for men's souls and had a rather vague authority in moral matters. In the nineteenth century, Western society showed a constant determination to reduce the role of the Church, and even to reject its presence altogether, a determination which has to be taken into account before one accepts the common assertion that 'Victorian England was religious'.[1] All over Europe

---

[1] Owen Chadwick, *The Victorian Church* (London, 1966), p. 1. He continued: 'Its churches thrived and multiplied, its best minds brooded over divine metaphysic and argued about moral principle, its authors and painters and architects and poets seldom

established Churches were either abolished or made as far as possible socially and politically powerless. The State took over the greater part of education and secularized its content so thoroughly that in England, for example, the compulsory 'act of worship' with which morning school still begins is quite unrelated to the curriculum, and often not more than nominally Christian. Civil marriage and divorce were introduced. The Churches felt increasingly that they were being pushed to the margin of society, that the hostility of a secular world was tightening its grip on them. This social pressure partly explains the appearance of new religious sects in England in the nineteenth century: one religious response to the growing isolation of religious institutions and ideas was to accept and intensify the isolation, to glory in the eccentricity of irrational opinion and divergent organization. This was also one reason for the popularity of the professional religious revivalist who, even if he did not succeed in invading and colonizing the surrounding non-Christian society, at least helped to restore confidence to those inside the Evangelical Pietist tradition.[2]

From the point of view of those outside the world of Evangelical Pietism, however, the professional revivalist was chiefly important at the political level. This was not because the revivalists showed any marked political preference in their

---

forgot that art and literature shadowed eternal truth and beauty, its legislators professed outward and often accepted inward allegiance to divine law, its men of empire ascribed national greatness to the Providence of God and the Protestant faith.' No doubt a case could be made; but who were 'the best minds', etc.?

[2] It is necessary to define what is meant by 'Evangelical Pietism'. The phrase is intended to cover the way in which both Anglicanism, through what is usually called the 'Anglican Evangelical' movement, and Dissent, through what is often called the 'Evangelical Revival', developed after the final collapse of the seventeenth century hopes of a permanent Puritan revolution. There was an ethos which could be found on both sides of the division between Establishment and Dissent, an ethos which showed remarkable affinities with the Pietist movement which developed in German Lutheranism in the late seventeenth century. All these groups had the same tendency to withdraw as far as possible from secular society, to organize on the basis of small, local *ecclesiola*, to ignore denominational control if possible, to use prohibitions in order to concentrate the life of the member entirely on the concerns of the tiny religious community. Evangelical Pietism was anti-intellectual, anti-humanist. It represented a late seventeenth century regrouping of the classical Protestant movements, once it was clear that the world at large remained firmly in the grip of Satan, and that the Second Advent, the only final solution to the problem of the Church and the world, was not going to take place as yet. The true importance of Wesleyan Methodism lay in its tendency not to conform to the Evangelical Pietist forms of belief and behaviour.

preaching. Part of their British constituency, however, was the Nonconformist world which was struggling to maintain its influence and position in a rapidly changing society; it did so by putting pressure on the Liberal Party, the only British political organization prepared to bargain for its votes. The revivalists mattered in this connexion because their visits played an important part in sustaining the self-confidence and identity of the Nonconformist section of society. The existence of a nation-wide, politically identified, socially coherent popular Protestantism was vital to the electoral fortunes of the Liberal Party in the last part of the nineteenth century.

The combination of intellectual change and social secularization also made men less willing to believe in the possibility of personal religious experience. This is a perennial problem, whose intensity has varied from one generation to another, and which in the eighteenth century had seemed to be solved by the revival of the classical Protestant religious pattern. In this pattern the individual was led to look for a supernatural personal deliverance from an acute state of allegedly divinely-inspired remorse at the thought of his own sinfulness. Belief in the efficacy of this traditional pattern (which may be seen vivildy at work in the spiritual autobiographies written by Wesleyan itinerant preachers in the late eighteenth century) dominated the English Protestant world until about 1830; so much so that the first American professional religious revivalist to visit England in the nineteenth century, Lorenzo Dow, who came in 1806 and 1818, was largely employed in helping to extend its grip in rural areas where a crumbling Anglicanism had for the moment lost its influence on the working classes in the countryside. Dow also played a vital role in the foundation of the Primitive Methodist Connexion, a Methodist body whose significance in the development of the Victorian working-class has not yet been properly understood.

By 1830, however, the classical Protestant tradition had begun to lose both its charm and its efficiency. Not only did the Oxford Movement start partly in reaction against the sterility of Charles Simeon's kind of Anglican Evangelicalism; but, at a very different level, a Broad Churchman like Benjamin Jowett of Balliol was also in full retreat from an Evangelical upbringing. For men of this kind, Evangelicals, Anglo-

Catholics and Broad Churchmen, the question of the validity of a specifically *Christian* and personal religious experience became acute. A generation of Anglo-Catholics after John Henry Newman claimed to have an overwhelming personal sense of the presence of Christ in the eucharistic elements. Broad Churchmen inevitably felt less certain and, although it might be said that the religious experience of Jowett, or, for that matter, Matthew Arnold, was christocentric, it would be difficult to decide how far either man felt that this was a relationship which involved a supernatural level of communication, and how far their sense of communion with Jesus Christ was simply a matter of being deeply affected by his recorded actions and teachings as mediated through the mind of the historic Church. The Evangelicals, on the other hand, remained faithful as they believed to the eighteenth-century tradition, vocabulary and all, and one reason for the nineteenth-century popularity of the American revivalist in England in the Evangelical world was that he claimed to be able to lead people into what might be called, in modern terms, an existential awareness of the realities underlying the classical Protestant pattern of religious behaviour. In his own terms, that is, he claimed to be able to produce the circumstances in which men would be open both to an invading sense of self-despair and to the divine intervention which brought them the assurance that their sinfulness was forgiven.

It may seem strange that England should turn to American experts for a nineteenth-century revival of religion but the situation becomes more explicable when one remembers that, whereas between 1800 and 1830 English Evangelical Pietism was declining, in America, on the other hand, this was the period of the second Great Awakening, which lasted from 1795 to 1835, and of the highly successful revivalism of the 1820s which is associated with the name of Charles Finney. Moreover, since it was in the United States that 'revivalism' first became fully self-conscious, it was natural that the first fully professional religious revivalists should have been Americans. To understand all this clearly, however, it is necessary to look briefly at the history of the word 'revivalism', which is itself ambiguous, and which has been used to describe two very different phenomena. On the one hand, it is used to describe familiar nation-wide movements covering two or three generations, like the eighteenth-century Evangelical Revival or the familiar 'Neo-Anglican' revival of the nineteenth century; on the other, the word is also used to describe the activities of itinerant missioners whose local 'revivals' might affect only a single church in a single city and last for no more than a few days. To understand how these two different uses of the word came about, one has to go back to the seventeenth century, to the time when the English Protestant tradition was finally breaking down into separate denominations. The Dissenting Churches of the later seventeenth century were gathered from the wreckage of the hopes of the Commonwealth period for a drastically purified English national church. In England and in the American Colonies, the Presbyterians, Independents and Baptists set up their distinctive patterns of autonomous local churches, tiny islands of pure religion in the vast wilderness of a fallen world. Each local church was commonly bound together by a Covenant, and the feeling of social solidarity, of belonging to a community complete in itself and needing nothing from its outside environment was so strong that great prejudice developed against anyone 'marrying out', as the saying was— that is, marrying someone who was not a member of the same sect.

These gathered churches soon faced the problem of survival. How were the children of those who were already members of the local church to be gathered in their turn into the religious community? In theory at any rate, the children could not be admitted unless they showed signs of conversion, and the problem was made all the more pressing because few people questioned that unconverted children would go to Hell when they died and stay there for all eternity. This was the theological level of parental anxiety, but there were other, perhaps equally compelling, reasons why parents should have become deeply concerned to see their children safely established in the ambit of their chosen sect. They felt that if they did so the children were much less likely to fall into bad company, to pursue unsuitable ambitions, or to repudiate the ideas and standards of their parents.

In the late seventeenth and early eighteenth centuries, the

American churches seemed to have found ways of coping with the problem. By means of the famous Half-Way Covenant, for instance, the children of members of the local church were allowed to become members themselves on the understanding that they must justify their admission in the long run by showing the appropriate signs of conversion. They did not find it easy, however, to fulfil this commitment, for in the Puritan tradition 'conversion' was defined in terms of the doctrine of justification by faith, and meant that a man had to recognize that he was helplessly guilty in the eyes of God and that he needed a forgiveness which was mediated only through Jesus, the Son of God. This human guilt was so far-reaching and all-pervading that man was almost defined in terms of it, becoming in himself evil and repulsive (fallen) in the eyes of his creator, God. Once he had admitted his condemned state, a man had both to accept in humble faith the forgiveness that God offered and also to confess that this acceptance was itself really another divine act for which he ought to be truly grateful. It was not enough to understand these propositions intellectually and grant one's assent to them, however; one had also to incorporate their spiritual sense into the core of one's being, emotionally and subjectively; one had to live through an experience of self-rejection that left one almost without God and without hope— and then, in the depths of the crisis, it was asserted, the truly religious man whom God wanted to save found that a new, personal level of meaning had been added to what before had been only an intellectual awareness of the forgiveness that God offered men in Christ. He then felt that Christ had died for him personally, that the Father no longer rejected him, that he was starting his life all over again. Without this new beginning, or 'conversion', he could not hope to escape damnation. He must learn to be utterly humbled, absolutely dependent on God, passive in the hands of Providence. His spiritual health required little in the way of sacramental support, but did necessitate the complete self-surrender, a surrender whose chief social consequence was not withdrawal from the world into a monastic community, in the medieval fashion, but a withdrawal from the secular world into the religious community of the sect. The best literary description of this process may be found in John Bunyan's *Grace Abounding*.

The late seventeenth-century evangelical pietist still believed that the kind of religious pattern which Bunyan set down ought to be the normal religious experience of the Christian, but he knew that few people spontaneously reproduced it in their own lives. As a result, signs of what is meant by 'American revivalism' can already be found before 1700. The New England of that period was made up largely of small, compact townships, many of them dominated by the Independent or Presbyterian tradition, which in England was rapidly becoming a minority way of life. Revivalism was originally a social event within one of these congregations; the first kind of revivalist was the local minister: one of the earliest was Solomon Stoddard of Northampton, Massachusetts, in the 1680s. The method was always the use of language combined with psychological contagion; the young people of a particular place were always tackled as a group as well as individually. The capacity of these New England townships to generate collective hysteria at this time may also be seen in the Salem witch-mania in 1692; revivalism grew as belief in witches declined.

In English Nonconformity this kind of revivalism, and therefore the use of the word 'revival' in this specific sense, hardly occurs between 1660 and 1730. Instead, the English non-Anglican religious institutions grew weaker; they faced the same problem of survival but they hit on no particular solution. Undoubtedly, the primary reason for this was the greater relative feeling of political and social failure which hung over English Nonconformity after the Restoration. The Baptist and Congregationalist Churches had to be recreated, partly by eighteenth-century impulses coming from the Wesleyan movement, partly by the social impact of the new industrialism of the nineteenth century,[3] before they recovered something of the self-confidence of early seventeenth-century Puritanism; English Presbyterianism never recovered at all.

As for the eighteenth-century Wesleyan movement, it had little in common with the revivals which had been happening in the American Colonies, so that to speak of a Wesleyan

[3] See C. Binfield, *So Down to Prayers*, 1977.

'revival' is to use the word in a different sense. The Wesleyan
Revival remains a historical problem and its origins are not
fully understood.[4] Instead of the limited, local, and, in the
long run, not very successful revival which Jonathan Edwards
produced at Northampton, Massachusetts, in 1736, the
Wesleyan movement (with occasional moments of intense
excitement) flowed gradually across England, a national as
much as a local event, forming a new, institutionalized
religious community, extending in time from 1738 to the
waning of the energy of Primitive Methodism in the mid-
nineteenth century, and sustained even further if one includes
the Salvation Army. The eighteenth-century Wesleyan movement did not revive the existing local parish or Dissenting
congregations on the American model; local churches were
the end-product, not the take-off point of the Wesleyan Connexion. The Wesleyan societies of the nineteenth century had
to face in their turn the problem of how to retain the children
of the congregation, but the original revival was among the
adults; it did not strengthen existing religious institutions—
it tended to weaken them—but formed new ones out of men
and women who had no deep sense of having belonged to a
religious community before, even though they might have
attended parish churches or dissenting chapels. For many
years, of course, John Wesley even resisted the development
of his societies into local churches on the Puritan or New
England model; he thought of them more as voluntary
associations for the pursuit of holiness. This is not to say that
local revivals did not ever happen, but this was usually in the
distinct social context of Anglican Evangelicalism: at
Haworth, for example, where Grimshaw, the incumbent, was
much more a seventeenth-century Puritan than a Wesleyan;
and at Everton, in Bedfordshire, where another parson,
Berridge, had his young people in an uproar for months in
1759.

During the late eighteenth and early nineteenth centuries,
however, the American use of the word 'revival' began to
change. Originally, whether the word was employed to
describe the internal excitement of a New England con-

---

[4] See J. Walsh, 'Origins of the Evangelical Revival' in *Essays in Modern Church
History*, ed. G. V. Bennett and J. D. Walsh, 1966.

gregation as it strove to save the souls of its children, or whether it was used to describe the steady seeping of the Wesleyan movement across England, 'revival' meant an event which was thought of as the direct, unpredictable work of God. A revival was an allegedly supernatural phenomenon; or, to put it the other way, the occasional, spontaneous occurrence of a revival, whether in the American or the Wesleyan sense, was regarded as important evidence both of the existence of a God who could be seen immediately at work in human life, and also of his benevolence towards the particular area concerned. With the new century, however, the atmosphere began to change. It is not altogether clear why this was so. Fundamental to the problem was the fact that the change took place in America before it happened in England. This may have been largely practical, for, at the beginning of the nineteenth century, war, economic crisis and social dislocation had led to the virtual collapse of American institutional religion. As in France after 1815, the religious counter-attack was self-conscious, and the methods of the Great Awakening were deliberately wheeled out to produce the Second Awakening in New England from 1797, and the Western revivals, which stemmed from the Cane Ridge Camp Meeting in August, 1801. As this new period of revivalism continued, the belief that revivals were events that could not be organized came increasingly under question; by the 1820s the nature of revivalism was being hotly discussed in the United States and the debate was brought to England in the 1830s.

The situation was clearly stated in a book called *The History and Character of American Revivals of Religion*, which was published in London with a preface dated 1 March, 1832, and written by the Reverend Calvin Colton, a New England minister anxious to promote the fortunes of the new revivalism. Colton said that he was writing because England had not yet made up its mind about the value of the American system. Information about East Coast revivals had appeared sporadically in British religious magazines for the previous few years.

Colton distinguished firmly between two types of revival. In the first, the old-fashioned kind, the hand of God has always been more undeniable. For nobody expected, nobody prayed, nobody tried for such a work—as far as appeared. And this till a few years past was the more ordinary character of revivals of religion in American churches, and Christians waited for them as men are wont to wait for showers of rain. . . . And it is only within the past few years that the promotion of revivals by human instrumentality has, to any considerable extent, been made a subject of study and an object of systematic efforts.

Colton believed in this second kind of revivalism. He dismissed the argument that men ought to wait for God's time as an 'expression of sloth';[5] and summed up his views in the assertion that revivals were now

> matters of human calculation by the arithmetic of faith in God's arrangements. . . . Formerly a visitation of the Spirit was unexpected and apparently unasked . . . now it is the divine blessing upon measures concerted by men and executed by men, where the instruments are obvious. . . . A host of ardent, devoted revival men has been raised up.[6]

For Colton, then, a revival was a historical event rather than a supernatural intervention. It seemed natural to him that the date of a revival should be fixed in advance, that posters should be printed and halls booked ahead of time, and that one might take for granted that, provided enough prayer had been offered, God was bound to co-operate. Indeed, if he refused, or seemed to refuse, this meant that there was a lack of faith somewhere in the religious community itself.

How the change took place is more difficult to say. In a sense American writers like Calvin Colton were only admitting what had always been true about the local New England revivals. It is obvious enough that Jonathan Edwards set out to preach his congregation into a state of religious hysteria and that his merciless analysis of the nature of everlasting punishment was carefully calculated to achieve his end. If no one had thought of the result as 'arranged', or as less than the work of God himself, this was partly because of the Protestant reverence for preaching. As long as the only technique used

[5] Colton, op. cit., p.6.
[6] Ibid., p.9.

was the technique of the sermon, it was possible for the Protestant to think of human instrumentality as absent, for the Puritan conception of the sermon meant that the human element in its composition and delivery could only, by itself, frustrate the will of God. The Word was only spoken with power when the external, divine Spirit of Power himself spoke a Word which was by no means easily identifiable with the human words which the congregation heard spoken by the preacher. But it was not of the evangelist as preacher that Calvin Colton was thinking when he spoke of *human* instrumentality; it was something more than preaching that he had in mind when he said that 'extra efforts and extra measures, in some form, are indispensable to a revival.'[7] What Colton had in mind was a device like the 'anxious seat', a device best described in his own words.

... It is not considered prudent to employ it except when there is manifestly a special degree of feeling in the congregation. On such occasions, and ordinarily towards the close of the meeting, a challenge is formally made on all who are willing publicly to signify their anxiety to secure an interest in the great salvation— to separate themselves from the congregation and come forward and be seated by themselves, that public prayer may be offered on their behalf and that they may receive advice and exhortation. And by this act they are known as inquirers[8] and treated as such. ... The individual who rises for such a purpose is apt to be so overwhelmed as to be unable to reach the place without the guidance and support of a second person; and immediately the sympathies of the whole congregation, except those who are hardened and resolved in sin, are roused to unwonted energy. A second, and a third, and perhaps a large number rise, one after another, and press forward under the same questions to the same place. And the common feelings increase. And when all have come whose feelings have urged them the minister rises and asks— And are there no more? No more? None others in this congregation resolved to renounce the world and seek after heaven? None others who feel the need of a Saviour? Dare you wait until tomorrow? Tomorrow, remember, is the thief of time and the

[7] Colton, op. cit., p.106.

[8] The term 'inquirer' is still used by revivalists like Billy Graham, with much the same basic sense. His inquirers, however, are not harangued in front of the main meeting in the style described here by Calvin Colton; they are taken aside and exhorted by themselves.

grave of souls. And another, and perhaps another, press forward to claim a place with those whose example has decided them. And now the offer is suspended and fervent importunate prayers are offered up on behalf of those anxious souls, who kneel weeping before the Altar of God. And the congregation weep with them. And they are counselled, exhorted and dismissed . . . and the effect of this step on them ordinarily is a speedy conversion. The same amazing power of the circumstances, instrumentally, seems to bring out their feelings, to enforce them to the crisis of submission to God.[9]

Here Colton was advertising to the British public a method of bringing tremendous emotional pressure to bear on a limited number of people who had successfully ('towards the end of the meeting') resisted the sermon. He was quite sure of what was being done, for he could speak frankly of the 'instrumental' power of the circumstances. When he said that the 'anxious seat' was used with caution he meant, as he said, that 'it is suited only to a very high state of feeling', that it would only work (that is, produce 'speedy conversions') if the meeting had been prepared very carefully for it. If the timing was right this was an 'extra measure' which would bring results. He gave an example from a revival which had taken place in the Mississippi Valley in 1831. At the climax of meetings, which had lasted several days, the baptized but unconverted children of believers were separated from the main body and pleaded with.

> Some of the children declined the wishful looks and heart-appealing expressions of their parents, and obliged their parents to go forward with them, weeping as they went. But most of them only stayed to sink down overwhelmed, not only with a sense of their unfilial conduct, but it is to be hoped also with a sense of the fearful choice that they had made, and to regret it in the bitterness of their souls.[10]

These examples of what the word 'revival' had come to mean in the United States by about 1830 are all the more relevant because they come from an American advocate of the revival system anxious to persuade the English public that in America

[9] Colton, op. cit., pp.96–8.
[10] Ibid., p.102.

it has been so fully demonstrated . . . that a community can enjoy a revival of religion without extravagance, and without disturbing the ordinary movements and relations of society—so far as they are innocent and proper—that opposition has greatly diminished.[11]

Thus usage of the term 'revival' had no real connexion with the kind of nation-wide movement from religious indifference to religious activity embodied in the traditional interpretation of the Evangelical Revival of the eighteenth century or, to a lesser extent, in the Oxford Movement of the Victorian era; nor had it more than a historical, emotional and, in the long run, purely mythological link with the Great Awakening as it was in the days of Whitefield and Jonathan Edwards. Here, instead, was a new tradition forming.

The new attitude which Colton was advocating was evidence of the degree of secularization which had affected the American Colonies by the end of the eighteenth century. He thought of revival, as has been said above, as a historical event rather than as a supernatural intervention, and his attitude reminds one that the founding fathers of the American Republic had been Deist, not Christian, in their outlook. The gradual emergence of the professional revivalist between 1740 and 1840 was a sure sign that the classical Protestant theology of the spiritual life was losing its hold on Western culture. John Bunyan had summed up that tradition in the late seventeenth century in the story of the Pilgrim whose burden of guilt fell away at the foot of the cross of Jesus, and serious Protestants did their best to re-enact in their own lives the mythology traced out in *Grace Abounding* and *Pilgrim's Progress*.

The vitality of this tradition in the less sophisticated, less wealthy areas of English eighteenth-century society largely explains the success of such preachers as George Whitefield and the two Wesleys. Such traditions of behaviour take a long time to die out completely in a fairly stable society, and the Pauline interpretation of Christianity, as re-interpreted by the sixteenth-century reformers, has not even now lost all its fascination, though it is no longer a creative force in European

[11] Ibid., p.61. Each fresh generation of revivalists has assured its public that this time, at any rate, there would be no emotion, no extravagance, in the meetings.

culture. Officially, the bulk of the nineteenth-century English Nonconformist churches, together with the Evangelical section of the Church of England, remained faithful to the classical Protestant pattern: what changed was that their response to it became more and more sluggish. In the eighteenth century, England had produced its own equivalents of the revivals in New England: there was an analogy, if not an identity, between the revivals of Jonathan Edwards and John Wesley. There was no such complete equivalent, however, to the second wave of American revivals which stretched from the 1780s to the 1830s, the period in which the professional revivalist came into his own as the expert who knew how to do what the normal minister could not do—engender in the congregation the signs appropriate to the classical Protestant pattern of the spiritual life.[12]

Once the 'revivals' had been demythologized, it was possible to approach the task of starting a revival as rationally as one would tackle any other problem, and so to think out and apply methods of reaching the goal. The goal might now be defined as the production in the 'unconverted' part of the congregation of certain signs or evidences of having been converted and it was natural, not least in the Romantic period, that the new technique should amount to the concentration in or on the individual of certain types of extreme emotional pressure. On the one hand methods like the 'anxious seat' stirred in the individual fear of the community and anxiety to conform to its standards and aspirations. Fear of parents, and a desire to conform to their will and gain their approval was also involved, as well as the subtler pressure of contemporaries. To sit in the 'anxious seat' was to feel wave after wave of communal pressure impelling one as an individual in a single direction. That the pressure contained much that could be called religious experience was not so obvious, and suspicion

---

[12] The nearest English equivalent to what happened in America was Primitive Methodism, a limited revivalist movement which was set in motion by the visit to north-western England of Lorenzo Dow (1806), which borrowed American methods like the camp-meeting, and which largely appealed to the social outcasts of rural England. For this very reason Primitive Methodism attracted very little attention (the employing classes in the countryside quickly grasped that it had no immediate political significance), won no social prestige and created few precedents, gained little ground in such expanding industrial and commercial centres as Manchester, and had burned itself out, revivalistically, by the end of the 1830s.

that the 'conversions' often represented social as much as religious conformity lay behind some of the criticism of the 'new' revivalism. Calvin Colton himself went out of his way to admit that what he called 'social sympathy' helped to spread a revival through the whole of a New England community. More important, however, was the deliberate exposure of the target group to a battery of influences and pressures not contained in the sermon alone. Despite much that was said to the contrary in the nineteenth century, a new revivalism testified to a decline in the importance of preaching: the address became a ritual with little specific content, and it was the closing appeal which gave the signal to the 'converted' to come to the front. Moody's addresses repay analysis, not because their content explains his success, but because their matter reveals unexpected features of his and the Victorian Protestant religious outlook.

The American professional revivalist, then, began as a specialist in treating the creeping paralysis which was affecting the classical Protestant world, its failure to keep alive its own distinctive kind of allegedly religious experience.[13] He had his own history as well, however, and American historians have discussed it in some detail. They have laid great stress on the career of Charles Grandison Finney (1792–1875), who has sometimes been regarded as the creator of modern mass revivalism.[14] Finney is said to have developed new techniques

[13] Revivalism, however, was not a purely Protestant phenomenon. The primary definition of a revivalist is perhaps that he offers certain types of solution, characteristically social and emotional, to the problem of the internal religious failure of a religious community. Roman Catholic revivalism also developed in the seventeenth century and was concerned to renew a serious religious life in people who had not made a confession or attended Mass for very long periods of time. Missions, as the Roman Catholics called them, were held in France between 1815 and 1830. One derivative from this tradition was Anglo-Catholic revivalism. Here the central experience (analogous to justification) was confession and absolution; this was held to be more objective. Cf. Chapter 7.

[14] See especially W. G. McLoughlin, *Modern Revivalism* (New York 1959), an incisive account of American Revivalism. Finney was born in Connecticut; at the time of his conversion in 1821 he had become a practising lawyer. He abandoned the law, and was ordained as a Presbyterian minister in 1825, the year in which he began to make a reputation as one of the most vehement revivalist preachers in America. His most famous revival was at Rochester, New York state, 1830-1. In 1835 he published his important *Lectures on Revivals of Religion*. The perfectionism which he developed about this time led to his virtual separation from the Presbyterian Churches; he became one of the staff of Oberlin College, holding revival meetings in the vacations. He visited England in 1849-51, and in 1858-60. On neither occasion was he outstandingly successful. Finney's *Memoirs* were issued posthumously in 1876. His career marked an

for the promotion of conversions, a new style of pulpit speaking, and to have transformed the American Churches' approach to evangelism.[15] From Finney, it is said, stem all the attitudes and methods of modern mass revivalism: Dwight Moody, Reuben Torrey, Billy Sunday and Billy Graham simply picked up and prolonged the tradition which Finney had created.

This interpretation must be treated with great caution. First, because although Finney claimed to invent 'new measures' he certainly did not invent 'mass evangelism', which was the product of a later nineteenth-century urban situation. Second, it was not his personal influence which led men to systematize revivals instead of leaving their occurrence to God: he was himself a by-product of the change of attitude. Third, American historians like McLoughlin leave out of account the role of the Baptists and Methodists at this period: if Finney succeeded in persuading American Presbyterians to employ revivalist methods which had horrified them in the camp meetings of the Second Great Awakening, one reason was the pressure of Methodist and Baptist revivalist success. Nor did American Methodist preachers need to borrow their Arminian theology from *Lectures on Revivals of Religion* when Finney finally published them in 1836: Finney's emphasis on what the sinner might do to save himself must have seemed to them no more than a belated admission within the ranks of Presbyterianism of what had seemed to them self-evident on the Western frontier for more than forty years. Finney shocked Asahel Nettleton, who maintained the traditional

---

important stage in the steady disintegration of American Calvinism, but McLoughlin exaggerates his centrality: Calvinism decayed all over the Christian world through its inner weaknesses, and in the United States the growth of the Methodist Societies between 1800 and 1840 was at least as relevant as the decline, relatively, of the Presbyterians.

[15] McLoughlin (op. cit.) compares Finney with Jonathan Edwards who, he says, was possessed with 'almost incredulous wonderment' at the Northampton Revival; Finney, on the other hand, did not believe that revivals depended upon miracles of divine origin. 'The difference between Edwards and Finney is essentially between the medieval and the modern temper' (p.11). But this is to compare as equals one of the major religious men of the eighteenth century with one of the minor religious figures of the nineteenth. Edwards was not medieval in mind: his steadily more critical view of the revivalism which he had practised in the 1730s, but which he came virtually to abandon at the end of his life, had obvious affinities with the spirit of the Enlightenment. Nor was Finney's adoption of the Holiness theology a sign of his being 'modern'.

Calvinist view of revivalism—that a preacher could only preach what had been revealed and trust that his hearers included some of those predestined to salvation—but it is not on record that he surprised Francis Asbury, the founder of the American Methodist tradition. Similarly, in England, the combined influences which had produced the Wesleyan Revival and the Oxford Movement had shattered Calvinism as a serious intellectual force in the religious culture long before Finney's *Lectures* (their pietist strictures on tea-drinking thoughtfully removed), were issued in London in 1840.

Of course, it is possible to distinguish between the 'new measures' American revivalism of the 1820s and the eighteenth-century revivalist style. Even here, however, Finney exaggerated his claim to be the herald of a new era. He asserted, for example, that

> even in New England it has been supposed that revivals come as showers do, sometimes in one town and sometimes in another, and that ministers and churches could do nothing more to promote them than they could to make showers of rain come on their own town when they were falling on a neighbouring town.[16]

This quotation comes from his *Lectures*, but I have already quoted a similar passage above from Calvin Colton's book on revivalism, published three years before and not acknowledged at all in Finney's text. Both Colton and Finney, however, were writing from a Presbyterian standpoint and describing what was true of the Presbyterian world alone. Outside it things went on differently, and the tremendously successful American Methodist camp-meetings of the first ten years of the nineteenth century could never have been held if there had been a universal conviction that revivals were God's limited gift to a particular local church, once in a generation.

The development of an independent tradition in England is also not hard to prove. A typical example would be William Bramwell, a Wesleyan Methodist itinerant who lived from

---

[16] W. G. McLoughlin (ed.), *Lectures on Revivals of Religion* (Harvard 1960), p.20. 'It used to be supposed that a revival would come about once in fifteen years, and all would be converted that God intended to save, and then they must wait until the next crop came forward on the stage of life. Finally, the time got shortened to five years.' Nothing could be more remote from the Wesleyan tradition, either in the eighteenth or the early nineteenth century. Nineteenth-century revivalists, however, rediscovered the practical common-sense behind the dictum.

1759 to 1818. Bramwell entered all his circuits with the kind of single-minded determination to produce revivalistic phenomena which may be observed in Charles Finney. One example must suffice, from his ministry in the Newcastle-upon-Tyne circuit.

In May, 1817, Mr Bramwell held a love-feast in the chapel at West Moor Colliery, when, after a few had spoken of their Christian experience he said, 'I am just thinking, there are some penitents here': and after having united in singing a verse for their encouragement, he commanded all who were determined to forsake their sin and come to Christ, to stand up and show themselves. Instantly there were fifteen or sixteen persons on their feet, all in tears. The first who rose was a stout young man who trembled exceedingly whilst he cried out, 'Oh, do pray for me'. Shortly afterwards, Mr Bramwell requested all to kneel down; it seemed that every individual was engaged in earnest prayer. In a few minutes the young man was set at liberty. . . . Mr Bramwell prayed again and several more were made happy. Mr B. then desired the people to sit down. We did so. In a little time, he again requested the remaining penitents to stand up; and this he repeated until there was not one left in unbelief. . . .

About six weeks afterwards, a love-feast was held at Cawe Hill. . . . I accompanied many of our friends, as many as filled six boats, and sailed up the River Tyne from Shields to Cawe Hill. As we proceeded we sang hymns which were responded to by multitudes of serious people who were travelling over the fields on each side of the river and getting to the same place. . . . Mr Bramwell opened the love-feast. After a few had spoken Mr B. requested all who were in distress to stand up, when about thirty instantly rose. After an exhortation had been given them prayer was made and several found peace with God. Mr Bramwell again and again requested those that remained in distress to stand up till there were none left. . . .[17]

This passage mentions most of the chief features of this kind of system which Finney advocated. There is the same basic reliance upon a powerful personality and upon a background of well-known assumptions about the nature of sin and conversion. There is the characteristic device—found also in the

[17] J. Sigston, *Memoir of W. Bramwell*, 1839, p.405. Sigston was a Wesleyan advocate of revivalism; he drew attention to Finney's *Lectures*, then just published in England, and said that 'Mr Finney entertains similar views to those of Mr Bramwell' (Ibid., p.590.) Bramwell had died in 1818.

'anxious seat'—of separating the most likely victims from the protection of the community, driving them into the centre of attention, and then of refusing them any chance of escape until they had given the expected signs of repentance and conversion. There is the same emphasis upon the need for an immediate response to the revivalist's demand for action. This demand for immediate conversion, immediate surrender, was one of the aspects of Finney's technique which his contemporaries criticized, and it is interesting that Bramwell had already met similar criticism from the Wesleyan leadership of his day. He became the focal point of a group of highly self-conscious 'revivalists' in the north of England. Bramwell, however, could point to John Wesley's example as a justification of his own approach. Wesley would lead an enquirer through arguments designed to prove the possibility of sanctification; he would appear for a moment to grant the traditional position that sanctification was a gift given by God on the death-bed; but he would then turn back and demand directly, 'And if then, why not tonight?'. This whole matter of the immediate response to the personal insistence of the evangelist suggests that Finney's technique was closer to that of the eighteenth century than to that of Moody and Sankey. This intensely personal approach almost completely dropped out during the last quarter of the nineteenth century, when anything approaching the bluntness of the 'anxious seat' would have been greeted with horror. Moody and Sankey dealt with their audience in the anonymous mass, as did their later twentieth-century disciple, Billy Graham.

Psychologically, Finney was always dealing with the same small New England town—the population of Rochester, New York, was about 10,000 in 1830–1. Finney's *Lectures* did not discuss mass evangelism: they were about how to promote revival in a place like Rochester. Indeed, he was less concerned with the technique of revivalism than was Calvin Colton, whose book was much briefer, more utilitarian in spirit and more detailed in its description of specific methods. Finney commenced the *Lectures* with a long section on what he called 'prevailing prayer'. He said in effect that God would revive a local congregation only if men put themselves in a suitably receptive state of mind, but he also said that the prayer of faith, defined as he defined it, was bound to prevail. This was the degree of his pelagianism. He gave a typical illustration of what he meant:

> Take a fact, which was related, in my hearing, by a minister. He said that in a certain town there had been no revival for many years; the church was nearly run out, the youth were all unconverted, and desolation reigned unbroken. There lived in a retired part of the town, an aged man, a blacksmith by trade, and of so stammering a tongue, that it was painful to hear him speak. On one Friday, as he was at work in his shop, alone, his mind became greatly exercised about the state of the church and of the impenitent. His agony became so great, that he was induced to lay by his work, lock his shop door, and spend the afternoon in prayer.
>
> He prevailed, and on the Sabbath called on the minister, and desired him to appoint a conference meeting. After some hesitation the minister consented, observing, however, that he feared but few would attend. He appointed it the same evening, at a large private house. When evening came, more assembled than could be accommodated in the house. All was silent for a time, until one sinner broke out in tears and said, if any one could pray, he begged him to pray for *him*. Another followed, and another, and still another, until it found that persons from every quarter of the town were under deep conviction. And what was remarkable was, that they all dated their conviction at the hour when the old man was praying in his shop. Thus this old stammering man prevailed, and, as a prince, had power with God. I could name a multitude of similar cases. . . .[18]

This was classical enough in content: the revival was at once God's work and that of a poor, ordinary man; the professional minister was sceptical: the result as miraculous as anything that ever happened to Jonathan Edwards at Northampton. It is true that this was not how Finney's own revivals started (or Edwards' for that matter), but this was how he liked to believe that they started, or would have started in an ideal, pietist world.

When Finney came to talk about new methods he mentioned only three, none of them especially new; the anxious meeting, the protracted meeting, and the anxious seat: none of these

[18] W. D. McLoughlin (ed.), *Lectures on Revivals of Religion* (Harvard 1960), p.70.

survived into the later mass evangelism in its early nineteenth century form. Apart from this, much of the book was made up of diatribes against his Presbyterian fellow-ministers and against the theological seminaries which in Finney's opinion unfitted them for the work of revivalism:

> When young men come out of the seminaries, are they fit to go into a revival? Look at the place where there has been a revival in progress, and a minister is wanted. Let them send to a theological seminary for a minister. Will he enter into the work, and sustain it, and carry it on? Seldom. Like David with Saul's armour, he comes in with such a load of theological trumpery that he knows not what to do. Leave him there for two weeks, and the revival is at an end. The churches know and feel that the greater part of these young men do not know how to do anything that needs to be done for a revival, and they are complaining that the young ministers are so far behind the church. You may send all over the United States, to theological seminaries, and find but few young ministers fitted to carry forward the work. What a state of things.[19]

Finney balanced this by sharp criticism of the laity for not providing secular society with perfect examples of the pattern of life of Evangelical Pietism. He gave a list of the causes of backsliding, and these included 'having too much worldly business'; 'being associated in business with an unconverted partner'; 'the influence of worldly companions; marrying someone who was worldly'; 'the fear of giving offence to worldly friends'; the neglect of 'secret prayer', of strict honesty and of reading the Bible.[20] Not only did revival ideally start inside the closely-knit community of the small-town Presbyterian Church, but its ideal product was a revivified Church of the same order within which the converts could be kept safe from contact with the corrupting outer world.

Finney's picture of revivalism, then, is that of a group of people (or in extreme cases a solitary blacksmith with a stammer) coming together and praying a local church revival into existence: it is a far cry from this to mass evangelism, as the phrase is generally understood. Perhaps it is also significant

[19] Ibid., pp.186–7.
[20] Ibid., pp.434–40.

that more recent revivalists have not set down their theories in a revival handbook; Moody sometimes made pithy comments to journalists, but he never even went so far as to edit Finney's *Lectures*.

The gap between Finney's *Lectures* and Moody's practice is sufficient to suggest that the line of division between ancient and modern revivalism should be drawn after 1860, at any rate so far as England is concerned. Between 1800 and 1860, the professional revivalist was certainly an American phenomenon, only slowly acclimatized in England and not often imitated. He still matured in the typical American situation before he tried his hand overseas, and therefore understood his job as the producer of a revival in the comparatively isolated, socially concentrated, pre-industrial American township. He was the inventor of new techniques. In a sense, he was bound to innovate, for conversions became more vital to him than they had usually been for the local pastor settled in a church. A professional revivalist who could not show conversions was not likely to stay in demand for very long. Between 1800 and 1850, revivalism was a folk-movement, contesting clerical conservatism. Certainly, the professional drew much of his support from laymen dissatisfied with the regular ministry and anxious to see in the revivalist's success proof of the regular ministry's inferiority. From this point of view the revivalist entered the scene as a radical, a dissolver of the existing religious patterns, a symbol of a long-standing discontent with the way in which the settled ministers dominated the older American and most of the English churches. It was not an accident that it was the Presbyterian and Independent ministers who lacked enthusiasm for the new professionals, whereas the more recent Baptist and Methodist groups showed less hostility. The professional revivalist emerged to some extent as part of the democratic Jacksonian impulse of the 1820s and 1830s to pull down what remained of the colonial structure and replace it with something more 'democratic' and more national.

This radicalism and anti-clericalism did not mean that the professional revivalists refused to be ordained—they were as anxious for ordination then as their successors are for doctorates today—but their ordination often took place in

defiance of the normal standards of entry into the ministry.
When Charles Grandison Finney was ordained under Presbyterian auspices at the age of thirty-two, he knew more about
the law than he did about theology and was accepted on the
strength of his reputation for conducting revivals. Indeed, if
the Presbyterians had taken his theological position rather
more seriously they might have spared themselves much later
trouble: in the 1830s Finney's position became more radical
as he developed a perfectionism alien to the Presbyterian
tradition and to the pessimistic view of man which had
obsessed America for so long. This radicalism was all the
more interesting in the history of the professional revivalist in
that, in the 1870s, Dwight Moody was by no means advertised
as a theological radical—indeed, his strongest asset in certain
quarters was his claim to stand guard over the Old Time
Religion, which had been betrayed by almost everybody else,
from the Higher Critics to the Anglo-Catholics. Moody
remained radical in another sense, however; he retained the
support of the anti-ministerial forces, their normal hostility
multiplied by horror—in England—at Pusey, Jowett or
Mackonochie.

In effect, the line of division between ancient and modern
American revivalism should be drawn after 1860 rather than
before it. This is to make the division come after the various
revival movements which spread from America to England in
the years 1857–60. There is no serious question of anything
like a Second Evangelical Awakening having taken place in
the Anglo-Saxon world in these years. There was certainly a
wave of religious excitement in the northern part of the
United States in 1857–8: Whitney Cross described these
revivals as the last nationwide awakening in the old manner,
and underlined their rural rather than urban characteristics.[21]
How far this American excitement was spontaneous it is hard
to say, but the campaign for an English revival in emulation
certainly was not.

The possibility brought Charles Finney and the American
Methodist professional revivalist, James Caughey, both of
whom had toured England in the 1840s, back again, together
with Phoebe Palmer, another American Methodist revivalist,

[21] W. R. Cross, *The Burned-Over District* (New York 1950).

who specialized in holiness revivalism. The British evangelical world resounded with reports and speeches about the full churches, crowded mid-day prayer-meetings and transformed factories which it was said were to be found in New York (and, later on, in Northern Ireland). It emerged that a few English imitators of American revivalism already existed— Richard Weaver, Reginald Radcliffe, William Carter, Algernon Blackwood and Captain Trotter, for example—all of them laymen, working without any great sympathy from the ministry of the Churches to which they belonged. Despite the efforts of these people, the much desired major English revival of 1859–60 did not take place, and the experiments of those two years showed how inadequate were existing methods to the new urban situation. The most that can be said is that it was at this time that the English Churches officially began to wake up to the way in which the new urban masses were slipping through the nets which were intended to catch and hold them. Even then, the established Churches hardly felt the need for revival within their own borders; they did not become aware of the hard fact of statistical decline in their own membership much before the end of the century. But it was obvious that a new world was coming into existence in which religion counted for very little, except perhaps on Sundays, when the shops still closed, factory overtime was uncommon, and the entertainment industry only a shadow of its present self. The increase in population, the increase in commerce (pietism always opposed the rise of capitalism), the increasing secularity of the general outlook combined to alarm the religious world; the joint attack by Evangelicals and Anglo-Catholics on Bishop Colenso and *Essays and Reviews* (both in 1860) expressed their sense of an uncertain future. This counter-attack on the theological front was clumsy and futile but the official Churches also tackled more directly the problem of the new, non-religious proletariat. New measures were consciously looked for, tried, found wanting, and replaced by others.

This was not done in the spontaneous manner character-istic of a powerful renewal of religious faith; instead the ecclesiastical *élite*, Anglo-Catholic as well as Evangelical, genuinely concerned about the religious condition of the masses, looked about for techniques with which to change the situation. To say that most of the methods employed failed is not to say that the Churches did nothing. It is too simple to accuse Victorian Christianity of not making contact with the working·class: it made contact, and was rejected.[22] Christians goaded and organized the religious middle-class into the gigantic financial outpouring of mid-Victorian charity; the money relieved some suffering but the patronage inherent in the system alienated the people it was meant to conciliate. Sunday and day schools were built for the education of the children of the poor, but the financial strain of their upkeep proved too much for the voluntary, religious system and the State, effectively a secularizing agent at this point, had to take over the burden of the day school education as early as 1870. Sunday schools reached the children of those outside the Churches successfully, but failed overwhelmingly to retain them for Christianity. Rarely has more effort been expended on the religious subjugation of a secular culture; but the effort was not a religious revival in itself and it failed to evoke one. This partly explains why Revivalism was pressed into service by both the Anglo-Catholics (1869) and the Evangelical community (1873).

When Moody and Sankey arrived in England in 1873 they succeeded as no other American revivalists had done before them, and that fact has to be set against any qualifications of the reality of their success. There *was* an American break-through. Moody faced audiences very different from those which Finney had known, even as late as 1860, when the old man had a last fling at Bolton. The change did not consist in the substitution of an Arminian for a Calvinist outlook—that had taken place long before. Both the Calvinist and the Arminian points of view had disappeared as conscious concerns of the laity, leaving a host of preachers hoist high and dry with their inherited platitudes, unable to make out why they drew no response from their inattentive hearers. One is reminded that when another great American revivalist of the earlier period, Lyman Beecher, published his *Autobiography*, in 1864, it seemed to the *Atlantic Monthly* a pointless question to

---

[22] Cf. E. R. Wickham, *Church in an Industrial City*. Victorian church leaders knew that they had lost control of the urban working-class.

ask whether 'a baby threw his bread and butter to the floor because of his federal alliance with Adam or because of a surfeit of plum cake'.[23] It was no longer a matter of whether or not men and women could respond for themselves to the unmerited grace of God. Damnation itself, if stated too directly as a would-be serious possibility, proved a bankrupt abstraction in the 1870s, one which stimulated no stronger emotional response in most people than hot denial. A much deeper anxiety about the function and reality of religion was emerging at the level of the ordinary man. Revivalism, and associated late nineteenth-century religious phenomena like the *glossolalia* of early Pentecostalism, a movement which began in the 1890s, revealed how badly people wanted to prove to themselves that God existed, that he did things here and now which could be seen and heard. Perhaps one of the reasons why music worked so powerfully for Moody, forming a vital component of the new revivalist techniques, was that audiences were able to accept uncritically in a sentimental musical form what they would have hesitated to accept in the clearer form of the sermon.

What was vanishing, and what has not reappeared in the twentieth century in a self-confident form, was an underlying belief that God revealed himself in the events of everyday life. Even in the late nineteenth century, of course, the doctrine of an active, identifiable Providence, a doctrine far more central to the vigour of the Evangelical tradition than has been commonly realized, was not quite exhausted. A revealing, pathetic example may be found at the death-bed of Samuel Butler, himself a bitter critic of both Evangelicalism and Darwinism. His sister, May Butler, was talking to Festing Jones, later Butler's biographer.

> I said it was not so much the great things in life, but the tiny ones which often made one feel how certainly there must be a God who knew and cared for us. I told him about my cold stopping your going; and Dr Lycett Burd being here when the telegram came; and Alfred's card coming just in time. He, Mr Jones, said he felt exactly the same, and that in many little ways he had been led and guided just right without his own will in these last days. I am sure that if not in the fullest sense a believer in Christian

[23] *Autobiography*, ed. B. M. Cross, p.xxxiv.

truth (he sees no difficulty in miracles) Mr Jones himself is very close to it.[24]

Thomas Hardy was not the only Victorian who might have felt that 'life's little ironies' was a better description of the pattern of events than May Butler's. Hardy might have quoted the incident of Harriet Butler's behaviour at the news of her brother's last illness. Butler was lying seriously ill at Naples and his servant Alfred was sent out to bring him back to England. The yacht of one of Harriet's married nephews was lying off the Italian coast and could have been used for the journey, but Harriet 'dare not expose a young man to the contaminating influence of the infidel',[25] and not until long afterwards did the young man know that he could have been of use. Of course, such things have always happened, but a few late Victorians still fastened on them as especially significant.

The real problem was how to make the non-religious religious without the aid of superstition. Some theologians, B. F. Westcott for example, tried to modify traditional Christian economic thought in a paternally 'Christian Socialist' direction, but they failed to convince enough people inside the Churches to make their proposals for an institutional change of heart attractive to those outside.

The Anglican Church experimented with freer, or more elaborate types of worship, sometimes in cathedrals and sometimes in theatres. The Free Churches, believing that the working-class disliked the atmosphere of the typical church-building, which had, after all, been re-emphasized by the Gothic Revival, built 'central halls' and 'institutional churches' instead: the intention was to make the interior of the hall look as unlike a 'church' as possible; the speaker stood behind a little table on a raised platform and the audience sang from hymn-sheets instead of from printed books. This form of service was worked out by Charles Spurgeon about 1860, but he started with considerable personal advantages over his imitators.

It was not surprising that the new pattern of American

---

[24] P. N. Furbank, *Samuel Butler (1835–1902)*, 1948, p.98.
[25] ibid, p.97.

revivalism, and Americans like Moody and Sankey, Torrey and Alexander, should have been pressed into service in the search for a solution. One new factor worked heavily in their favour. Since the Civil War the professional revivalists had added a new technique of great potential value—a new kind of popular religious music. The Civil War had given its first great opportunity to the nascent music industry; when it ended, composers and song-writers found a new market for their talents among the religious. As a result of what might be called the industrialization of religious music, the nineteenth century probably heard more new hymns and tunes than ever had been composed before. Few of them had much value, but the revival music which Sankey and his successors brought across the Atlantic had a much wider appeal than the songs which Lorenzo Dow had published in a little paperback in 1807, and they enabled the revivalists to establish a temporary basis for their mission within at any rate the lower-middle-class section of Victorian popular culture.

From the point of view of the official Churches, however, the professional revivalists, even in their last and most persuasive version, failed at the most important test; they did not make any marked contact with the world beyond the organized Churches. The reason for their failure was perhaps basically that what the Americans brought with them, disguised to some extent by the use of what was then very up-to-date music and a highly colloquial style of preaching remote from the rhetoric of the mid-century, was yet another approach to the traditional American problem, how to convert the children of the members of the Church. Some of Sankey's most popular hymns promised the return of the black sheep of the family, the prodigal child, or pictured the reunion in heaven of the ideal family group, including those children who had died in their infancy. Inside English Protestantism, this approach was subtly urbanized by Moody, so that it penetrated far more widely than the efforts of Finney and Caughey. Outside the religious world, the effect was slight. In effect, the professional revivalists were still trying to solve the problems of non-Christian urban society in the later nineteenth century with techniques adapted to the problems of seventeenth- and eighteenth-century young people living in a small, rural, closely-knit community. They were using methods which depended for their success on the pre-existence of a Christian community in order to tackle a situation whose central difficulty lay in the absence not only of a Christian community, but of any community at all. The collapse of cultural unity—political, religious, moral—was well on the way by the close of the century. The degree of success which Moody and Sankey enjoyed depended upon their ability to conjure up for a brief period in the Islington Agricultural Hall in London the appearance of a Christian community on something like an urban scale; this achievement put them into a different class from their predecessors. It was not, however, a permanent achievement, and it was one geared to the structure of the official Churches.

2

The English Tradition: Primitive Methodist Revivalism and American Influence

THREE American revivalists made an impression in England between 1800 and 1860. Lorenzo Dow and James Caughey were Methodists; Charles Grandison Finney had abandoned the Calvinism of his early ministry by the time he came to England. Lorenzo Dow deeply influenced the first phase of Primitive Methodism, a movement which began in the opening decade of the nineteenth century as a revolt of farmers and farm-workers against the inadequacies of the Anglican parish-system as they knew it in the south-west, parts of the Midlands and Yorkshire; Primitive Methodism had a membership of about 100,000 by 1850, the largest new denomination to form in England since the eighteenth century. James Caughey came in the 1840s, when Wesleyan Methodism was splitting into warring camps, and he became a hero of the 'Wesleyan Reformers', who made approval of revivalism a test of loyalty; Caughey also affected William Booth, later General of the Salvation Army. Charles Finney had more in common with the Congregationalists and Presbyterians, but his *Lectures on Revivalism*, which mattered much more in England than his own preaching, were read widely in the 1840s when George Eliot, for example, had to free herself from his teaching. Finney, however, like Phoebe Palmer (who arrived in England at the very end of this period and was less publicly known than the earlier trio), had become a holiness revivalist; an approach which had limited success until the mid-1870s when another American, Robert Pearsall Smith, was to triumph where his predecessors had failed.[1]

[1] Smith, T. *Revivalism and Social Reform in Mid-Nineteenth-Century America* (Nashville 1957), and D. Dayton, *Discovering an Evangelical Heritage* (New York 1976), relate American perfectionism to social reform and early feminism, but few signs of this

38

Lorenzo Dow was fortunate in that he landed in England before Methodism had completely spent itself. He acted as a catalyst to the final wave of Methodist expansion: he did this by offering a particular revivalist style and music to men and women in the English countryside who had grown tired of what was currently available—and those whose image of rural Anglicanism is conditioned by infrequent visits to show-piece churches should seek out some of the small, dark, uncomfortable, badly-designed and poorly-built erections which still do duty in the more isolated parts of counties like Dorset. Social conditions were propitious for the rise of a new movement. In the previous century Anglican Evangelicalism and Wesleyan Methodism had appealed to distinct social groups, leaving whole sections of the population untouched. Evangelicalism seemed to thrive in watering-places and under fashionable, if respectable, protection; Wesleyanism developed into an essentially urban denomination with a bourgeois imagination. As it became more respectable, more institutionalized and more hereditary in its membership, Wesleyanism became less able to expand socially and by 1800 had ceased to compete with Anglicanism in many rural areas. At this point, however, the psychological possibility of what has been called 'the revolt of the field' was just emerging. Rural workers and many of the poorer farmers were becoming conscious of a need for greater self-respect and for more respect from others; they wanted more economic security as well. The evidence suggests that in the first half of the century Primitive Methodism prospered as the religious expression of this demand for change, but ceased to prosper in the second half of the century as it lost contact with the wave of social protest which consolidated itself in trade unionism and in the exploitation of the County Councils Act of 1884. The camp-meetings of 1807 reflected the desire of many of the poorer people in the country areas to set up a religious society of their own, as outside the normal religious structure as they themselves were outside the recognized social system; and this was

---

appeared in England. See also Nancy Cott, *The Bonds of Womanhood, Woman's Sphere in New England 1780–1835* (Yale 1977); and Ann Douglas, *The Feminization of American Culture* (New York 1977).

to be true of other groups which rallied to Primitive Methodism before 1850—coastal fishermen in East Anglia, for example, and especially miners in the Midlands and the northeast. The camp-meetings were a declaration of social independence, in fact, quite as much as of religious intent.

It would be simple, but mistaken, to interpret this by saying that Primitive Methodism was a religious sect—that is, a group which creates a separate community of social identity by explicitly rejecting the ladder of economic success of the classes immediately related to it in favour of a sectarian identity as such. Looked at this way a sect represents the social withdrawal in religious terms of a defeated, often urban group which prefers to deny the propriety and validity of those goals whose achievement baffles it, and seeks to convince itself instead that in the final, glorious consummation of all things members of the sect will inherit the earth for so long promised to the meek.

This kind of explanation does not, however, account for Primitive Methodism down to 1860. For the movement, whether of agricultural labourers or miners, was aggressive; it did not offer a way of escape from an undesirable social situation, but revealed a will to change it; in the first half of the century, the tiny Primitive Methodist chapels could function as citadels from which attacks were mounted on the social and economic enemy. This came out clearly, for example, in Tremenheere's official report on the strike in April, 1844, at the Marquis of Londonderry's collieries in the villages near Durham. One of the witnesses the Commissioner questioned said:

> During the strike they had regularly once a week prayer-meetings at the chapels in the colliery villages to pray to God to give them success. The men said they went 'to get their faith' strengthened. I attended one of these meetings. There were about sixty miners present. Prayer was offered up for God's blessing and support during the strike, and that He would give them the victory. Everything that could be collected up in the Bible about slavery and tyranny, such as Pharoah ordering bricks to be made without straw, was urged upon them.[2]

[2] *Report of the Commissioners into the state of the Mining Districts*, 1846.

Similarly, at the Seghill Colliery, Charles Carr said:

I asked during the strike several of the leading local preachers why they did not show the men they were wrong, which as reasonable men themselves they must know they were; but if they interfered at all they were against us. The Primitive Methodists were the worst of the people at the time of the strike. One of them, a local preacher, who was in our employ underground, told me that 'according to his religion he could not go to work'.[3]

As a working-class religious movement, however brief, Primitive Methodism expressed the miners' rejection of the assumption of the traditional society, an assumption with which Tremenheere himself entirely agreed, that the function of religious groups was to encourage social obedience. Since the mine-owners felt themselves not to have any real control over working conditions, including the size of wages, they did not regard the men as entitled to protest against some kind of tyranny. Tremenheere reported in favour of assisting the expansion of the Church of England in the colliery districts, in order to establish clergy who would explain the true economic situation to the ignorant and misguided men. He rejected the propriety of a working-class religious body, in whose chapels the miners might pray for divine support for their strike. He did not think of Anglicanism as class-based, but as the proper religious expression of society as a whole. He was bound to be horrified when he was told at another big colliery, at Seaton Delaval, for example:

The three leading men in the strike here were William Dawson, William Richardson, and John Nicholson: they were pitmen. They were Primitive Methodists and local preachers. They frequently assembled the people, from 100 to 400 together, on the road-side, and offered up prayer for the success of the strike, and also that the men who were brought from a distance to work in the colliery, the 'black-legs' as they called them, might be injured, either lamed or killed; and they rejoiced when anything did happen to them. Several accidents did happen to the new hands; four Welshmen got burnt, one got his arm broken, one had his ankle dislocated, and others met with trifling injuries. Those men I have named encouraged the people to rejoice at

[3] Ibid., p.25.

these accidents, and met the men themselves, and abused them. Those three men, of course, were discharged. About one third of the whole number of our hewers (heads of families) belong to the Primitive Methodists. The Wesleyans were very quiet, and were among the first to offer to go back to work.[4]

The inspiration of these attitudes at the religious level was partly the Old Testament, in which God was known to act fiercely, drowning Egyptians and having the occasional Agag hewed in pieces before an altar in Gilgal, and partly the wilder, apocalyptic side of the New, in which Lorenzo Dow had revelled. There is no sign here of a religious force which helped men to come to terms with a changing and developing class structure and to find peaceful solutions to problems of conflict—the kind of role which Professor Harold Perkin, for example, has suggested for the non-Anglican denominations in the first half of the nineteenth century.[5] In fact, Primitive Methodism over-committed itself in the mining areas in the 1840s, putting God to the political test of results, promising a divine army which never came, like the French, whom one Durham local preacher, according to Tremenheere, firmly believed were on the point of invading England to save the strikers. It is difficult to agree with Professor Perkin that early Victorian denominations helped to stabilize society in a hierarchical sense; they seem rather to have split in terms of the developing class system, expressing, and even, as in the case of Primitive Methodism, actually increasing, instability. Primitive Methodism promised too much, with the result that the political defeats of the working-classes in the 1840s cost the denomination much of its original support; the aggressive demand for social change ceased to look for religious expression but turned more exclusively to trade unionism, while those who became Primitive Methodist were now more often sectarian-minded, their politics a generalized, essentially middle-class Liberal Party politics.[6] The enthusiasm for

[4] Ibid.

[5] H. Perkin, *The Origins of Modern English Society, 1780–1880* (1969).

[6] The links between Methodism and trade unionism have been exaggerated: cf. R. F. Wearmouth, *Methodism and the Trade Unions* (1959). As denominations, both Primitive and Wesleyan Methodism avoided any serious commitment to the Unions in the second half of the century. There was a Nonconformist tendency at that time to talk as though the Free Churches disposed of the working-class vote, but this was never true.

revivalism dwindled at the same time, and Lorenzo Dow was totally forgotten.

Dow did not entirely create the revival which produced Primitive Methodism.[7] The institutional founder of the new body was Hugh Bourne,[8] who was brought up as an Anglican on an isolated farm in the parish of Stoke-on-Trent. His father doubled as a small farmer and timber-merchant; Bourne became a timber-dealer and carpenter. He spent some years under conviction of sin in a manner recognizably eighteenth-century, before justification released him when he was alone one Sunday morning in the spring of 1799; he was about twenty-seven. From then on he moved steadily from an almost quietist mysticism, which sometimes brought him into close contact with Quakers, and especially the Quaker Methodists of Warrington, led by Peter Phillips,[9] to a more aggressive idea of evangelism nearer to the Methodist tradition. In a manuscript Self-Review, dated 17 August, 1800, intended for a blacksmith at Mow Cop, in Staffordshire, Bourne said that even after his conversion,

> whether it would be best for me to join the Quakers or the Methodists, I could not tell: as I had received benefit from both: but one thing seemed to point me to the Methodists, and that was, when I went among the Quakers, there was no persecution, which there always was when I went among the Methodists.[10]

As early as 1803, when his extant *Journal* begins, Bourne had linked the ideas of revivalism and persecution. In February,

[7] For Dow (1777–1824), cf. *The Travels of Lorenzo Dow*, written by Himself, 1806; *Thoughts on the Times and Camp Meetings*, Liverpool 1807; and *Vicissitudes in the Wilderness*, or 'The Journey of Life Exemplified' in the *Journal of Peggy Dow* (4th ed. Liverpool 1818). Dow had taken part in the Second Awakening which began in the 1790s; in 1802 he converted one hundred people in a three-hour meeting at Western, up-state New York, the place where Finney later first attracted attention in 1825. Dow met his 'rib', Peggy, at Western, and returned there four times before 1817. For the American background, cf. Whitney Cross, *The Burned-Over District* (New York 1950).

[8] For a short life of Hugh Bourne, cf. J. T. Wilkinson, *Hugh Bourne, 1772–1852*. I am taking a different line of interpretation.

[9] For Peter Phillips (1778–1853), a life-long friend of Bourne, and leader of the Quaker Methodists, a tiny group dedicated to the impossible task of reconciling Wesleyan and Quaker ideas, cf. A. Mounfield, *A Short History of Independent Methodism*.

[10] The manuscript of the self-review, and of the journals, were kept in the library of Hartley Victoria College, Manchester, and passed into the possession of the University of Manchester when the college was closed in 1973. The closure of this seminary marked the termination of all direct links with the Primitive Methodist tradition.

1803, for instance, he heard a young itinerant called Butler, of whom he noted:

> he seems a zealous young man, wishes to be a revivalist. . . . Was saying to him that I was not able at all times to rebuke sin, and to take up the Cross in reproving sin. . . . He replied, If we be servants of Christ we must take up the Cross. I said, If Mr Butler means to keep clear of the blood of all men he must take up the Cross. He said he looked for it. I said he would also be persecuted by Methodists. This he was unwilling to believe. I told him the people here had been persecuted and had stood it out against both preachers and people: a number which had opposed them and had prevailed so far as to bring the revival to an end. . . . I told him we had had persons convinced and converted too in the middle of the noise when one could scarce distinguish one word. But such earnest ways of carrying on meetings was disliked by the greater part of Methodists.

The background of this passage lay in Bourne's local circumstances. He was living near Mow Cop on the outskirts of the Burslem Wesleyan Methodist Circuit, and the 'preachers' referred to were the full-time Wesleyan itinerants stationed there. He and others had been stimulated by the accounts of the American Second Awakening which began to appear in the *Wesleyan Methodist Magazine* from 1802, and the last of which was published in 1806.[11] These articles described the early camp meetings, and what seems to have first attracted the little group in Staffordshire was that the meetings went on for several days, an example of abandoning everything except religion which appealed strongly to their intense pietism. They wanted to concentrate on religious exercises in the same way, and it is clear that the Wesleyan Methodist ministers stationed at Burslem felt obliged to interfere; and this interference, which went as far as stopping a revival under way in his opinion, was what Bourne was discussing with Butler.

At this stage the idea of 'revivalism' still lacked shape in England: when it was not simply nostalgia for the excitements of early Wesleyanism, it amounted to a naïve invocation of direct supernatural action, and clearly often ended in

[11] Op. cit., 1802, pp.422–5; 1803, pp.125–32; pp.82–93; pp.268–85; pp.326–33; pp.417–19; 1804, pp.233–4; 1805, p.573; 1806, pp.94–5.

collective dissociation, accompanied by phenomena familiar in later Pentecostalism, such as speaking with tongues (not always recognized as such but one element in Bourne's reference to noise 'when one could scarce distinguish a word'), hallucinatory visions (common, as we shall see, both to Bourne's group and to the 'Magic Methodists' in the Forest of Delamere), uncontrollable weeping, trances and so forth.[12] The Wesleyan itinerants, already a professional group whose experience went back to the 1740s—it involves a serious, ecclesiastical kind of misunderstanding to speak of them as 'becoming ministers' after John Wesley's death in 1791— were not over-impressed by the religious content of such meetings, and alarmed by what seems to have been a wave of such activity running across the industrial north Midlands at this time. In 1802–3 'Christian Revivalists' emerged briefly in the Macclesfield area; another revivalist group formed in Manchester, to be dispersed by Jabez Bunting[13] in 1806; between 1800 and 1807 Bourne in Burslem and William Clowes in Hull slowly developed what was to become Primitive Methodism; and there were the Forest Methodists in Delamere. All these were fringe groups which found social relations with the larger Wesleyan chapels difficult. Politics may also have come into it. Bourne's followers were not only noisy, but working-class—he had drawn in colliers from the local pits—and democratic, and in the midst of the Napoleonic War, which was certainly not fought to make England safe for democracy, open-air gatherings of any size must have seemed incautious to the Wesleyan ministers immediately concerned. William Miller, the superintendent who was appointed to the Burslem circuit in 1805, sympathized with revivalists but objected to open-air meetings on anything

---

[12] For Pentecostalism, cf. W. J. Hollenweger, *The Pentecostals* (Zürich 1969, E.T. 1972), a fascinating history of modern institutionalized Pentecostalism; but Hollenweger does not sufficiently consider the cross-cultural appearances of these phenomena, which are by no means purely 'Christian', and familiar long before the recent movement in Western Churches.

[13] For Bunting, cf. *The Age of Disunity*, by the present writer (1966), and W. R. Ward, *The Early Correspondence of Jabez Bunting* (1972) and *Early Victorian Methodism*: the Correspondence of J. Bunting 1830–1858 (1978). Professor Ward, however, is over-critical of Bunting, whom he sees as fatally distorting an 'open' Wesleyanism in a closed, 'priestly' direction. Wesleyan ministerial feeling was more collective than he thinks, and more in touch with the eighteenth century, and John Wesley's own attitudes to what 'revivalism' meant when run in this way.

approaching an American scale. Moreover, the years in which Primitive Methodism grew, 1800–17, were years of lower-class poverty and violence; riots, many of them food riots, were common in 1800–1; and in February, 1803, Edward Despard and six London guardsmen were executed for allegedly trying to organize national insurrection;[14] 1811 to 1817 was the period of intensive Luddism. The hysteria of the war years worked both ways, inflaming the minds of both governors and governed with dreams of conspiracy; religion offered some people alternative kinds of ecstasy, which, as has already been suggested, could move surprisingly close to politics in troubled times.

Bourne, at any rate, was angry at official dislike of revivalism; he continued to read the articles about camp-meetings, and cultivated a more and more intensely subjective spirituality. He and others developed their own private rules for Christian growth, as might be seen in the case of William Clowes,[15] who

> shut himself up in the chamber with the Bible to see what the Lord would do for him. He felt the spirit of burning when he went up; but the Lord gave it to him until it filled every part of his body at once, burning to his finger-ends, and his eyesight seemed for a while to be taken away. He says that in his work and everything, he gives up all to God, and he has full and perfect patience, and submission to the will of God in all things. . . . This man is such an example of living by faith as I scarcely ever met with and which I am not able at present to follow: but he is uncommonly strict: and if he happens to drink water without asking the Lord to make him truly thankful, it drives him to God for pardon.[16]

The reference to the 'spirit of burning' supplies the clue to the kind of dissociative behaviour which was common among these people. One may compare it with an example from Yucatan Pentecostalism in 1969:

[14] Cf. E. P. Thompson, *The Making of the English Working Class* (1968). He rightly emphasizes the turbulent underside of English society in these years. Dow's revivalism gave form to one reaction to conditions of social tragedy.

[15] For Clowes, Bourne's ablest associate, cf. J. T. Wilkinson, *William Clowes, 1780–1851* (1951).

[16] *The Memoirs of the Life and Labours of the late Venerable Hugh Bourne*, by J. Walford, 1855–7. This passage comes from a lost manuscript of Bourne's journal, for 1805, which was in Walford's possession while he was writing.

The beginning of January, I started going to church, and at the beginning of February, I received the Holy Spirit. I had prayed for it, and then I felt the heat, the heat of the Lord, it reached up to my neck, and I saw a great light, it was like one of those very large lamps, and I began to weep. Then I began to speak in tongues, and I began to pray and pray.[17]

Sensations of burning or heat are one possible element in dissociative behaviour, made more likely in this case because the New Testament Holy Spirit is frequently spoken of in terms of fire. The early nineteenth-century Methodists could draw on well-known eighteenth-century examples of mass dissociative behaviour taking over in the course of evangelistic efforts, as at Everton, in Bedfordshire, in 1759, when the local vicar, Berridge, and John Wesley, were jointly responsible for releasing the outbreak. Wesley's description of the interior of the parish church on a Sunday afternoon in May, 1759, illustrates the kind of tradition from which their cultural expectations sprang in 1800:

> When the power of religion began to be spoken of, the presence of God really filled the place. . . . The greatest number of them who cried or fell were men: but some women, and several children, felt the power of the same Almighty Spirit and seemed just sinking into hell. This occasioned a mixture of various sounds, some shrieking, some roaring aloud; the most general was a loud breathing, like that of people half strangled, and gasping for life; and indeed almost all the cries were like those of human creatures dying in bitter anguish. Great numbers wept without any noise. . . .[18]

Neither Berridge nor Wesley understood what was happening; they fitted the phenomena into their obsessive theological system of conviction of sin followed by the release of justification by faith; they failed to recognize the phenomenon of speaking with tongues when they had it in front of them, no doubt because they had very precise images of what *glossolalia* should be like, and perhaps because they judged the state of

[17] F. D. Goodman, *Speaking in Tongues* (Chicago 1972), p.54. Her examples also come from poor, desperate but not psychotic people.

[18] Quoted from J. Wesley's *Journal* (1759), in *Showers of Blessing*, or Sketches of Revivals of Religion in the Wesleyan Methodist Connexion, Robert Young, 1844. Young defended both Caughey and Phoebe Palmer (v.i.).

those in dissociation from the outside appearance of extreme discomfort. At one stage John Wesley may himself have become temporarily involved:

> I saw a thin, pale girl weeping with sorrow for herself and joy for her companions. Quickly the smiles of heaven came likewise upon her, and her praises joined with those of the others. I then also *laughed* [italics mine] with extreme joy; so did Mr B—ll, who said it was more than he could well bear. So did all who knew the Lord, and some of those who were waiting for salvation; till the cries of those who were struck with the arrows of conviction were almost lost in the sounds of joy.[19]

The psychological possibility of such events—as distinct from the historical memory of them—had died out in Wesleyanism by the middle of the nineteenth century, and Primitive Methodism did not retain the pattern much longer. This was why the Ulster revival of 1859, in which dissociation was once again identified with supernatural intervention, struck so many English evangelicals as bizarre, and was defended by others only as a matter of duty. In the meantime men like Hugh Bourne, William Clowes, and James Crawford (who lived from 1758 to 1839, dominated the Magic Methodists among whom visions and trances were common, but who withdrew from Primitive Methodism in 1813, perhaps because of rivalry with Bourne), were ripe for the eccentric and intense leadership of Dow.

Dow landed at Liverpool on 24 December, 1805, where he preached for the first time under the aegis of the Methodist New Connexion. Peter Phillips heard him and took him off to Warrington. His appearance was striking. George Herod wrote:

> The first time we were introduced to him we thought he was the most singular person we ever beheld. In stature he was about five feet ten inches; he was not amply supplied with bone and flesh considering his height; he had small features—his eyes were light brown and very penetrating. The colour of his face was sallow, Yankee-like; he had a hat in Quaker fashion—with a low crown and broad brim—a black spencer upon a blue double-breasted coat; his trousers were of the same colour. His hair reached to the

[19] Ibid., p.31.

bottom of the cuff of his coat sleeve; and his beard covered his breast.[20]

His style was equally and deliberately startling. When he preached in a house at Frodsham in 1806

his manner became the subject of much talk and the people watched his words very closely. A very fine looking young female was in the congregation, having a beautiful rose fixed to the bosom of her dress—in the middle of his sermon he paused, and stepped from his stand, and went direct to the young woman and took the rose from her dress—it immediately shed, leaving the stem in his hand; he said to her, 'in less than twelve months you will fall like this rose by death'. He then returned to his stand and resumed his discourse. The young female before the meeting closed was brought into the enjoyment of true religion, and in a few months after sickened and died, triumphant in the faith.[21]

Herod had no reservations about the propriety of this. A later American revivalist, James Caughey, well-known in the 1840s in Methodism, also enjoyed making prophecies about the fate of his hearers (v.i.). Herod told a similar story about Dow's visit to England in 1818.

On September 14th he preached at the opening of the East Bridgford Chapel. In the middle of his sermon he made a rest, then came down and passed through the congregation to a young man who stood on the outside and who had only recently been converted. He laid his hand on the young man's shoulder and said, 'How long halt you between two opinions respecting your call to preach the gospel? You are called of God and woe unto you if you preach not the Gospel.' He then told him he would meet great opposition through life etc. At the close of his address, or rather, prophecy, he laid his hands on the young man's head and offered up a fervent and solemn prayer. This to the congregation was completely new; yet the greatest decorum was maintained whilst the preacher was performing the ceremony of ordination. He then returned to his stand and resumed his discourse. . . .[22]

The drama no doubt depended on prior knowledge, picked

[20] See *Biographical Sketches*, by George Herod, published in the 1850s. Herod, a Primitive Methodist itinerant, who died 30 August, 1862, met Dow in 1818.
[21] Herod, op. cit., p.183.
[22] Ibid., pp.187–8.

up in conversation, of the people concerned. In the spontaneity of the ordination scene can be traced the confluence of revivalist, Quaker and popular ideas about the divine spirit, all of which came together in the belief that anyone could do anything provided that he was moved to do so directly by a supernatural prompting and empowering. Dow moved easily in such an atmosphere, and he had other attractions as well. He was a personal revelation of the revivals which were going on in the United States, a country of which the English working-classes approved through most of the nineteenth century; they did not share the middle- and upper-class contempt for republican America. Dow knew how camp-meetings should be conducted because he had taken part in them; he was eager to talk about them, moreover, and to start them in England, because he believed that the American revivals heralded a new outburst of religious life which would sweep through the whole Protestant world. Americans with an ideological mission have become familiar in the nuclear age; Dow was less heavily armed, but he still affected English popular religion profoundly.

Dow had published in Dublin, his first port, and also in Liverpool, a number of brief tracts exalting the camp-meeting system. Bourne bought some of these publications from him and made good use of them. He read, among others, the extraordinary diatribe which Dow had written in Liverpool in 1807. It was called *Queries, Observations and Remarks, or Thoughts on the Times and Camp Meetings etc with a Word to the Methodists*, and it was sub-titled 'his last European publication'. Dow's thoughts on the times commenced with a highly cryptic interpretation of the relations between Bonaparte and the Pope worked out in terms of the Book of Revelation. Into this apocalyptic pattern the American camp-meetings fitted as another sign that the Spirit was being poured out at the End of the Times.

> In the present state of things may we not view some prognostic of events now in the womb of time, but which futurity not many years hence shall more particularly exhibit to view? The spirit of missionary enterprise, with the great outpouring of the Spirit of God, or revivals of religion, particularly in America, I think deserve notice; also the shaking of the nations in the sweeping off

of the wicked by sword, famine and pestilence, which are the scourges of the Almighty. And I think that what we have seen is but a token of what is to come; and that God will not withdraw these things until the inhabitants of the world learn righteousness.

Dow then turned abruptly from the speculative and gave details about the American camp-meetings. What probably caught the attention of Bourne and his friends was the juxtaposition of this with a short paragraph headed, 'A Word to the Methodists'. This was written as though Dow was a person of some consequence, and ran:

> Being about to sail to the land of my nativity, I entreat all into whose hands this may come, to pay attention to the following remarks; whilst a ministry are kept poor, they have generally a more godly simplicity; and, of course, purity. Secondly, there is need for a pious body frequently to have recourse to their first principles; therefore, not amiss to read the old magazines, to see if there is any contrast, etc., etc., etc. . . .

Given his personal impact, these random shots hit a bigger target than Dow may have realized, at any rate in 1807. There was certainly a connexion between Dow's appeal for a return to first principles and Bourne's attempt to revive 'primitive Methodism'. The more lasting effect of Dow's personality on the Staffordshire group becomes clear from Bourne's manuscript Journal. Through 1810 and 1811 many members of the new Church (for so they already regarded it), were accustomed to have visions, this being one possible aspect of dissociative behaviour. They believed themselves to be directly inspired by the divine Spirit, and on at least one occasion a man in a vision was told that another member was suffering from unbelief, which was admitted by the offender. These visions, however, also served another, odder purpose: they revealed who were the leading members of the group. In one of the earliest of the visions of this type, recorded on 6 May, 1810, when Nancy Foden 'went into vision', 'it appeared to us that the man who stood above James Crawford, dropping honey from his fingers, was Lorenzo Dow'—this was four years after Dow had gone back to America. On that occasion James Crawford was 'the second trumpeter', Clowes the fifth, and Hugh Bourne the seventh. On 20 April, 1811, Hugh Bourne recorded that 'the head of the Church now stands as follows: James Crawford 1, Lorenzo Dow 2, Mary Dunnel 3', etc. William Clowes was again fifth and Bourne sixth. The visions happened frequently at this time, and at the end of May, 1811, Hannah Mountford saw another list, in which Crawford was still first and Dow second. On 30 July, 1811, when Hannah Weston was in vision, Clowes had moved up to third place. At this point the visions ceased, as one would expect to happen after they had continued for a certain length of time. The cessation was hastened, however, by a quarrel between Bourne and Mary Dunnel, who had usually been third in these vision-lists of the trumpeters: Bourne accused her of lording it over the people in 'the old Wesleyan manner', and allegedly proved her, in December, 1811, to have three husbands living at once. Like most famous Methodist leaders, however, Bourne was no democrat (except when criticizing Jabez Bunting), and it is significant that a similar breach took place with James Crawford in 1812, leaving only William Clowes, who had his own base in Hull, as a serious rival to Bourne himself. As far as Dow was concerned, the interesting side of the visions was the status which Dow retained in them; his being second to Crawford reflected the immediate prestige of the Delamere Forest group. Dow did not return to England until 1817, and died in 1824; he was forgotten because the very nature of the early movement was forgotten after 1850.

Dow's criticism of the Wesleyan ministry was bound to appeal in north Staffordshire, where the would-be revivalists constantly found themselves at odds with the local itinerants. Many Methodists resented the changes which took place in Wesleyanism after the founder's death in 1791. There was a struggle for power between the itinerants and a more Nonconformist section of the laity which had caused a division in 1797, when the Methodist New Connexion was formed. A New Connexion chapel stood in Hanley, and knowledge of what had happened only ten years before affected the judgement of both the Wesleyan ministers and the laymen in the Burslem circuit between 1807 and 1810. Bourne was actually expelled from the Wesleyan Connexion by the Burslem Quarterly Meeting on 27 June, 1808; Hanley and Burslem are only a few miles apart.

The picture of American camp-meetings which Dow printed by the side of his appeal for a return to the primitive past suggested the obvious alternative of romantic simplicity and religious passion. He wrote:

> Having tent equipage of blankets, sheets or coverlets, sewed together, and etc., and the night before the meeting, several companies will arrive and pitch their tents, and spend most of the night in devotion, for a blessing on the meeting. Early the next morning, the people will be flocking in by hundreds. At twelve o'clock the trumpet sounds, all hands repair to the stage, except one person to a tent. The meeting is opened by singing, prayer and an introductory discourse; an exhortation or two subjoined; and then the meeting dismissed until evening. The remainder of the day is spent in preparation for the night; when you may see a hundred fires; with candles, lamps, lantherns, and etc., suspended from the boughs of trees, and parties taking their tea, coffee, etc. The trumpet sounds for meeting; at the close of which, an invitation is given for mourners to come forward to be prayed for: perhaps a distressed soul, who has walked many miles with a burdened conscience, comes forward with streaming eyes; and others follow the example: and whilst the preachers are joining with them in prayer, the meeting is generally crowned with the cry of a new-born soul. Thus the work breaks out and continues for hours, though most have retired to their tents. At dawn of day the trumpet sounds for family prayer at every tent. At sunrise, for a general prayer meeting. At eight, twelve, three and candlelight for preaching.

This was in line with the descriptions which Bourne had been reading for some time in the *Wesleyan Methodist Magazine*:

> The order of our religious exercises was as follows: an horn was blown in the morning to collect the people to a general prayer meeting at eight o'clock. After this was ended, viz. about ten o'clock, preaching began. The like order was observed in the afternoon, one sermon was preached at a time, generally two or three exhortations were delivered. During this time the minds of the people were affected in an extraordinary manner. Many fell down slain, so to speak, with the sword of the Spirit, the Word of God, and groaned, like men dying in the field of battle, while rivers of tears ran down their cheeks. A number of souls were quickened and comforted on Saturday and through the Sabbath.

... Oh, my dear sir, if you had been there you would have been astonished. In one place you would have seen a poor sinner leaning with his head against a tree with the tears running from his eyes, while some went to him and pointed him to the Lamb of God. If you had turned your eyes in another direction you would have discovered a grey-headed father and his two daughters all down upon their knees together among the leaves and dirt, crying to God to have mercy on their souls. . . . The appearance of the place at night was very solemn, and at the same time, romantic. When going to the place a person heard the preaching, singing and other exercises of devotion at some distance off, and coming by a winding path through a thick wood, all of a sudden he beheld a large congregation of people, and a whole train of fires all round them. Candles and lanterns hung on the trees in every direction, and the lofty oaks, with their spreading boughs, formed a canopy over our heads, while everything conspired with the solemnity of the night to make the place seem awful.[23]

Bourne could not see why the *Wesleyan Methodist Magazine* should print such letters if the practises described in them were improper for Wesleyans. He adapted the system for English use as an open-air method of revival. There was no camp, of course, for few of the people interested would have been free to attend one. These English meetings took place on a Sunday, the one day when the rural workers were comparatively at liberty; they lasted from dawn to dusk, and were often rounded off with a love-feast in a convenient local chapel. Bourne developed a strong interest in technique, and he did not believe in the sort of revival meeting in which everything hangs on the personality of a single speaker. At his camps there were a number of preaching-stands, usually waggons; he defended this on the ground of variety and because it made it easier for everyone to hear. He also arranged teams of what he called 'pious praying labourers'; after the preachers had spoken for about an hour these teams 'went out', as the expression was, and held prayer-meetings for the next hour which centred, if possible, on anyone who had been affected by the preaching. Sometimes he introduced what he called 'reading services': this meant that, instead of preaching, the speaker read to the crowd around him some poignant

[23] *Wesleyan Methodist Magazine*, May, 1804, pp.235-6. The camp was near Baltimore.

biography, together with an obituary from a religious magazine, the kind of article which always ended with a long-
drawn out, triumphant death-bed, full of cries and quotations
from remembered revival songs. Then there was singing,
used on Bourne's principle, 'Let a little singing be occasionally
intermingled to vary the exercises'. As we shall see, this was a
point at which Dow's assistance proved vital.

All this variety of approach was based on Bourne's study of
American examples; it is interesting that when the camp-
meetings reached a crisis between 1816 and 1819 Bourne again
solved his difficulties through the use of American precedents.
The details of the crisis are obscure. There are two distinct
references to it in the *History of Primitive Methodism* which
Hugh Bourne originally began in 1819,[24] and he seems to have
made no attempt to relate them to one another. The earliest
reference is in chapter four, where he speaks only of Derbyshire in 1816; the other comes in chapter six and refers to the
state of affairs in the enormous Tunstall circuit in 1819. In
both versions Bourne said that after the first few years the
camp-meetings had degenerated into a monotonous programme of tedious sermons, many of them more than an hour
long. The praying services had been dropped, so that the
course of the camps became nothing but sermon after sermon.
Bourne commented that all this had nearly driven the converting power out of the Tunstall circuit. What makes these
accounts slightly confusing is that Bourne spoke as though
the evil had been coped with by the time of the Mercaston
camp-meeting in the passage in chapter four, whereas in
chapter six he said that this defective manner of holding
camp-meetings had been started in Tunstall at the end of 1816
and that it was not finally abolished until the March quarterly
meeting in 1819. Both statements could be true, but Bourne
did not write as though this was what he intended to say.

John Petty, in the first serious account of the denomination,
History of the Primitive Methodist Connexion (1860), solved the
problem of these two passages by the omission of any reference
to the problems of the Tunstall circuit. More important,
however, was that neither Bourne nor Petty (who was

---

[24] This account was read to the Hull Annual Conference in 1820; published in the
Primitive Methodist Magazine, and printed separately in 1823.

presumably following Bourne closely at this earlier stage of his book) referred to the visit of Lorenzo Dow to the Midlands in 1818, a visit which certainly influenced the course of events. Bourne's unpublished diary for 1818, which survived the disappearance of most of his private journals for the years between 1813 and 1840, contains entries which show that the two men met. The diary, which was brief and obviously written in haste, contains the note:

> Sunday 19 (July) Camp Meeting at Tunstall Lorenzo Dow was there. We had some rain at noon with thunder and lightning. Monday 20 July was at Tunstall, we had a number of preachings. Lorenzo Dow spoke at five in the morning and five in the evening.

If Dow attended camp-meetings at Tunstall in 1818 he may well have made criticisms, and suggested remedies.[25]

The only direct confirmation of Dow's visit is to be found in George Herod's *Biographical Sketches*, published in the 1850s. Herod heard him at Bingham, where he held an open-air service in the market place on Sunday afternoon, 14 September, 1818. Herod wrote:

> He commenced by singing one of his American hymns, which the people had been accustomed to sing for some months past; thus hundreds joined in the grand chorus of hallelujahs. After delivering a very pointed and pithy discourse (for it was full of Jesus Christ) he saw that a great many were deeply wrought upon by the Spirit and the word; he therefore immediately went into the centre of the congregation and requested the people to draw back and form a circle; he then stood and invited the penitents to come forward and receive a blessing of pardon; and in a few minutes the whole space was filled; he then enlarged the space by requesting the congregation to go further back; but this was also soon taken up—we should judge that not less than two hundred were on their knees seeking pardon. He then commenced prayer and very soon his voice was lost among the groans and cries for mercy; and in less than half an hour we should suppose one hundred souls were brought into gospel liberty.[26]

In chapter four of his own *History*, Bourne attributed his

---

[25] The diary, at one time in the library of Hartley Victoria College, Manchester, is now in the keeping of Manchester University.

[26] Herod, op. cit., pp. 188–9.

success in handling the camp-meeting crisis to the fact that he had read Joshua Marsden's *Narrative of a Mission to Nova Scotia*, in which he found a description of a New York camp-meeting which Marsden had attended, at which the Americans had not only listened to four or five preachers a day, but had interspersed the sermons with prayer-meetings. In chapter six, he made no reference to outside inspiration, but said that in March, 1819, the Tunstall quarterly meeting drew up camp-meeting regulations according to which the time of the gatherings should be equally divided between preaching and prayer. Dow, who had visited Tunstall, Nottingham, Leicester and many other smaller places, sailed to America from Dublin at the end of March, 1819.

The most likely explanation of all this lies in Bourne's character. By the time that he wrote the *History* Bourne had become rather complacent about his share in the establishment of Primitive Methodism. He was a jealous man; he felt uneasy about William Clowes and bitterly criticized his colleague's *Journal* when it was published as long after as 1844. The use of a portrait of Bourne as a frontispiece to the 1823 *History* caused unfavourable comment at the time, because it seemed to imply that Bourne was the sole founder. In writing the *History* he certainly did not want to draw further attention to Dow. Bourne's biographer, Walford, who wrote in 1855-7, accepted the tradition in playing down Dow's return, and was inclined to think that Bourne was 'dissatisfied' with Dow at this time, perhaps because he was travelling, for part of the time, with the Yorkshire Quakeress, Dorothy Ripley. Herod, in a better position to know, said that Dow 'had written and published a pamphlet upon the happiness of a married life, and some of the views it contained were now opposed by Mr Bourne'.[27] This comment applied to September, 1818. Bourne, though occasionally tempted to marry, set a high value on celibacy. What Bourne had effectively obscured, however, was that when his own efforts to reform the English camp meeting system had become ineffective, it was Lorenzo Dow's return which had set the Connexion moving again.

In Primitive Methodist legend, the first English camp-meeting was held on Mow Cop, in Staffordshire on 31 May,

[27] Herod, op. cit., p.187.

1807; it was not really, however, a camp-meeting at all. It took place only on the Sunday, without much preparation, and the number of people who came—between two and four thousand—took the organizers completely by surprise. As Bourne said, 'We had no previous plan. It was like Judges, 21,25 : every man did that which was right in his own eyes.'[28] John Riles, the Wesleyan superintendent of the Burslem circuit, sanctioned this meeting, in the hope that it would satisfy the local demand for 'a day's praying'; before the Norton meeting, however, which happened in August, the Wesleyan Conference had met and forbidden camp-meetings altogether.

Dow's converts were prominent at Mow Cop. One of them was an Irish lawyer living at Knutsford, whose speech was chiefly about what he had lost in the recent Irish rebellion. Another was a former Deist 'who had been preferred in the army and had left a leg in Africa. . . . He shewed the happiness of our land and the gratitude we owed to God for being exempted from the seat of war'. Bourne may have included these statements in the hope of soothing those who felt that any large popular gathering must be politically disaffected, or open to agitators who would exploit the ignorant poor. In fact, Mow Cop had attracted too many people for either the organizers or the authorities, and patriotic speeches calmed no one, especially in the Wesleyan Connexion. There had been four speakers in operation at once at the height of the occasion; by four in the afternoon the meeting began to disperse and only one preacher was still on his feet at six. At seven, however, 'a work began among children, six of whom were converted, or born again, before the meeting broke up'.[29]

Myth apart, Mow Cop was no more than a large open-air meeting for which there was plenty of eighteenth-century precedent in the history of the Evangelical Revival. Much more like camp-meetings were those at Mow Cop (19–21 July), and at Norton-le-Moors (23–25 August), 1807. This was because they took place at the time of the annual parish feast

[28] *Observations on Camp Meetings*, with an account of a camp meeting held on 31 May, 1807, at Mow, near Harriseahead. By Hugh Bourne, 1807.
[29] Ibid. Bourne seems not to have been prominent on this occasion.

or wake, when whole villages had a holiday, fairs were set up
and there was a drastic break with the normal rhythm of life.
The Norton meeting had been planned for months as a
deliberate offset to what seemed to the Staffordshire pietists
the wickedness of the wakes. How successful these camps were
it is hard to say: in the case of the second Mow meeting,
Bourne claimed that 'upwards of sixty souls were hopefully
converted from sin to holiness in life and conduct'.[30]

The Norton camp mattered much more than the previous
ones because in the meantime the Wesleyan Conference had
said that 'it is our judgement that, even supposing such
meetings to be allowable in America, they are highly improper
in England and likely to be productive of considerable
mischief, and we disclaim all connexion with them'.[31] The
Wesleyan Conference then consisted only of itinerant
ministers. The superintendent of the Burslem Circuit required
the local preachers, who were laymen, to promise that they
would have no more to do with the system.

No doubt the Wesleyan Conference intended to make only
a local decision in which local factors counted for almost
everything; there was no conscious idea of opposing 'a
revival of religion'. As has already been suggested, however,
the Wesleyan leaders knew that some of the Methodist laity
wanted a more democratic system of church government; they
had survived one secession in 1797, but feared another. They
knew that both Independent Methodists (from Macclesfield)
and Quaker Methodists (from Warrington) had attended the
second Mow meeting, and they must have been told by the
Burslem ministers of the links between Bourne, Phillips and
Crawford. Lorenzo Dow had been free of their control; what
he said in a political style on this occasion we do not know,
but when he was in England in 1818 George Herod heard
him 'contend for the superiority of Republicanism over other
forms of government', a sentiment natural to many (though
not all) Americans at this time, but unlikely to have commended him to the Wesleyans if they were given similar
reports about him in 1807. Revivalism, in any case, threw up

[30] Walford, op. cit., p.151. Bourne said the immorality of the wakes was never the
same again, but attendance at the Mow camp declined on the Monday and Tuesday,
which suggests that the wake was still drawing well.
[31] *Minutes of the Wesleyan Methodist Conference*, 1807.

groups of laymen who resented outside control, and in this resembled the Sunday School movement.[32] Jabez Bunting was serious when he said that 'schism from the body will be a less evil than schism in it',[33] and similar earlier exclusions had not had very drastic consequences. The miscalculation was not about revivalism, but about the social context of this particular group, which was much less accessible to Wesleyan pressure than the urban revivalists in Manchester and Leeds who had failed to find a leader in William Bramwell. The Burslem ministers no doubt expected that Bourne would form a tiny sect of earnest pietists who would withdraw happily into the obscurity of their own private hierarchy; the decisive factor was probably the camp-meetings themselves, which at the crucial moment expanded the numbers involved and jerked what would otherwise have been as little noticed a body as the Quaker Methodists, or the Methodist Unitarians (who also sprang up and withered again between 1800 and 1850), into a wider social and political environment, in which it briefly flourished.

Bourne's determination to persevere with the Norton camp-meeting therefore marked a vital stage in the emergence of Primitive Methodism; if this camp-meeting had failed, the Wesleyan itinerants would probably have been justified as the latest outburst of revivalism died down. Bourne showed his awareness of this, saying in his journal that

> my sufferings were heavy and my sorrows were great, but by labours and diligence I got all things ready by Saturday evening, 22 August, 1807; and we had a course of praying, and the Lord was with us, and I so far copied after the Americans as to sleep all night in one of the tents.[34]

Even so, almost the first thing that he heard at six o'clock the following morning was that the Tunstall Wesleyans, on whom he had depended for preachers, had decided to obey their

---

[32] For Sunday Schools in these years, cf. W. R. Ward, *Religion and Society in England, 1780–1850* (1972); his statement that Mow Cop 'had no political significance' (p.76), seems much too confident; his suggestion that Wesleyan theology was showing signs of becoming 'a bore' misses the point; revivalist theology differed very little in content or repetitiousness from Wesleyanism.

[33] T. P. Bunting, *Life of Jabez Bunting* (1887), i. p.248.

[34] Walford, op. cit., p.161.

Superintendent and to abandon the meeting. Again Dow came to the rescue, this time in the shape of one of his converts, a Dr Paul Johnson, who had heard of the Norton meeting from the Irish lawyer who lived at Knutsford and who now arrived, believing 'that the Lord required that he assist'.[35] The atmosphere in which Bourne and his friends were living at the time is shown by his comment on Johnson's advent:

> Dr Johnson being much in the Quaker way, we could not tell when he would preach, but all fell in well. When he stood up his voice filled the field, and his preaching took surprisingly with the hosts of potters. He appeared to suit the meeting and the people more than any other preacher. I myself had experienced reluctance to preaching, but the discourse of a pious sister at Delamere Forest had very much removed it, and now the remarks of Dr Johnson who had received good under my preaching, cleared away the remainder of my reluctance.[36]

Johnson, whose intervention sustained the meeting, stayed until the Monday evening; significantly, on the Tuesday the meeting did not commence until noon and lasted until about six in the evening. Walford agreed that without Johnson's unexpected coming the Norton meeting would have collapsed, clearly because no one else could carry the burden of speaking. Bourne had not quite the qualities of leadership with which he credited himself, and on this occasion his nerve evidently gave way at one point. William Clowes had stayed at home altogether. In practice, it was another twelve months before Bourne was finally expelled from the Wesleyan society, but this was the time when the breach was made. It is sufficient to add an account of a camp-meeting held at the height of the revivalistic fervour of the 1820s.

> August 13, 1826, I, with brothers J.H. and J.R. attended a camp meeting at Kingsmoor, about five miles from Tenby. A little after nine we opened with a prayer meeting. I then spoke a little respecting the nature of camp meetings. Then Brother R. spoke; Brother H. read a memoir out of the Magazine; I exhorted a

[35] Johnson was no stranger to revivalism, however; he had attended Dow when he was ill in Ireland, and according to Herod (op. cit., p.184) had come over to England with him in 1806 and had preached in Cheshire and Lancashire. Such men did not usually stand by silent when there was a revival going on.
[36] Walford, op. cit., p.116.

little, and we went out into praying companies after which we again attended at the stand until dinner. At the opening after dinner I spoke a little on the origin and success of Camp Meetings; and Brother H. read another memoir. . . . I then made a few remarks and we went out again; the power of the Lord was abundantly manifested and there was much weeping. We came again to the stand, and I spoke on the nature of godly sorrow. We went out again and the Lord was with us. After which Brother H. preached and I exhorted and we concluded. In the evening we held a love feast at Hill, about half a mile from the camp ground. I spent a few minutes explaining the nature of love feasts; and after the bread and water had gone round we commenced speaking. And though not more than three or four of our members present had even been at a love feast, yet there was no backwardness in speaking, for the friends (chiefly colliers) spoke in the simplicity of their souls (not losing a moment) till the Spirit of the Lord descended in such a manner that weeping and groaning, mingled with shouts of praise, were heard in every part of the room: I then exhorted them to be looking to the Lord for faith, for that He was now come with His converting power. Immediately, a man fell on his knees and cried for mercy, I then stepped down and pointed him to the Saviour of sinners, and shortly he rose up and shouted the praises of God. I then went to another who was in great distress: but her sister wished to have her out, saying she was overcome with the heat of the place. I desired her to let her alone, telling her that she would soon see her rejoicing in God. However, with difficulty I got her away, and her sister in distress cried, 'Pray for me'. I told her to plead the merits of Jesus who died for her; his all-powerful name again prevailed and she was filled with glory and with God.[37]

This was the rhythmical alternation of sermon and story, prayer and love-feast which Bourne wanted. By 1826, the new Primitive Methodist 'itinerant' was orchestrating the whole, seeking to push the group to the point at which, in the phraseology generally adopted, 'the power of the Lord (or of the Spirit) was abundantly manifested', the point at which the group took off emotionally and followed the patterns of behaviour which, in the example quoted, the revivalist had carefully set out beforehand. In this instance the expectancy was increased because in a love-feast, the materials of which

[37] *Primitive Methodist Magazine*, 1826.

were simply bread and water, those present were able to talk about themselves, 'testifying', as they put it, which meant that they described, with reference to their own lives, experiences of guilt and forgiveness which others could then imitate. As in later Pentecostalism, and still in the eighteenth-century tradition, there was positive encouragement to those taking part to release their feelings by shouting, singing, weeping and physical movement; and as Bourne had protested to Butler, those who were familiar with such meetings could see an ordered, if excited process, repeated again and again, in which the participants were 'taken out of themselves' in genuine sensations of peace, harmony and joy. Much of what happened was analogous to the euphoria generated in twentieth-century youth festivals dominated by popular music and strong guiding personalities; the moral value of either revivalist meeting or pop-festival depended on the teaching which accompanied the emotional and physical release, though there was no guarantee that those who were converted by the Primitive Methodists or uplifted by the pop-festivals would change their personal behaviour as a result. Potters, miners and rural workers had few opportunities for satisfactions of this kind in the early nineteenth century. What has been called 'mass evangelism', though it might be better described as 'lower-middle-class evangelism in large groups', the urban revivals of the 1870s, organized by Moody and Sankey, repudiated these aims and substituted more genteel techniques; the older tradition reappeared, however, in the early holiness meetings of the Salvation Army in the late 1870s, and in the Pentecostal groups which were forming by the end of the nineteenth century.

As far as the American contribution to all this was concerned, the new music which Lorenzo Dow brought with him from the United States proved very important. Dow published the words, and taught the tunes, of what he called *A Collection of Spiritual Songs used at the Camp Meetings in the Great Revival in the United States of America*. More than one edition came out in England. The earliest known preface is signed 22 February, 1806; this is found in a copy reproduced by George Herod[38] as printed by H. Forshaw in Liverpool in

[38] Herod, op. cit., p.216.

1806; this must have been soon after Dow landed at the close of 1805. A second preface is dated Dublin, August, 1806, and implies that Dow published a second edition there; this has sometimes been taken for the first edition. The Dublin date-line is also found, however, in a copy printed by James Smith in Liverpool in 1807. Herod's original version was titled Part One, and the order of the songs was not the same as in the Liverpool version. 'My soul's full of glory which inspires my tongue' stood first in the 1806 collection and twelfth in 1807. The second song in the Herod version, 'One night as I lay musing the Spirit said to me Go blow the Gospel trumpet and sound the Jubilee', was not in the 1807 book. The date of the 1807 edition may have been in April, when Dow printed other works; the price was sixpence.

This was not only the first specifically revivalist song-book to be issued in England but also the first, though by no means the last, to attract attention on the ground that the songs in it had been used successfully in American revivals. Hugh Bourne bought a copy in April, 1807, and liked it so much that he reprinted twenty-one and a half of the twenty-three songs in his own first hymnbook, which he published in 1809, and enlarged to contain seventy-seven songs and hymns in 1821.[39] Nineteen of the original twenty-three songs were also reprinted, without mention of indebtedness to Dow, however, in the *Collection for Camp Meetings, Revivals etc for the use of the Primitive Methodists*, the volume which became known to the new denomination as the Small Hymnbook. It contained one hundred and fifty-four hymns. The vitality of Dow's songs proved remarkable. Richard Weaver (*v.i.*), for example, who carried on the tradition of the singing evangelist which Dow had incarnated, used them in the London theatre services he held in 1860, and printed some of them in his own revival songbook.

The songs which Dow printed expressed religious ecstasy with rough vigour, and in doing so both suited the kind of meeting which has been described, and helped it on to its fruition. 'The Dying Pilgrim' is one example:

[39] *A General Collection of Hymns and Spiritual Songs for Camp Meetings and Revivals*, selected by Hugh Bourne. Newcastle-under-Lyme, printed at the office of C. Chester, 1809; according to his manuscript journal, the book had been published by February, 1809.

My soul's full of glory which inspires my tongue,
Could I meet with angels I'd sing them a song.
I'd sing of my Jesus and tell of his charms,
And beg them to bear me to his loving arms. . . .

Oh Heaven, sweet Heaven, I long to be there,
To meet all my brethren and Jesus my dear.
Come angels, come angels, I'm ready to fly,
Come quickly convey me to God in the sky. . . .

I'm going, I'm going, but what do I see;
T'is Jesus in glory appears unto me.
To Heaven, to Heaven I'm gone, I'm gone,
Oh glory, oh glory, 'tis done, 'tis done.

John Adam Granade, the Billy Sunday of the Second Great Awakening which lasted from about 1792 to about 1801, probably wrote these words;[40] he lived from 1775 to about 1806. The other celebrated composer of camp-meeting songs was John Leland (1754–1844), who was a Baptist minister.

The theme of ascending to glory is found in many Southern camp-meeting songs; no doubt they were popular partly because the core experience of the meetings was one of being lifted from one plane to another, or of being released from one's normal self into what seemed for the time being to be limitless freedom. This was not necessarily a religious experience: the movement and imagery of the song just quoted obviously exploit a possible sexual reference at the same time as they exalt a religious one—the American camps, lasting for days and bringing together masses of normally isolated farming families (as at Cane Ridge in 1801 in Kentucky, the most famous of them all), were known not only for the 'outpouring of the Spirit', but for the comment that sometimes 'more souls were begotten than saved'. Other songs crystallized the crisis which revivalists believed to face all human beings, and especially human beings at camp-meetings. Thus the last stanza of the 'Camp Meeting Farewell' ran:

[40] For the music of the camp meeting songs, cf. *Spiritual Folk-Songs of Early America*, collected and edited by G. P. Jackson (New York 1937).

Farewell, farewell, fare you well,
Poor careless sinners too,
It grieves my soul to leave you here;
Eternal vengeance waits for you,
Oh turn and find salvation near;
Oh turn, oh turn, oh turn,
And find salvation near.

The case for the religious element in the whole social experience which the camps devised (and which could never be properly or fully reproduced among English working-class people in the early nineteenth century because of the quite different social and geographical conditions), was put in terms of this threat that men who were not 'saved' would be perpetually 'damned'. The Liverpool edition of Dow's songs made this clear in detail:

Will mercy then her arms extend?
Will Jesus be thy guardian friend
And Heaven thy dwelling-place?
Or shall insulting fiends appear
And drag thee down to dark despair
Beyond the reach of grace?

A Heaven or Hell, and these alone,
Beyond the present life are known,
There is no middle state;
Today attend the call divine,
Tomorrow may be none of thine,
Or it may be too late.

Using this simple theological framework, with its clear contrast between exaltation and misery, the Southern revivalists implanted a religious tradition, chiefly Baptist and Methodist, which has begun to crumble only in the second half of the twentieth century. The whole process offers an example of what Emile Durkheim called 'collective effervescence',[41] by which he meant a kind of frenzy which seizes on a small or larger social group, and which he identified in the central mass outburst of the French Revolution as well as in

[41] Cf. E. Durkheim, *The Elementary Forms of the Religious Life* (London 1954).

some religious rituals. In such times of intense communal activity, Durkheim thought, collective representations were impressed on people's minds, and sometimes, as in the French Revolution (we should now also think of the Russian and Chinese revolutions), new symbols were created in this existential sense. If one applies this idea to the history of revivalism, Cane Ridge would stand for an effervescence of this kind, because the great revivals did stamp on the South an ordered, sub-christian culture from which that society has never yet broken entirely free, and whose impact can be measured in the writings of the Southern novelists, in Faulkner, for example, or in Flannery O'Connor. Mow Cop, on the other hand, would stand for failure by comparison, for it was not to be through the agency of revivalism that the consciousness of the English working-class was to be modified in the first half of the nineteenth century; it was rather the working-class which temporarily penetrated Primitive Methodism with something of its own political ambitions and so gave the Connexion its hour of social importance in the 1840s. In so far as there was a collective movement in the American South in the early years of the nineteenth century to create an ordered society at the level of the poorer white population, this communal impulse seems to have worked through religious institutions; in England, the nineteenth-century urban working-class turned away from organized Christianity as a political instrument after 1850; a new working-class religious outlook developed, which used some Christian symbols, but rejected the characteristic doctrines of evangelical Protestantism.

This explains why, when Moody and Sankey launched urban mass evangelism in the 1870s, they did not find an audience at the working-class level. They drew their hearers from more direct descendants from the Evangelical Revival, the drapers' assistants of the world of the Y.M.C.A., the middle-class students of the slowly expanding group of new universities, and from other social groups uncertain about their identity, caught between rich and poor, longing for upward social mobility, if they could but find the way to rise. In the changed circumstances Sankey, whether he knew it or not, was already muting the 'Old Time Religion', as one can see by comparing Lorenzo Dow's vigour with Sankey's sentimentality. Sankey sang:

> Meet me there, oh meet me there,
> No bereavement we shall bear,
> There no sighings for the dead,
> There no farewell tear is shed;
> We shall, safe from all alarms,
> Clasp our loved one in our arms,
> And in Jesu's glory share:
> Meet me there—oh, meet me there.

Dow's tone was quite different:

> Hark, listen to the trumpeters,
> They sound for volunteers;
> On Zion's bright and flowery mount
> Behold the officers—
> Their horses white, their garments bright,
> With crown and bow they stand;
> Inlisting soldiers for the King
> To march for Canaan's land.
>
> It sets my heart all in a flame
> A soldier I will be,
> I will inlist, gird on my arms,
> And fight for liberty.
> They want no tories in their band,
> That will their colours fly;
> But call for valiant-hearted men
> That's not afraid to die. . . .

Dow called this 'Zion's Volunteer', though the reference to the tories suggested that the American War of Independence was as present to the writer's mind as the struggle for a more spiritual freedom. One of the tunes to which it was sung was called 'We'll End this War'. William Booth printed it in his *Revival Hymnbook* of 1875, changing 'tories' to 'cowards' as Primitive Methodist editors had done before him. Sankey's songs rarely evoked a military image; they usually implied that the faithful were permanently quartered in a rest camp well behind the lines; Dow's on the other hand, relished images of conflict and violence:

While glory bright inspires the fight,
We'll slay the bloody sons of night
And thus we'll take the field.[42]

The obvious link between the two collections was the word 'glory', which stands out again and again in the American songs which Dow used and in their later imitations. 'Glory' rapidly ceased to have any exact meaning: it seemed, when used with any exactness at all, to express a sense of being overpowered and simultaneously empowered by the Divine Spirit. The term appeared even more frequently in the Primitive Methodist *Small Hymnbook* than in Dow's collection:

I'm glad I ever saw the day—sing glory, glory, glory,
We ever met to sing and pray—sing glory, glory, glory,
I've glory, glory in my soul—sing glory, glory, glory,
Which makes me praise my Lord so bold—sing glory, glory, etc.

I hope to praise him when I die, sing glory, glory, glory,
And shout salvation as I fly—sing glory, glory, glory,
Sing glory, glory through the air—sing glory, glory, glory,
And meet my Father's children there—sing glory, glory, glory.

The tradition of spontaneity for which 'glory' stood was almost all that survived of early Primitive Methodism by the end of the century, and it sometimes survived in unexpected places. In her biography of Temple Gairdner, the Anglican missionary to Islam, Constance Padwick recorded this picture of the Oxford of the 1890s:

Bawling down the High Street, not fifty yards from Walter Pater's window, swung a line of undergraduates arm in arm. Some with faces tense with an act of daring and others strangely lighted with an inward joy, they chanted to a totally undistinguished tune:

It is better to shout than to doubt,
It is better to rise than to fall,
It is better to let the glory out
Than to have no glory at all.

[42] Dow, Liverpool edition, no. 11.

The crude words struggled up to Heaven past the twisted columns of St Mary's, past the carved front of All Souls, past Queen Anne, in whose day approved religion was more decent and composed, with less resemblance to intoxication.[43]

Constance Padwick was referring to a time when the Keswick Convention had brought together for a time many diverse elements from the nineteenth-century tradition, but the link with the early years of the century was unmistakable: the 'shouting' and the 'glory' both belonged to American revivalism rather than to English evangelicalism. The 'crude words' lacked the vivacity of the original—Dow's second song, for example, which included:

> Oh then we'll shine and shout and sing
> And make the heavenly arches ring
> When all the saints get home;
> Come on, come on, my brethren dear,
> We soon shall meet together there,
> For Jesus bids us come.

It was no accident that where Dow had called his songs 'spiritual', Sankey labelled his 'sacred'.

By 1850 the American impulse had exhausted itself in Primitive Methodism, which in its turn had become an established religious denomination which would survive until the not very successful unification of the chief branches of Methodism in England in 1932. The middle-class evangelicals who earnestly discussed the possibility of introducing American revivalism into England took very little notice of what was actually happening among miners, potters and agricultural labourers. By the close of the 1830s, however, the turbulent American East, so often and so willingly revived, had lost its appetite for salvation; slavery was becoming the topic of a new age; Calvin Colton himself turned away from revivalism and became a secular politician, his vision of the world's coming redemption thoroughly secularized. From about 1840 down to the eve of the Civil War, the American professional revivalist was not in great demand in his own country, and it was natural that some of the better known should look for an audience in England.

[43] C. M. Padwick, *Temple Gairdner of Cairo* (1929), p.2.

3

1859: The Failure of English Revivalism

I. *1859*

THE dividing line between the old and the new revivalism may be drawn in the years 1857–62, when in America and Northern Ireland the old forms of pietist renewal showed themselves capable of a last major outburst of popular feeling, but in England attempts to encourage similar signs of revival failed almost completely. Once again American professional revivalists sailed to England and once more the results of their work were marginal. This was hardly surprising, for the Church of England was still the most powerful religious body in the country, and Anglican parishes had no American-style tradition of recurrent 'revivals'; no religious movement could hope to be 'national' if it hardly moved the Church of England at all. In the second place, in England differences between rural and urban areas were becoming steadily more pronounced; village depopulation went on while the towns grew in size and wealth, presenting a religious problem to which neither the existing religious institutions nor the traditional kinds of revivalism had adjusted. It would be wrong to suggest that in 1859–60 either the professional or the amateur revivalists succeeded in England.

A wave of religious feeling had swept across Protestant America between the autumn of 1857 and the winter of 1858. The movement was not unconnected with the commercial crisis of 1857; it did not originate with the professional revivalists though they soon joined in. For the last time as a significant national phenomenon, the traditionally Puritan areas went through the phases of being convicted of sin, brought to repentance and finally converted. In the background lay the fact that the Roman Catholic Church in the

United States, which had numbered about 50,000 members in a single diocese in 1800, had grown by 1860 to be the largest denomination in America, with more than two million members in forty-four dioceses.

Evangelical Protestant tradition has always linked the events in America with the similar outbreak of religious feeling in Northern Ireland in 1859–60, on the principle that both historical sequences were caused by the Holy Spirit, who is then represented as the cause of an allegedly great revival which spread from the United States to Northern Ireland, from Ireland to Scotland and Wales, and finally to England.[1] In fact, the chief resemblance between the American and Irish revivals was that they both occurred in communities which felt themselves threatened by a resurgent Roman Catholicism; no Americans transferred the revival from America to Ireland, as Lorenzo Dow had attempted to do more than fifty years before. The wave of American religious feeling had spent itself by the close of 1858 and the first stirrings of the Northern Irish movement did not take place until the spring of 1859. Moreover, the style of the two revivals differed, for the chief characteristic of the Irish revival was the variety of physical phenomena which accompanied it; in the United States these phenomena hardly occurred at all.

Inevitably, the American movement was reported in the British religious press, and the stories led to the usual speculation as to why this religious excitement seemed to happen so rarely in England. John Angell James, the now very elderly minister of Carr's Lane, Birmingham, but still devoted to the possibility of an English revival, gave a paper on the subject to the Congregationalist Union in May, 1858. He called it 'American Revival and the Duties and Hopes of British Christians'. No doubt, he said, circumstances differed in the United States, where there was no State Church, and no overwhelming pressure through caste and social formality to accept a limited view of serious religion. This new American revival, however, ought to satisfy even the most conformist British critics, for it was said to be the result of

[1] See J. E. Orr, *The Second Evangelical Awakening* (1949). Though widely known, Orr's book did not make a convincing case for the view that what happened in the 1860s was comparable in size and significance to the eighteenth-century evangelical revival.

no exciting means, no forcing hothouse growth, no fervid appeals to passion or imagination; it was attended by no wild outcries, no physical convulsions, no bodily disorders, no frenzied emotions; all, with few and small exceptions, is deep solemnity and in strictest harmony with the profoundest devotion.[2]

This was the one kind of revival of which James really approved, and in writing in this way he helped to pass on the image of the American revival of 1858 as a spontaneous outbreak of religious seriousness directly caused by the Holy Spirit through a handful of devotional prayer-meetings; a revival without a revivalist; surely the most respectable kind, and the only one which many people in England were ready to defend theologically. The terms in which James wrote, his rejection of wild outcries, bodily disorders and physical convulsions, though meant as criticism of what had often been reported of other American revivals, foretold unintentionally the reception that the Irish revival would obtain. Despite his contacts with America, James remained sceptical of the human element in revivalism; it was as though the steady failure of revivalists between 1830 and 1850 to rouse the English congregations into a general revival had convinced him that they had been making the wrong approach, that Finney and his imitators were mistaken in their methods, that one could, after all, only wait until God in his own good time poured down the Spirit from above. 'I want God's work, not man's,' he wrote, repudiating much that he had said in the 1830s and 1840s; 'I like not the minute, artificial and man-devised inventions to which some have resorted, as if all things were to be done by rule and measure, and by a spiritual machinery, the products of which are to be brought out upon principles of arithmetical calculation'—words which deliberately contradicted what Calvin Colton had done his best to popularize. 'I want no revivalist preachers; and yet if God had qualified some men more than others to be evangelists, I see no objection to their being employed occasionally to assist, but not to supersede, the pastor.'[3] This new revival, however, was the exception and the whole emphasis of James' last speech on the subject, in which he seemed to imagine the

[2] J. A. James, *Collected Works*, ed. by his Son, Vol. IX, p.537.
[3] Ibid., p.551.

Lord walking on the Atlantic with his face towards Great Britain, was upon prayer as the one permissible instrument for starting revivals. In this, as we have seen, James stood closer to Finney's *Lectures*[4] than he probably remembered in 1858; he had met, and not been over-impressed by, Finney in the meantime.

The Ulster revival began to attract attention in March, 1859, and the form in which news of it reached the English religious public may be judged from an extract from the pro-revivalist *Wesleyan Times*,[5] which reprinted a long description of the more extraordinary phenomena from the Irish *Ballymena Observer*:

> The external symptoms in one case have been minutely described to us. The person affected was a married woman, of middle age. She appeared to be greatly excited and feverish; her pulse was quick, there was a hectic tinge upon the cheeks, her eyes were partially closed and bloodshot, and her face was streaming with perspiration. Her appetite was entirely gone, and for the space of fifty-six hours she was unable to taste anything but water. After the first four hours of racking pain and incessant cries for mercy she became more composed, but remained prostrate for nearly three days . . . during the prostration of this woman she was visited by hundreds of neighbouring people. She had never been taught to read or pray and was unable to distinguish one letter of the alphabet from another, yet she prayed with intense frequency. . . . This case, like many others, was accompanied by visionary scenes; illusions certainly, but of a very extraordinary character. Among other things she maintained that a Bible traced in characters of light appeared to be open before her; and that although unable to read a spiritual power had endowed her with the capacity to comprehend the meaning of every word in it. It is an undoubted fact that she repeated with literal accuracy, and as if reading from the volume, a very large number of quotations from

[4] Finney published a letter in the *Wesleyan Times* (24 January, 1859), claiming that 'the present great work in America is a striking exemplification of the justness of the views expressed in my lectures on revivals. . . . Prayer, closest prayer, social, public, earnest, agonizing, prevailing prayer'.

[5] The *Wesleyan Times* was the organ of those Methodists who had parted company with the Wesleyan Connexion in the troubles of 1849. Their slogan was 'a free Church and a free Ministry', and they supported revivalism partly because they knew that the Wesleyans were suspicious of it. The use of the name 'Wesleyan' in the title is confusing, but the chief journal of the Wesleyan Connexion proper at this time was still *The Watchman*.

the Old and New Testaments . . . but these perceptions gradually faded in her progress towards recovery and entirely disappeared on her restoration to ordinary health. . . .[6]

The *Observer* went on to describe a more general outbreak in an open-air prayer-meeting near the town at which within half an hour twenty people were prostrated in a similar manner. Some of the victims were removed on cars; seven further cases occurred as the groups returned home and, over the three following days, the total of those affected rose to about one hundred and fifty. The only clergyman present at the original meeting was the Rev. Mr Robinson of Brough-shane; he had not been one of the speakers but worked until midnight among the prostrated, 'expressing his opinion that the power of God had been mightily manifested on the occasion'.

The tone of the *Observer* itself hinted at doubts which the sophisticated were bound to feel, but the mid-nineteenth century lacked the vocabulary with which to make sense of these occurrences: the Evangelicals disliked criticism of what they felt must, theoretically, be the work of the Holy Spirit. They tried to apply the common-sense criterion that the phenomena were valid if the associated 'conversion' were lasting, but the difficulty then was that there was no lack of observers willing to say that the results were excellent in almost any case. The kind of dissociative behaviour which is really being described here is familiar to students of religion in many cultures and against many different religious back-grounds; it is not uncharacteristic of individuals and groups under stress, as an adaptive mechanism; it is not necessarily a sign of mental disorder, indeed, 'in many cultures, the emotionally disturbed are directed by their healer-priest to join possession cults in order to be healed, in recognition of the pyschotherapeutic property of dissociative behaviour'[7] (culturally interpreted, of course, as spirit possession). In themselves, however, the phenomena, which may include

[6] *Wesleyan Times*, 30 May, 1859.

[7] Cf. F. D. Goodman, *Speaking in Tongues*, A Cross-Cultural Study of *Glossolalia* (Chicago 1972), p.xxii. Miss Goodman researched in Pentecostalist groups in Mexico City and Yacatan; the description of how she herself succumbed on one occasion to the dissociative state makes a revealing comment on the way in which mid-nineteenth-century Irish Protestants were said suddenly to collapse in a trance-like condition.

speaking with tongues (*glossolalia*), as seems to have been the case in the instance quoted above, tend to die out in the individual as he becomes accustomed to them, and cannot in themselves be regarded as having any kind of supernatural origin. Against their Irish background one might explain them partly in terms of the socio-economic pressures on the Irish groups involved, and partly in terms of their conforming to the expectations of the religious groups concerned. This behaviour did not require an external revivalist to set it off, nor did it require the revivalist's theological system to justify it. What counted here was the experience, not the linguistic expression of it, and it was this non-intellectual aspect of what happened which bothered the Evangelicals almost as much as the secular-minded, for the Evangelicals themselves liked to reduce religious phenomena to verbal equivalents.

In July, 1859, the *Wesleyan Times* carried another despatch from Ulster which described an evening meeting outside Belfast. When prayer was asked for,

> a little boy ten years old commenced to the astonishment of everyone, and he had not long begun when a poor woman, who had been under strong conviction for three months, came forward and shouted 'O Jesus', which she repeated again and again until she sank from exhaustion. A Mrs Hudson, converted about a fortnight before, commenced then with power to pray for her. Mr Doherty then got up and addressed them on Ezekiel's vision, with which all were well pleased. The scene of tumult round the woman was so great that I gave out the hymn, 'Come, Holy Spirit, on us breathe' and sang it, which seemed to tranquillise the excitement.[8]

The *Wesleyan Times* (which was not anti-rationalist, its political articles were intelligent and forceful on the Liberal side) printed this letter with apparently complete approval: the Free Wesleyan temperament responded to the spontaneous lay action, and to the idea that recent converts were the best people to counsel those in distress. The symbolism of the little child was no accident: in revivalist circles the converted child who saved his parents played as vital a role as did the

[8] *Wesleyan Times*, 11 July, 1859. It has sometimes been said that the British press distorted the Ulster revival for the relish of the English public by printing stories of this kind, and that this explained the failure of the movement to spread into England. But the *Wesleyan Times* wanted the revival to spread.

Virgin Mary in contemporaneous Roman Catholic exhibitions of religious excitement. What the Evangelicals saw in the Ulster excitement was at least the chance that God was about to stir up an equivalent of the eighteenth-century Revival in England. What oppressed them in the mid-century was not an eighteenth-century feeling that the institutional Churches had become idle and corrupt, but a sense of powerlessness at the rise of new, aggressive movements inside the Churches: the Broad Church rationalists, the ritualistic and romantic Anglo-Catholics, the pre-Vatican 1 Roman Catholics, eager for the reconquest of England. The Evangelical counter-attack on the 'Papal aggression' of 1850 had collapsed; J. H. Newman's encounter with the notorious Achilli had ended in another public Evangelical defeat. In the same vein the *Wesleyan Times* lamented the damage done to Methodism by the schism of 1849–57: the Methodist ministry had lost prestige during the struggle, and successful revivalism offered a way of restoring the familiar Wesleyan feeling of expansion.

There might have been more hope of success if the Evangelical world had not been divided into three groups: the American revivalists, several of whom visited England in 1859; the professional clergy and ministers, most of whom remained unimpressed by accounts of what had happened in Ulster; and a small number of English lay revivalists who thrived on the state of alienation which was growing between the regular ministry and sections of the laity. The usual organ of the lay revivalists was the *Revival*, but papers like the *Wesleyan Times* gave them publicity and support. In June, 1859, for example, a leading article which praised Caughey also referred to Miss Marsh,[9] who was preaching in a barn near her father's house every Sunday; and to groups of lay evangelists travelling in the north of England. In July, 1859, another leader launched a spirited attack on the 'learned ministry', a favourite target in Methodist literature.

The American revivalists in England in 1859 were Charles Finney, James Caughey and Phoebe Palmer. Of these Finney was the least successful, probably because he was now about

---

[9] Catherine Marsh (1818–1912) was a famous Evangelical propagandist, who wrote *Light for the Line*, or the Story of a Railway Workman, and *Memorials of Captain Hedley Vicars* (about God and the Crimean War), as well as the *Life of the Rev. W. Marsh*, her father, a well-known Evangelical Anglican.

seventy years old. He preached in Edinburgh for two months in the autumn of 1859 without attracting much attention.[10] He spent the remainder of his visit during 1860 in Bolton, where he preached from January to April, and Manchester, where he stayed from 25 April to 27 July. At the beginning of August he returned to the United States. These were attempts at full-scale local church revivals of the true American type, and I shall consider the value of this approach when I describe in detail James Caughey's long spell at Rochdale between December, 1860 and April, 1861. Despite the glowing account of his work which Finney gave in his *Memoirs*,[11] he does not seem to have made a great impression, and in July, 1860, newspaper reports were finding excuses for him. 'The season has been in some respects very unfavourable to revival work; trade has been brisk, the working and many of the middle classes have been busily employed until a late hour.' Whitsuntide had been a sad drawback.[12] The *Revival* spoke of about 2,000 'conversions' in Bolton, which was not unlikely, if one takes 'conversion' to mean all those who were in any way affected by the meetings: Caughey averaged 90 a week for 20 weeks at Rochdale a year later. About 45 per cent of Caughey's total might have been called 'converts' and there is no reason to suppose much difference in Finney's case. At the farewell tea for Finney, given at Chapel Street, Salford, in August, 1860, the Rev. R. Best of Bolton said that he hoped to have admitted one hundred new members to his church by the end of the year, and this puts Finney's work in the right perspective. This was one of the rare instances where one can say what was paid to the professional revivalist for his services, for at the Salford tea Finney was given a purse of a hundred guineas for himself and another of thirty guineas for his wife, who had conducted meetings for women. The total

[10] Cf. *Wesleyan Times*, 26 October, 1859, where a correspondent lamented Finney's failure, saying that he had seemed less impressive in Edinburgh than his prestige had led people to expect. A defence appeared in the next issue, but only underlined the truth of the chief points made: Finney had been virtually ignored by the Scottish ministry; only one other church had asked him to speak; he had had about 300 inquirers; he was strongly opposed by Andrew Bonar, no doubt as an ancient Perfectionist. He made a brief visit to Aberdeen, but then admitted defeat and went back to England.

[11] *Memoirs of C. G. Finney* (New York 1876, posthumous), from p.468.

[12] *Wesleyan Times*, 6 August, 1860. Even Finney's Sunday evening meetings failed in Manchester.

came to about the same amount as Caughey received at Rochdale.

Caughey was in a different situation from Finney. He started with the advantage in 1860 that he was a household name and popular hero among the Methodists who had broken away from the Wesleyan Connexion since the 1830s; they supported him as a fellow sufferer at the hands of the despotic Wesleyan ministry; they regarded his revivalism as a hallmark of their own cause and as evidence of their spiritual superiority over the Wesleyans. He came back to England just after the long Methodist civil war was ended, when the Free Methodists were anxious to settle down and strengthen their new societies. He could draw on the memory of great successes in the 1840s, when Finney had achieved little more than he did in England in 1859–60. Above all, whereas those who heard Finney speak in England always reacted in the same way—they found him lacking in oratorical skill but impressive in the cumulative construction of an argument— Caughey had at his finger-tips exactly the florid, vulgar rhetoric which the Arnoldian Philistines relished in the mid-century. Finney was too full of 'Americanisms' for their taste, without catching the familiarity which was part of Spurgeon's charm. Spurgeon, however, who was just coming into vogue in 1860, could also become very florid. By the time that D. L. Moody reached London, in 1875, taste had changed, his 'yankeeisms' proved attractive—whereas they were always quoted against Finney—and his crisp, direct manner, now felt to be 'manly', seemed preferable to the older revivalist style. Nevertheless, the emotional quality of Moody's and Caughey's sermons was similar: Moody's language was plainer but the vulgarity of feeling was the same.

The printed sermons of the period do not always reproduce what the revivalist said. In Caughey's case, however, there has survived a reliable newspaper report of a sermon which he preached at Bethesda New Connexion Methodist Chapel in Hanley on 26 January, 1858. Caughey chose two texts and they were typical: 'Grieve not the Holy Spirit of God' (Eph. 4:30); and, 'They rebelled and vexed his Holy Spirit, therefore he was turned to be their enemy and he fought against them' (Isa. 63:10). The reported address concluded:

'A third dissuasive is, if you resist the Holy Spirit of God—if you grieve Him—He will turn round and grieve you. If you dare to do so, He will retaliate, grieve your conscience, and break your peace. He has plenty of means to do this: through your wife, through your daughter, through one of those boys. Those near and dear to you may help to fill the ranks of the bloated drunkards or the felon's cell. It may be done through your creditors, who may press you hard—through your debtors, who may turn out to be villains, thieves, bankrupts and endorsers of bills which may prove good for nothing. And all this because you grieved the Holy Spirit. All this may occur before the Holy Spirit departs from you. You have good health, a good home, kind friends— for what purpose? Another dissuasive was, that if they grieved God's Spirit, God would grieve them. He would have them mark his words, that when he should be gone and the Atlantic should roll between them, he should hear, in the cases of some before him, they had had feverish nights and restless days and bereavements, which should lead them to think of him, for they were on his heart like fire, he was as sure of it as that the Bible was at his grieving heart. They should mark what he said, for he had been alone with God; and he believed he was speaking His will; and that if Jesus the Son of God stood where he stood he would say so. He would ask no excuse for flights of fancy, but in the name of the God of Daniel he would say, with prophetic cry, that God would take that husband, that wife, that child . . . and he would make his appeal to them that night. . . . He would call out the names of some persons, not told him by human lips; although he had heard no audible voice—but it had been brought to his mind that there were men in that audience—some there whose position was fixed—men there who would not join the church, men who would not be affected if he talked until the red blood came out of his mouth. (Sensation.) God had spoken—the word had gone forth—their pews would be vacant. He had said to him: 'Do not trouble yourself about them, others will hear you, do not waste your words upon them'. 'In all probability', added the preacher, 'they will live and die as they are. They turn their backs upon love-feasts and fellowship meetings and they set a bad example to the young men around them. Do you ask me who they are? I would not tell it—but I shall have letters from Hanley, telling me of the occurrence of what I say. God is going to weed certain men out of Bethesda, one, two, three, four.' (Sensation.) These had not been mentioned to him by an audible voice nor had he seen any angelic form, and yet it was true. After some kindred observations

Mr. Caughey went on to relate some remarkable judgements which had overtaken persons who did not give heed to religious impressions—for Balls. He did not mean that dancing was the worst thing in the world, but he did mean to say that whatever led a person to reject the Divine influence ought to be shunned. He concluded his remarkable discourse by offering prayer on behalf of his hearers, that they might turn that night—and added: 'The Spirit, the Bible and the Church call upon you to yield yourselves—I offer you salvation through the Blood of the Lamb'.[13]

Here one sees the demands of professional success actually corrupting the methods of the revivalist, whose defence probably was that conversion justified the means. On the basis of the evangelical doctrine of 'special providences'—itself intended to demonstrate the existence of God from the events of everyday life—Caughey had manufactured a weapon of peculiar intensity. He manipulated every kind of event, from the death of one's wife to the dishonesty of one's friends, so as to make one feel more guilty, to make one feel punished by God himself. He did not invent this attitude, but he used it cruelly. Nineteenth-century evangelicals of all denominations interpreted their misfortunes as the result of God's hostile reaction to their sins. When the dying Elizabeth Fry knew that her eldest son and his daughters had died of fever, she began to ask herself what sins her family had committed which might explain such tragedies. Caughey, however, had adapted what was primarily meant as a system of self-examination to the rhetorical needs of his revivalist technique; he substituted immediate punishment in the present world for threats of punishment in a world to come, perhaps on the ground that his hearers might be prepared to risk eternal punishment, but were scared of bankruptcy. Many in his audience who did not believe in these supernatural threats must still have enjoyed speculating as to the identity of those being attacked, whose names, of course, Caughey never actually mentioned. Other, more neurotic, people sometimes identified themselves with his threats, suffering intensely in

[13] *Wesleyan Times*, 3 January, 1859, borrowed from *The Staffordshire Sentinel*, which also printed an early account of the American revivals. Four thousand people were said to have heard Caughey's sermon; 950 gave their names as having received blessings from Caughey's meetings.

F

consequence. The combination of sensationalism, silliness and sentimentality says little for the sophistication of the audience.

It happens that we are in a position to study in some detail Caughey's visit to Baillie Street Chapel, Rochdale, from 2 December, 1860, to April, 1861. The records of the chapel survived until closure in the 1970s, among them the Revival Register—two large notebooks in which were entered, day by day, the names, addresses, ages, Christian background and actual experience (described as either 'justification' or 'sanctification') of those who came forward in the revival meetings.[14] Baillie Street was typical of the kind of Nonconformist society which asked for Caughey's assistance. Rochdale Wesleyanism had been deeply torn by the internal strains of the Old Connexion: Baillie Street had been built in 1837 by seceders to the Wesleyan Methodist Association, with which it entered the Methodist Free Church in 1857, just before Caughey's return. The chapel was paid for with money raised by issuing shares in the Society as a company, which even paid out interest for a few years before the shares were redeemed. For some years after the schism of 1837, Rochdale and the neighbouring town of Bury made up one circuit of the Association, but they parted in 1841, when the Baillie Street Circuit began on its own with a membership of 1,663, on trial, 111. The circuit did not prosper immediately, and by 1845 membership had dropped by 1,017, on trial, 80; then things improved and by 1852 membership had risen to 1,327; in 1853 the figure was 1,452. In 1859, not long before Caughey came, the membership, 1,747, exceeded the original total for the combined membership of Rochdale and Bury. Surviving membership returns presented to the Leaders' Meeting show the situation on the eve of the invitation to Caughey.

September 1859: 1,748 members; on trial 27; deaths 9; backsliders 8; removed 12.
December 1859: 1,763 members; on trial 140; deaths 5; backsliders 19; removals 15.
March 1860: 1,772 members; on trial 163; deaths 9; backsliders 11; removals 19.

[14] The existence of the registers had been forgotten; I found them at the back of a disused cupboard.

June 1860: 1,811 members; on trial 92; deaths 8; back-sliders 12; removals 32.

September 1860: 1,823 members; on trial 76; deaths 9; back-sliders 11; removals 19.

December 1860: 1,825 members; on trial 67; deaths 2; back-sliders 5; removals 24.

Caughey, that is, did not come to Rochdale to revive a declining or faltering church. Between September 1859, and September 1860, Baillie Street had added 75 members, despite 31 deaths, 53 backsliders and 85 removals. The problem which faced these ex-Wesleyan societies was survival: only a rising membership could guarantee a voluntary local chapel against the weight of its financial liabilities.

The surviving Leaders' Meeting Minute Book from Baillie Street records the steps which led to Caughey's invitation. Efforts had been made by the Dissenting ministers in Rochdale in the spring of 1860 to arrange for some joint action in the town. In May, 1860, the Minute Book says that the Free Churches were considering house to house visitation in order to survey the religious state of the population. In July, 1860, Baillie Street arranged its own camp-meeting. In August, 1860, a deputation reported that Caughey had agreed to come to Rochdale when he had finished preaching in Sheffield, probably in the following October. (The Stewards Cash Book reveals that the deputation called on Caughey in Liverpool and that their expenses came to £1.) In November, 1860, the Rochdale Dissenting ministers, having finished their survey, proposed that town missionaries be appointed; and the same Leaders Meeting was told that Caughey had been delayed by success in Sheffield and would now arrive (as he did) in December, 1860. One has the impression that Baillie Street wanted to act alone; the minute-books do not mention any suggestion of joint services with other bodies, nor was this a condition which Caughey made himself.

Meeting on 19 November, 1860, the Leaders' Meeting decided to advertise the services in the *Rochdale Observer*, and to have 2,000 handbills printed; weeknight meetings were to start at 7 p.m.; stewards were appointed to cope with strangers in the gallery and in the bottom of the chapel. The December Leaders' Meeting met on the Monday night after Caughey's first service (2 December): 24 had been justified and 21 had been sanctified on the Sunday evening. In the New Year a special collection for expenses was taken, on 27 January, 1861: one had already been taken on 23 December, 1860. At the same meeting, 21 January, 1861, it was decided that boards should be obtained to carry through the principal thorough-fares of the town to announce the revival services; this continued until the beginning of March. There seems to have been no definite contract with Caughey himself: he was asked to continue on 21 January, 1861, and again on 4 February. On 18 March, 1861, the Leaders regretted to have learned from remarks made by Caughey in the pulpit on the previous day that he now intended to leave Rochdale: once again he was 'persuaded' to go on. On 25 March, 1861, he was allowed to use Baillie Street for a temperance meeting, and on 8 April the Leaders authorized the formation of an Adults Temperance Society. This same April meeting came to a final under-standing with Caughey, who remained until Whitsun, by which time his total of justified and sanctified had risen to 1,800. The Baillie Street officials retained a lasting admiration for Caughey and tried without success to induce him to return to the town when he travelled in England in 1867. The April Leaders' Meeting also fixed Caughey's remuneration at £120, to which must be added board and lodging and other incidental advantages.

Statistically, the first membership figures to show the effect of the revival meetings were those of March, 1861. The membership proper was still only 1,869 (removals 20, back-sliders 16, deaths 20), but there were 359 members on trial, an increase on the quarter of 292. At this point the Revival Register shows that the total number of those recorded as either justified or sanctified had risen to 1,506. Of these 279 claimed sanctification and were probably members already. 568 of the total were described as belonging to the Methodist Free Church, though this did not necessarily mean that they were members at Baillie Street.

The main effect of the revival, however, came in the figures for June, 1861, when Caughey had already quitted Rochdale. The membership now stood at 2,144, an increase in a single quarter of 275. This may be compared with the 359 actually on trial in March, of whom 292 had been added in the previous quarter. Those on trial in June, 1861, numbered 545. Caughey's total of saved and sanctified had been 1,800, of whom 326 claimed sanctification. This meant that about 1,474 had been in some sense 'justified': rather more than half of these—the 545 now received on trial and the nearly 300 new members who had already been accepted—had moved closer to Baillie Street as a result of the experiment.

The 545 members on trial did not, however, really represent the potential of a further advance to the 3,000 member mark. In fact, the figures rose slowly: in September, 1861 to 2,253, an increase of 109, with 296 still on trial, backsliders 18, removals 22 and deaths 6; and to a peak figure of 2,308, a further increase of 55, in December, 1861, with 246 still on trial, removals 42, backsliders 27, and deaths 5. If one takes the membership of December, 1860 as a base-line, when it was 1,825, and compares this with the peak figure of 2,308, the increase is only 483, about a quarter of the total contained in the Revival Register. This makes a fair comparison with previous years, since the number of removals and deaths remained reasonably steady, and the increase in the number of backsliders may be attributed to the revival itself. After December, 1861, the membership figures were:

March 1862:   membership 2,305 (loss of 3); on trial 214—loss of 32; backsliders 20; deaths 19.
June 1862:   membership 2,302, on trial 213; removals 30; backsliders 24; deaths 7.
September 1862: membership 2,281; on trial 159; removals 18; backsliders 31; deaths 6.

There were 75 backsliders in this period. More briefly, the figures continued:

December 1862: 2,284; March 1863: 2,280; June 1863: 2,307; September 1863: 2,293.

Even in 1870 the membership still hovered about the 2,000 mark, but with a tendency to drop which was never reversed. By 1893, circuit membership had dropped to 1,093; in 1935, when the Baillie Street Circuit was radically altered, it was 1,101. From June, 1861, in fact, when the membership stood at 2,144 and the number on trial was 545, there was no considerable increase above what would have been normal in earlier years. In the long run local tradition concluded that

> after the mission, wonderful as it was, reaction set in and years elapsed before the church and circuit returned to their position of steady work and reliance upon God for the gathering in of souls. ... The mistake was that the special and the extraordinary were so protracted as to exhaust time and energy and to impress the mind with the thought that ease and indulgence might rightly follow.[15]

Caughey's activities in Rochdale suggest the limitations of the older form of American revivalism. He gave a boost to the membership of Baillie Street circuit, which had been growing steadily in what was a favourable period and area for Nonconformity. This increase did not prove the basis for further advance, for from the 1870s the circuit declined, and the characteristics of Baillie Street became a combination of political radicalism, pacifism and theological liberalism, as though in conscious reaction against the pietism of the past. Only Caughey's teetotalism remained as a mark of his passage, but then teetotalism became the circumcision of later nineteenth-century Nonconformity. The Revival Register underlines the true nature of what he did. Out of the 1,800 names recorded, 1,236, or about 68 per cent, were those of women and girls, and there were at least 243 girls aged 14 and under; of the 564 males, about 112 were boys aged 14 or under.

In these terms the actual course of the revival becomes interesting. The totals registered for the first six weeks were 104, 131, 121, 73, 55, 36. This fall then checked, and a steady level was maintained from the seventh to the seventeenth week. The second six weeks ran: 79, 76, 91, 112, 97, 91, whilst the thirteenth week produced the peak figures of 135. (Billy Graham would not reckon these high totals for a mass evangelist, but one has to remember that Caughey was drawing his converts from an audience of about two thousand, whereas when Graham visited Manchester in 1961, for example, he drew an average attendance of about 18,000 a night). The totals for the fourteenth to the twentieth weeks were 113, 66, 126, 47, 71, 68 and 78. The average for the

[15] *A Centenary History, 1837–1937*, Anon., Rochdale 1937, pp.47–8.

twenty completed weeks was 90 a week. The meetings closed on 21 April, 1861. Examination of the Revival Register reveals that between the eighth and the sixteenth weeks, when the first wave of conversions had fallen away critically, the second wave of success depended partly on bringing in numbers of children up to 14 years of age. After the seventh week, moreover, the number of females, excluding girls aged 14 and under, did not vary much from one week to another. Children aged 14 and under in the grand total of 1,800 came to just under 20 per cent, but in the peak week, the thirteenth, 46 out of 135, or 34 per cent, were children. Anyone who has seen a whole modern Sunday school class taken to a revival meeting and sent forward *en bloc* in answer to the appeal can imagine what was probably happening.

2. Types of Revival Conversion Experience

If one takes Rochdale as a typical example, it is safe to say that in the period 1859–62 neither Finney nor Caughey nor Phoebe Palmer (for whom see more particularly chapter 8 on Holiness Revivalism) did more than provoke a small number of local church revivals, most of them on a smaller scale than the one at Rochdale. They elicited no response which could be called an 'Evangelical Awakening'[16] or an American revivalistic breakthrough. Caughey, indeed, affected the British religious scene much more importantly in the 1840s, when he helped to weaken the internal structure of Wesleyan Methodism and so to produce the Wesleyan Schism of 1849, an event whose consequences for English popular religion were greater than historians have realized.[17] Nevertheless, from the accounts of the meetings which the Americans held, it is possible to work out some of the attitudes which filled those who supported them. At first sight, newspaper reports of revival meetings resemble one another monotonously, but closer examination shows that the most significant variable was the kind of 'conversion-type' which was brought forward to illustrate the individual meeting and awaken the reader's

[16] Unless this were understood in the sense of an evangelical awakening to a need for new methods.

[17] Recent attempts to meet the need include W. R. Ward, *Religion and Society in England* (1972); H. Perkin, *The Origins of Modern English Society* (1969).

approval. These English conversion-types can be classed under five headings, none of which echoes the dissociative phenomena common in the Ulster revival. An analysis of these conversion-types enables one to answer the questions: what satisfaction did the audience find in revival meetings? what were they hoping would happen? how far were their hopes religious?

There were, to begin with, *conversions to teetotalism*.[18] By 1859 teetotalism had already become a highly organized movement: the United Kingdom Alliance had been founded in Manchester in 1853, under the inspiration of the triumph of the Maine Law agitation in the United States. Teetotalism spread through the evangelical pietist world like a kind of cement; for some at least the new cause had the advantage that the Higher Criticism could not touch it. The irrational self-contradictory element in the leadership, which Dr Brian Harrison has brought out so well, can be explained if one assumes that actual abstention from alcohol was never the end, but only the means, of the great campaign. Of course, the United Kingdom Alliance would have liked to see England dry, but only as a symbol of a social victory; the sort of practical compromise which would have reduced drinking would not do, because such changes implied no significant social gain for the religious middle-class and its dependents. Teetotalism symbolized for such people their repudiation of the social values of those whom they were expected to regard as their social superiors, as well as their contempt for the social values of the working-classes; it offered a new and simple way of criticizing both the aristocracy and the proletariat. It is sometimes said that teetotalism prospered because it could be offered as a universal, non-political solution to every social problem, and so united people who would have come together under hardly any other banner; this was potentially true, but in the course of the Victorian period teetotalism became more socially confined than this analysis suggests. If one assumes that a religious sub-culture was slowly separating from the main body of English culture in the late nineteenth century, then aggressive teetotalism characterized much of the

---

[18] See Brian Harrison, *Drink and the Victorians* (1971), the best guide to a subject riddled with prejudice.

Protestant, though not only Nonconformist, part of that sub-culture. The development of teetotalism was one of the ways in which that sub-culture identified itself, though the survival of teetotalism was not absolutely necessary to the survival of the sub-culture in the twentieth century. Revivalism played an important part in recruiting for the cause and in helping to make the Nonconformist chapels in particular into a kind of teetotal closed-shop.

An example can be found in the reports of the Newcastle-upon Tyne revival conducted by Dr Walter and Mrs Phoebe Palmer in the autumn of 1859. The Palmers were American Methodists, well-known for their advocacy of sanctification. There was considerable prejudice in England against women who spoke in church, and the accounts of the Palmers' meetings usually suggest that Dr Palmer read a lesson, one of the local ministers preached, and that Mrs Palmer then walked to the communion rail with deliberate modesty, 'not to preach according to the modern acceptation of the term'—or so the highly conservative Wesleyan Methodist newspaper, the *Watchman*, put it—but simply to say a few words to the people. When she had finished, she would invite those who wanted to consecrate themselves to come forward to the rail to be exhorted and prayed for. At Newcastle, late in September, 1859, a report, sent to the *Watchman* by a well-known Wesleyan minister, Robert Young, said that

> on the last Sabbath evening an influential member of the congregation, who has for some years been connected with the liquor traffic, an extensive brewer, at the close of the service, responding to the invitation to the rails of the communion, asked permission to make a statement—a request which was at once complied with. Addressing the large congregation, he referred to the benefit he had derived from the services during the week, and publicly declared that the effect of these services on his mind was a resolution to take immediate steps to dissociate himself from the traffic with which he had been connected *and to be done with it for ever*. The effect was electric. A thrill of joy went through the assembly, and 'Glory be to God' gushed from many a grateful heart. This fact has made a deep impression on the community.[19]

Phoebe Palmer, of course, was a holiness revivalist, and

[19] *Wesleyan Times*, quoting *The Watchman*, 3 October, 1859.

teetotalism formed a central part of her interpretation of the theme. She used what was called 'the altar phraseology': she encouraged her penitents to offer themselves entirely to God— 'to lay their all on the altar'—and then to believe that they were sanctified because God had accepted and sanctified their offering. Alcohol was something that people could give up if they had a strong motive to do so; social motives operated very strongly in the evangelical middle-class between about 1850 and 1880. To become a teetotaller showed that one had sacrificed for one's religious beliefs and also enabled one to distinguish, with overtones of superiority, one's own social groups from others. The Nonconformist world in particular stood badly in need of sources of superiority, in order to induce prospering Nonconformists not to abandon their religious position in favour of Anglicanism. As this illustration shows, there was great rejoicing if a man like the Newcastle brewer symbolized his loyalty by shutting his brewery.

It is significant that, in the same *Wesleyan Times*, there was another story which claimed victory over alcohol through revivalism. In an account of the Ulster Revival given to a London audience by the Rev. Richard Parrott, the proof that what was happening there was 'a second Pentecost' was a story about the conversion of a man who had been 'the very terror of the neighbourhood in which he resided—a notorious drunkard, blasphemer and debauchee—who, while in a state of intoxication had caused the death of a fellow creature, and who has several times attempted the life of his wife and children because they attend a place of worship'. Readers were assured that the tale took twenty minutes to tell and had been listened to with breathless attention. Sensationalism, the feeding of the moral superiority of the audience, evidence that God sided with revivalism and teetotalism: the ingredients remind one of Caughey's methods as well.

The emphasis on the family in this last story leads on to the next conversion-type: the *reunion of families* and the *child-leader* image. These themes were effective in 1859 and worked wonders for Moody and Sankey in the 1870s. In the developing urban culture of England in the nineteenth century, the church/chapel related family group acquired fresh value as a centre of order and relationships in a chaotic society. One of the uses of revivalism lay in attempting to strengthen this kind of family, which was usually to be found in the various layers of middle-class society. A stable, family-centred life unhampered by too many middle-class values always attracted the working-classes, but in their case the kind of pressure which the local church/chapel could exert on the family was normally replaced by that of a street-based community.

Accounts of revivals frequently included the story of the conversion of a whole family, sometimes at a single meeting, sometimes in a series of conversions dispersed over several. Another common feature was that one of the younger children had been responsible for the conversion of one of the parents. A deep sentimentalization of the Old Testament saying that a little child should lead them underlay much Victorian popular religion: doubtless the high infant mortality rate had something to do with it, but there was also the need to find an effective personal image of Jesus to offset the deadening results of traditional Protestant salvation-theology, which robbed Jesus of personality and reduced him to a counter in a supernatural transaction. Temperamentally conservative, revivalists and evangelicals could only repudiate the Liberal Protestant Lives of Jesus, which introduced a new charge of humanity into the image of Jesus;[20] they preferred, under the sway of the sentimentalizing tradition, whose role in Victorian popular culture should never be ignored, to think of Jesus in terms of the little child. There is a good example in the account of a revival directed by Dr and Mrs Palmer at Banbury in December, 1860:

A little deformed girl stepped up trembling to Dr Palmer as he was in charge of the meeting and with tearful eyes requested that the prayers of the congregation might be asked for her father. The father of the child was a confirmed drunkard and in an evil hour had thrown that little daughter downstairs and deformed her for life, and now she comes and entreats the prayers of the pious on his behalf.[21]

[20] Strauss's *Life of Jesus Critically Examined* had been published in 1835; George Eliot's translation was issued in 1846; Ernest Renan's *Vie de Jésus* appeared in 1863; Nietzsche's *AntiChrist*, the most brilliant psychological portrait of them all, in 1895.
[21] *Wesleyan Times*, 24 December, 1860.

Another instance comes from the Palmers' visit to King's Lynn, in North Norfolk, in 1860.

The first to the altar of prayer was a lady of the Established Church, and her four daughters and their governess, all of whom were made blessedly assured of pardoning mercy. . . . On Tuesday evening special requests for prayer on behalf of ungodly children, and brothers, and friends, gave fresh (without needing it) or increased impetus to the glorious work. And the last night was indeed a glorious time. The first seeker up to the communion, in the sight of a vast company, was the youngest son of the lady already referred to, who came forward as soon as Dr Palmer gave the invitation. The communion rails were speedily filled, also the large vestry, in which I found the elder boy of this lady, both of whom were made blessedly happy.[22]

Both these incidents happened in Wesleyan Methodist chapels. Here is one from a simpler social background, a Primitive Methodist chapel at Northwich, in Cheshire.

One of the finest scenes ever seen by mortal eye was that of a little boy, the son of pious parents, who felt that the prayers neither of father nor mother could wash away his guilt. He therefore sought for pardon, and prayed in a most sublime and yet simple manner until he obtained the desire of his heart. It so happened that just at that moment his sisters were groaning under their load of guilt: 'God, be merciful to me, a sinner', on which he immediately turned round and said, 'Sister, why don't you believe? God cannot, neither will He, save you until you do believe'. 'Yes,' cried one, 'I can, I will, I do believe that God, for Christ's sake, has forgiven me'. 'Then', cried the little boy, 'it is done'.

As told, the story stressed both the unity of the family and the child-leader image. If the revivalist could commit the children to the parents' inherited Protestantism, he would simultaneously bind the family tighter together in loyalty to the parental point of view. Fear of what might divide the family was also fear of what might weaken the sect, however: in 1860 the comparatively radical *Wesleyan Times* deplored the results of allowing Methodist boys to join the Volunteers, the militia hopefully expected to beat off a very hypothetical

[22] Ibid., 29 October, 1860.

French invasion. The paper exhorted Methodist parents to provide antidotes to the evil social outcome which was bound to follow if Wesleyan boys mixed with the children of other social groups against a military background. Families which were deliberately training their children not to mix in a wider world than the sect welcomed revivalism as a possible way of reconciling them to the narrow limits of a sectarian life. Revivalism worked, not by 'conversion' as much as by persuading the converted that their religious experience justified their being alienated from general society, and also necessitated sabbatarianism, teetotalism and other restrictive practices. It is in this light that the Evangelical attempt to ban novels and Sunday visiting is best interpreted. Such bans were the work of ministers eager to please their more powerful laymen. When these rules were enforced, they cut children off from alternative forms of behaviour, even in fiction, and prevented them from having any contact with non-church/ chapel people on Sundays, the one day when this was generally possible. Inevitably, the restrictions bore hardest on the least sophisticated sections of the lower middle-class. Some children always fought back, however. When George Williams, the most probable founder of the Y.M.C.A., required two of his sons, on holiday at Lowestoft, to give away tracts before they played by the sea, the boys simply handed the tracts to each other as they walked along; when they had exchanged them all, they buried the bundle; the play on the words 'give away' is a typical stratagem of the Evangelical mind.[23]

At the popular level, the child-leader type found perfect expression in a song written by the American, Philip Bliss (1838–76) about 1870:

I should like to die, said Willie, if my papa could die too;
But he says he isn't ready, 'cause he has so much to do;
And my little sister Nellie says that I must surely die,
And that she and mama, then she stopped because it made me cry.

But she told me, I remember, once while sitting on her knee,
That the angels never weary, watching over her and me;

[23] C. Binfield, *George Williams and the Y.M.C.A.* (1973), p.352. Williams was a successful draper.

And that if we're good—and mama told me just the same before—
They will let us into heaven when they see us at the door.

There will be none but the holy—I shall no more of sin;
There I'll see Mamma and Nellie, for I know He'll let them in;
But I'll have to tell the angel, when I meet him at the door,
That he must excuse my papa, 'cause he couldn't leave the store.

Nellie says that very soon maybe I shall be called away;
If Papa were only ready I should like to go today;
But if I should go before him to that world of light and joy,
Then I guess he'd want to come to Heaven to see his little boy.

This masterpiece of sentimentality was number 415 in Sankey's *Sacred Songs and Solos*, and had been sung in England by Phillip Phillips before Sankey's time. Its emotional punch sprang from the way in which it could awaken both the sense of having been rejected by one's own father in the past and the sense of guilt at having rejected one's own child in the present: theoretically, the revivalist might even release this pent-up feeling and reconcile father and child. Symbolically, however the song worked in a different fashion, with Willie a semi-divine figure who invokes against a cruel adult world all the forces associated with childhood in the New Testament, an infant Jesus consciously exploiting his own pathos. If the perfect Evangelical child behaved like this, it was because the child Jesus would behave like this, and there does seem to have been a period in the second half of the nineteenth century when Evangelicals found this sentimentalized version of Jesus a possible way of humanizing the cult-figure.

In reports of nineteenth-century revival meetings, another conversion-type was that of *conversion from Roman Catholicism*. The theological function was obvious: the anxiety of the Protestant to be proved right by the actual surrender of the Roman Catholic, who would then repeat as his own description the standard Protestant denunciations of Rome. Conversions to Protestantism also offset the movement, faithfully reported in religious journals, of Anglo-Catholic priests to Rome, and compensated for the failure of the riots at St George's in the East, London, where Anglo-Catholicism remained entrenched. In the north of England, moreover, acute tension existed between the Protestant community and the newly confident Roman Catholicism which had grown up since emancipation and the restoration of the Roman episcopal hierarchy. Fear of Rome ran high; well-known Anglican Evangelicals like Hugh McNeile of Liverpool and Hugh Stowell of Salford made anti-Popery their stock theme to their supporters. There were still odd corners of the Church of England where little groups of clergy searched the pattern of contemporary history for evidence that would link either the Papacy or Napoleon III with the Book of Revelation. There was a flood of 'prophetic literature' in 1860, partly because political changes in Italy encouraged Evangelicals to foresee the collapse of Papal power. 'Islam sees all her frontiers falling in,' wrote William Arthur, 'Rome, her centre heaving beneath her: humanity, sighing under the feet of both, does not ask, "Will they fall?", but "When?".'[24] The adventist Mildmay Conferences became famous in Anglican circles in the later 1860s; adventism and anti-Roman Catholicism were not inevitably one, but they often combined in pursuit of the Beast. Protestant orators talked boldly about Protestant truth which was bound to drive out Roman lies in free competition, but they also knew that Protestants could no longer rely on the State to guarantee them against the failure of their oratory. When the Palmers visited Newcastle upon Tyne, in north-east England, with its large, poor Roman Catholic community, they provided evidence of the power of revivalism to overthrow the influence of Rome. The Rev. Robert Young reported that

at one of our evening meetings a youth, brought up in the Romish faith, asked permission to speak, which being granted, he with deep feeling gave a brief account of his change of opinion and conversion to God, which had taken place a few evenings previously. He referred to his mother with filial affection and spoke of her prayers to the Virgin Mary on his behalf; but said she thought more of the Pope than of God, and he earnestly prayed that the light which had discovered to him his sinful and dangerous state might also shine upon her.[25]

[24] William Arthur, *Italy in Transition* (1860), p.436. A Wesleyan minister and popular writer, Arthur drew on a recent tour of Italy for this book, but the Papacy was one of his favourite topics.
[25] *Wesleyan Times*, 17 October, 1859.

A similar example may be drawn from Finney's tour of 1860. He came to Manchester in mid-April of that year, and an account drawn from the Congregationalist paper, the *British Standard*, gave two specimens of his success. The first of these was a conversion-type which has already been discussed: the drunkard who had been given up by his friends but who had been converted by Finney—'his family can hardly believe their eyes'. The second was that of a Roman Catholic 'who came into Chapel Street Chapel the other evening in his working clothes and was convinced and converted to God'. Finney was not the only revivalist who claimed to have converted Roman Catholics in Manchester, as much a centre of the body as Newcastle upon Tyne. Richard Weaver assured readers of the *Revival* that he knew 'many Roman Catholics, and bigoted ones, who were thankful to God that they ever came to the Free Trade Hall'.[26]

In such cases the revivalist proved publicly to the satisfaction of many English Protestants that they were right to believe that a Roman Catholic was not a Christian; in declaring that he had now been converted to God, the Roman Catholic admitted that his previous views had been so wrong that his condition had been damnable.

Another example may be drawn from the Palmer's visit to Banbury in December, 1860. Once again a Roman Catholic convert was put forward as proof of the value of the revivalists' work. A Roman Catholic woman had told Dr Palmer that she had come four miles to the meeting hoping that she would receive pardon, but that she would have to go back; she asked him to request the evening meeting to pray for her. Palmer 'laboured with her for some time after the service endeavouring to point her to Him whose prerogative it is alone to forgive'—this was meant as a hit at both the Roman and Anglo-Catholic priesthoods—and she went away 'looking to Jesus'.[27]

A more remarkable example can be found in the biography of Reginald Radcliffe, one of the English lay revivalists. In September, 1860, there were riots in Glasgow in which Roman

---

[26] *The Revival*, 30 November, 1861, referring to a visit he made to Manchester in October, 1861.
[27] *Wesleyan Times*, 24 December, 1860.

Catholics seem to have tried to prevent a Protestant minister from preaching in the open air in the Bridegate. An enormous rally was held in reply on Glasgow Green on 5 September, 1860, at which Radcliffe and Richard Weaver were among the principal speakers. Radcliffe's biographer continued:

Inquirers adjourned to an old building, Parry's Theatre, where the Lord manifested His presence. A girl, among others, was stricken there; when she found Christ she rose up happy and said, 'May I pray?' She knelt down with two other girls, one on each side of her and said, 'O Lord, forgive me for striking the minister that Sabbath; and forgive my companion on the right and my companion on the left'. At these words one of her companions fell down stricken. From this prayer I suppose that she was one of those who had attacked Mr McColl in the Bridegate, and she was likely a Roman Catholic, as she added, 'May I never bow down to graven images again'.[28]

All the characteristics of the Roman Catholic conversion-type were evident here. There was the suggestion that the Roman was an idolater; that Roman Catholics hated the preaching of the Gospel and might be expected to strike Protestant ministers; there was the spectacle of the persecutor being compelled, by God, through the revivalist, to confess her sinful action. The story is worth finishing, for another reason.

The companion who was stricken appeared unconscious except when the name of Jesus was uttered. I watched her with deep interest for about an hour, when she began quite suddenly, but slowly and sweetly, to sing 'Happy day, happy day, when Jesus washed my sins away'. She afterwards rose up; and then such a strange and beautiful light spread over her face, one could easily believe that what she said was true. 'Jesus had come to her'.[29]

The incident is interesting because it establishes the resemblance, in Mrs Radcliffe's mind at any rate, between the phenomena which accompanied the Ulster revival and those which followed her husband's preaching in his early years. Hardly any other cases of this trance-like condition were reported in England in 1859–61, even from meetings which

[28] *Recollections of Reginald Radcliffe*, by his wife, n.d., p.94. Radcliffe died in 1895, however, and the book was issued soon after.
[29] Ibid.

Radcliffe and Weaver conducted. It was not surprising in itself that a Catholic girl should suddenly feel the enormity of having struck a kind of priest; nor was it remarkable that individual Irish immigrants should yield to the social pressures of an alien and frequently hostile community and desire to conform to it, making a change of religious affiliation a symbol of a wider change.

Conversions to Sabbatarianism constituted another conversion-type, designed, like conversions from Roman Catholicism, to show the rightness of dearly-cherished Evangelical positions; once again revivalism, because of the swiftness with which it obtained affirmations, could reveal God in action on the pietist side. The nineteenth century had seen a renewed campaign to achieve a complete Sunday shut-down of all forms of employment and secular leisure, and this had largely succeeded, partly because this was an issue which united the whole sub-culture, Protestant, Catholic and sectarian, and partly because the campaign fitted into a wider middle-class desire for the establishment of urban public order. (This second reason also explained some of the toleration of teetotalism.) The sabbatarian movement had made the alleged day of rest into one of restless religious activity for all church/chapel-goers, who were effectively stopped from having direct contact with the secular culture. Revival stories often showed how converts had been enlightened about Sunday, and now understood that an Evangelical Sabbath helped on the Kingdom of God. Dr and Mrs Palmer provided an example of indirect pressure of this kind in an incident which was reported from one of their meetings at Leamington Wesleyan Chapel in November, 1860.

> One dear man and his wife found the blessing of perfect love, and were so happy that they longed for the morning that they might go and tell their friends what great things God had done for them. The wife went to a woman who kept her shop open on a Sunday and induced her to close it, saying that if she were a loser at the end of the month she would make it up to her.

The significant point was that the woman who believed that she had been directly perfected by an act of God translated her new condition into sabbatarian terms; it is possible, of course, that she had some financial interest in the shop. She certainly did not expect to have to pay out any money, because Evangelicals argued that if one obeyed the divine law and treated Sunday as a day of rest, God would protect one against unfortunate consequences; if an Evangelical baker refused to bake on a Sunday God would see to it that he did not suffer any financial loss. Indeed, the attitude still survives: I have known a present-day sabbatarian maintain publicly that if the State honoured God by refusing to allow British Railways to operate on Sundays, God would see to it that the deficit on the railways disappeared.

Another mid-nineteenth-century example comes from the biography of Richard Weaver:

> One Sunday afternoon, when Weaver was conducting a Mission in Swansea, walking down the street he saw a fruiterer's shop partly opened, and several customers standing inside waiting to be served. His quick perception and ready wit led him to go into the shop, and addressing the woman in charge, he said: 'Mrs, I see someone is dead here, you have the shutters up.' 'No sir,' said the astonished woman, 'there is no one dead here.' 'There is,' thundered Richard, 'and the burial will be in Hell.' Without another word he walked out and went on to the meeting. The woman became so terrified that she refused to serve the customers, shut up her shop, and followed the evangelist to the Albert Hall. There that afternoon she was converted, and returning home told her husband what had taken place. His reply was a murderous attack upon his wife for closing the shop. The police came on the scene, arrested the husband, removed the poor woman in an unconscious state to the hospital, where her right leg was amputated. The husband was tried at the Assizes and sentenced to a term of imprisonment. A few months ago, Mr James Jones (one of Richard's spiritual children) was visiting at Bristol, and saw the one-legged woman bright and happy, rejoicing in that Christ whom she had received as her Saviour in the Albert Hall under such remarkable circumstances.[30]

In so far as we are discussing the image of mid-nineteenth-century revivalism, the truth of this story does not matter; it probably represented what Weaver would have liked to do

---

[30] James Paterson, *Richard Weaver's Life Story* (n.d.), pp.235–6; Weaver died in obscurity in 1896.

and what he would have liked to happen. In the story, at any rate, the revivalist was pictured providing a martyr for the Sabbath, though whether the martyr was the man or the woman later judgement might hesitate to say. Weaver had no doubt that the woman was the martyr; as long as one could believe implicitly the truth of the final assertion—that the one-legged woman was still rejoicing in Christ—the Evangelical found no problem in the presumable disintegration of the husband, nor would he have seen much relevance in the view that what the story really illustrated was that one should hesitate before interfering in the lives of other people.

The success of the American and British revivalists in the early 1860s, and the limitations of the success as well, may be traced to their ability to provide examples of these types: conversions from Roman Catholicism, conversions to teetotalism and to sabbatarianism, family conversions, examples of the child-leader and so forth. They did not create these demands, they satisfied them; they did not remould English Evangelicalism, they responded to what it already was; they staged a simple but dynamic social situation in which it became possible for individuals to accept personal transformation along the lines of one of these types. It was a narrow, centripetal society which was dominated by these demands. A pattern of promises also emerged from them: one's family (seen from the parents' point of view) would become more harmonious, the drunkard would be made sober, the Roman Catholic would become a Protestant, respect for the Sabbath would be imposed on society: there was a crescendo with an inevitable evangelical climax—if all these promises were fulfilled, the Advent of Christ would be at hand. There is little evidence to show that mid-nineteenth-century revivalists were employed to reconcile the poor to their poverty, to teach them to look for their reward in heaven. They did not often preach to the really poor, in any case; and, in Evangelical thinking, poverty was more frequently reckoned a consequence of sin than a means of grace.

3. Weaver, Radcliffe and the English Revivalist Network

Reference has already been made to some members of the

small group of British lay revivalists which had been quietly forming during the 1850s, and their work must now be examined in more detail. There were full-time revivalists, like Reginald Radcliffe, Richard Morgan (later an evangelical publisher) and Richard Weaver, and part-time preachers like Stevenson Blackwood, Captain Trotter and Admiral Fishbourne. Of these, Weaver, born in 1827, had finally been converted in 1852 and started to preach at New Mills in Derbyshire in the same year; Radcliffe, born in 1825, must also have begun to preach in the early 1850s; and Morgan, born in 1827, had been converted in Bristol in 1849 by a sermon preached by a retired minister of Lady Huntingdon's Connexion. Among the part-time evangelists, who came from a higher social class, Captain Trotter had been born in 1808, was converted in Paris in 1839, and began to preach in 1852; Lord Radstock, born in 1833, the son of a vice-admiral, arrived in the Crimea just after the fighting ceased and was converted before he returned to England; S. A. Blackwood, born in 1832, also came under evangelical influence while serving before Sebastopol and was converted after he came back to England in 1856. Of the two most prominent Scottish lay evangelists of the period, Duncan Matheson, born in 1824, was converted in 1846 and worked in the Crimea as an agent of the Soldiers' Friend Society; and Brownlow North, born in 1810, was suddenly converted in 1854, on which he gave up shooting and fishing: only a man diabolically inspired could kill salmon on the Sabbath.

All these men were committed to an aggressive evangelical way of life long before the Ulster Revival of 1859. American influence mattered more than Irish, for the publication of Finney's *Lectures* in England, and James Caughey's long visit in the 1840s, helped to stimulate the group's development. A more important factor was the rise between 1830 and 1850 of a 'new evangelicalism', lay in spirit, urban in concern, disaffected from the ministry, indifferent to denominational frontiers, expressing its distrust of traditional religious institutions by the formation of new ones, which were kept out of the control of the clergy as far as possible.

One such institution was the London City Mission, started by a layman, David Nasmith, in 1835: by 1850 the Mission controlled 235 lay agents each with his own district, in which he visited from house to house, reading the Bible and preaching in all but name. He was paid £60 to £70 per annum in the 1850s and was independent of the local ministry and ecclesiastical structures; he was usually slightly inferior in social origin to the ordained. The significant comparison is with the Church of England Scripture Readers (whose Association was started in 1844): there were 97 of them in 1850; they were paid about the same as the City Missionaries; they were linked directly to parishes; the bishop's sanction was needed for an appointment; no Reader remained in a district against the will of the incumbent.

The City Mission was a sign of the need to break out of the parochial strait-jacket and to free the would-be evangelist from clerical control. It was all very well for James Rowsell, of St Peter's, Stepney, to tell a House of Lords Committee in 1858 that he treated his parish as a family gathered round the House of God; he wanted more curates, not City Missionaries, as one would expect. But Abraham Hume, a tougher Anglican from Liverpool, told the same Committee that the parochial system had worked disastrously in Liverpool, leaving the parishes of the poorer part of the population hopelessly ill-equipped in every way, even to their having church buildings twice the size that was needed.[31] This conflict, which is fundamental to Anglican history in the Victorian period, and in which the ecclesiastical leadership took the wrong decision and backed the parish system in an essentially unreformed shape, has hardly surfaced in histories of the Church of England, in which the assumption is still made that it is only in the twentieth century that the parish has become a questionable ideal. In fact, one has the impression that criticism of the system mounted until about 1860, but that after that the individualistic preference for 'a parish of one's own' finally conquered. The leaders of the City Mission regarded the church building boom of the 1870s and 1880s as a matter of putting the wrong kind of building in the wrong place at too high a price, and they never forgot the opposition of both Anglican and Dissenting ministers to

31 *House of Lords Select Committee* on 'Deficiency of Means of Spiritual Instruction' 1858. Rowsell's evidence, qu.1125; Hume's, qu.461.

the Mission in the first instance. Although the Oxford Movement was re-emphasizing the doctrine of the Church, the reverse process went on among evangelicals, who measured the high claims made for the Church against this institutional failure to support their schemes.[32] In effect, the evangelicals freed themselves from traditional ecclesiastical restraints, while inventing a new, looser and more relevant urban structure in which revivalism could operate happily.

The City Mission lived a sharply Protestant life of its own— 'no peace with Popery' was one of its mottoes. Its historian wrote in 1885 that

> it is a pleasing duty to add, that in our quiet way, the plague of Popery had been stayed among the people in those sections of London where Ritualism has had full sway in the Established Church. While there has been fighting in the law courts to legally free her from the papal influence developed within her, we have guarded the public from priestly effort. In the parish of St Alban's, Holborn, four missionaries have kept the poor under constant visitation, and have protected them in great numbers from perversion, and so in other parishes. Where the testimony is pure, the Mission has ever worked in harmony with the clergy; where it has been otherwise, the enlightening power of the Bible has been extended to the people.[33]

The importance of the conversion from Roman Catholicism has already been indicated in discussing the images of successful revivalism; conflict with Anglo-Catholicism became acute as the century progressed; the tendency of both revivalists and the new lay evangelicals to set themselves up as judges of the clergy comes out very clearly in the above passage.

Other vital elements in the formation of a network of organizations which lay outside the control of the mainstream Churches were the foundation of the Young Men's Christian Association in London in 1844, initially among young men in

[32] J. W. Weylland, *These Fifty Years*, Jubilee Volume of the London City Mission (1885), pp.17–18.

[33] Ibid., p.321. By 1895 the Mission had 481 agents, more than the Wesleyan itinerancy of 1795. In looking at the committee lists of this kind of organization one should not be misled by the almost inevitable presence of Shaftesbury and other prominent laymen, or by the appearance of an interdenominational neutrality. Institutions based in the evangelical sub-culture always had a definite character of their own: it was the lay agents who gave the London City Mission its real flavour.

the drapery trade and never moving towards a working-class clientele;[34] and the spread of teetotal bodies which led to the establishment of the United Kingdom Alliance in 1853.[35] Once again the leadership was effectively lay, and clerical opposition to teetotalism widened the gap between the two parties. An alliance had formed between the American revivalists and the teetotallers as early as the 1840s, when both groups lacked social prestige; the alliance was natural, for Americans already took teetotalism for granted as part of any Protestant Church's programme; neither Caughey nor Finney had any hesitation on the subject.

The growth in the 1850s of an English revivalist tradition owed more to the support of this new evangelical network than it did to the ministry of the mainstream Churches, or, indeed, the organized Churches as such. In their turn, the English revivalists set up their own contacts, so that the revivalist and new evangelical structures became overlapping while remaining independent. What became a highly organized evangelical sub-culture played a fundamental role in the breakthrough of Moody and Sankey in the 1870s, for the Americans found a highly organized English constituency prepared for them.

Central in this process was the publishing business of R. C. Morgan, who in later years was accused of 'creating a vogue for undenominational missions—indeed, almost a new set of undenominationalists, admittedly devoted and eager in soul-winning, but seeking isolation rather than unity of heart and purpose in the wider life of the Churches'.[36] Morgan, however, thought nothing of the 'wider life of the Churches'; his son was equally mistaken in saying that his father's sympathies were 'pan-denominational'.[37] Morgan's loyalty was to certain Protestant doctrines, not to institutions.

Morgan began to publish *The Revival* as an eight-page weekly on 30 July, 1859. At first he sold only about 8,000 copies, but here the evangelical network came to his rescue,

---

[34] H. Williams, *Life of George Williams* (1906); C. Binfield, op. cit.

[35] Brian Harrison, op. cit.: 'Pledge-signing often marked an important stage in the conversion process and often itself sparked off a revival' (p.171). Harrison underestimates the extent to which revivalists spread the new movement.

[36] R. E. Morgan, *Life of R. C. Morgan* (1909), p.190.

[37] Ibid., p.191.

for when the paper was advertised at the Barnet Conference of 1859 the sale soon shot up to about 80,000. This was the Conference started by William Pennefather at Barnet in 1856, which became better known as the Mildmay Conference after he moved to St Jude's, Mildmay, in North London, in 1864. The annual meetings, which joined the practical and the apocalyptic, were another crossing-point for all varieties of new evangelical. The date, 1856, was also important: the influence of the Crimean War on Victorian evangelicalism has been underrated, largely on account of the irrelevant concentration on the year 1859. In that year Morgan published revival hymnbooks for both Richard Weaver and Joshua Poole; they sold well, without touching the sales reached by Sankey in the later years of the century. Poole's book was called *The British Revival Hymnbook*; it contained 120 hymns; Poole was the son of a Wesleyan sadler in Skipton, and was born in 1826. Weaver's book was called *Richard Weaver's Hymnbook*: it had 80 hymns, 10 of which came from the first Primitive Methodist songbook. From this point of view, Weaver looks like a last flourish of the working-class end of the Primitive Methodist revivals.

Morgan's attitude to the organization of religion typified that of the revivalist group. In the early 1860s his father, who lived in what was then the village of Wood Green, in Essex, ran open-air meetings, Sunday by Sunday, for the trippers who came out from London in brakes and piled into the 'Jolly Butchers' as soon as they caught sight of the country. About 1865 he built himself a hall, of which R. C. Morgan was to be the self-appointed pastor for forty years. He first spoke there himself in 1867; in 1884 he had a baptistery put in, but before that when he wanted to baptize someone he simply borrowed a nearby Baptist Chapel. One ran up one's institutions to suit the needs of the moment; the historic Churches only cumbered the ground. *The Revival* naturally supported the English revivalists, with Weaver as its early hero and the Americans rather in the background. Morgan also backed the Free Methodist, William Booth, in the earlier, less successful stages of his career. Morgan had been a member of the East London Special Services Committee from its beginning in 1861; this Committee, which was another independent lay body, gave Booth his first foothold in London in 1865, when he preached in a tent erected on the Quaker's Burial Ground in Whitechapel. When Booth formed the Christian Mission in 1867, Morgan gave his name as a referee. In starting the Salvation Army, however, Booth revealed how little he really believed in freedom, spontaneity and reliance on the Spirit. The military analogy in which the 'General' sunned himself concealed a clerical origin: Booth's absolute power over his 'soldiers' reflected the authority which as a young man he had seen, or thought he saw, in the hands of the Wesleyan ministry of the 1840s.

Nothing could have attracted Morgan less. He preferred Richard Weaver, whom he once described as having converted more people than any revivalist since George Whitefield. Weaver, Morgan said, was the most prominent of the working-men preachers, and he spoke of having heard Weaver sing 'My heart is fixed, eternal God/Fixed on Thee, Fixed on Thee' in a way that thrilled him as no hymn had before or since.[38] Weaver, born in a Shropshire mining village in 1827, started work in the pit at seven and worked intermittently as a miner from then until 1852; part of the time, however, he supported himself by singing and fighting. In later years he was often described as a converted prize-fighter; he denied this publicly in 1860, but admitted that he had been famous in the colliery districts as 'Undaunted Dick'. In 1852 he went to live with his brother George at Biddulph; this brought him among Primitive Methodists, and his first conversion and preaching soon followed.[39] After a relapse into more fighting and drinking, his lasting conversion came after a vivid dream in which he dreamed that he was cast into the material flames of Hell for ever. He wrote:

[38] *The Revival*, 1 September, 1860. In June, 1860, William Carter, another 'working-man preacher', was reported in the *Revival* as wishing to contradict the statement that he was 'a London chimney-sweep'. The idea that he was just an ordinary sweep had led to objections to his preaching in some places; a correspondent stated that Carter was 'a highly-respected master-sweep'. The real cause of this sensitivity was that both men had now been adopted into evangelical-pietist society.

[39] If Wesleyan Methodism had been able to use William Booth, and Primitive Methodism had been able to absorb the energies of Weaver, both might have had a better chance of retaining contact with the poorer classes at what was probably, in the 1860s, the turning-point of the century for both. That they could not do so, however, depended upon causes far too complex to allow one to suppose this a simple, or personal, alternative.

I required something more powerful than visions of Hell to save me from my life of sin. Weeks after that dreadful dream I was still a slave to Satan—led captive by the devil at his will. One night I was sparring with a black man in a boxing saloon. We stood up foot to foot and I let drive. The blow went home, and the blood ran down his black face. As I stood there looking at his blood, the Spirit of God brought that word of God to mind, 'The Blood of Jesus Christ, His Son, cleanseth us from all sin'; and that other word, 'The same Lord over all is rich upon all that call upon Him'; and that other word, 'For whosoever shall call upon the name of the Lord shall be saved'. 'Here, Charlie,' I said, 'pull off these. Never again shall a pair of boxing gloves be put on my hands.'[40]

If one omits the second and third quotations from the Bible one has one of the more convincing conversion stories of the nineteenth century. A man's life summed itself up and changed direction in a single blow. This type of conversion-experience was recognized by William James; it is also discussed by a phenomenologist like Merleau-Ponty, who stresses this quality of character-accumulation, as opposed to Jean-Paul Sartre's picture of an individual whose character is all the time future-directed. After this conversion Weaver married, claiming to have been guided to his wife in a dream, and joined the Openshaw Wesleyan Society in Lancashire. But although he and two or three other Wesleyan colliers who lived in Haughton Green, near Hyde, held cottage meetings in the village, the Wesleyans, like the Primitive Methodists, could not contain him. It was the revivalist network itself which found him out, gave him religious work, and then brought him into contact with Reginald Radcliffe, who was as loosely attached to the Church of England as Weaver was to the Methodists. For a brief period between 1855 and about 1862 Weaver became well-known.

Reginald Radcliffe, born in 1825, had also begun to preach in the 1850s. The sixth son of a Liverpool lawyer, he is said by his wife to have grown up in 'Liverpool's palmy days, when Dr McNeile was valiant for the truth, and the Rev. Haldane Stewart was an epistle known and read of all men.'[41] Those

---

[40] J. Paterson, *Richard Weaver's Life Story* (1897), pp.57–8.
[41] *Recollections of Reginald Radcliffe*, by his wife, p.10.

were the days when Liverpool Anglicanism was dominated by aggressively anti-Roman Catholic evangelicals, while more sophisticated middle-class Protestants took refuge in Unitarianism and the Gaskells. The pressure of the huge Roman Catholic community made the local Anglicans more sympathetic to lay preachers than they were in other places; Mrs Radcliffe describes a meeting on the Exchange Flags at which McNeile, 'our Protestant champion', preached for Radcliffe 'on a little raised platform beside the monument commemorating Nelson's naval victories'.[42] Already as a young man Radcliffe knew some of the Anglican evangelicals who had not quite lost sight of the eighteenth century idea of 'irregularity', and when he travelled to London to preach in the open-air was given an introduction to William Pennefather, then at Barnet; several years later Pennefather offered to pay Radcliffe the cost of sending one of his tract distributors to Barnet Fair. Both Pennefather and McNeile accepted the parish system, which the eighteenth-century 'irregulars' had sat very light to, but they anxiously looked for ways of supplementing it.

Nevertheless, the Anglican system could make little use of Radcliffe in the 1850s. His spiritual home was the Liverpool Town Mission and its band of lay agents. Even this was not independent enough for him, and in April, 1855, he took the Teutonic Hall in Lime Street. On Sundays there he ran a series of half-hour services from ten o'clock in the morning until half-past nine at night. Men were despatched into the street to sing and pray in order to gather groups into the hall, a method which the Primitives had made familiar. 'Towards eight o'clock on Sunday evenings, when the congregations were dismissed from the churches, there was often a great crowd, and many Christians came to help.'[43] The comment underlined the alienation of the revivalists from the mainstream churches.

Radcliffe soon organized a team of Bible-sellers and tract-distributors. Among them was John Hambleton, an ex-actor, said to have been converted in California during the Gold Rush and so half an American contribution to the English

[42] Ibid., p.20.
[43] Ibid., p.19.

School. He first met Richard Weaver when they were selling Bibles in Hyde market-place in 1855. Weaver and other colliers visited the market to buy food; they listened to the colporteurs and offered to sing for them. Just before Easter, 1856, the colporteurs announced that Radcliffe himself would preach in Hyde on Good Friday. On the day Radcliffe failed to arrive, so Hambleton called Weaver up on to the platform and told him to speak as well as sing. Weaver succeeded: in fact, he took the stall over from Hambleton. Radcliffe now visited Weaver and engaged him to travel through the villages around Chester distributing tracts and dissuading the people from attending Chester Races.

Radcliffe and Weaver did not team up immediately; in practice, Weaver seems to have drifted into the post of town missionary at Prescot, in Lancashire. The revivalist fortunes of both men were made by the Scottish evangelical, Brownlow North. North, as his biographer acknowledges, did his most effective preaching in Scotland in 1856–8, before either the American or Ulster revivals had affected the situation. He combined hell-fire preaching with an irreproachable social position—a grandfather was Bishop of Winchester and he himself was a grand-nephew to Lord North, George III's Prime Minister. Radcliffe went to Aberdeen in November, 1858, as the result of a private invitation, and found himself conducting services in a small mission hall linked to a local Congregational church at the same time as Brownlow North, at the height of his fame, was crowding a chapel belonging to the Scottish Free Church, the revival-minded Presbyterians who had seceded from the Church of Scotland in 1843. The two men met, and North evidently guaranteed Radcliffe's soundness to the Scottish revivalist network, which revolved round the pietist Duchess of Gordon, who spent much of the year at Huntly, close to Aberdeen. Radcliffe stayed at Huntly in 1859 and was sent into the Highlands in the Duchess' travelling carriage with Hector Macpherson as Gaelic interpreter and Duncan Matheson as fellow preacher. It was only in the summer of 1859 that the Established and Free Churches of Scotland reconciled themselves to the idea of a lay preacher. Things did not differ so much in England, where Baptist Noel told the Baptist Union in May, 1860, that 'God had been teaching the Church that other men were fully as able to preach the Gospel to the people as were preachers'.[44] That the Methodists had institutionalized lay preaching for more than a century did not count, but somehow confirmed their inferior social status. And only the Methodists, loyal to their past, ever doubted that much of their lay preaching was very poor stuff.

Baptist Noel[45] was a mild, earnest man who had disappointed political Dissenters when, having left the Church of England in 1848 because he disapproved of the union of State and Church, and having published a six-hundred page attack on the principle of an English establishment, he quietly refused to join the Liberation Society or to speak on its platforms. In his Presidential Address to the Baptist Union in 1855, he said that political action was always dangerous to Christians and especially to ministers of religion, and that a visible deepening of the piety of Dissenting ministers and people would do more in a few years to free the Church of England from the State than thirty years of political warfare. Charles Miall, the would-be architect of disestablishment who did so much to destroy the religious influence of Nonconformity, thought this 'very illogical and unsound',[46] but Noel's real objection to the Anglican establishment was the way in which, he believed, it prevented the evangelization of the country.

He was a warm supporter of lay preaching, and it was certainly he who, having heard of events in Scotland, invited North and Radcliffe to preach in London. They came in the third week in December, 1859, and stayed until May, 1860. Radcliffe himself was Noel's guest and gave his first address in Noel's Baptist Chapel, which was in John Street, Bedford Row, on 18 December, 1859. Both North and Radcliffe spoke

[44] *The Nonconformist*, 2 May, 1860.
[45] Noel was Anglican minister at the proprietary chapel at St John's, Bedford Row, for twenty years before he became a Baptist; he published his *Essay on the Union of Church and State* in 1849. He became President of the Baptist Union again in 1867; he deplored Spurgeon's negative attitude to Biblical Criticism in the Downgrade Controversy. He died in 1873.
[46] Cf. C. Miall, *History of the Free Churches in England* (1891), p.511. The revival of Dissent as politics divided nineteenth century Nonconformity more than church historians seem to have realized; dislike of the new political attitude drove men like George Williams over to the Anglican Church. For Miall, see C. Binfield, *So Down to Prayers* (1977), pp.101–24.

at the Marylebone Presbyterian Church; Radcliffe also spoke at the Congregational Chapel in Kentish Town; most of their meetings, however, were held in theatres and in the Riding School, Bayswater. It is significant of the role of the Y.M.C.A. that North's first engagement was to speak to the Association at Exeter Hall on 20 December, 1859, and that a number of other meetings were held at the Marlborough Street Y.M.C.A.

Noel and Radcliffe were also involved in the midnight meetings for the reclamation of prostitutes which were started at St James' Restaurant, Piccadilly, on 8 February, 1860. A note in the *Nonconformist*, 15 August, 1860, gave the results of the season. Seven meetings were held in Regent Street, two in Euston Road, one in Islington and one in Bishopsgate, and two were held for Frenchwomen. About 2,000 women were said to have attended, 180 to have been reclaimed; of these 91 were then in homes; the average age was twenty-two. These figures are more exact than those given by Kathleen Heasman in *Evangelicals in Action* (1962).

When Radcliffe returned to Aberdeen he held similar meetings there in 1860. This led to one chance conversion, for, when Radcliffe's invitations were distributed, one was handed to a woman who was standing in the street who was in fact perfectly respectable; she went to the meeting all the same and was converted. Evangelicals always delighted in what they regarded as providential touches. This Evangelical effort fell off in about 1866; the Anglo-Catholics started similar attempts in the Missions to London of 1874, making use of the female orders.

North and Radcliffe aroused much more controversy in London than might be supposed from evangelical accounts of the period. It is a fundamental weakness of J. E. Orr's *The Second Evangelical Awakening* (1949) that the author gave no attention to the way in which the campaign to work up an English revival in 1860–1 split the Evangelical world, though one ought to expect such a division in view of the growth of the 'new evangelicalism' after 1830. But Orr's book was committed to a unitary view of 'evangelicalism', and his chapter on 'Opposition to the Revival' was concerned entirely with defending the reputation of the Ulster Revival against the criticisms which were in fact made by contemporaries on the

proper ground that it had encouraged hysterical phenomena.
Orr, however, would have found it difficult to talk about a
'second evangelical awakening' if he had first had to admit
that the main body of evangelical Anglicans remained either
indifferent or hostile to the English lay revivalists, and that on
theological as well as on more personal grounds.

The trouble really began when Radcliffe rashly accepted an
invitation to preach at the Whitefield Tabernacle on 22 April,
1860. The Tabernacle was the headquarters of the would-be
prince of Independency, Dr Campbell, whose influence on his
denomination was much less constructive than that of John
Angell James. Campbell united stupidity and arrogance to a
remarkable degree, and he treated the unsuspecting Radcliffe
as he had done Finney ten years before, cutting him up in an
article. Many of Campbell's flattering invitations to the pulpit
were intended to supply him with easy copy for the *British
Banner*, the journal which he edited and liked to think of as the
conscience of Congregationalism. He warned the world in
general against Radcliffe's style of revivalism; no one had
thought to warn Radcliffe against Campbell's style in journalism. Campbell quoted a certain Dr Belcher, an American, as
saying that the Churches of the American East had been
ruined by revivalism. He attacked every detail of Radcliffe's
meeting, comparing it adversely with both the American and
the Ulster styles of revival, in which, he said, prayer had been
the principal method.

All this was reversed in the exhibition of Mr Radcliffe at the
Tottenham Court Road Chapel; he expounded, after a fashion,
for half an hour; he preached an hour and a half; and he prayed
for five minutes. The thing was quite original. The sermon was
so incoherent that it might have been preached backwards. He
spent no small portion of his time in asserting that the people
must all perish unless they were 'born again'. In no instance
[Campbell retorted] do the Apostles threaten men with perdition
as the penalty of not being born again, apart from personal
transgressions. . . . In no cases did the Apostles enjoin men to be
born again as a duty, under the penalty of perdition.[47]

[47] Cf. *The Record*, 4 June, 1860. It is significant that Campbell dismissed Radcliffe as
the worst kind of *American* revivalism. Radcliffe also offered a convenient chance to
point out that those who had objected to lay preaching were splendidly justified.

The importance of this article was not that Campbell wrote it—the world was used to his bullying impersonation of orthodoxy by 1860, but that the *Record*, the journal of mainstream Anglican Evangelicalism, reprinted it in full on 4 June, 1860. The *Record* added that complaints had been received at the *Record* office about Radcliffe's style of preaching. He had been criticized because he had brought forward an uneducated youth, said to have been converted at a revival prayer meeting, to address his audience on the subject of his conversion and religious experience, which he was said to have done in an unconnected and over-excited manner. 'This', the *Record* said, 'was very strongly to be condemned, as likely to have a very injurious effect on any new convert, from its tendency to foster spiritual pride, and to affix moreover to the whole work of revival a character of ranting fanaticism.' As for Radcliffe himself, the *Record* thought that he had been pushed forward by mistaken and indiscreet friends into a false position, a hit at Noel as a lapsed Anglican Evangelical whose views on establishment were anathema to the *Record*.

A brief description of Radcliffe at this time is to be found in his biography, where he is described as coming to a meeting 'in company with the Hon. and Mrs Baptist Noel, at whose house he is residing—you would have little imagined on looking at the busy man in grey tweed shooting suit and blue silk necktie loosely thrown round his neck in sailor fashion, that another Paul had come from a distance to proclaim with words of fiery eloquence the tidings of salvation'.[48] No such Pauline figure had arrived in the *Record*'s estimation.

The *Record*'s attack coincided with Richard Weaver's return to London. He had come briefly in March, 1860, when he had addressed a special meeting of chimney-sweeps; his success led to an invitation to Sheffield, and it was from there that he now arrived back in the capital. Radcliffe afterwards took the credit for bringing him back, and there is no reason to doubt the truth of the claim. Weaver's first meeting, however, was managed by the master-chimney-sweep, William Carter, another 'workingman revivalist', as their propaganda called them. Weaver did not relish the cards which Carter had caused to be printed as advertisement. They read:

[48] Mrs Radcliffe, op. cit., p.112.

To Prize-Fighters, Dog-Fanciers and Sporting Men of all Kinds
Come and Hear
Richard Weaver, known as 'Undaunted Dick'
the converted prize-fighter, from the mines of Lancashire. He
will sing and preach in Cumberland Market, Regent's Park, on
Sunday morning, June 3, at eleven o'clock, and in the evening
at six o'clock. He will narrate his wonderful conversion and
other striking circumstances of his life. He will also sing and
preach every evening in the same place at seven o'clock, and on
the following Sunday, 10th June—in the morning at eleven
o'clock and evening at six o'clock.

Carter's advertisement looked forward to the successful
vulgarity of the Hallelujah Circus and other tricks of early
Salvation Army propaganda. A free, spontaneous, lay
revivalist style was now surfacing in England. It took two
forms: the restrained but importunate gentility of the
Y.M.C.A. world, and the unrestrained, popular rhetoric of
Weaver which, whatever he chose to believe, suited Carter's
cards, and also reminded one of the romantic wildness of
Lorenzo Dow. Weaver's addresses linked with the theatre of
the period, still committed to 'strong acting' and calamities
elaborately staged, to sentimentality and a low-priced pit.
This may well have been the last point in the nineteenth
century at which the popular tradition and the religious
tradition could speak in much the same language; certainly
the *Record*, in rejecting Radcliffe (and Weaver by implication)
was assuming that revivalism must keep clear of the popular
style, eschew the vulgar, and go for the draper's assistants.

R. C. Morgan disagreed, and in the *Revival* for 16 June,
1860, published what amounted to a descriptive defence of
Weaver.

We have listened to him with unbounded pleasure. The salvation
which is in Jesus is to him a river to swim in (Ezek. xlvii.5).
Somewhat startling indeed is the originality of his words and
deeds: but wait it out and you'll say, it has been good to be here.
'Salvation,' he cries aloud, 'isn't in sacraments. Many go from
the communion-rail to Hell. It isn't in having the Bishop's hand
laid on your head; it isn't in going under the water; it isn't in
groans and tears and prayers. It's in the blood of Christ. Look at
Him. I'll get out of sight.' And he hides himself behind the

extemporised pulpit. 'Souls-saving blood. Sin-cleansing blood; peace-speaking blood; devil-confounding blood'. . . . He long and with all his heart labours for the salvation of souls. 'My friends tell me I'm killing myself. I have come to London because I love you working-men: and now I'll preach to you, if you carry me from this waggon to the grave. A kind brother said he would pay my fare to London if I could trust the Lord to keep me when I got there; and bless the Lord I *can* trust Him. Hold up your hands all who are on the Lord's side. Now, all who are anxious, hold up your hands. Who'll volunteer. Don't be ashamed. One hand is up. Bless the Lord. Another hand—another. Come up here you dear souls and we'll pray with you and talk with you. Now all kneel down. If you would get to Heaven you must kneel. They get on best who kneel most.' Let it not be supposed that levity accompanies all this. Indeed, no. We have attended no meetings more solemn or more rich in results.[49]

The *Revival* was fond of quoting Weaver's aphorism: 'Spurgeon believes in final perseverance, but if you don't begin you can't finish';[50] and also 'You see on the bills I'm called the converted collier: that's better than Reverend'.[51] He said on one occasion: 'I have not been ordained; no Bishop's hand has been on my head: but I have got the Blood upon me';[52] and 'The Devil's paw can't touch you through the Blood—Jesus never lost a battle yet. Infidelity must lie at his feet; Puseyism and Popery must fall before Him'.[53]

These slighting references to the ministry and the sacraments help to explain why the Anglican *Record* attacked Radcliffe and Weaver, and also remind one that there is not much substance in the claim sometimes made that nineteenth-century revivalism contributed to the rise of the ecumenical movement. The history of the Western religious tradition since 1789 shows two antithetical themes: one, a growing belief in the value of a united Christian Church, which would compensate for the break-up of Christendom; and the other, steadily increasing disillusion with ecclesiastical institutions,

[49] *The Revival*, 16 June, 1860.
[50] Ibid., 4 August, 1860.
[51] Ibid.
[52] Ibid., 13 October, 1860.
[53] Ibid.

an attitude which expressed itself in falling membership in all Churches in the course of the twentieth century. The Ecumenical Movement, which reached a climax in the formation of the World Council of Churches in 1948, has had the moral and political prestige, whereas historians have neglected the anti-church movement, in which many different strands also merged. At the theological level, for instance, Søren Kierkegaard, the most brilliant writer of modern Protestantism, dismissed the institutions of Christianity as a perpetual threat to the religious life of their members.[54] At the close of the century, a typical Protestant view was that of Harnack, who regarded the Church as a voluntary association of no central importance in the Christian life.[55] Much more influential in revivalistic circles were the Plymouth Brethren,[56] a breakaway from Anglicanism in the late 1820s. The Brethren combined adventism, revivalism and a disbelief in the existence of a historical Church. Most revivalists thought of the historic Churches as the enervating and over-intellectualized environment within which they had to save primitive Christianity.

Weaver stood in a long tradition. John Wesley had made scathing attacks on the Anglican ministry of his day, and on people who relied on their baptism for salvation. Baptist Noel's essay on Church and State included a long digression on the section of the clergy which he believed to be unconverted itself and uninterested in converting others. D. L. Moody made similar references to baptism, in deliberate contrast to the Anglo-Catholic appeal for a renewal of baptismal vows at the climax of parochial missions. Weaver was also giving vigorous outlet to the lay revivalist's sense of being an outsider; he was bitter because the professional ministry refused to take seriously the conversions which he claimed. At the same time the revivalist was driven by the uncertainty of his situation; he had to keep up a flow of conversions, and this made him anxious to convince his

[54] S. Kierkegaard, *The Attack on Christendom* (1854). He belonged to the Lutheran Pietist, not the Anglo-Saxon revivalist, tradition; the two had in common their emphasis on the subjectivity of faith.

[55] A. Harnack, *The Essence of Christianity* (E.T. 1900).

[56] For the influence of the Brethren, see R. Sandeen, *The Roots of Fundamentalism* Chicago 1970).

audience that its problems could be solved only then and there in the penny theatre where they sat—they must not escape to renew their baptismal vows elsewhere, or to attend communion more frequently. It was not even enough if they made an inward act of contrition as they sat in their places. The emphasis in reports of revival meetings at this time on movement, on weeping, on groups of people huddled together in prayer, on openly expressed action, was intended to contrast with the formality of most public worship as evidence that the revivalist had brought the powers of the supernatural back into the religious situation. The visible, physical consequences of the revivalist's appeal was the dramatic equivalent of the elevation of the Host in the Roman Mass; in Protestant terms some 'new evangelicals' found what they believed to be the observable actions of God more impressive than the invisible action of the Eucharist. When apologists said that there was no 'emotion' in the revival meetings, they meant *human* emotion as such; they were prepared to defend even the more extreme Ulster phenomena once they had persuaded themselves that these resulted from supernatural forces.

This did not exhaust the case against Weaver, however. The *Wesleyan Times* backed revivalism, but not as uncritically as did the *Revival*. The Free Wesleyan paper summed up its impressions of Weaver in October, 1860. He had begun, the writer said, by preaching from a cart in the market near the Tottenham Court Road when the evening weather was fine enough, or in a penny theatre. Later, he had used St Martin's Hall (which R. C. Morgan, in his biography of Weaver, said was hired by the *Revival* itself for two weeks, half the cost of the second week being guaranteed by a gentleman who had recently been converted by Radcliffe); he also used the Rev. J. Fleming's schoolroom in Kentish Town, which Radcliffe had occupied earlier in the year. Weaver was described as thirty-six and not strong, despite a pugilistic career in which he had allegedly never been beaten; he was below medium height. 'His utterance', the paper said, 'is an almost continuous shout, and the expression harsh to the ears of Londoners, especially as the Staffordshire accent is decidedly marked.' He had recently preached at the Victoria Theatre for about an hour from the text in Genesis, 'The Lord shut him in': this was a reference to the closing of the Ark which left the lost outside, a favourite image with revivalists as late as Billy Graham.

> Weaver called for a show of hands to show who were on the Lord's side. About half the entire number gave the required signal, which was accompanied by shouts of 'Glory' and 'Praise God'. Those who were anxious were asked to raise their hands, but only two of them did, and the service closed with prayer and sacred song led by the preacher to a very lively tune, the chorus being many times repeated with extraordinary animation.[57]

According to Morgan[58] Weaver had been advertised to speak at the Victoria Theatre on Sundays in September, and he had tried to do so by travelling down from Scotland by train and then returning. After one Sunday he broke down and the network replaced him with William Carter, but the group retained the theatre for two further weeks at which Weaver appeared, and it was one of these meetings which the *Wesleyan Times* was describing. The incident showed how determined the *Revival* group was to create a London movement, rather than keep a spontaneous one in being; it also indicated how railways were extending the range of revivalists, if not necessarily their effectiveness.

In a leading article entitled 'Revival Preaching' (23 June, 1860), the *Revival* defended Weaver's style. Weaver, Morgan said, did not try to please people by toning down the realities of Heaven and Hell. Instead, he talked about Hell and the torments of the damned in an imagery derived from the dense darkness of the coal-pit, the flames of the firedamp, and the suffocating vapour of the choke-damp. Thousands, Morgan wrote, perished every day, their epitaph written by God as 'damned, damned'. The *Revival* quoted with approval Weaver's outburst: 'How many of you mothers are suckling your children for Hell? One says, I am not. Yes, you are, if you're not a child of God by faith in Jesus Christ.' Morgan sincerely believed that Darwin, Colenso and Benjamin

---

[57] *Wesleyan Times*, 1 October, 1860.
[58] Morgan, op. cit., pp. 115–16.

Jowett were endangering men's salvation; Weaver's methods were abundantly justified, on the other hand, if he 'converted' people.

Despite the efforts which were made in 1860 to float an English revival, Radcliffe and Weaver found it worth their while to spend most of the second half of the year in Scotland, where the demand for revival meetings continued unabated. When the *Record* published a second critical article about them, it referred largely to their Scottish campaign. The writer deliberately said that Brownlow North avoided most of the errors common among lay preachers, but this was probably a tribute to North's social background. Of Radcliffe and Weaver, however, he said that most of their apparent conversions in Scotland were very short-lived; he blamed this on a sentimental, one-sided preaching which appealed too much to the emotions. Of Weaver in particular he said that

> one of the devices resorted to for the purpose of arresting the attention is to sing a hymn to a merry, jovial tune. Mr Weaver probably adopted this extraordinary plan for the purpose of arresting the attention of the poor colliers to whom he was accustomed to speak in the mines. But this plan can hardly be commended, and whilst a merry jig revolts good feeling, and is calculated to dispel solemnity, it seems utterly repugnant to the dignity of the everlasting gospel.[59]

As for Reginald Radcliffe, the writer thought that he was gradually becoming more doctrinal in his preaching, but that earnestness and zeal would never make up for an effective understanding of the Christian message, and he deprecated the talk of those who were saying that with enough Norths and Weavers one could convert the whole of Scotland.

The *Record*'s next mention of Weaver reinforced the points made in this article. This was a report from Dunlop, in Scotland, where the parish church was said to have been filled with people singing songs from Richard Weaver's *Revival Hymnbook*. In one corner of the church people were singing to the tune of 'Wait for the Waggon', while another group not far distant was singing to 'Betty Baker'. The *Record*'s corres-

[59] *Record*, 31 October, 1860.

pondent had clearly been shocked by the sight of 'young men and women, boys and girls, embracing each other in transports of religious delirium—swaying their bodies backwards and forwards—standing on the seats and stamping their feet to the tune, and holding forth at the pitch of their voices: "Christ for Me".'[60]

Weaver printed no music in his hymnbooks and in Scotland, where instrumental music was still hardly used in churches and where congregational singing was still slow and mournful, such excitement, which reminds one of a group of twentieth-century teenagers reacting to popular music, had a shattering effect. Anticlericalism, hell-fire sermons and folk-tunes—the similarity to the mixture which William Booth improved by the addition of the working-class brass band, is interesting. Weaver did not anticipate Booth, however; this was the tradition of the street-singer and entertainer adapted to revivalistic purposes. Booth was not strictly speaking a revivalist at all; his aim was to found local chapels; he always intended to occupy the ground.

At the close of 1860 Weaver was the central figure in a larger London scheme. Exeter Hall was hired for revivalist services by a committee which wanted to put on William Carter, Reginald Radcliffe and Weaver himself. Only one meeting took place, after which the proprietors of the Hall cancelled the arrangements. The *Record* said on the day after the meeting that some of the incidents alleged were so objectionable that the editor wanted to make further enquiries before printing an account.[61] Revival tradition has omitted mention of the veto, as in Morgan's life of Weaver, where Morgan wrote that on the first night Weaver spoke at Exeter Hall, but afterwards at the Surrey, City of London and other theatres. An account in the *Nonconformist* made clear that Weaver was the principal speaker, that his address lasted an hour, on top of a lengthy prayer for the salvation of London and the annihilation of Puseyism, infidelity and so forth. The *Nonconformist* compared him to the American teetotal orator, William Gough, and described how he paced from one side of the platform to the other, telling stories, and alternately

[60] Ibid., 2 December, 1860.
[61] *Record*, 3 December, 1860.

imploring his hearers to accept the mercy that he offered, or threatening them with the awful consequences of refusal. When he called upon those who had 'found Christ' to hold up their hands about a third of those present did so, and later on a few responded to the invitation to volunteer for Christian service.[62] The plan to give Weaver greater prominence ended by re-emphasizing the divisions in the evangelical ranks.

The *Record* did not consider Weaver properly awakened at all. After their exclusion from Exeter Hall, he and his friends held a rally at the Surrey Theatre at which about 3,500 people were said to have attended. Weaver evidently tried to conciliate his critics a little, for the *Record* said that 'there was nothing of denunciation in the speaker', a comment which suggested that it had been Weaver's dismissal of the clergy and the sacraments which had given most offence. The *Record* reporter, however, launched a theological assault which went to the heart of revivalism in practice. He quoted statements by Weaver such as: 'Only believe and you are saved'; 'You may be saved while this arm is lifted up'.[63] Evangelicals of the *Record* tradition disliked the way in which revivalists like Weaver, whilst seeming to increase the tension and seriousness of religious experience, actually relaxed it; Weaver (they felt, and the same would apply to later critics of Moody and Graham) vulgarized the apprehension of conversion so that what ought (as they understood it) to have been an aweful and triumphant appropriation of the forgiveness of God became a sentimental, simple assent to the idea of 'being saved'. Weaver, the writer complained, never really made it clear that 'saving faith' included surrender of the heart, and must be seen in the conduct of life, not just in the raising of an arm.

Nor was the *Record* inclined to modify this opinion. About a year later, another leading article, devoted to criticizing revival meetings, said:

There is too often a great display of that which plays upon the passions; a style of language is employed which savours far more of man's wisdom than of scriptural truth; and in pressing upon

---

[62] *Wesleyan Times*, 3 December, 1860, should also be compared.
[63] *Record*, 10 December, 1860.

the audience the great duty of faith in a Saviour, it is sometimes done in terms which would imply that some dexterous volition of their own would, at any moment, transform them from unconverted sinners into children of light. . . . While faith is greatly insisted upon, repentance, as binding upon the unconverted class of hearers, is overlooked. . . .[64]

Coming from an unimpeachable Anglican source this criticism was painful, and it was probably one reason why, early in December, 1861, a Conference was held in the Y.M.C.A. Rooms in Great Marlborough Street, London, 'for those believers who have been led to go out into public places of resort, or to theatres, etc. . . . to preach the gospel.' Captain Trotter[65] presided; Reginald Radcliffe, Hambleton and William Carter represented the full-time lay revivalists; among the part-timers were Stevenson Blackwood, H. F. Bowker (a leading London Y.M.C.A. supporter since the 1840s, who was Chairman of the Keswick Holiness movement in the 1880s) and Captain Wilbraham Taylor, as well as Trotter himself. This conference gave further evidence of the split in the evangelical world. Speaker after speaker defended the way in which the revivalists asked their hearers to 'come to Jesus': sorrow for sin would be awakened afterwards, Bowker said, if only they would respond to the invitation. Radcliffe, whose background was Anglican, regretted the hostility of so many of the clergy; but the conference speakers

[64] *Record*, 27 November, 1861. The issue of 30 October, 1861, had attacked the meetings which Denham Smith, another English revivalist, was holding in Geneva. Samuel Garratt, a London Evangelical clergyman, had replied to this: he said that faith in Christ produced repentance; but he was Calvinist, scornful of dating revivals in advance; cf. *Life*, etc., ed. Evelyn R. Garratt, 1908. He thought that the Irish revival was a sign that God was willing to revive the English Church, but that the Church responded too late.

[65] Trotter, born in 1808, an Harrovian, entered the Life Guards 1825; in 1833 he married a daughter of Baron Ravensworth; left the Guards 1836, converted in Paris 1839. In 1840, a new vicar, Myers, came to Barnet, where he lived; Trotter noted: 'Second Advent doctrine received by grace, May 4, 1840'. He obtained Sunday off for Barnet postmen in 1842. He employed his own lay agents in the Barnet area. Dallas started the Irish Church Mission in his house. In 1851 he started the Army Prayer Union, and also visited Italy with the Earls of Roden and Cavan to plead for the release of the Madiai, imprisoned in Tuscany for distributing Protestant Bibles. Gave his first address, in the Windsor Theatre, 1852. He built the new Christ Church, Barnet (1845); this was the scene of the first Barnet (Mildmay) Conference in 1856. The Duchess of Gordon (*v.s.*) had attended this Conference in 1860, before the Huntly meetings at which Radcliffe spoke. Paralysed in 1868, died 29 October, 1870. Cf. *To Die is Gain*, with a brief notice of the late Captain Trotter, by William Pennefather, 1871.

could not explain this hostility, or how it was that the Ulster revival had not spread to England. That it had not done so they knew quite well by 1861.

It is not difficult, a century later, to see why there was no 'second evangelical awakening' in England between 1858 and 1862. In the first place, to speak of an 'awakening' was to imply a previous slumber of the kind documented (and probably over-documented) in the case of the eighteenth-century English Churches. Now to talk in this fashion of the various English denominations in the first half of the nineteenth century would have been absurd. Anglican Evangelical-ism might be narrow; Anglo-Catholicism might be irrelevant; Methodism might be internally divisive; *Essays and Reviews* (1860) might symbolize theological ideas execrated by Evangelical, Anglo-Catholic and Methodist alike—but no one could say that early Victorian Christianity had fallen asleep. Rarely, if ever, in a single society, have more people spent more time, money and thought on religious activities. Even from a statistical point of view the sudden expansion of the Baptist and Congregational Churches between 1800 and 1860 was as impressive as the much more frequently quoted figures from the Religious Census of 1851 which showed that working men in the larger, industrial towns were not attending churches at all.

This activity deprived the would-be revivalists of the advantage of contrast. Moreover, by about 1860 the leaders of the institutional churches were well aware of the gap between their largely middle-class clientele and the working-class which had been growing in numbers and self-consciousness and separation from the rest of society since the end of the eighteenth century. In the rapidly expanding towns, schemes such as the series of London theatre services, which were officially sponsored in 1860, were tried in the hope of making contact with the poorer people. The evidence suggests that such measures had no permanent success; working-class contact with the religious tradition was partially restored after 1870 as the new Board Schools became efficient; teachers and schools did far more than the Churches to keep alive in the mass of the population some idea of the Bible and the style of Jesus. It is difficult, however, to speak of an 'evangelical awakening' when the middle-classes were not asleep religiously, but the working-classes remained unconvinced by all the varieties of Christian experience to which they were exposed. The pressure of Evangelicalism on Victorian society rose to a climax between 1860 and 1870, then declined between 1870 and 1914; the years around 1860 do not especially stand out, and the methods used to maintain pressure after 1870 became political as much as religious.

Nevertheless, the public success of revivalism, particularly of Moody and Sankey in London, and to a lesser extent of Smith in Brighton, came in 1875, when the Americans at last made the impact for which Caughey, Finney, Phoebe Palmer and many others had been striving since the days of Lorenzo Dow. A comparison between the 1860s and the 1870s explains what happened. In 1860, for instance, the ecclesiastical leadership had only just grasped the extent of the dechristianization of the towns; they still thought of their own denominations as strong and expanding. They were ready to experiment with urban evangelism, as long as they controlled it themselves, but were inclined to regard the revivalists, American and English, as meddling where they had no status. By 1875 the situation had changed enough for the revivalists to receive wider support.

In 1860, again, the Ulster revival prejudiced English observers against revivalism. This was not because a hostile press misinformed people about what was happening in Ireland; the newspaper stories were true enough, and the essentially 'physical' phenomena which they contained sounded unconvincing in mid-nineteenth-century England as evidence of the presence of a Divine Spirit. Strong as Garrat's evangelical stomach was, he attached small importance to the Ulster marvels in themselves, but defended them by claiming that God was using them to draw attention to the revival. For the time being at any rate, middle-class evangelicalism had become too sophisticated for this kind of phenomenon, though the furious excitement of the Holiness meetings of the Salvation Army in the 1870s won a few middle-class sympathizers; and by the 1890s desperation for visible results was driving some evangelicals back towards physical manifestations, and so to a readiness for early Pentecostalism, in which 'physical' events, 'healings' and '*glossolalia*', abounded. Moody found the right combination for the 1870s when he encouraged Ira Sankey to form the massed choir whose singing probably provided the degree of physical release which his London audiences wanted.

In 1860 no leader like Moody emerged. Finney never dominated in England, and Phoebe Palmer, her immense American Methodist reputation useless in England, had to be satisfied with a prolonged provincial tour. Weaver, whatever the *Revival* said, did not survive the assaults of the *Record*, and lapsed into obscurity after brief notoriety. Weaver's failure, decisive at the Exeter Hall, mattered; one has only to compare it with the slow but steady climb in Moody's reputation in England between 1873 and 1875. Weaver nearly hit on the right mixture of popular music and direct speaking; but it was Sankey who was to introduce England to a new kind of religious music, and Moody who knew how to manage a revival as no one ever had before.

Two other factors counted heavily. One was the split in Evangelicalism, between the *Record* and the *Revival*, so to speak, which deprived the revivalists of help where they expected to find it. The older Anglican Evangelicalism, which traced its descent back to Henry Venn of Huddersfield, Charles Simeon of Cambridge and William Wilberforce, disliked revivalism as a system, distrusted the revivalist as a professional, and doubted conversions as a matter of spiritual method. Faced by revivalism as something lay, American, and even—as in Phoebe Palmer's case—not masculine, they withdrew on positions of strength, demanding, both in 1860 and again of Smith and the holiness group in 1875, the moral guarantees which they summed up in repentance. Revivalism looked like a short cut as far as they were concerned, and the same instinct made them reject perfectionism. They did not deny that poor men had souls, but they retained an eighteenth-century objection to listening to their social inferiors preach; by 1860, however, their confidence in a university-trained ministry had been weakened by the rise in Oxford and Cambridge of Anglo-Catholicism and Biblical Criticism. They preferred overseas missions to revivalism, though sometimes the underlying reason was the conviction that once the gospel had been preached to *all* the nations, the Second Advent would occur.

Interwoven with this clash of generation and tradition, social feeling and theology, was tension inside the churches as institutions. A full-time professional priesthood identifies the 'Church' with itself, developing an employer-role which inevitably casts the laity as employees. Wealthy Anglican lay evangelists like Captain Trotter and Stevenson Blackwood could supply the social guarantees which Radcliffe and Weaver did not possess, but the strength of their social position led to further difficulties with the clergy, and to the career of a man like Lord Radstock. Born in 1833, the son of a vice-admiral, Radstock went to Harrow and Balliol, and was converted in the Crimea. He was a great renouncer: he associated the conversion of his sisters with giving up shooting, for instance. He solved the problem of his right to preach without ordination by asking God to give him three instances of the value of his doing so within twenty-four hours; he received them in the form of unsolicited letters, and went on preaching. He held missions of his own, in Brighton Town Hall in 1867, for instance, and in Scarborough in 1869; he also spoke on the Continent. In about 1873, he became a healer in the manner laid down in the Epistle of James, working through repentance, confession, prayer and anointing. Radstock was perfectly willing to associate with professional revivalists; he was present, naturally, at Smith's English holiness meetings; but he could not mediate between revivalist and ordained minister. Without widespread Anglican ministerial support, revivalism could not become more than a marginal factor, and this support remained minimal in the 1860s. One further cause of this was that so many of the lay revivalists had links with the Plymouth Brethren, a para-ecclesiastical body whose hard core was mostly ex-Anglican, but whose ethos had developed in reaction against Anglican tradition: the Brethren dispensed with a priesthood and cared nothing for the visible Church in the present dispensation. Anglicans, for whom the 'Church' had a personal rather than an institutional existence, found the ruthlessly negative attitude of the Brethren horrifying. In most ecclesiastical circles the mid-nineteenth-century Brethren were feared as a solvent of loyalties as well as a source of strange doctrine; in the 1870s, however, the influence of the Brethren waned as their original creative leadership aged and was not replaced.

The rise of the professional revivalist increased this normal tension between ministry and laity. Americans like Finney and Caughey expected that the majority of ministers would oppose them. Although the Wesleyans, for example, had a much-vaunted system of lay preachers, and liked to boast of the elasticity of their system, they finally expelled Caughey from their pulpits despite his standing as an American Methodist minister, and in 1860 similarly forbade the circuits to receive the Palmers as lay revivalists. The difference in the 1870s was that Moody conciliated the ministry as far as he could. He advanced the theory that the revivalist was the expert in salvation who won the converts and then left them to the churches to nurture. The theory was not more than half-sincere, and, as we shall see, was repudiated in action by many of his supporters. Moody was freer to make terms with the ordained ministers because he had broken with the pattern of the local church revival as his English operation went on, and had set out to gather his own mass audience in centres like the Agricultural Hall, Islington, or the Bingley Hall in Birmingham. The Free Church ministers in particular had to face the fact that they could not stop their members from going to Moody's meetings, and so they preferred to sit on the platform at Moody's back, with the chance of being asked to offer a prayer in the course of the evening. Moody was not able to keep this power over the ministry, however, on his two later tours in England, for he did not repeat his 1875 triumph.

A final factor was the growth of Protestant fear of Anglo-Catholicism, which had not reached its full height in 1860. The Protestant riots in St George's in the East, London, in 1860, which occupied at least as much space as revivalism in the newspapers, suggested that the Ritualists had been thrown onto the defensive and that public opinion would now halt the Catholicizing movement. Revivalist propaganda, as we have seen, frequently claimed the conversion of Roman, but not of Anglo-Catholics. It was after Anglo-Catholic mission priests had taken a prominent part in the Mission to London in 1869 that the revivalists were called in to stop them from establishing a popular version of what had hitherto seemed to be a middle-class sophisticated medievalism. The doubts and fears and ironies of *Essays and Reviews* seemed the enemy in 1860, and no one supposed that either Finney or Weaver would be able to save Jowett.

4. *The French Connexion*

In order to set all this in perspective it is worth comparing what was being attempted in England in the mid-nineteenth century with what was happening at the same period in France. This was made possible by Christiane Marcilhacy's brilliant study of the diocese of Orléans during the episcopate of Mgr Dupanloup, famous for his resistance to the proclamation of the doctrine of Papal Infallibility in 1870, and bishop of Orléans from 1849 to 1878.[66] The bishop set out to re-christianize his diocese, in which religious observance had dropped to a very low level in the mid-century. His principal weapon was the traditional Roman Catholic evangelistic mission, which Dupanloup often called a 'parochial retreat' in order to avoid the hostility stirred up by memories of the missions of the Restoration period, when the State had turned out both the local civil administration and the local military to support the Church's demand for corporate penitence and repudiation of the Revolution. Dupanloup had four groups of mission priests in his diocese: Pères de la Miséricorde, Lazaristes, Missionaires Oblats de l'Immaculée Conception and La Compagnie de Marie; in fact in any period of his episcopate he had between twenty and thirty mission priests living in his area, a situation without parallel in England, where no bishop or other ecclesiastical organizer approached him in his practical grasp of the needs of the situation and where professional revivalists, very different in attitude to the mission priests, remained few in number and uncontrolled by authority.

In 1861 Dupanloup drew up a code for mission work in which he stressed the difficulty of successful evangelization. 'Après un si longtemps d'égarement loin de la Religion, il faut les convertir une fois, deux fois, trois fois, et puis cela

[66] C. Marcilhacy, *Le Diocèse d'Orléans sous L'épiscopat de Mgr Dupanloup* (1963).

finit par durer',[67] a view very different from that of the typical English revivalist. Dupanloup's strategy included simultaneous missions in a number of neighbouring parishes, a method which was imitated by the Anglo-Catholics in the Mission to London in 1869. There should be a second mission to each parish within two or three years. The mission-priests should try to form new *confréries* in the hope of holding their converts together; they should leave prominent signs of their passage by setting up roadside Calvaries, an idea reminiscent of the missions of the Restoration when a parish planted a cross in a great public ceremony to mark the rededication of the village community to the Church; Republicans normally planted trees of liberty.

A mission might last between a fortnight and six weeks. The preachers were told to take as their subjects mortal sin, death, the reception of the last sacrament, eternal punishment, prayer, contrition, confession, the right attitude for communion, and so on. Christiane Marcilhacy commented that 'l'enseignement n'est pas Christologique mais est centré sur le salut individuel, selon l'optique religieuse du xixe siècle.'[68] In other words, even though Dupanloup's missions were prompted by the recognition that the dechristianizing process had advanced a long way since 1789, the assumption of the preaching remained that the audience understood and believed in the Catholic faith as such. Indeed, the idea of seriously 'converting' people in public meetings is possible only on that assumption. Each mission was to include major ceremonies such as a service for the parish dead with a blessing of the cemetery—this seems a harking back to the romantic revivalism of Lamennais in the Restoration missions; the renewal of baptismal vows, and a closing eucharistic celebration. In France, as in England, singing was important: mission-priests sometimes wrote the words of new religious songs themselves and set them to popular tunes known to the peasants.

The best results of Dupanloup's system were felt between 1858 and 1862, but by 1865 a definite falling-away had taken place. The shock effect had spent itself, the more elaborate

[65] Marcilhacy, op. cit., p.283.
[68] Ibid., p.286.

processions and other spectacles had become familiar; political change in the later years of the Second Empire made it easier for an undercurrent of hostility to the Bishop to express itself. As late as 1867 the number of Easter communicants tended to rise after a mission, but after that date the chief effect of the missions was on the already committed. The overall results in the diocese were as follows: between 1852 and 1868 the percentage of the adult male population of the diocese making an Easter communion rose from 3.8 per cent to 5.8 per cent; the number of women rose from 20 per cent to 28 per cent. In figures these percentages meant an increase in the number of men from 3,361 to 6,278, and in the number of women from 18,302 to 27,779. The increase did not spread itself equally over the diocese: two out of the four *arrondissements* which comprised it contributed disproportionately to the increase, and the evidence suggests that the greatest progress took place in the areas which had remained more strongly Catholic during the previous half-century. One factor which hampered Dupanloup was the rigorism of his clergy. 'Une jeune fille qui se permet d'aller danser n'est pas admise à la fréquentation des sacrements.'[69] On the other hand, priests were sometimes willing to oblige men who feared the mockery of their neighbours if it were known that they had attended mass, by saying mass for them privately before daybreak.

Christiane Marcilhacy's conclusion was that Dupanloup's drive to win his diocese back to the Roman Catholic faith was a comparative failure; this was all the more significant because the efforts at Orléans were better thought out and sustained over a much longer period than any similar campaigns in England in the nineteenth century. Commenting on Marcilhacy's book, Gabriel le Bras, the sociologist of religion, said:

A toutes les causes de l'échec final (dont elle montre qu'il ne fut pas total) Mme Marcilhacy ajoute le manque d'adaptation du clergé. Nous pensons qu'il ne pouvait, à cause de sa formation, de ses préjugés, comprendre les inévitables transformations du monde et de sa condition sociale; ses moyens intellectuels ne lui eussent permis, les comprenant, de s'adapter. Nous pensons

[69] Marcilhacy, op. cit., p.313.

surtout que la religion n'a été, ne sera jamais que le privilège d'une élite, où se rencontre des paysans, des ouvriers et des savants, et que le rêve d'une reconquête massive (a fortiori d'une reconquête) suffirait à classer Mgr. Dupanloup parmi les romantiques.[70]

Most of these criticisms would have applied on the British side of the Channel at the same period, though it might be argued that the new English 'theological colleges' for the training of ministers, which were being set up in most denominations in the second half of the century, produced men a little closer to the mood of the cultural crisis than did the French seminaries which, apart from their grave intellectual limitations, used practical methods appropriate to the training of monks, not parish priests.[71] Yet it is significant that this effort at what Le Bras correctly pointed out would have been reconquest should have been made in both countries between about 1848 and 1880, with various methods but with similar results.

---

[70] *Archives de Sociologie des Religions*, vol. 18 (1964), pp.202-3.

[71] Nevertheless, some of the least satisfactory features of the English colleges can be explained only on the view that they also were designed for the production of quasi-monastic celibates, and this was as true of Nonconformist as of Anglican colleges. There was no 'Protestant' concept of training for the priesthood in England, but a tendency to follow Roman methods without understanding their rationale.

4

Moody and Sankey

WITH the coming of Moody and Sankey to England
in 1873, one passes from the margin to the centre,
from comparative American failure to comparative
American success, from the local chapel to the Islington
Agricultural Hall and the Royal Opera House, from the
religious press to *The Times*. It is true that Queen Victoria
refused to attend Moody's meetings and that the Archbishop
of Canterbury, A. C. Tait, did not offer the gesture of support
to Moody which a later Archbishop, Dr Fisher, was to make to
Billy Graham in the twentieth century. Evangelicals preferred
isolation, however, and its leaders could comfort themselves
with St Paul's assurance that God used the small things of the
world to confound the great. In the meantime the London
campaign of 1875 was the greatest public triumph that a
foreign revivalist had ever achieved in England: after the
Wellington Boot and the Gladstone Bag came the American
Organ.

Moody was born in 1837, Sankey in 1840. Both men were a
product of that powerful network of formative influences in
nineteenth-century Protestantism which lay outside, and was
often opposed to, the society of parishes and chapels which
has tended to absorb the church historian's attention: both
were largely products of the initial evangelical phase of the
Young Men's Christian Association, which we have already
seen in action in England in 1859–60. Moody made his
American reputation as an organizer and fund raiser for the
Y.M.C.A. in Chicago and elsewhere, and it was through a
Y.M.C.A. conference that he met Ira Sankey for the first time
in 1870. It was on Sunday School and Y.M.C.A. business that
Moody visited England in 1867 and 1872, when he showed no
outstanding gifts as a religious speaker. The fact that all the
Moody biographies say little about these earlier trips suggests

how slight an impression he made on most of those who met him. It is known that in 1872 William Pennefather, then an old man, invited him to return in 1873, and Moody's later success gave this invitation the lustre of a kind of prophecy, but no organization had been set up to greet him and the evidence implies that Moody exaggerated the significance of a casual, or polite, remark.

What is more interesting is Moody's evident determination to preach in England. He did not, like James Caughey, attribute this to a direct command from God; indeed, he did not commonly discuss the matter at all. That he should want to become an itinerant revivalist was not surprising in view of his American background, and in coming to England he was hoping to do exactly what he did, to break out from the ranks of evangelical preachers and establish himself as an independent power. From this point of view, it is interesting to compare him with William Booth. At first sight the obvious difference is that Booth, without overwhelming personal public success as an evangelist, set up in the years immediately following Moody's English tour of 1873–5 a self-perpetuating denomination, whereas Moody, whose personal public success was much greater than Booth's, set up no permanent institutions in England.

Further examination, however, suggests that the difference is less than might be thought. Moody made more skilful use than did Booth of the evangelical pietist network to which reference has been made in our discussion of the so-called Revival of 1859, and so was able to run his initial English campaign virtually without a personal organization; but as, in the 1880s, his energy and evangelistic prestige diminished, he did in fact work hard to give his achievement permanent form. In the 1880s, for example, when his popularity was declining, he persuaded a group of Chicago businessmen to provide a quarter of a million dollars in order to found a training centre for evangelical laymen who would penetrate the factories of the new industrial cities and prevent the spread of non-Christian and anti-capitalist influences. Professor James Findlay has underlined the political nature of Moody's appeal in this period: he told businessmen that the working-classes must be evangelized by Christians if they were not to be evangelized by atheists and Communists. Similar arguments were being used in England by Mrs Booth to attract middle-class support for the Salvation Army. Neither instance should be treated too seriously, however; in both cases the revivalists instinctively used the arguments which were likely to produce subscriptions. Moody certainly obtained the money and in 1887 the Chicago Evangelization Society was founded; buildings appeared in 1889, when Reuben Torrey became Principal, and by 1895 there were five hundred students. This was the original Moody Bible Institute which became the centre of a still-surviving international group of Bible Institutes. Whereas the Salvation Army, after a bright beginning, faded rapidly as fear of working-class irreligion decreased, the Bible Institutes prospered because their financial independence of the main-stream Churches enabled them to become strongholds of pietistic resistance to the spread of the various kinds of liberal Christianity. This outcome of Moody's work should be kept in mind when one considers modern attempts to present him as somehow an early apostle of the ecumenical spirit. Of course, the professional revivalist wanted the various denominations to combine at his meetings: the alliance increased both the size of the audience and the personal prestige of the revivalist himself; but this 'evangelical alliance' was a means to an end only, and once the end was achieved, Moody's own institutions followed.

This is not a detailed history of nineteenth-century revivalism but a discussion of its significance; it is therefore sufficient to indicate briefly what Moody and Sankey actually did in England.[1] Moody held his first British service at York in June, 1873. From 20 July to 24 August, 1873, he stayed in Sunderland, using the Victoria Hall instead of the customary church or chapel buildings in the hope of conciliating Anglican opinion. By Anglican definition Moody was a Nonconformist, which made it difficult in theory—and in practice impossible—for him to preach in Anglican consecrated buildings, while the Nonconformist buildings which

---

[1] For an excellent survey of the literature on Moody, cf. J. F. Findlay, jnr., *Dwight L. Moody* (Chicago 1969), pp.5–25. Findlay did not treat Moody's English career at length, but his book superseded other biographies. There is nothing comparable on Sankey, who wrote his own biography (published 1906). My own analysis of his songbook (*v.i.*) is the first serious treatment of him.

he could have obtained permission to use without much opposition themselves presented fresh problems to Anglicans who wanted to hear him. In London, Moody was to speak in secular buildings from the start. He could not hope to build up the mass revivalism on which he had set his sights unless he could unite Anglicans and non-Anglicans in the same audience; he was also aware, from his Y.M.C.A. experience apart from any other sources, that the pietist network stretched through all the English denominations, regardless of their official views of one another. Anglo-Catholic revivalism, on the other hand, had already established itself (see chapter 7), and was bound to oppose or ignore a non-sacramental approach; the Anglican liberals not only doubted the permanence of the results of revivals, but also disliked the theory of the atonement which figured prominently in Moody's preaching.

At the end of August, 1873, Moody moved on to Newcastle-upon-Tyne, where he collaborated with the American Negro Fisk Singers,[2] who were then touring Europe; so far the Americans had attracted little response, but Sankey was beginning to find his touch with an English audience. Even so, Anglican Evangelical interest remained lukewarm, and Moody had to move on at regular intervals, staying at Darlington from 13–20 October, 1873, at Bishop Auckland from 30 October to 2 November, and at Carlisle from 15–22 November. A complete change of background followed, when he travelled to Scotland: he held meetings in Edinburgh from 23 November, 1873, to the beginning of February, 1874, and in Glasgow from 8 February to 15 May, 1874. In just over six months he at last established a reputation, which he then consolidated by a visit to Northern Ireland, which was always a safe port of call for a visiting evangelist. He spent September and part of October, 1874, in Belfast, and 18 October to 26 November, 1874, in southern Ireland, in Dublin. From there he returned to England at long last, opening at Manchester on 28 November, 1874, with very little now left to chance. The evangelical world had com-

---

[2] Findlay, op. cit., pp.328–9. Moody could finance a large-scale operation only by accepting the existing social system: when he began to preach in the Southern States after 1875 his meetings were segregated in deference to white pressure.

mitted itself to his coming, convinced partly by his success in Scotland and Ireland and partly by the zealous propaganda of R. C. Morgan, who had distributed thirty thousand copies of his paper, *The Christian*, free in advance telling the story of the Dublin revival. This was not the only use that Moody made of *The Christian*. He also raised a fund of £2,000 which was spent on providing a three-month free subscription to *The Christian* for every minister in Britain. This scheme had actually started after Moody and Sankey had reached Edinburgh in the closing weeks of 1873. As Morgan supported the Americans without any reservation, this meant a widespread free advertisement for Moody. Moody consciously aimed at making himself a representative, symbolic figure, the centre and source of revivalistic effort in Britain. In the same fashion he launched through *The Christian* an appeal for ministers all over Britain to join in midday prayer-meetings for revival. This plan started on 5 January, 1874, and undoubtedly met with some response, though it is equally true that many copies of *The Christian* must have gone straight into the fire.

Diligent propaganda, such as no professional revivalist had employed in England before, together with the preparations made by the evangelical sub-culture and the prestige gathered in Scotland, all help to explain Moody's London triumph. In Scotland, his success depended on local factors. The Americans automatically stood outside the religious gang-warfare of Scotland, which had been stimulated rather than started by the Presbyterian schism of 1843. Moody's own ethos was Calvinist if anything; he sounded a note of underlying pessimism which commended him to traditional Scottish piety without over-committing him theologically—indeed, he was still attacked, both in Scotland and in England, by the handful of ministers who still remained faithful to the stricter forms of Calvinism. Like many nineteenth-century Calvinists, he was deeply influenced from about 1870 by premillennialism, the belief that the millennium would only come at the end of a long period of social and moral deterioration, a view quite the reverse of the optimistic devotion to progress which is so often attributed indiscriminately to all Victorians. Premillennialism owed much to the tireless advocacy of the best known leader of the Plymouth Brethren,

J. N. Darby, who pursued power and the interpretation of Biblical prophecy with equal intensity; Moody came under his direct influence from at least 1872, and always preached on the Second Coming in the course of a revival.[3] Moody's premillennialism did not figure so prominently as to become an obstacle to his revivalism in the 1870s; on the other hand, it enabled him to draw support from another of the 'undeclared sects' of the period.

In the Scottish Lowlands, where relations between the State and Free Presbyterian Churches had been embittered for a generation, it is possible that the presence of a neutral revivalist—and Moody wanted to be as neutral as possible—offered the chance of a new beginning which was consciously taken. The battle between the two Scottish parties had been as much political as religious; it had distracted them from much that was happening in Protestantism elsewhere, so that Moody's own indifference to the Victorian religious crisis, an indifference which might be sincere but was nevertheless shallow, helped him to profit from a Lowland Scottish mood of nostalgia for great days before the schism of 1843. Scottish religious elders were still committed to a pre-critical attitude to the Bible; the persecution which drove William Robertson Smith from his post at Aberdeen because of his moderately liberal opinions on the Old Testament took place after Moody's visit, between 1876 and 1881. In the Highlands this conservatism took a sharper tone and was even more isolated from the main cultural stream of the time. In Montrose, for example, Sankey was criticized for his complacent attitude to his own singing, and John Kennedy Dingwall, a hyper-Calvinist leader in the Highlands, disputed Moody's offer of free salvation as obstinately as a minority English Calvinist like J. K. Popham of Liverpool was to do a little later.

Moody opened his Manchester campaign, the test of his ability to stage a revival in England, on 28 November, 1874, and it is evidence of how far the ground of his success was already assured that he was mentioned in *The Times* as early as

---

[3] The best modern account of the nineteenth-century premillennialist movement is in E. R. Sandeen, *The Roots of Fundamentalism*, (Chicago 1970). Premillennialism might have been important if its doubts about human progress had led to serious social criticism, but this was, in men like Darby and Moody, a purely self-indulgent pessimism.

1 December, 1874, in a report which noted with approval that 'emotion', as that term had been understood in the 1859 revivals, especially in Ireland, was missing from his meetings. Indeed, the absence of the phenomena associated with 'Irish' revivalism was the key to the degree of 'establishment' support that Moody obtained. He spoke in the Manchester Free Trade Hall and reports claimed audiences of 15,000 to 17,000 on Sundays and 10,000 to 12,000 on weekdays. These figures were estimated, but if one assumes that they were approximately correct, it may be added that Billy Graham, the latest in the succession of important American professionals to visit England, was not drawing substantially larger audiences than this in Manchester eighty years later, despite the advantages of modern transport.[4] Almost, if not quite, unnoticed by the many historians who have studied the Moody revivals, the crisis of his English campaign now came and passed, leaving him, contrary to most historical judgement, defeated.

At the start of the Manchester meetings Anglicans were not conspicuous, and on 4 December, 1874, Moody actually issued a circular lamenting that 'not more clergymen of the Church of England have attended our meetings'.[5] Even when Anglicans did come to the meetings, they almost all belonged to the Evangelical wing. Moody intended to pass on from Manchester to Sheffield, but the meetings proposed there almost broke down because of High Church Anglican

---

[4] The Billy Graham organization held meetings at Maine Road Football Ground in Manchester from 29 May–17 June, 1961, excluding Sundays. The official report said that 'a total of well over 400,000 people (approaching almost 25,000 per night)' attended the 18 meetings. The figures given suggest a minimum average of 22,000; there was no absolute check on numbers; the attendance was higher at the weekend; the ground was stated as holding 52,000 for the Crusade. The official number of enquirers was 'almost 18,000'. A follow-up questionnaire, answered by 106 churches, referring to 1,250 enquirers, suggested that 237 of them were considered by the ministers concerned to be 'outsiders'. This was 19.3 per cent, or one in five. Perhaps more significantly, it represented an average addition of about two people per church. In his biography, *Billy Graham* (1966), John Pollock admitted that 'the Manchester Crusade did not set the North aflame or fire the nation, as had been the hope of the Team and of those who had invited them' (p.299). He went on to blame 'the failure of the churches to involve themselves fully, from the start' (ibid.), but this argument was not open to the professional revivalist in whose tradition Graham stood, whose *raison d'être* was that he claimed to be able to *revive*.

[5] *Narrative of Messrs. Moody and Sankey's Labours in Scotland and Ireland, also in Manchester, Sheffield, and Birmingham, England*, compiled from *The British Evangelist* and *The Christian* (New York 1875), p.99. The preface was signed February, 1875, before the London meetings started.

opposition, and a vast inter-denominational visitation campaign had to be cancelled by Moody himself once he realized that Evangelical clergy also objected. In Scotland Moody had managed to bridge the gap between the opposed groups of Presbyterians as far as attendance at his meetings, but there is little evidence that he repeated this act of outward reconciliation in England. In these early stages of his English adventures Moody did everything that he could to unite Anglo-Catholic and Evangelical behind him, because the full support of the State Church would have transformed his revivals into something of a national movement, but he was faced with a situation of greater religious complexity than existed in either Scotland or Ireland, and he had little to offer beyond a degree of religious neutrality. He could not say what his Anglo-Catholic critics wanted him to say, partly because he did not really believe them and partly because to have done so would have meant forfeiting much of his Evangelical Anglican support; he had no sympathy at all for the religious problems of men like Matthew Arnold and so could not take any positive step towards the Broad Church laity and clergy.

Moody tried to solve the problem by angling for the support of what he called the 'High-Lows', a small group of men who combined an Evangelical insistence on the need for instantaneous conversion with a more High Church emphasis on the importance of the Eucharist, and whose views were, therefore, at first sight, related to those of the Anglo-Catholic revivalists, to whom a separate chapter has been devoted. The most remarkable of the 'High-Lows' was Adam Clarke Smith (the Christian names suggest a Wesleyan ancestry), the Vicar of St John's, Middlesbrough. In 1874, at the time of the Anglican Mission to London he wrote to the *Guardian*, the High Church periodical, suggesting that Anglican Bishops should incorporate the mission system into their diocesan agencies, an idea of which he may well have derived from knowledge of French Roman Catholicism, where men like the famous Archbishop of Orléans, Dupanloup, regarded it as part of their episcopal duty to organize the evangelization of their dioceses and employed the Catholic mission orders as their agents. In his letter[6] Smith said that everyone should

---

[6] *Guardian*, 25 February, 1874.

read *The Revival of the Priestly Life in France in the Seventeenth Century* (by 'The Author of "A Dominican Artist"') 'wherein much is said concerning missions'.[7] If the bishops did not like the Anglo-Catholic mission system, Smith said, they might form two bands of mission preachers in each diocese, 'since it is clear that there are two types of mission working in the Church'. It is important to notice that Smith was taking for granted the gulf between the two kinds of evangelism. Now, in March, 1875, he wrote to the *Guardian* again to say that he had taken part in the meetings which Moody had held in Liverpool in February, 1875, and to point out that Moody had publicly declared that he would welcome the assistance of the 'High-Lows'. In Liverpool Moody had also been helped by Hay Aitken, the son of Robert Aitken of Pendeen,[8] who was a popular preacher like his father and who also combined some Evangelical and High Church traits.

None of this amounted to much, however. Smith had little personal prestige and Hay Aitken's influence lay chiefly in the Evangelical circles which supported Moody in any case. W. D. Maclagan and G. H. Wilkinson, the most important Anglican clergymen who shared something of Smith's approach, had been deeply involved in the Anglo-Catholic missions to London in 1869 and 1874 and both were still committed to the system which had dominated those efforts. Writers about Moody have not grasped clearly enough that whatever his merits as an evangelist he came too late as far as the Anglo-Catholics were concerned; to them his methods seemed irrelevant. Maclagan and Wilkinson did not believe that the sacramental life of the Church could simply be grafted on to Moody's approach as the personal choice of the parish priests, without its mattering that Moody paid little attention to the doctrine of the Church in what he said. Moody, indeed, often implied that infant baptism was more of a snare than a sacrament; he disapproved of auricular confession, which he thought of as beyond the Protestant pale. Moody was not, as Maclagan and Wilkinson saw it, making possible recon-

---

[7] 'The Author' was H. L. Sydney. The Dominican artist was a Frenchman, Père Besson, painter and missionary, who died in the Middle East in 1861 on a mission to the Nestorians. Both books are examples of the Anglo-Catholic preference for French Catholic sources.
[8] *v.i.*, pp.245-6.

ciliation between the Evangelical and Anglo-Catholic wings of the Church of England, but only asking the High Churchmen to subordinate their views of repentance, conversion and the Christian life to his in order to make him the effective symbol of the Catholic Church. All the compromise, they felt, was to be on their side; they were to add their prestige and agencies to Moody's organization; in return, they would run the risk of finding that contact with the Moody meetings would gradually weaken their hold on their own parishioners. Moody had not enough to offer to make this prospect alluring, and his inability to widen his base beyond what was essentially evangelical support meant that in England his revivals were never more than a sectional drive. In this sense Moody had already failed before he reached London.[9]

From 17–31 January, 1875, Moody preached in Birmingham, where it was a sign of the steady growth of his prestige in Free Church circles that he gained the backing of John Angell James' successor, Robert Dale, then perhaps the best known Congregationalist minister in England. Dale published an article in defence of the Americans in *The Congregationalist* in March, 1875, which was reprinted as a pamphlet, and, at a later stage, he was to publish 'The Day of Salvation' (1875), a furious reply to the refusal of Tait, the Archbishop of Canterbury, to countenance the American professionals. This was a sign, however, of the limitations of Moody's position, for Dale was playing a leading role in the national campaign, which had been launched in the previous year, for the disestablishment of the Church of England; Moody surrendered Bingley Hall, which had been built for the annual Birmingham cattle show, for one night of his meetings in order that John Bright and Dale might hold a

[9] The extreme Anglo-Catholic Society of the Holy Cross decided: 'To mission preachers like the Rev. R. R. Bristow there was much in the (revival) Movement that called for assistance as far as it was allowable, and to one who knew the criminal world and the dark side of life like the Rev. J. W. Horsley, there was in spite of its one-sided doctrine, a wish of God-speed to it, in the face of London's immorality. It was felt that while Catholic priests were bound to stand aloof from it, it should be in passive sympathy and prayer and not in censoriousness, and so while recognizing the defective doctrines of the teachers and their imperfect methods of dealing with individual souls, the Society resolved that, although it was prevented from any active co-operation, yet it would pray earnestly that both the preachers and hearers might be rightly guided into all truth' (J. Embry, *The Catholic Movement and the Society of the Holy Cross*, 1931, p.52).

political rally in which they both advocated the end of the Church Establishment. This was not likely to commend Moody in most Anglican circles. Politically, Dale and his associates needed a large-scale religious movement which would multiply the number of Free Churchmen as badly as the Welsh Nonconformists needed a revival in 1904 in their struggle against the Anglican Church in Wales. Dale's support for the Americans was genuine, but he was a man in whom religious and political feeling were integrated. Once again, however, Moody's revivalism had meshed with a sectional impulse, not an ecumenical one.

The climax of Moody's whole career lay between 9 March and 21 July, 1875, when he held the London revival to which we shall return in a moment. On 5 August, 1875, the Americans sailed from Liverpool for the United States. Moody made two further visits, much less important, to England, in 1881–3 and in 1891–2. In 1881 he started at Newcastle in the October, was at Cambridge in the November, and moved swiftly on to Edinburgh; in 1882 he stayed in Glasgow for four months, apart from which he visited in England: Plymouth, Bristol, Oxford, Torquay, Exeter, Southampton, Portsmouth and Brighton; while in 1883 he went to Birmingham, Manchester (in March), Leicester, Nottingham and Leeds. It is significant that no second attempt was made to carry out a London campaign, despite the repetition of the long visits to Edinburgh and Glasgow. Moody's last trip to England in 1891–2 was on a very small scale, as might be expected, for he was now a very tired man, carrying too much weight, and perhaps expecting results to come too easily. He held a six-day mission at the Polytechnic in London, and then travelled on via Manchester to Scotland, where he spent four months, speaking, it is said, in over ninety different places. Moody died in 1899; Ira Sankey, who gave up regular singing in the mid-1880s, visited Britain without a preacher in 1901. What stands out about the later trips is that they were visits to Scotland rather than England.

When one examines Moody's London revival of 1875, it becomes evident that he owed a great deal to the careful preparation of the ground by the evangelical sub-culture, which saw his coming as an opportunity to demonstrate its own strength, a demonstration all the more desirable in view of the Anglo-Catholic advances of the previous years. This support was not given without some misgivings as far as the Anglican Evangelicals were concerned. The *Record*, in a leading article on revivalism published as late as 11 January, 1875, when it was already known that Moody was to hold meetings in the capital, said that the progress of the Americans was being watched with interest and hope, but the paper went on to rebuke R. C. Morgan's *The Christian* for the lack of caution with which it accepted the revivalists' claims, and for recommending a book like *Showers of Blessing*, by Dr Knox of Belfast, which described Moody and Sankey's recent tour of Northern Ireland. The book contained an instance of an eleven-year-old boy preaching, of which, the *Record* said, that the evil likely to result for the child far outweighed any conceivable good which might arise from his having done so. The *Record* also said of a story, which was very much in Moody's habitual vein, called 'The Man Who Lost His Dog and Found His Saviour', that the title 'is so painfully revolting as to border on blasphemy'. The point of the story, of course, was that because the man lost his dog he was induced to attend one of Moody's meetings, where he was converted. By 1875 such stories fell somewhere between the older category of 'providential instances' and a newer category which might be called 'religion and chance', or some other title which suggested a strange combination of luck and divine guidance. *The Christian* was also rebuked because it said that the Scriptural Clock, a simple toy which Moody had devised for persuading children to read biblical texts, had become a favourite amusement among young people. 'Does it not seem a breach of the commandment against taking God's name in vain?' asked the *Record*. This seems a pompous comment, but it underlined the vulgar streak in Moody's original approach.

All these criticisms depended upon a degree of evangelical austerity foreign to the revivalist tradition: the revivalist was a showman, not a shaman. The attacks expressed an Anglican horror of social concessions which might be regarded as admissions of social decline: religious institutions based in the middle class only make concessions to vulgarity after they have been forced to recognize a loss of social standing. When, a week later, a correspondent wrote to the *Record* to say that Moody advocated the views of the Brethren, whose eschatological position was premillennial and who dismissed out of hand any doctrine of the Church and Ministry which was intelligible to Anglicans, the paper repudiated the suggestion. This approval of theology as distinct from style was not casual, for in the same period the *Record* constantly warned its readers against Robert Pearsall Smith, the American holiness revivalist. That a letter also appeared (1 February, 1875) deploring the refusal of the Scottish Episcopal Church to countenance Moody's visit no doubt implied a certain satisfaction that High Church principles led to a refusal to evangelize.

Moody's London visit was planned in advance by a Central Committee which deserved much of the credit for the final result. On 29 January, 1875, the *Record* reported a meeting of about a hundred ministers to organize the East End of London in preparation for Moody's coming. The ministers met at the Beaumont Institution in London, and among the evangelicals present were the Rector of Stepney, J. Bardsley; Mr Kennedy of the Stepney Meeting; the Rector of Limehouse, S. Charlesworth; Dr James of the Wesleyan Chapel in Bow Road; the Rector of St Matthias, Poplar, L. G. Kitto; C. Horel of the Baptist Chapel in Commercial Road, and W. Tyler of the Mile End Congregationalist Chapel. Delegates from the Central Committee for London were present and an East End sub-committee was formed. Another report, on 12 February, largely taken from *The Christian*, described a meeting of the Central Committee at which the chairman, Thomas Stone, said that the Committee had taken the Agricultural Hall, Islington, for ten weeks from 1 March, 1875, at a rent of £50 per week, and Exeter Hall for two months for the use of a midday prayer-meeting. The speaker emphasized that the Committee wanted to organize an outer ring of revival meetings, subsidiary to Moody's, but vital to any idea of a general London revival, and for these they must take big public halls: churches and chapels would not do.

The Agricultural Hall needed considerable fitting-up for the purposes of a revival. A contractor, Mr Sharman, put in 12,000 new chairs in addition to the 2,000 which belonged to the place, together with accommodation for another 2,000 people on forms (*The Times*, 10 March, 1875). 'The platform at the West End is arranged in steps, giving the appearance of a gigantic infant-school'; these steps could hold about 1,200 people (the *Record*, 12 March, 1875). In the centre of the north side was a platform for the speakers and for a choir, which was originally trained by Joseph Proudman of the Tonic Sol-Fa Association. The *Record* estimated that the hall would hold 23,000; *The Times* gave a more precise figure, 21,320. On week nights the Islington Hall never seems to have been filled, and at times may have been as much as half-empty. Although Moody began with a sounding-board as big as a barn-door many people complained that they could not hear properly. In the meantime, a hall was being built in the East End, on Bow Common, which it was said would be ready by the end of April and would hold 8,000–9,000 people. This attempt to set up a major centre of the revival meetings in East London reveals how anxious many members of the Central Committee were to employ Moody (who no doubt felt himself as employing them) to lead the Churches in a campaign to evangelize the London poor, of whose existence they were well aware because they had been serving on committees to help them in various ways for many years, and about whom they had both religious and political fears. Moody's second important failure—his first, as we have seen, was his failure to unite the divided parties in the Church of England in the work of revivalism—was in this task of bridging the gap between evangelical Protestantism and the London poor. This in its turn caused disagreement between him and the lay members of the Committee.

The risk that some members of the Committee felt that they were taking was underlined in February, 1875, by a report that Moody had run into trouble in Liverpool. He was alleged to have said that a young man who had refused to attend one of his meetings had fallen down dead in his hotel the same night. No such occurrence had taken place in Liverpool but his hearers were left with the impression, rightly or wrongly, that he was referring to the meetings which were then being held. When challenged to produce his evidence Moody apparently defended himself by saying that he was really talking about an incident which had happened in the north of England in the fall of 1873 (the *Record*, 19 February, 1875). To anyone acquainted with the revivalist tradition, the incident had a familiar look: it was normal for a professional revivalist to tell his audience that, if they did not accept conversion that very evening they might well die before they had another chance and would therefore, being unconverted, go to Hell. This was a conventional way of threatening damnation. James Caughey's more reckless method had been to inform his hearers that he knew on the authority of the Holy Spirit that someone listening to him would die before midnight that night. For the revivalist this was a case where the end, conversion, justified the means, fear. Moody would have denied that he was saying that God had struck the man dead because he refused to go to a revival meeting, but he was really relying on his audience making this connexion for themselves. The *Record*, which disliked such tactics, reacted on the level of taste, not theology; not for the last time, Moody seemed vulgar.

Nevertheless, as the Islington meetings began, the *Record* gave Moody its approval. This was despite such letters as that signed 'Vetus' which was published on 22 February, 1875, which suggested that Moody was an antinomian who said in effect that all that men had to do in order to be saved was to accept what Christ offered. This criticism recalled the standard Anglican Evangelical objection to the English revivalists of the previous generation, that their doctrine of repentance was defective. On 10 March, 1875, however, the paper made its official pronouncement. A leading article said that Moody had come to London at a critical moment in the city's development. The condition of the town was chaotic and that of the labouring classes desperate, and much ought to be done by Government to improve matters. In the meantime, however, there were souls to be saved and this was the specific job that Moody had come to do. The writer mentioned the criticisms of the Vicar of Kingston, A. Williams, and of Dr Duncan of Edinburgh, who feared what he called 'an American anti-nomianism', by which Duncan meant an undue exaltation of the human will. Duncan's evidence for this was the way in which Moody pressed men to make their decision on the spot, a demand which was central to professional revivalism but totally unacceptable to the Calvinist tradition which was bound to declare that a man could not be saved by his own decision. Moody's teaching, however, did not disconcert the *Record*, which even suggested that it might be altered, a view which implied little knowledge of either the American revivalists or the theological position which they inherited. As for his attitude to the Church and his lack of ordination, lay preaching, the *Record* said, 'may be intended to combat that spirit of sacerdotalism which has grown up amongst us to such proportions under the fostering aid of Ritualism'.

The conclusion was clear, that Anglican Evangelicalism would support Moody as a counter to the Anglo-Catholic movement. Moody's apparent success in obtaining conversions undoubtedly weighed heavily with the *Record* as well. It must have been a relief to Moody that the *Record* did not repeat the hostility to professional, lay revivalism which it had shown in 1859. Too much Anglican history lay in between, however, and it explains why the paper was tempted to make the highly uncharacteristic comment that Moody's theology might be ignored for the moment and perhaps modified later. One must not exaggerate the extent to which the Evangelicals were compromising their standards, however, for the *Record* firmly opposed Pearsall Smith throughout 1875 on theological grounds, well before his moral failings had destroyed his immense popularity in the pietist world.

Moody opened at the Agricultural Hall on 9 March, 1875. Preparatory services had been going on there since the beginning of the month. He commenced his activities with the first of the midday prayer meetings held at Exeter Hall. The list of prominent laymen present showed the extent to which his financial support and influential backing came from the fringes of institutionalized religion, not its centre. Many of the laymen mentioned could trace back their private history in the evangelical sub-culture for many years, and their names have been mentioned in the discussion of the revivalism of 1859–61. George Williams and Edwin Hodder, for instance, were the London businessmen who had created the Young Men's Christian Association and were responsible for its strongly evangelical tone. Moody had just served them well in

Manchester, where he had called on his abilities as a fund-raiser to find money with which to buy a museum in the centre of the city and to convert it into what became the permanent headquarters of the Y.M.C.A. in the city. Admiral Fishbourne (1811–87) and Lord Radstock (1833–1913) were wealthy, eccentric Anglican laymen.[10] Their Anglicanism was a matter of social class; they both did exactly as they pleased ecclesiastically. In his later years Fishbourne published many tracts attacking the Church of Rome; Radstock had already taken up faith-healing, on the basis of the Epistle of James, as early as 1873. It was characteristic of both that they also attended Pearsall Smith's Holiness Conventions in 1875. Radstock was a revivalist in his own right in the Evangelical seaside and watering-place tradition: he had conducted personal missions in Brighton, for example, in 1867, and in Scarborough in 1869.

Samuel Morley was a Congregationalist, a Liberal M.P., and a successful businessman who devoted part of his profits to religious causes. He had backed William Booth financially in his troubled middle period when he had forsaken the chapels of the Methodists and had not yet established the citadels of the Salvation Army. There was also the publisher, R. C. Morgan, and the rather younger Quintin Hogg, a West India sugar merchant, at whose London house Moody spent much of his time. More prominent socially was Lord Cavan, an Etonian of an Ulster family which went back to the Plantation;[11] Lord Cairns (1819–85) was an Orangeman, lawyer, the son of a captain in the 47th Foot, who had been made a baron in 1867 and was Conservative Lord Chancellor from 1874 to 1880; W. F. Cowper-Temple (1811–88), was the second son of the fifth Earl Cowper, who had left the army in 1835 to become a Whig M.P. and who had taken a vigorous share in the troubled politics of Victorian education. Cowper-Temple probably preferred Pearsall Smith to Moody and Sankey; he was also Lord Shaftesbury's brother-in-law.

The campaign which followed made different impressions on different people. Perhaps the best example of what Moody

[10] For the weaving together of Evangelical families implied here, see C. Binfield, op. cit.

[11] Cavan had served in the Dragoons; he died at Weston-super-Mare in 1888.

and Sankey sounded like to the Victorian intellectual world may be found in an article which the *Spectator* published in March, 1875.

> Messrs Moody and Sankey appear to be business-like, amiable, at heart modest, and thoroughly sincere men, without any knowledge to speak of the difficulties which beset the faith of modern Christians, and a simple sort of conviction that the right way to get over any difficulties there may be is to get up some how or other a sufficient tide of emotion to float ordinary persons over them. . . . Though the chief impression left by Mr Moody's preaching is the impression of a narrow, but well-defined stamp of conviction on a somewhat hard substance, he is capable of pathos, and even tenderness now and then, which produce the more effect from the sudden contrast they present to his wide-awake familiarity with both man and God.

Moody's influence on other evangelical ministers the *Spectator* thought less striking.

> At the prayer meeting in Exeter Hall on Wednesday there was something quite melancholy in the wordy aridity which was the only result of competitive praying. . . . The mode in which the Revivalists use the favourite Biblical paradox of God's weakness being mightier than man's strength is a thoroughly false one. It is perfectly true that what seems the grandest is often the hollowest thing in human life. But it is not a bit true that great revolutions of faith or practice are wrought by the help of what any wise man would call genuine emptiness or silliness. The Revivalists talk as if want of learning, and the ignorance which rather boasts of want of learning, were a positive advantage in the realm of faith.

This was well put, and reminds one of Kierkegaard's dismissal of the Protestant innkeeper who wanted to begin his spiritual life at the point of insight which Martin Luther reached only after half a lifetime's experience.[12] The *Spectator* continued:

---

[12] 'Let us see what happened to Luther. After a score of years, filled with fear and trembling and temptation, which were so terrible that—note well—scarcely one individual in each generation experiences it in this way, his human nature reacts, if one may put it so, and this fear and trembling are transfigured into the most blessed and happiest cheerfulness and joy. How remarkable! But what happens now? This principle is then generalised in Protestantism, thus and only thus (for only this is true

But the revivalists in part calculate carefully enough within the limits of their experience. . . . Mr Moody's favourite illustrations —like the blank cheque on heaven which he said that God had given to Moses, and which Moses filled up, first for water, when the people were perishing of thirst, then for manna, and so on— are as carefully chosen to fix the attention of common people as is Mr Sankey's music. . . .

Nevertheless, the *Spectator*'s correspondent thought that the revivalists were preaching to the wrong people and limiting their effect by their attitude to the Bible.

As far as we can see, the people who are now filling Exeter Hall and the great Hall at Islington are people who already have quite as good if not better teaching than Moody and Sankey can give. Mr Spurgeon, for instance, is a much more vigorous preacher of the same order as Mr Moody, and probably quite as good a man. Smaller halls in East London or Saint Giles are the places where these men could produce the best effect. They will never come near to Mr Newman Hall or Mr Baldwin Brown in the depth and manliness of their religious teaching.[13]

The Times also commented on the meetings, saying that Moody was straightforward, racy, full of American humour, often, it had to be owned, a little vulgar. 'It is not pleasant sometimes to hear venerable narratives and events around which a halo of hallowed imagination has gathered presented as if they were good American stories picked up the other day in Chicago.' His success, however, was hardly surprising, for

---

Christianity) is Christianity to be presented. The immensely powerful tranquillising means which Luther discovered in the extremity of his *angst* . . . this is what is to be proclaimed as the sole means for all' (*The Last Years*, ed. R. G. Smith, 1965, p.319). Kierkegaard gave the example referred to here: 'O dear Luther—these are two entirely different things—a scholar who has used the best twenty years of his life . . . for the most intense study, and in his forty-eighth year, at the pinnacle of knowledge, has not found the satisfaction he sought . . . closes his books and says, "No it is not knowledge that matters"—is not this a very different thing from an innkeeper, who was just passing and heard the scholar . . . and this innkeeper could not even read his own name . . . is it not a very different thing when the innkeeper goes on his own way, takes what he heard as a result, and says, "It is not knowledge that matters"?' (ibid., p.317). This is the most damaging criticism of professional revivalism, that it organized a mistaken systematization of Luther's personal experience into the basis of its appeal: in mass evangelism every man was to reproduce Luther.

[13] Spurgeon, Hall and Brown were Free Church popular preachers, all probably superior to Moody in style and content.

when Moody told his audience that they needed saving 'a vast number among them know that this is perfectly true, whatever may be its precise theological interpretation. . . . Mr Moody called to this struggling, confused mass to follow him, and to follow him in a direction which on the whole is guaranteed by ancient and sacred experience, and he is obeyed' (*The Times*, 16 March, 1875).

Neither of these reports was especially hostile. Moody belonged to the class of evangelical speakers for whom there was (and is) no such thing consciously as a problem of communication—though the *Spectator* pointed out that his style did communicate, even if the method jarred on *The Times*' sensibility. If the *Spectator* objected to the way in which he sometimes implied that ignorance and a lack of education were an advantage in matters of faith, Moody, though hardly aware of it, stood in a tradition which went back at least to the early days of the German Pietist movement in the late seventeenth century when Francke, in particular, analysed the process of justification and concluded that, in the course of the experience, one had to put aside the arguments of reason and temporarily at least tread the power of the human mind underfoot. The Holy Spirit did not work through human reason, but human reason often rejected the promptings of the Holy Spirit. One must therefore listen to the leadings of the Spirit and resist the questionings of reason. This kind of analysis lay behind talk about 'heart-religion' and also underlay the constant pietist contrast between formal, cold religiosity, a condition in which reason still played the dominant role, and the experience of the justified man, whose heart had been warmed by the Spirit and who knew how to keep reason in its place. This older terminology does not fit into the late Victorian period but the basic ideas had remained unchanged through generations of revivalistic preaching.

The Times and *Spectator* reporters may also be forgiven for not grasping what was really new in Moody and Sankey's revivalism. *The Times* rightly said that Moody's teaching was at once traditional and vague, nicely calculated to be seized on by hearers already more than half committed to his position. The *Spectator* was also correct when it said that as a speaker Moody only offered another example of a style familiar in the pulpit of a man like Spurgeon. What was more original came out clearly in a report which the *Guardian* reprinted on 17 March, 1875, from the *Daily News*, a paper somewhat prejudiced in Moody's favour because of its close contact with the Nonconformist world to which he owed much faithful support. The *Daily News* reporter said:

> The secret of Mr Moody's power was very apparent; it was the faculty, by a rapid succession of human touches, of producing a vivid picture of the subject he wished to convey. Concluding his sermon abruptly Mr Moody called for a moment or two of silent prayer. Presently, while all heads were bowed, the faint notes of the organ, scarcely louder than the silence, were heard, and before one could decide for certain whether it was actual music or not, Mr Sankey, in the softest pianissimo, was singing
>
> > Come home, come home,
> > You are weary at heart,
> > For the way has been dark,
> > And so lonely and wild:
> > Oh prodigal child,
> > Come home, oh, come home,
>
> and at the end of each verse the well-trained choir, in little more than whispered melody, took up the refrain, 'Come home, come, Oh, come home'. Organ, soloist and choir in the most skilful manner, gradually increased their force of sound until the last verse poured forth in full volume. It is difficult to describe the effect the music had on the faces of the congregation who, still retaining their bowed position, were with one accord looking with transfixed eyes towards the platform.

It would be difficult after all these years, and in the absence of even the kind of scrambled gramophone record which gives a rumbling echo of Tennyson charging with the Light Brigade, to evoke the kind of spell which Sankey cast in London in 1875. Here was a kind of carefully prepared special effect which no one had really exploited before for religious purposes: Anglo-Catholicism had been seeking to bring warmth of feeling, colour and ritual back into worship, but was here outbid by a frank combination of the sentimental and theatrical traditions in a secularization of the subjective hymns which had produced much of the effect of the

eighteenth-century evangelical revival. Seventy years later
there were still chapels in the north of England where even
the most thinly attended evening service was felt to be in-
complete without a solo, and very often the solos were still
those which Sankey had sung. In the 1870s the last popular
religious culture of British Nonconformity forms before one's
eyes and Sankey, much more than Moody, determined its
ethos.

There were those, of course, who had their doubts about
the propriety of his singing at all, and had to fall back on such
distinctions as that made by the Vicar of Walworth, D. G.
Copeland, between singing religious music purely for display,
and singing it with a truly religious purpose: Sankey, one
gathered, fell into the second category. The *Guardian* carried a
long report of the Good Friday services at Islington in 1875 in
which it 'deprecated his anything but graceful habit of swaying
to and fro as he plays—obviously unnecessary with an
instrument as easily played as one of these cabinet organs'.
Ruder still, the reporter said that Sankey had 'the style of a
careful, if second-rate ballad-singer'—clearness of enunciation
was one of his great merits. He succeeded, the reporter
thought, because he chose attractive songs with which his
audience was in sympathy (this was acute) and because of the
skilful use of the organ. If one appreciates the extent to which
Sankey was secularizing religious music rather than sanctifying
secular music (and we shall consider this in more detail later in
the chapter) the reference to a ballad-singer seems not unfair.

Nevertheless, Sankey was doing more than these commentators admitted. Anyone who has attended modern mass
revival meetings, where the music is handled with less
subtlety than it was in Sankey's time, knows that the singing
of gargantuan choirs has an immediate appeal for many
people: Sankey, accidentally at first, stumbled on a formula
which sufficed mass evangelism for two generations. It was
all very well for the *Guardian* to say that when contrasted with
the rendering of a hymn like 'The Church's One Foundation'
under the dome of St Paul's, the song of the Agricultural Hall
was decidedly wanting the elements of solidarity, real fervour
and musical dignity, but this was prejudice; and *The Times* on
16 March, 1875, came nearer the mark when it said that the

tunes were at least melodious and that 'melody from thousands of human voices sweeps individuals into the swell like the waves of the sea'. Novel, sentimental songs sung with an emphasis on the words and sentiment, sung plainly with no kind of concert arrangement, but supported by mass choral singing, played a vital part in the Americans' success. Sankey's *Sacred Songs and Solos* remained an active symbol of the revival campaigns long after the printed volumes of Moody's sermons and addresses had been wholly forgotten.

This technique was essentially new. Finney and Caughey had spoken in England, Phillip Phillips had sung in England; Moody hit on the idea of combining his addresses with the use of a skilful singer whom he saw as playing a subordinate role. Sankey, less subordinate than Moody had expected, developed the massed choir. The outcome was modern mass evangelism proper, for the device of the choir and the popular song provided the binding element necessary if the revivalists were to control and manipulate crowds of the size which came to the Agricultural Hall. There were an estimated 15,000 at Islington for the first evening meeting (the *Record*, 10 March, 1875). On the first Sunday, 14 March, 1875, a morning meeting was held at eight a.m. for Christian workers which was attended by about 8,000 people, while about 12,000 came to the afternoon meeting for women (the *Record*, 15 March, 1875). Of this meeting the *Guardian* said that the majority of the women, though not all fashionably dressed, were well-to-do, and that the galleries were filled with young girls who appeared to have come on from Sunday Schools (the *Guardian*, 17 March, 1875). By 17 March, 1875, the evening attendance at Islington, having fallen a little at first, had risen to an estimated 20,000 (the *Record*, 19 March, 1875). There was no way of establishing the exact figures. The total of 20,000 cannot be taken as an average figure: a *Record* correspondent who went to Islington just before Moody stopped using the Hall reported an audience of about 12,000 (the *Record*, 25 April, 1875). At the close of the first fortnight it was stated that 335,000 people had gone to the Islington and Exeter Halls. The final attendance figure claimed for all the services, including those held later in the West and East End, was 2,530,000, a gross total which was not corrected to allow for the large number of those who went to meeting after meeting. A modern writer has suggested that perhaps a million and a half people saw and heard Moody and Sankey in London in 1875.[14]

Modern American studies of Moody, like that of James F. Findlay, do not perhaps attach sufficient importance to such figures as evidence of a large-scale, long-sustained demonstration of strength by the evangelical sub-culture. The demonstration was ambiguous, however. There was a powerful lay element, often close to Brethrenism, which supported Moody as a way of expressing distrust of traditional Churches and their ministries. Yet Moody also drew support from many Anglican Evangelical and Free Church ministers, who saw in the revival system a means of consolidating their respective hierarchical societies; to some extent this involved the Free Churchmen in looking for reinforcement in their religious, social and political struggle with the Church of England itself. A strange alliance of Free Church laymen and ministers hoped increasingly after 1870 to make the Liberal Party the organ of political power for which Nonconformity, as they interpreted it, lusted; for them revival campaigns and political campaigns overlapped, as they did for instance in the career of R. W. Dale, because to keep Nonconformity in being required the constant renewal of a religious as well as a political programme. Men like Dale, Hugh Price Hughes and Robertson Nichol did not foresee the rapid decline of the Free Churches after 1900; they thought that social and political equality would release the creative power latent in Nonconformity. If one thinks in these terms, what the non-Anglican religious sub-culture needed after 1900 was a fresh form of revivalism which could maintain simultaneously the religious vitality and social identity of the groups concerned. Moody succeeded at this level in 1873–5; in the twentieth century the only comparable movement was the Welsh revival of 1904–5.[15]

---

[14] J. C. Pollock, *Moody without Sankey* (1963), p.150. The average for the first fortnight in London was about 24,000, very similar to the figure claimed as an average for Graham's Manchester meetings at Maine Road Football Ground in 1961.

[15] For the Welsh Revival, cf. B. Hall, 'The Welsh Revival of 1904–5, A Critique' in *Popular Belief and Practice*, ed. D. Baker (1972), pp.291–302. My own impression is that the 1904 Welsh movement resembled the Irish revival of 1859 as far as 'phenomena' were concerned; that Evan Roberts played a charismatic role quite different from Moody's professionalism; that Welsh Nonconformity's need to make a quantitative

Revivalism unaided, however, could not reverse the social forces which caused the disintegration of the English Free Churches after 1900.

The extent to which Moody attracted the poorer classes of London was therefore important, not least in the eyes of those who invited him, who put great faith in evangelism as a way of creating a social basis for evangelical pietism. Full weight must be given to the criticisms which Lord Shaftesbury voiced at a meeting of the campaign organizers and sympathizers at the Opera House in London on 7 April, 1875. Shaftesbury had not been invited to join the original committee, no doubt because he had always preferred to combine social and evangelistic work instead of confining himself to revivalism, in Moody's style. He did not hear Moody speak until 26 March, 1875. He was not overimpressed by the Americans but very impressed by the number of men and women whom they influenced; even here, however, he had reservations.

At the Opera House meeting it emerged that the Committee was not entirely satisfied with the audience that was being drawn to Islington. The Bow Road Hall was to open in the middle of April to attract the East End working-class and on 25 March, 1875, the *Record* had announced the culmination of negotiations to use Her Majesty's Theatre for a West End meeting for three months at a rent of £1,000. Moody does not appear to have really favoured these West End meetings; he only wanted to use the theatre for afternoon Bible readings of a type familiar among the well-to-do Brethren. But at this 7 April meeting he found himself less in command than usual. As well as Shaftesbury, there were Samuel Morley and Algernon Blackwood, and the twenty-eight-year-old Lord Kinnaird.[16] The clerical element seem to have taken little part.

---

case for itself as the people's Church, as distinct from an 'alien' Church of Wales, explained the strong support and direction given to the first movement. The revival marked a stage in the disestablishment of the Church of Wales, much as R. W. Dale hoped that Moody's campaign would reinforce his own disestablishment campaign in England.

[16] Sankey stayed with the Kinnairds in 1875. They were Scottish evangelical Presbyterian bankers, who had connections with the Y.M.C.A. and the Y.W.C.A. (which Emily Kinnaird helped to found), and with the inner London, largely Scottish Presbyterian congregations at Crown Court and Regent Square. They formed another part of the non-Anglican wealthy London society which supported Moody.

The laymen asked Moody to give up Islington and hold evening meetings in the West End theatre as well as in the Bow Road. Moody, who at this stage was tempted to renew the lease of the Islington Hall by a fortnight to the end of May, at first refused to accept the plan, saying that he would rather preach to 20,000 in the Agricultural Hall than to 3,500 in Her Majesty's Theatre. Someone appears to have said that not more than a third of the Islington audience could hear what he said distinctly, which he also denied, no doubt disliking the inference that many people were prepared to go largely for the sake of the music and massed singing. The first sounding-board had proved a failure, and the *Record* reported on 25 March, 1875, that a great piece of canvas had been stretched across the breadth of the hall in the hope of making Moody audible. There must have been some truth in the allegation.

Shaftesbury then made his own criticisms. The Gospel, he said, should not be localized. The poorer people were not going to Islington—a statement which fits in with contemporary reports, which on the whole agreed that the Islington audience came mainly from inside the Churches, and did not belong to the poorer sections of the community. As far as the upper and middle classes were concerned, Shaftesbury said, there were many who would not go to Islington either, and he added with rather brutal frankness that such people needed the Gospel just as much as 'the crowds of the North End who again and again repeated their visits to the Agricultural Hall'. Samuel Morley, who believed in revivalism more than Shaftesbury did, strongly supported him nevertheless, and Shaftesbury rose again 'and made what has been described to us as the most earnest and powerful appeal to Mr Moody, which carried with it, as appeared from the cheering, the general if not unanimous sympathy of those present' (the *Record*, 7 April, 1875). Shaftesbury said that all kinds of upper-class people would come in from the West End to the Opera House 'as well as many shopkeepers and tradespeople with their dependants, who cannot or will not go to Islington'. The Committee, in fact, did not think that they were having an evangelical equivalent of the Anglo-Catholic Mission to London, but that Moody was simply rallying the faithful round himself at his Islington centre. They were afraid that Moody and Sankey had become no more than an elaborated version of the method which drew a weekly congregation of several thousand to hear Spurgeon in the Metropolitan Tabernacle.

Dissatisfaction with his achievements in North London can hardly have pleased Moody, who must also have been disconcerted to find his lay supporters taking such an independent line. 'But after he had left the meeting he distinctly stated that he was not at all shaken by Lord Shaftesbury's arguments', said the *Record*. In fact, however, the lease of the Agricultural Hall was not extended, though Moody continued to preach there until 9 May, 1875, only a week before the Hall was surrendered. From 9 May, however, he preached at 7.30 p.m. in the Bow Road Hall to perhaps 9,000 people, and then travelled to the West End to the Haymarket where the Opera House held perhaps as many as 5,000 for a service at 9 p.m. These figures would imply a rather smaller total audience in the second stage of the meetings, which lasted until 21 July, 1875. This turn of events suggests that the evangelical laymen made their point effective in the long run; they insisted that Moody must try and provide for every section of the population. Books on Moody's English visit have failed to make this clear.

How successful the Bow Road meetings were is hard to decide. The *Guardian*, on 23 June, 1875, when the Etonian controversy was at its height (*v.i.*), printed a letter from C. N. Edgington, who was Vicar of Trinity Church in the Bow Road. He said that he had attended one of the services at the Bow Road Hall during a week in which an especial effort had been made to bring in the working-classes. Only about one fifth of the hall was filled, which strictly speaking meant an audience of less than 2,000.

> I watched the people as they came in and saw but few of the working class. The Congregation have consisted of ordinary church and chapel goers, clergymen, Dissenting ministers, and visitors from the country. Had the revival at all succeeded in making its way among the class whom neither the Church nor Dissent had hitherto reached it would have disarmed a good deal of opposition.

Edgington was not an unbiased witness, of course. He summed up Moody's teaching as a religion of

> mere emotionalism and sensationalism, with its antinomian theories, its instantaneous conversions, its arbitrary divisions of converted and unconverted, its preaching of terror and damnation, its test question of 'Are you saved?' and its confessional in the guise of the inquiry room.[17]

There were, as J. C. Pollock pointed out in *Moody without Sankey* (1964), letters on the other side, but the later history of the East End suggests that the outcome of Moody's preaching there was not remarkable.[18] For example, *The Bitter Cry of Outcast London*, a twenty-page penny pamphlet published anonymously in 1883, took for granted that 'while we have been building our churches and solacing ourselves with our religion and dreaming that the millennium was coming, the poor have been growing poorer, the wretched more miserable, and the immoral more corrupt'. One result of the controversy caused by this essay, which may or may not have been written by the Secretary of the London Congregational Union, was that the Government set up a Royal Commission on working-class housing: this was more positive than the work of the revivalists. Ecclesiastically, the

[17] The content of the East End meetings varied. The *Methodist Recorder*, 30 April, 1875, said that on the previous Sunday Hay Aitken had preached 'a wonderful discourse, leaving both the Socinian and the mere Ritualist no ground to stand upon'; this hardly sounds like the perfect address for the East End, but the reporter was unsympathetic to the American style of speaking. Another report on 28 May, 1875, said that on the Thursday night Sankey had given out Temperance as the subject; he had sung 'The Death of the Drunkard's Wife' and read portions of Scripture bearing on it. 'An earnest prayer followed that East London might be purged of its curse of drunkenness.' Then a vivid description of a shipwreck introduced the 'Lighthouse Hymn', the audience joining in the chorus, 'Some poor struggling seaman you may rescue, you may save'. Moody then preached, but there was no account of the result, which at any rate suggested that the meeting was unremarkable. In June, 1875, the Rev. C. Melville Pym replaced the lay Henry Varley at the Bow Road; he was a retired army officer who filled his addresses with battlefield stories. The *Methodist Recorder* leaves the impression of a typical late nineteenth-century downtown mission-station, in which middle-class helpers were making an unusual effort, without unusual success.

[18] Cf. P. J. Keating, 'Fact and Fiction in the East End' in *The Victorian City* ed. H. J. Dyos and M. Wolff, vol. 2 (1973), pp.585–602. Keating shows how middle-class writers in the 1880s established the stereotype of the East End as a city separate from the West, passive, mean and hostile. Moody and Sankey were accepting an older Victorian attitude, which still treated London as a whole, and therefore sent missions to the East as well as the West part of the city. But there was no special sense of the East End as early as 1875.

Forward Movement, which characterized the efforts of London Nonconformity in the last fifteen or so years of the century, came partly as a response to the 'Bitter Cry'—in the sense that the Wesleyan Methodist and other East End Churches were annoyed by the pamphlet's criticism of what they had done in the past, and partly because the circumstances to which the pamphlet itself testified stimulated further denominational experiment in the shape of the Wesleyan Central Halls and the 'Institutional Churches' of Nonconformity. These efforts did not consciously build on the revivalists' campaign, nor were they assisted by another American descent on the East End in this period. And when one turns to Charles Booth's patient survey of the religious life of London, made at the very end of the period, one finds that he is chiefly exercised to explain the non-Christianity of the poor.

This may sound like carping criticism but the point is not without importance. As Lord Shaftesbury seems to have realized, Moody and Sankey had become the symbolic centre of what had turned into a demonstration of the strength (and weakness) of middle and lower middle-class Victorian pietism, a social group which resented and feared the growing secularization of late nineteenth-century society, and longed to see the restoration of the religious dominion over the nation as a whole which was believed to have existed in the past; in this sense the gathering of the evangelical legions behind Moody (or for that matter the superficially apolitical Pearsall Smith) had a distinctly political flavour about it. Throughout the Victorian period this religious section of the middle classes attached great importance to having its moral and social attitudes not only respected, but if possible, obeyed by other groups; this corporate need for approval explains the development of what came to be called the Nonconformist 'Conscience' and its Anglican equivalent. The impulse has continued into the present century, but television and the cinema, more than any other form of mass entertainment, have driven home to this stubborn minority the extent to which English society as a whole ignores (and already in the Victorian period largely ignored by the time of Moody), their codes and customs, and is indifferent to their approval and disapproval. Anxiety to make their presence felt explained why Shaftesbury, Morley and Algernon Blackwood, for example, wanted Moody to conduct meetings in the East End and also in the West End. Moody, however, as an American, could hardly be expected to grasp the meaning of the social aggression of the evangelical world; he had the professional revivalist's liking for large numbers; twenty thousand in Islington sounded much better than three and a half thousand in the Opera House and it was only natural that he should see less imperfection in his methods than others saw. He retained, in any case, a pessimistic, premillennial streak which made him doubt the possibility of changing social situations, whereas Shaftesbury obviously took the optimistic side, as did such powerful leaders of late nineteenth-century Nonconformity as the Wesleyan Hugh Price Hughes.

Moody differed from many other revivalists, however, in that he made no serious attempt to find out how many people were converted or otherwise influenced by his campaigns. It was a sign of his supremacy as a professional that he dispensed with any kind of official statistical proof of his effectiveness in London—no subsequent revivalist of any prominence has been able to follow his example. His share in the success of the meetings was two-fold: his speaking, to which we shall come back; and the tactical skill, often pure showmanship, with which he preserved the feeling of variety, the expectation that something unusual might always happen, in the months of the London meetings. He thought that English religious gatherings were badly organized, lasted too long and were dominated by diffuse, aimless addresses; his own services were briefer, under tighter control, and he and Sankey both spoke in a style which at the time seemed plain and direct, though a century later one may be more conscious, in reading Moody's printed addresses, of the strong element of pietist rhetoric that they contain. He did not reduce his meetings to a single, invariable plan. On the opening Sunday of the London campaign (14 March, 1875), he held a meeting for men only in the evening at Islington, which about 17,000 attended, a figure which was itself proof of skilful preparation. At the end of the formal assembly, about half of these stayed for the after-meeting. On this occasion Moody gave no address but instead asked for silent prayer, and, once this had begun, asked those who wanted the company to pray for them to rise to their feet. Many did so, theoretically cloaked in the anonymity of the closed eyes of those whose heads were bowed in prayer. This appeal he repeated many times, after which he asked those who seriously wanted to become Christians to go into the adjoining concert-hall. Several hundred entered what now became the inquiry-room including, of course, those with workers' tickets who were to counsel those who might be in distress (the *Record*, 15 March, 1875). Here one sees techniques already familiar to Finney and Calvin Colton: the separation of the half-committed from the protection of being lost in a crowd, and then the bringing of the pressure of the whole group to bear on the scattered, standing individuals. This was a variant of the 'anxious seat'. Moody's skill lay in his ability to ring the changes on methods of this kind, so that his audience was prevented from relaxing.

Moody's flexibility in handling audiences also helped to preserve their primitive character, the sense in which, despite the lines of ordained ministers on the platform, they were an anti-clerical alternative to the traditional form of institutionalized English Protestantism. This mattered to Moody, because he could not afford to break entirely with the picture of the revivalist as the focal point of dissident lay evangelical pietism—by doing so he would have sacrificed much of his most devoted support. He attracted larger audiences than any revivalist in England before him by keeping the balance between this dissidence and institutionalism, between the lay and the clerical. He was helped, of course, by the greater tolerance of lay evangelists which had penetrated Anglican Evangelicalism since the 1860s. His flexibility took many directions. Sankey tells the story of how on one occasion, in the intense silence which followed after he had sung a solo, a child's voice was heard, saying, 'I wish that man would sing again'. Moody heard it and turning to his colleague immediately said, 'Mr Sankey, you've got your order to sing again', and sing he did.[19] When the Americans visited Edinburgh in 1874 the American negro Fisk Jubilee Singers were also there. Moody concealed them in the gallery, and at a

[19] D. Williamson, *Short Life of Ira D. Sankey* (n.d.).

given signal they began quietly to sing, 'There are angels hovering round'. His informality cannot have surprised those who knew Spurgeon, for instance; Spurgeon himself was quite ready to overlook the normal Baptist objection to instrumental music in religious services when it was a question of having Sankey sing in the Tabernacle. But Spurgeon held his great congregation much more by doing what was expected of him: Moody packed the Agricultural Hall by being less predictable.

As a master of the surprise effect Moody had a freedom denied to Spurgeon. At the evening meeting at Islington on 12 March, 1875, he suddenly swung round to face the large array of ministers, belonging to many denominations, seated on the platform and said: 'I ask you ministers of religion whether God may not be found here tonight?' The whole body on the platform as with one voice replied, 'Yes'. The force of the sound took the audience by surprise and seemed much to impress them. Then Moody, turning back to the audience, said, 'I appeal to some of you whether you have not found him here'—to which there came responses of 'Yes, Yes'. Moody then cried, 'Oh, may thousands in London find him', to which many in the audience replied, 'Amen' (the *Record*, 15 March, 1875). How many ministers were present on this occasion it is impossible to say, but at Islington on 23 March, 1875, there were said to have been sixty Anglican clergymen alone (the *Record*, 24 March, 1875). The weight of this phalanx of clerical authority gave powerful indirect support to the bulky, rather carnal figure of Moody, and on such an occasion he turned this visible image of ecclesiastical approval to his own advantage, making his personal ascendancy and independence felt at the same time.

The Eton affair made an odd climax to Moody's London campaign. The origin of the scheme is not seriously in doubt. In London Moody was on close terms with Quintin Hogg, a West Indian sugar merchant, then about thirty years old, and another of those ardent laymen whom the Church of England could accommodate with difficulty in the late Victorian period. Hogg, indeed, made little of the Church of England; his biographer confesses that he was often criticized for his irregularity as a church-goer—in his later years he started the

Polytechnic Movement which, like the Y.M.C.A., was much more evangelical in its earlier years than it later became, and spent his Sunday mornings in preparing for an afternoon religious class with the boys there. Like many Victorian laymen he solved the problem of allegiance by creating an institution of his own to which he gave his primary loyalty. Hogg had been at school at Eton and so had his brother-in-law, John Graham, who actually had a boy at the school in 1875.[20] The idea that Moody should preach to the Eton schoolboys must have arisen in this circle and would have seemed natural to Quintin Hogg, who had spent much of his spare time in establishing a Ragged School at Long Acre in London, at which the conversion of the boys took first place.

Graham and Hogg went down to Windsor on 12 June, 1875 and saw the Provost (Goodford) and the Headmaster (Hornby). They came away convinced that the school authorities would take no step to prevent Eton boys from attending a meeting to be held in a tent pitched on private land near the College on 22 June, 1875. At a later stage, both the Provost and the Headmaster were anxious to deny that they had encouraged the scheme at all. Their position was difficult. No one could actually forbid Moody to preach at Windsor in private grounds if he wanted to, and there had been no question of his seeking to preach in the College Chapel itself. From Moody's point of view the plan was excellent. If he succeeded in preaching to some of the boys he would have put his prestige as a revivalist on a higher level socially than ever before; and if, as actually happened, there was opposition to his preaching in Windsor at all, he would be in the comfortable position of alleging social persecution.

More important than Moody's intentions were those of the Anglican Evangelical group of laymen. Their campaign to win social recognition for Moody had not been very successful. The Archbishop of Canterbury, approached by the

[20] The Grahams were another non-Anglican family of London business people. William Graham, Quintin Hogg's father-in-law, admired Moody, 'but he also possessed a fine collection of paintings and Moody had been affronted by his nudes'. The Graham family attended the Congregationalist Westminster Chapel, and its minister, Samuel Martin, advised that Christians 'should not give offence to each other, and a particularly offensive picture of bathing boys was redeemed by the painting in of towels' (C. Binfield, *George Williams and the Y.M.C.A.* (1973), p.302).

Evangelical Lord Chancellor, Cairns, as an intermediary, had refused to give his unqualified approval of the meetings. The Queen, approached by the Dowager Countess of Gainsborough, a member of the Court, replied briefly:

Dear Fanny, I received your letter yesterday on the subject of Moody and Sankey, the American Evangelists. It would never do for me to go to a public place to hear them, or anything of that sort, nor, as you know, do I go to any large public places now. But independently of that, though I am sure they are very good and sincere people, it is not the sort of religious performance which I like. This sensational style of excitement like the Revivals is not the religion which *can last*, and it is not, I think, wholesome for the mind or heart, though there may be instances where it does good. Eloquent simple preaching, with plain practical teaching, seems to me far more likely to do *real* and *permanent* good, and this can surely be heard in the Established Church or amongst Dissenters, if the Ministers are thoroughly in earnest.[21]

This letter was not published, of course, but that of the Archbishop of Canterbury was,[22] and the fact that the Queen had refused to visit one of the theatre meetings was not a secret. In these circumstances Moody's agreement to hold a meeting at Windsor and to invite Eton boys to come to it seems to have taken on, especially in the eyes of some Anglicans, the appearance of an inexcusable defiance of the Crown, the Church of England and the social order which symbolized itself in such institutions. There seems to have been a rumour that Moody meant to stay at Windsor and hold more than one meeting, and there is nothing incredible in this; Quintin Hogg's biographer says that 'one of the clerical dignitaries of Windsor even went so far as to assert that "the American was only coming to preach Republican doctrine, and asked that a reinforcement of troops should be sent in readiness to defend the Castle".'[23] This improbable story may suggest the hysteria which was generated. A letter to the Archbishop of Canterbury, A. C. Tait, has survived in the Lambeth archives, dated 19 June, 1875, from Darby Griffith:

[21] *Letters of Queen Victoria*, 27 April, 1875.
[22] *v.i.*, pp.207–8.
[23] Ethel M. Hogg, *Quintin Hogg* (1904), p.88.

. . . I have on good authority that Moody and Sankey are to be allowed to erect a tent for the performance of their services, in South Meadow, on Thursday next, at Eton College. I venture to think it to be a breach of faith with parents who have sent their sons to Eton to be educated in the principles of the Church of England, that, without their consent, their sons should be exposed to religious excitement of this character.[24]

It is also clear that Knatchbull-Hugessen, a High Church friend of Oscar Browning, who had recently lost his position as Under Secretary of State for the Colonies through the fall in 1874 of Gladstone's Government, and who also had a boy at Eton, happened to visit the school on the fatal 19 June, 1875, heard about the proposed meeting and reacted furiously. There followed a series of rather absurd protests, in *The Times* and even in Parliament; the Eton authorities hastily denied that they had in any sense consented to the affair; Moody's advisers substituted a simple gathering in a private garden in a house in Windsor on 22 June for the tent in a field which they had planned originally; some boys from the school went to hear him but there is no trace of any great excitement. Professor Findlay takes an exaggerated view of all this:

A great hue and cry erupted in Parliament. Members of the House of Lords especially opposed Moody's plans. As long as Moody spoke of saving 'the masses', obviously by the means of personal evangelisation or through support of charitable organisations that in turn reflected upper- and middle-class values, as long as his revivals seemed designed especially to appeal to the great body of evangelical churchgoers, the aristocracy could look on with a certain indulgence. But going to Eton meant that the evangelist was invading one of the sacred precincts of the upper classes, an upstart American preaching undesirable doctrines to young innocents being groomed carefully by the Church in religious tradition and faith. It could not be. . . .[25]

The explanation is over-sophisticated. It was not so much Moody as his wealthy backers, who had their own aristocratic connexions and who for the most part sat lightly to Anglican-

[24] The letter is preserved at Lambeth in the Tait Papers. Griffith's address was 19 Wimpole St.
[25] Findlay, op. cit., p.179. There were letters in *The Times* on 22, 23 June, 1875.

ism, who were giving offence. On the strength of Moody's undoubted public success in London they were seeking to assume a religious (and inevitably social) leadership which they did not possess and which other, especially Anglican, circles were not prepared to grant them. For Moody, uncommitted to the English social system, the Eton rebuff was easily passed off as an example of the way in which Truth was constantly persecuted by the World. For his English friends, the overall failure, which Moody's visit to England compounded, to impose their evangelical system on society, was decisive. It is significant that so many of his admirers could turn almost immediately to Pearsall Smith's narcissistic perfectionism; as far as Anglican Evangelicalism was concerned, the acceptance of the new Holiness Movement marked the close of what one might call the Shaftesbury era, a period in which Evangelicalism, whatever its faults, had always struggled to evangelize and change the surrounding, secular society. Now Evangelicalism turned in on itself, not only withdrawing from society but seeming to abandon it to its fate. Premillennial influences, which came from the Brethren as well as from Moody, no doubt made it easier to feel that history had no positive value, but there was also a loss of nerve so deep as to call in question the effect that Moody and Sankey were really having on some of those who followed them closely in 1873-5.

When Moody returned to England in 1881-3, his advisers gauged his value more accurately. As a whole, the tour failed, attracting little publicity. The organizers did not repeat the experiment of a full-scale, centralized London campaign; they did not press their social claims in places where they were not wanted. Instead, they took Moody to Cambridge in November, 1882, and then to Oxford, meeting with some success in Cambridge where Anglican Evangelicalism had rooted itself deeply since the eighteenth century. Moody had been averse from speaking to university students in earlier years, in America as well as in England, because of his own limited education; in fact, he did not attempt to work seriously among students until 1886, and then under Y.M.C.A. encouragement in the United States. The opposition which he met in both British universities in 1882 stemmed from local dislike of the Anglican Evangelical groups of students. He was much less effective than was to be another American, John Mott, when he visited English student groups in 1894.[26]

---

[26] Mott was an American Methodist layman; he began his religious career in the Y.M.C.A.; in 1895 he became secretary of the World Student Christian Federation, which he had done much to form. He was chairman of the Committee which called the famous Edinburgh Missionary Conference of 1910. That Mott (and Moody) should have had some success in late nineteenth-century Cambridge is not surprising: many undergraduates still came from small professional and clerical groups in which religious obscurantism remained strong. Mott was not a revivalist, but a manipulator of young people already in the tradition.

5

Moody's Preaching and the Revival Meeting

1. Moody's Preaching

MOODY'S preaching has never been adequately analysed.[1] His contemporaries thought of him as an effective speaker rather than as a great one, and found various explanations of a success which some of them resented. Commentators emphasized his brevity, for he took twenty minutes when most other preachers took at least twice as long; they also stressed his conversational, even ungrammatical language, which contrasted with the florid style still popular in the pulpit; they noted his constant use of anecdotes to fill up his paragraphs and keep his audience's attention. No one described him as original, because Spurgeon preached in a similar manner and had held his own mass congregation at the Tabernacle for many years, but the total impact of Moody's addresses was innovatory. He could not be quoted to any great effect, and it was Sankey's solos which his hearers remembered, but he had the clarity of a man who had a powerful impulse to dominate, and his occasional brusqueness, very different from the normal gentility of the evangelical pulpit style, communicated power as well as the sincerity of his convictions.

Moody's admirers admitted weaknesses in his preaching, doing so all the more readily because they thought that this showed that 'the work is to be attributed to the special blessing of God'.[2] W. H. Daniels, writing as the London campaign of 1875 drew to an end, said that 'the power which attends the ministry of these men is of God . . . they are

---

[1] See, e.g., *The Pulpit Speaking of D. L. Moody*, a thesis by R. K. Curtis, the substance of which was published in *They Called Him Mr. Moody* (1962). I have not followed Dr Curtis in my own analysis of Moody's preaching; McLaughlin, op. cit., is too brief on this topic.

[2] *Record*, 25 April, 1875, in a leading article on the Americans.

honoured in this pre-eminent fashion because they speak and
sing the simple gospel of Christ, instead of any doctrine and
fancies of their own'.[3] Moody's public success became proof
of the technical skill of his preaching.

There is another explanation of Moody's success still
current in evangelical circles; it derives partly from something
that Moody said himself and partly from an article which the
American literary critic, H. L. Mencken, wrote about thirty
years ago. 'It was by putting the soft pedal on Hell,' Mencken
said, 'that Moody beat all his competitors.'[4] Mencken was
not the first to say this, but he gave wide currency to a myth
about Moody's theological development to which Moody
himself contributed. It may be traced back to a story according
to which Henry Moorhouse, an English member of the
Plymouth Brethren, visited Moody in Chicago in 1868 and
persuaded him to preach more about the love and less about
the wrath of God. Actually, in one of the earliest forms of the
tradition, the biography by Daniels, it is implied that what
Moody learned from Moorhouse was a style of preaching
(though it would have been more accurate to say a style of
conducting prayer meetings) which was very closely tied to
the text of the Bible, and in the manner of the Brethren themselves. There was probably some truth in this version of the
incident, for Moody's sermon, 'The Blood', for example, was
certainly an address of this type, reviewing a long series of
texts from the New Testament about the blood of Christ. In
general, however, the addresses which Moody used in 1875
did not show this characteristic; what stood out was the huge
number of anecdotes, contemporary in character, and not the
number of Biblical references. Moody often told the story of
Moorhouse's visit to Chicago himself, explaining how before
this he had not realized how much God loved mankind; 'this
heart of mine began to thaw out; I could not hold back the
tears. I just drank it in', his son quoted him as saying.[5] After
this he modified, according to his own account, the way in
which he preached, and it is some confirmation that in 1875,
for example, the *Record*, which was not over-friendly towards

[3] Daniels, *D. L. Moody and his Work* (1875), p 381.
[4] Cf. *The American Mercury*, September, 1930, 'The Scourge of Satan'.
[5] R. K. Curtis, op. cit., refers this passage to *The Great Redemption* (Chicago 1889);
W. R. Moody gave no source.

the Americans who, after all, were not Anglicans and not episcopal in origin, said that Moody preached 'a genial gospel, no mere system of terror'.[6]

Nevertheless, such statements are not the whole of the truth. Mencken was right—as far as Moody's preaching in England was concerned, at any rate—only in the sense that Moody substituted for the early nineteenth-century pictures of legions of devils and lakes of fire which might still be found in the hymns of the Primitive Methodists or the preaching of James Caughey, Reginald Radcliffe and Richard Weaver, a subtler system of terror.[7] There was no question of any revolution in Moody's revivalist theology, as can be seen if one examines one of the best-known and most frequently used of his addresses, 'The Blood'. Moody, like other revivalists, used the same address again and again; the published version must be regarded as a basic outline into which he could insert new, topical illustrations to suit a particular occasion and city.

The most striking thing about 'The Blood' was how it was organized to compel the hearers to act, not just listen; they had either to agree to do what Moody was asking them to do, or deliberately refuse to do it. This was the essential structure of all his revival sermons, and distinguished them from the kind of sermon preached by R. W. Dale and Liddon. The note was struck at the beginning of 'The Blood':

> The blood has two cries, it cries either for my condemnation, or if you will allow me to use a stronger word, for my damnation; or it cries for my salvation. If I reject the blood of Christ, it cries out for my condemnation; if I accept it, it cries out for pardon and peace.[8]

All through 'The Blood' Moody implied that this demand for response was made in the context of a universe which was

---

[6] *Record*, 25 April, 1875.

[7] I discuss the extent to which Moody was still a hell-fire preacher later in this chapter; here I am concerned only with the qualifications which have to be made to the idea that Moody succeeded by preaching about a God of Love.

[8] *The London Discourses of Mr. D. L. Moody* as delivered in the Agricultural Hall and Her Majesty's Opera House. From the notes of special shorthand writers; James Clarke, London, 1875. There were several later official publications of this sermon, in England and the United States. Note the qualification, 'if you will allow me to use a stronger word': nevertheless, 'damnation' had been mentioned, and given its full force as 'condemnation'.

both cruel and arbitrary and yet completely in the control of its creator. Jesus had acted as he did in order to save men from the crushing retribution of this hostile world-order, but those who were listening to the address had to realize that they could escape an eternity of suffering only if they accepted for themselves the substitutionary death of Christ.

> The sinner is justified with God by his matchless grace through the blood of his Son. Justified, that means, just as if he had never committed sin. What a wonderful thing; not one sin against him. It is as if he owed someone a debt and when he went to pay the debt was told, 'There is nothing against you, it is all settled'. 'Why,' he would say, 'How is that. I got some things from you not long ago and I want to pay the bill.' 'There is nothing against you.' 'But I am sure that I got something here.' 'There is nothing against you in my ledger; someone else must have come in and paid it.' That is substitution. Now I know who paid my spiritual debts. And God looks at his ledger and there is nothing against us. Christ was raised up for our justification. It is a good deal better to be justified than pardoned. Suppose I was arrested for stealing £1,000, tried and found guilty, but suppose the judge had mercy on me and pardoned me. I should come out of prison but it would be with my head down. I had been found guilty, I could never face the world again. But suppose I was accused of stealing it, but it could not be proved, and when the case came on, it was found I had done nothing of the kind. Then I should be justified.

The final illustration showed the slackness of Moody's thought. That Christ could be said to have paid for our sins did not mean that the sins had not been committed, whereas in Moody's example the man who left the court 'justified' had not stolen a thousand pounds at all, and would have been more accurately described as innocent. Like Radcliffe and Weaver in the 1860s, Moody was sometimes criticized for not sufficiently emphasizing the need for repentance; but he was not deeply interested in repentance, what he wanted from his hearers was an obedient act of will, and the strong element of fear in his 'converting' addresses was intended to exact this obedience. The content of the act was not easy to define. He was not trying to awaken a feeling of remorse, or the 'conviction of sin' which would lead to a desire first for repentance and then for justifying faith; he simply narrowed down the possible response to his preaching to one of two courses of action. In the case of 'The Blood', one either accepted the Blood or one trampled on it, and Moody so arranged his address and the concluding appeal that one was left with the impression that unless one had positively come out in favour of the Blood then one *had* trampled on it.

> Sinner, let me ask you what are you going to do with the blood of God's only Son? I tell you it is a terrible thing to make light of the blood, to laugh and ridicule the doctrine of the blood. I would rather fall dead on this platform than do such a thing. It makes my heart shudder when I hear men speaking lightly of it. Some time ago a very solemn thought came stealing over me and made a deep impression on my mind. The only thing that Christ left upon earth was his blood. His flesh and bones he took away. But when he went up on high he left his blood down here. What are you going to do with the blood? Are you going to make light of it, to trample on it. . . .

By talking in this fashion Moody left the meaning of the act of submission which he required very vague, so that people might fill it with their own religious feelings and aspirations. He demanded that one declared oneself for or against God in a universe in which God had absolute control, and in which it would be dangerous indefinitely to defy him. 'The Blood' did not sound like a sermon about the love of God; it posed a threat—that one had better get into line with God's mercy quickly, because there were very definite limits to the liberty of the subject.

To some extent, then, Moody solved the revivalist's problem of how to obtain decisions by simplifying the decision which had to be taken. He also appealed to the hesitant in his audiences by the brusque and confident way in which he dealt with some of the more serious objections to Christianity. In 1875 he used two famous addresses called 'Excuses'. In these, for example, he disposed of Victorian difficulties with the Bible in no time at all:

> Only the other night a lady came to me in the inquiry-room and said, 'There are so many things in the Bible I cannot understand.' No doubt about that. God says, the carnal man cannot understand spiritual things, and the Bible is a spiritual book. How can

the unregenerate heart understand the Bible? Well, when God put salvation before the world he put *that* very plain. The word of God may be darkened to the natural man, but the way of salvation is written so plain that the little child of six years old can understand it if she will. . . .[9]

And so he had moved in a few sentences from the admission that the Bible contained difficulties—though that was really the result of one's own sinfulness, not of the Bible's teaching—to the very different statement that a six-year-old child could grasp the nature of salvation if she really wanted to. With equal confidence Moody went on to say that

> 'of all the infidels and sceptics I have ever met speaking against the Bible I have never met one who has read it through. There may be such men, but I have never met them. It is simply an excuse. There is no man living who will stand up before God and say that kept him out of the Kingdom. It is the devil's work trying to make us believe that it is not true, and that it is dark and mysterious. . . . Young men, the Bible is true. What have these infidels to give you in its place? What has made England but the open Bible. . . .'

In such a passage Moody was not trying to offer either a serious or an honest argument. He must have known of men like Charles Bradlaugh, the professional sceptic, who regarded the Bible as the best weapon with which to attack Christianity, and who could have exchanged text for text with Moody on any significant theological topic. Moody was not interested in the problems which other people found in the Bible, but was anxious to shift the issue back to his chosen ground, the need to make a decision, a decision which, however vaguely Moody defined it, the six-year-old girl could perfectly well make, '*if she will*'. One senses a hard core to his character, a need and a will to dominate, which overcame the resistance of some of the uncertain and under-educated among his hearers.

In the second part of 'Excuses' Moody dealt in a similar fashion with a man who said that he could not believe.

> Not long ago a man said to me, 'I cannot believe' . . . 'Whom?' I asked. He stammered and said again, 'I cannot believe.' I said,

[9] *The London Discourses of Mr. D. L. Moody*, etc. 'Excuses' was often reprinted.

'Whom?' 'Well,' he said, 'I can't believe it.' 'Whom?' I asked again. At last he said, 'I cannot believe myself.' 'Well, you don't need to. You do not need to put any confidence in yourself. The less you believe in yourself the better. But if you tell me you can't believe in God, that is another thing, and I would like to ask you why.'

Here Moody gave the momentary impression that he was about to answer a serious objection seriously, but in fact threw the hypothetical questioner into a false position which was intended to imply that anyone who said that he could not believe did not even understand his own problems. Only after strengthening the faith of the audience in Moody himself as the all-conquering apologist did he revert to the original question, which he handled with the same ruthlessness:

Why don't you be honest and say at once that you *won't* believe? There is no real reason why men can't believe God. I challenge any infidel on the face of the earth to put his finger on one promise that God has ever made that he has not kept. The idea of a man standing up in the afternoon of the nineteenth century and saying that he cannot believe God. . . . My friend you have no reason for not believing him. . . . Some men talk as though it were a great misfortune that they do not believe. They seem to look upon it as a great infirmity, and think they ought to be sympathized with and pitied. But bear in mind that it is the most damning sin in the world. 'When He, the Holy Ghost, is come, He will reprove the world of sin, and of righteousness, and of judgement; of sin, *because they believe not on me.*' That is the very root of sin; and the fruit is bad because the tree is bad.

One would hardly suppose from this that Moorhouse's visit to Chicago in 1868 permanently enlarged either Moody's sympathy for mankind or his appreciation of God's love; here he was trampling on other men's difficulties much as he accused others of trampling on the blood of Christ. Each objection was systematically referred to a conscious act of the will, in order to justify the demand for a contrary, submissive act of will at the climax of the address. If the truth about the 'infidel' was that he was refusing to believe what he had no ground for disbelieving, then it was fair to insist that he change his mind on the spot, deliberately; if his unbelief could also be

called 'sinful', he had no business to ask for reasoned argument, any more than he ought to expect sympathy. It followed
that Moody was not obliged to offer argument or to extend
sympathy; he was free to attack the 'infidel' on the one hand,
and to flatter his audience on the other by suggesting that the
majority of those before him knew better than to follow the
promptings of an unrighteous will.

In taking this line Moody was setting precise limits to his
own success. These limits meant that Moody contributed little
more than his own self-confidence to the defence of evangelical
Christianity in the late nineteenth century. He could not
expect the Victorian intellectual world to take him seriously,
whether Christian or agnostic; he lacked both an imaginative
understanding of agnosticism and a sufficiently sensitive interpretation of Christianity. Success, when it came in 1873–5,
came rather too suddenly and easily, and he probably never
gave Sankey full credit for the influence of his singing.
Evangelical biographers of Moody (and there have been few
others) still regard his critics as either deficient in religion or
misinformed about what Moody said and did. No doubt some
ministers criticized Moody because they did not like successful
competition; Anglicans who had already condemned both the
revivalism of 1859–60 and the Anglo-Catholic experiments of
1869 were not likely to alter their opinions because of Moody's
campaign. It is arguable, however, that there was not enough
open criticism and discussion, that the co-operative silence of
most religious leaders implied that Christianity could be
understood as Moody defined it, which meant in turn that
Christianity could be rejected in terms of what Moody said.
The silence also implied a social judgement, however: that the
views of Moody and his supporters did not really matter,
above all at the level of discussion; popular religion did not
count, precisely because it was popular. It would require a
long and patient search to find many passages in which the
professional clerical theologians examined and judged the
value of Moody's statements; it was the lay theologian,
Matthew Arnold, who was willing to comment on popular
religion.

That this social gulf existed, however, explains why the
Archbishop of Canterbury, A. C. Tait, was willing to refuse

official approval to Moody's meetings. In an open letter which the Anglican Evangelicals must have wished that they had not provoked, Tait said that enquiries he had made prompted him to conclude that the American revivalists were not entirely sound doctrinally. 'I am not alluding,' he said, 'so much to any depreciation of the ordinances which Christ established for the edification of his Church'—a reference to Moody's public dismissal of the importance of the rite of infant baptism—'but rather to the allegation that in the discourses of the missionaries there are unwise and untrue representations of the almost universal necessity of instantaneous conversion, and an ignoring of the full Scriptural teaching as to the nature of repentance.'[10] This comment was certainly not unfair, as can be seen if one examines another of Moody's addresses, 'The New Birth', which he used in London in 1875, and which started from the text, 'Except a man be born again he cannot see the Kingdom of God'.

Moody began this address with the uncompromising statement that there was no question upon which the Church and the world were more confounded than that of regeneration. He gave a list of what he regarded as the principal misunderstandings of the idea. Regeneration, he said, was confused with church attendance or church work.

> If you go down in the dark alleys and by-ways of the city and do all the good you can, preach God's word and show God's love to those abandoned beings—I tell you that is not regeneration. No, no. It is a false idea that you can get regeneration by scattering the seed of God by the wayside.

Nor would being baptized do any good—and the paragraph which followed showed what Tait had in mind when he wrote his open letter.

> You may be baptised into the visible church, and yet not be baptised into the Son of God. Baptism is all right in its place. God forbid that I should say anything against it. But if you put that in the place of regeneration, in the place of the new birth, it is a terrible mistake. You cannot be baptised into the Kingdom of God. If I thought that I could baptise men into the Kingdom of

[10] Davidson and Benham, *A. C. Tait*, vol. 2 (1891), pp.510–19.

God it would be a good deal better for me to do that than preach.
I should get a bucket of water and go up and down the streets
and save men that way. If they would not let me do it while they
were awake I would do it while they were asleep; I would do it
anyway.

Moody's English supporters did not always admit that he
talked like this, but at the time his views were clearly reported
in the newspapers, and the vulgarity of the concluding
sentences quoted above touches the deeper reasons for the
unfavourable reaction of many Anglican clergy to Moody.
Tait could not possibly have shown approval of this tone, or
of the travesty of High Anglican baptismal theology in the
passage as a whole. Moody, of course, was simply saying what
he would have said in the United States, as he did when he
passed on in this address to comment on the Eucharist in the
same style. Attending communion was no guarantee of
salvation—'*that* is not being born again—that is not passing
from death into life. Jesus says plainly—and so plainly that
there need not be any mistake about it, "Except a man be born
of . . . the Spirit, he cannot enter the Kingdom of God". What
has a sacrament to do with that?' It was probably not an
accident that Moody failed to quote the whole of the
Johannine passage, which speaks of a man being born '*of
water* and the Spirit', a reference which links Spirit and
sacrament tightly together as far as the author of the Fourth
Gospel was concerned. The professional revivalist, however,
was bound to persuade his congregation that what they
needed was cataclysmic change, not a process of growth in
which the Spirit of the 'new life' gradually overcame the
resistance of the old. At the social level, moreover, Moody
was appealing for the support of the 'new evangelicals', who
had become tired of the pretensions of the clerical hierarchy
to every kind of ecclesiastical leadership.

In view of the claims which have been made about the
ecumenical spirit of Moody's evangelism, it is worth docu-
menting his use of the 'New Birth' and his attitude to the
institutional Church while he was in London in 1875. A *Times*
reporter who heard him preach the sermon in March, 1875,
said that like most of the American's addresses, it was short,
pointed and largely made up of anecdotes. 'A vigorous attack

on mere church-going or on mere praying may be looked for at any moment, be the subject of the address what it may.' Moody, the reporter said, treated religion as essentially a simple matter, a question of the New Birth. 'Mystery', he represented Moody as saying, 'Why—it is going on at your right hand and at your left—it is the Lord's everyday work. I care nothing for baptism—nothing for mere church-going. These are all right as far as they go, but you must go beyond them for the new birth.'[11] The attitude of *The Times* hardened as the meetings continued and a week later another article said that as a rule Anglican clergy had not attended them, adding that 'Dean Stanley did, and he has been fully described, even to the putting on of his spectacles, for his pains'. The writer also insisted that the revivalists had been attacking worthy parish priests who refused to give them outright support. The article (26 March, 1875), written just before Good Friday, said that the normal solemnities of the day would be regarded as 'mere formalism' by Moody's followers.

Of course, Moody's language could be interpreted as no more than a vigorous statement of the importance of the existential approach to religion, but neither the historical context—Moody was speaking at a moment when English religious society was torn apart by the dissension of Evangelical, Anglo-Catholic and Nonconformist—nor the general tenor of the address on the New Birth warrant such an interpretation. Moody meant to assert the absolute necessity of conversion in the dramatic, conscious, instantaneous, traditional evangelical pietist sense. 'When I was born in 1837,' he said, 'I received my old Adam nature, and when I was born again in 1856 I had another nature given me.' He said that it was impossible to serve God properly unless one had first made up one's mind to be born again—'you must have your salvation before you can work it out'—a deliberate exclusion of any possibility of process. He did not attempt, however, to describe how the New Birth was obtained, beyond saying that 'all men have to do is to accept the work of Jesus Christ', and, in spite of his attacks on other people's alleged religious formalism, this willingness to believe often seemed to amount to little more than a willingness to assent publicly

[11] *The Times*, 19 March, 1875.

to the proposition that Christ had died for men's sins. The force of will that a man had frequently to summon up before he could give public assent to this idea became confused with the existential quality of faith; twentieth-century revivalism was to move on beyond Moody largely by devising situations which reduced the strain which 'inquirers' felt in bringing themselves to the point of making the affirmation. In Moody's own case, however, it was already significant how vague the address on the New Birth became in its second, theoretically more positive part: there was nothing about repentance, nothing likely to lead men to repent, but only the constant repetition of the statement that the New Birth was mandatory, varied by appeals to the evidence of those whose lives had allegedly been transformed by their 'conversion'. At the climax there came nothing more definite than the exhortation, 'Let us get our heart in the Kingdom of God'. Moody, in fact, like his successors, was leaving it open to his hearers to give what sense they liked to 'conversion', as long as they regarded the event as fundamental to their existence, an act distinguishing them from their own private past, and also from all other people who had not similarly been 'converted' and got their hearts into the Kingdom of God. The first distinction was traditional in the American religious world from which Moody and Sankey came; the second was much more important in the later nineteenth century, for it was by producing in the 'converts' this feeling that they had been separated from the ordinary (not necessarily the 'secular') society in which they lived, that the revivalists helped sectarian evangelical Protestantism to survive for another generation in the inimical conditions of the new urban culture.

Moody's success in pressing for immediate response was so great, however, that little open criticism was published in 1875. One of the rare examples came from the obscure hand of the Reverend J. K. Popham, then the pastor of the Particular Baptist Chapel in Shaw Street, Liverpool. Popham was the kind of Baptist who found Charles Spurgeon dangerously liberal in his theology. Any of Popham's contemporaries who read his pamphlet probably dismissed it as old-fashioned and wrong-headed. Most Evangelicals no doubt felt that what was good enough for the *Record* (if with certain qualifications) ought to be good enough even in Shaw Street.[12]

As a Calvinist who would have been at home at the seventeenth-century Synod of Dort, Popham naturally criticized Moody on the ground that he talked in terms of human free will instead of stating clearly that salvation was the divine prerogative. It was because Moody did not understand this, Popham claimed, that he could exhibit 5,000 converts at the Bingley Hall in Birmingham and say sorrowfully that many of them would fall away after he had departed. Popham objected to Moody's description of regeneration as 'coming to Christ as a poor, ruined, lost sinner'—a dead soul, Popham said, could do nothing of the kind, any more than the hundredth sheep, whose salvation Sankey so often celebrated, could have returned to the fold of its own volition. Popham said that Moody had no proper sense of sin, but seemed to think of it as something external which could be dropped at will: he had no idea of the corrupted state of human nature. This last point had theological force, for in his addresses Moody's catalogue of sinners was usually limited to drunkards, prostitutes, and young men or women who had abandoned the safety of the evangelical family for the dangers of the big city; there was also the steel-hearted, impenitent sinner, often a man in late middle age, whose sins were reducible to a final obstinate, wilful refusal to accept the New Birth. Moody could rely on a handful of stock portraits, not even closely related to the majority of the audience in front of him, because his demand for an act of will in Christ's favour was so loosely related to the need for repentance that he had no especial need to stir up feelings of remorse for actual wrong-doing in the hearts of his hearers. In consequence his addresses implied that sin took place in a society remote from the experience of the crowd in the revival hall; if emotion were awakened it was rather the sense of not having been a sufficiently loyal member of the separated community of believers, whose sign and seal was the claim to have been 'converted'. Moody's audience consisted of people drawn from every branch of the pietist world, from the Evangelical

---

[12] Popham came to Liverpool in 1874; he moved on to Brighton in 1882, staying there until his death in 1937. See I. Sellers, *A History of the Liverpool Baptists* (1962).

section of the Church of England to its mirror-image, the Plymouth Brethren, and his demand for an act of will in Christ's favour made its impact on those that were most aware of having (to whatever extent) repudiated the claims of their birth-sect upon them. Moody's frequent references to 'praying mothers' sound like symbolic allusions to the rights of the sects.

Popham's analysis would have been put in different terms, but as he saw it a preacher could only describe the relationship between God and man as it was understood in the hyper-Calvinist tradition; there he had to leave matters, because to try to do more, to take the responsibility for demanding an immediate response to what one had said, was to interfere with the working of the Holy Spirit and so to produce results which must be false.

> Assuming that it is the will of God that every creature should be saved, which is not true, men have made the conversion of sinners an art, and have resorted to all sorts of unscriptural methods to compass their ends. Sadly forgetful of him who said, I kill and I make alive, they are madly bold in their efforts to wrest God's special work out of his hands. We have the new doctrine of regeneration by faith, singing theology, sudden conversions, the inquiry room, sensational advertisements such as 'February for Jesus', 'Liverpool for Jesus', 'Body and Soul for Jesus', etc. And when these new appliances have done their work, the task allotted to them, we have an exhibition of the work done.'[13]

Popham's scorn knew no limit:

> by the galvanizing apparatus now in use at the Victoria Hall, they succeed in evoking 'mere' emotion, and these galvanized but dead saints are then called Christians. Oh horrible blasphemy.[14]

Popham's attitude was typical of the small Strict and Particular Baptist world; this separatist group saw the whole culture external to itself as morally and religiously inferior; the mere size of Moody's triumph was enough to discredit

---

[13] *Moody and Sankey's Errors versus the Scriptures of Truth*, J. K. Popham, of the Particular Baptist Chapel, Shaw Street, Liverpool, 1875, p.9.
[14] Ibid., p.10.

him as far as Popham was concerned; and if one was justified in taking as one's standard the theology of the seventeenth-century Calvinist Baptist tradition, there was no great problem in showing Moody's deviation from the truth. Popham's beliefs corresponded much more closely than Moody's did to the 'old-time religion' which Moody ostensibly championed, and it is now time to examine Moody's use of the ideas of Hell and Heaven, ideas which remained traditional realities for the Baptist, but emerged in a strangely altered form in Moody's addresses.

Moody was preaching in London in 1875 at a time when the educated Protestant laity was slowly driving the doctrines of Hell and eternal punishment into the background of official theology; his career fell between this movement and the reassertion of these doctrines in their older form in Pentecostalism after about 1900. The original operative force was less Biblical than moral criticism, beginning with the Enlightenment. The movement which shuddered at the conditions of life in eighteenth-century prisons and rejected altogether the use of torture as a punishment was unlikely to tolerate the theological claim that finite human sin both deserved and received everlasting retribution at the hands of an angry God. Criticism of the Bible then weakened the argument that, nevertheless, the doctrine of eternal punishment must be accepted, despite its horror, because the Scriptures clearly taught it. Ingenious apologists, like F. D. Maurice, tried to save the form of the doctrine and the face of the Scriptures by showing that the words of the New Testament might be interpreted in such a way as to leave 'eternal' not quite meaning 'eternal' and 'punishment' not quite meaning 'punishment'.[15] As the authority of the Bible lessened, however, people lost interest in this kind of facile solution. A passage from a letter written by J. H. Newman in December, 1849, shows how difficult the subject had become by the middle of the nineteenth century:

As to what you say about eternal punishment, it is to me, as to most men, the great crux of the Christian system as contemplated

[15] The best summary of Maurice's views was his own, in a letter written to the Anglican theologian, F. J. A. Hort, and republished by Maurice's son in *Life of F. D. Maurice*, vol. 2, p.13.

by the human mind—it is to me what the doctrine of pre-
destination is to Ward. But then, *is there to be no trial of faith?*
Another consideration is our utter ignorance of what is meant by
eternity—it is not infinite time. Time implies a process—it
involves the connection and action of one portion upon another—
if eternity be an eternal *now*, eternal punishment is the fact that a
person is suffering;—he suffers today and tomorrow and so on
for ever—but not in a *continuation*—all is complete in every time—
there is no memory, no anticipation, no growth of intensity from
succession. . . . If I be right, then, the question is merely, should a
soul suffer, should sin be punished, which few would deny. . . .
I would add, it is the turning-point between Christianity and
pantheism, it is the critical doctrine—you can't get rid of it—it is
the very characteristic of Christianity. We must therefore look
matters in the face. Is it more probable that eternal punishment
should be true, or that there should be no God; for if there be a
God, there is eternal punishment (*a posteriori*).[16]

Given Newman's final assertions, which would have been
widely accepted among the orthodox, both Catholic and
Protestant, it was hardly surprising that so many early
Victorian intellectuals gave up Christianity in despair. Some
writers in the Evangelical tradition tried to save the 'essential
truth' of orthodoxy by suggesting that the impenitent wicked
were not sentenced to perpetual punishment but annihilated.
An Anglo-Catholic theologian, like Pusey, saw in the
Protestant embarrassment over Hell a chance to press the idea
of Purgatory as an acceptable alternative. There was never
any official, institutional ratification of the changing attitude
of the majority of middle-class Christians, any official admission that the lay majority had stopped believing in the
doctrine of eternal punishment altogether; the problem of
authority in religion had become too acute for the ecclesiastical leadership to demonstrate publicly, by changing its
teaching about Hell, that the leadership might have been
doctrinally mistaken in the past. Theologians also recognized
the danger inherent in allowing that one of the foundation
beliefs of orthodoxy could be abandoned under social and

[16] *The Letters and Diaries of J. H. Newman*, ed. Dessain, vol. XIII, letter to J. M.
Capes, 2 December, 1849. G. Rowell, *Hell and the Victorians* (1974), discusses Roman
Catholic attitudes to Hell at length, but fails to mention revivalism.

intellectual pressure. A new consensus developed slowly, according to which 'Hell' could perhaps be defined as exclusion from the presence of God, an exclusion which was not, however, the will of God himself, but the choice of the individual. This consensus, which did not finally form until the present century, never received official confirmation, but it was vaguely supposed that an appeal to 'the development of doctrine' might cover the situation. The change was all the more important, however, because what was involved was the dropping of past teaching, and not in any real sense its development.

The radical nature of this change, the gradual displacement of the fear of damnation in the middle-class imagination profoundly affected the position of the professional revivalist. As a group, the professional revivalists were conscious of the crisis through which British religion was passing. Men like Moody instinctively sided with the laity on most issues; they normally supported whatever was anti-clerical, in the mild nineteenth-century British sense, in the Churches. Most revivalists therefore followed the mood of the period, making no great attempt to protect the 'Old Time Religion' in detail, quietly abandoning the damnatory rhetoric which had still been used by Weaver and Caughey in the early 1860s. Here can be found part of the explanation of the growth of the Holiness movement, with its revivalist methods, after 1860 and especially after 1875. Phoebe Palmer, Pearsall Smith, William Booth, the Keswick Anglicans all took part in schemes 'to deepen the religious life' as it was often called at the time. At one level this was a protest at the secularizing process at work in Victorian society—a similar protest expressed itself through Anglican monasticism, again after 1860. Neither protest was very effective, since the new monasteries were usually built in rural areas, just as the annual Keswick Convention met in the Lake District, a symbolism of retreat rather than rebuke. At a second level, the appeal to an allegedly objective spiritual experience, that of being instantaneously sanctified, was intended to replace, at a morally unchallengeable point, the kind of ecstatic personal state associated in the past with conversions at fear-motivated revival meetings.

Moody, however, was never strongly drawn to such

solutions, though he sometimes experimented with the holiness theme. When in England he published, for example, *Power from on High*, five addresses on 'success in Christian life and Christian work'. His other chief English publication outside the field of his normal salvation addresses, was *The Second Coming of Christ*, which chimed in with the late nineteenth-century Evangelical interest in the subject. Moody wanted a mass movement, and neither adventism nor perfectionism lent itself to large-scale revivalism. To the extent that he always hoped to draw the poorer classes of the new cities to his meetings, conversion had to remain his aim. His ability to compel his hearers to accept the need for a decisive act to be made before they left the meeting, depended to a large extent on the latent fear which he released in them. For this he relied on the residual force of the traditional Christian vocabulary and imagery; he talked about Hell and Heaven because of the reserves of feeling which such terms could still release, especially in that part of his audience, often the majority, which had been trained to take such language seriously in the sectarian atmosphere of small Victorian chapels and local mission halls.

This does not mean that Moody escaped the influence of either secularization, or of the current moral criticisms of the older forms of Protestantism. It was in response to these influences that he largely secularized the popular ideas of Heaven and Hell, or rather accepted and vulgarized the secularization of them which was already spreading.[17] He brought Heaven down to earth and identified it with the culture of so many of his hearers. As Matthew Arnold wrote, this view of Heaven made it 'a kind of perfected middle-class home, with labour ended, the table spread, goodness all round, the lost ones restored, hymnody incessant. "Poor fragments all of this low earth", Keble might well say.' Arnold's description accurately lists the main themes of the revivalist songbooks, and of Moody's addresses on salvation and Heaven. Moody actually printed a volume of addresses entitled *Heaven*, which described its hope, its inhabitants, its

---

[17] Elizabeth Stuart Phelps, *The Gates Ajar* (1868), was the American 'novel' which heralded the domestication of Heaven; it sold 100,000 in England by 1900. See the edition by Helen S. Smith (Harvard 1964).

riches, its happiness; it had sold about 50,000 in Britain by 1900, having probably been printed about 1882.

Moody secularized Hell as well, partly by making only rare references to its cruder aspects, such as the Devil himself, and partly by emphasizing, not the pains of Hell so much as the pain of the act of God which condemned one to go there, an act thought of in subjective terms as an experience of parental rejection. Moody differed from his predecessors in as much as he talked much more than they did about Heaven; he felt his way towards a new synthesis of the traditional ideas whose temporary success tells us something about the state of English popular culture in the last quarter of the nineteenth century. Early in the twentieth century this precarious combination of Heaven and Hell collapsed: when Billy Graham spoke in England in the 1960s, for example, he was still making appeals to latent fear which bore a close resemblance to Moody's; he constantly threatened his audiences with disasters which united the nuclear peril and the Second Coming; but neither his addresses nor his music, which had declined in every sense since the Victorian period, showed much trace of the late nineteenth-century bourgeois heaven. It seems as though, as serious belief in the possibility of Hell waned, the visualization of Heaven offered a temporary substitute; and this becomes less surprising if one recalls that the growth of Liberal Protestantism meant a shift to a benevolent conception of God who might be supposed to want all his children happy in one big family. At the next stage, however, as belief in the existence of God also waned, belief in Heaven became as difficult as belief in Hell; ideas of damnation, moreover, probably served more psychological purposes than did images of Heaven. There are not many people left in England today who can sing 'Shall we gather at the river?' unselfconsciously, and the number who could was always smaller than the equivalent number in America. Nevertheless Moody and Sankey, and more especially Sankey, persuaded many people to enjoy singing it again and again, not only in the uplifted atmosphere of the Islington rallies, but also to the strains squeezed out of the American organ in the gas-lit parlours of that side street England the memory of which still haunts the lingering death-bed of Nonconformity.

The extent of the change becomes obvious if one compares this situation with the attitude of the Primitive Methodists to the idea of damnation in the early nineteenth century. They had sung with gusto about Hell as a place not far from Staffordshire. In Lorenzo Dow's book of songs were such verses as:

> My scarlet crimes did now appear
> Which sank my soul in black despair;
> My dreadful pains no tongue can tell,
> I thought I felt the pains of Hell.
>
> I thought I saw the burning lake;
> My frightened soul began to quake;
> I cried aloud, Lord, I must go
> To languish in eternal woe.

Dow's songbook also contained the warning songs which Primitive Methodist processions sang as they marched slowly along village streets to fulfil Hugh Bourne's command that they oblige people to hear the words of the gospel even if they refused to come out of their houses.

> Stop, poor sinner, stop and think
> Before you further go.
> Will you sport upon the brink
> Of everlasting woe?
>
> On the verge of ruin stop,
> Now the friendly warning take,
> Stay your footsteps or you'll drop
> Into the burning lake.

By 1914 the Primitive Methodists had almost ceased to sing such words. They were still singing them in the 1870s, however. In October, 1872, for instance, when George Edwards, the Norfolk agricultural labourer who succeeded where Joseph Arch had failed and organized a national union of agricultural workers, took his first service as an exhorter in a Primitive Methodist chapel, his third and closing hymn was 'Stop, poor sinner'. His wife had helped him to learn the words off by heart because he was unable to read. When Edwards told this story in his autobiography he commented, 'Needless to say, I have long ceased to use the hymn, it was too horrible for my humanitarian spirit.'[18]

This change also helps to explain the answer to the question raised by Professor Inglis about Primitive Methodism: why was Primitive Methodism more successful among nineteenth-century working-class groups than were most other religious bodies? and why was the sect unable to maintain its hold in the later part of the century?[19] The answer would seem to be that Primitive Methodism should not be treated as an unchanging entity. In the early nineteenth century it embodied an outbreak of the 'old evangelicalism', suited to the environment and outlook of the English rural worker. After about 1860, a new self-respect, self-education and social aggression, which had been developing for some time within the villages, gradually destroyed the social conditions which had made the sect possible. The leaders became urban, and middle rather than working-class in their outlook; the demand for a hell-fire religion and the will to supply one disappeared. Primitive Methodism remained as an institution; it is a rare thing historically for a religious corporation to go into voluntary liquidation; but the leaders were not deeply concerned to find a new relationship with the agricultural labourer. It is also important to realize that the picture of Primitive Methodism given by writers such as R. F. Wearmouth was misleading.[20] It was true that some miners' leaders in the late nineteenth century had a Primitive Methodist background, but many of them were not *persona grata* with the ecclesiastical leadership of their sect, men who clung to the theology of an earlier period and disliked the political theology of this generation of trade union leaders.

An intelligent working-class radical like George Edwards changed his mind about hell and damnation in the 1880s, released from the grip of tradition by the discovery of fellow-rebels like the Anglican Canon Farrar, but the American revivalists never came to such a clear-cut decision. In his edition of Finney's *Lectures on Revivalism* Professor McLoughlin

[18] George Edwards, *From Crow-Scaring to Westminster* (1922), p.33.
[19] Cf. K. Inglis, *The Churches and the Working Classes in Victorian England* (1966).
[20] See especially, R. F. Wearmouth, *Methodism and the Trade Unions* (1959). Wearmouth wrote extensively on Methodism and the working classes in the nineteenth century.

writes as though, after about 1835, most professional revivalists took the other side from Finney and emphasized the love
of God instead of the wrath. This was not the case in England,
where the most prominent American revivalist between 1840
and 1860, James Caughey, defended the doctrine of eternal
punishment and constantly threatened his audiences with the
wrath of God. When someone suggested to him in 1842 that
an infinite penalty was too great for what was only a finite sin,
Caughey replied that a sinner dying continued a sinner through
all eternity. 'The torments of hell can no more put an end to
the soul's sinning than a pump in a river could drain it dry.'
Applied to damnation, Caughey's rhetoric sounded like this:

> Hear me, oh you careless ones. . . . Already you are performing
> those mysterious circles, verging rapidly to the maelstrom of Hell.
> Sin, like the intoxicating cup, fascinates you. Again and again the
> report of our solitary signal gun has boomed in your ears. We have
> approached within hailing distance. We offer you assistance. . . .
> Your circles in the fatal influence are becoming narrower. The
> parting ray of salvation, perhaps the last one, is now falling on
> your head. Let your numbers be lessened. . . . Will nothing avail?
> Darkness is gathering round you fast. We may see you no more.
> God have mercy on the doomed then. But hear it earth and
> heaven and hell, angels, men and devils—they doom themselves.
> See, see, the doomed, the doomed. Farewell. Perhaps before
> morning trembles over our sky you may have disappeared under
> the skies of blackness and darkness for ever and ever.

Caughey's urban audiences swallowed his threats for the
sake of their melodramatic utterance. The English lay
revivalists about 1860 used much the same language as that of
the early Primitive Methodists. Their paper, *The Revival*,
warmly applauded. 'Mr Weaver knows the terror of God', the
editor wrote, 'lest the blood of murdered souls should stain
his skirts.' Even in 1860 the old-fashioned nature of this
approach helps to explain Weaver's limited impact in London.
His speciality was the death of the unbeliever, a favourite
subject of eighteenth-century preachers, and an admirer
recorded the effect of one of these addresses on one occasion:

> Infidelity is dark, dismal, dreadful. Listen to yonder dying

sceptic. Death is coming and it grows darker. Now for the grand secret. Dark, dark, dark. 'I think I have been deceived. Oh, the waters are cold. Oh, what's that? The devil has seized me. What a fool I have been. I am going down the stairs into the eternal vaults. I hear the howling of the damned and I see the flames of hell. Oh, the devilish infidelity. My feet are already in the flames. I am lost, lost, LOST.' As Weaver uttered each of the last three words in our Church he descended one step of the pulpit stair, striking it so heavily with his heel that the dull thud was a weird accompaniment to the despairing shriek, 'Lost'. It was awful.[21]

Faced by the menace of *Essays and Reviews* (1860), Samuel Wilberforce fell back on the same tactics in a sermon which provoked J. M. Ludlow to exclaim:

Do you think that any man fit to be called a man could ever be worked on for any good purpose by that highly wrought picture of a doubter's death?

He compared Wilberforce with Job's three comforters and said,

There is the same hardness and want of sympathy with one of the most acute, I would almost say the most sacred, of human miseries; the same use of threats and bullying to crush struggles which need rather the tenderest help.

Wilberforce was about fifty-five years of age in 1860; the parallel with Weaver is interesting because it shows that Weaver was not simply an isolated survival from an earlier popular religion; on the other hand Wilberforce was a good example of how under-educated a member of the nineteenth-century Anglican episcopate could be. The classic defence of this style of preaching might be found in an Exeter Hall lecture given to the Y.M.C.A. by Baptist Noel in 1850:

If the sinner is not sinking into Hell—why, smoothly and blandly flatter him. But if the fact is that every unconverted man will sink into Hell unless he is regenerate by the Holy Spirit, then tell him the truth. . . . It is reasonable that they should be alarmed.[22]

[21] *Richard Weaver's Life Story*, ed. Rev. J. Paterson of the White Memorial Church, Glasgow, n.d. but after 1896, when Weaver died.
[22] *Twelve Lectures delivered before the Y.M.C.A. in Exeter Hall* (1851), p.186. Noel's lecture was called 'A Revival of Religion'.

The bridge between this rhetoric and a plainer style may be found in the preaching of Spurgeon (1834–92), who had no doubts about the reality of damnation.

> You man yonder—who is it that died but a few days ago? The woman that loved you as she loved her own soul; she idolized you; she thought you an angel. Shall I say it before God and to your face—you ruined her. And what next, sir? You cast her off as though she were but dirt and threw her into the kennel with a broken heart. And being there, her God having cast her off—for you were her God—she fell into despair, and despair led to dreadful consequences, and to direr ruin still. She is gone, and you are glad of it, you will hear no more of her now, you say. Sir, you shall hear of it, you shall hear of it, you shall hear of it. As long as you live her spirit shall haunt you; track you to the filthy joy you have planned for a future day; and on your death-bed she shall be there to twist her fingers in your hair, to tear your soul out of your body, and drag it to the hell appointed for such fiends as you are.[23]

Or on another occasion:

> If, after once having put your hands to the plough you look back, you are unworthy of the Kingdom; but what are you worthy of? Why, those reserved seats in Hell. . . . There are such, and let me quote a passage that proves it. We are told in one place of darkness 'reserved' for some who were 'wandering stars', for whom 'is reserved the blackness of darkness for ever'. When you turn back you turn back to those reserved places where the darkness is more black and the pain is more terrible.[24]

As a speaker Moody could not compete with the vigour of Spurgeon's style, but he certainly preached about damnation in all the major centres of his mission when he came to England in the 1870s. He had a sermon specifically on the subject, which was printed, without his permission, as a sermon about Hell, and others which resembled it, such as 'Saved or Lost'. In England, at any rate, these addresses were

[23] 'Am I clear of his Blood?", sermon preached at the Metropolitan Tabernacle, July, 1862.
[24] 'Turning back in the Day of Battle', sermon preached at the Metropolitan Tabernacle, n.d.

not reprinted very often after 1875, and Moody did not include the two mentioned above in the volume of addresses which he published himself in 1875. This volume, later republished by Morgan and Scott as *Where Art Thou?* contained: Where art Thou; There is no Difference; Good News; Christ seeking Sinners; Sinners seeking Christ; Excuses (two); The Blood (two); and Heaven. Both are to be found in *The London Discourses of Mr. D. L. Moody*, issued by James Clarke in 1875, 'as delivered in the Agricultural Hall and Her Majesty's Opera House, from the notes of special shorthand writers'. This volume contained: 'God's Human Instruments; Christ Seeking the Lost; Saved or Lost; The One Alternative; Man seeking God; The Call to Self-Examination; The New Birth; A Sermon of One Word; The Jailer's Question Answered; The Master's Parting Commission; Excuses (two); A Sermon about Hell; A Sermon about Heaven; The Healer of Broken Hearts; The Right Kind of Faith; An Answer to the Great Question; A Call to Slumbering Professors; The Blood (two). This was not an official publication; it is significant that *D. L. Moody, His Life and Twenty-Two Addresses*, edited by W. R. Moody and A. P. Fitt, also omitted the more directly damnatory sermons. This was hardly a question of dishonesty, but rather suggests an awareness of the changing climate, in which Moody himself, while prepared to use the sermon on the doctrine of damnation for revivalistic purposes, was not over-anxious to appear in public to be doing so.

When Moody preached about Hell he made no concessions but played on the remnants of fear in the minds of his hearers. A contemporary account of a meeting at Manchester in December, 1874, when he used the printed sermon Hell, said that in former days Moody's words would have provoked wild enthusiasm and emotion; 'we seemed to be looking across the gulf that divides time from eternity and beholding the torments of the self-destroyed victims of a broken law and a rejected gospel'. That night the inquiry-rooms were full. Once again one notices the insistence that the victims are 'self-destroyed': this was partly because the revivalist was proposing to save his converts from this terrible fate; and partly because of the need now felt to save God from the reproach of actually condemning anyone to eternal punishment.

The text of the sermon on Hell was Luke 16.25: 'Son, remember'. As one would expect, Moody, who began by saying that if he didn't believe in the existence of Hell he would have burned his Bible and caught the next boat home to America, described Hell in terms of the break-up of a human family, an image which formed a natural antithesis to his image of Heaven as the centre of family reunion. The existence of Hell meant that a time was coming for the families before him when husband and wife, parents and children might be parted for ever if any one of them died without accepting Christ. And once this family unit had been shattered it could never be recreated. 'There will be no Bible in the next world,' Moody said, 'no teachers, no friends, no Church. . . . You may have a praying wife now that weeps over you . . . but there will be no wife there to weep over you.' Hell, in fact, was the absolute opposite of a respectable Victorian home, and Moody seemed almost to exult in this prospect of separation, to feel a kind of power implicit in his own utterance when he made assertions of this kind about another world. Moody told the story of a woman who had tried to prevent her daughter from entering the inquiry-rooms because she did not want her to associate with Christians—a word which had a special sense in Moody's language, of course, meaning those who shared the 'new evangelical' point of view. 'Is there such a mother here tonight?' he continued, 'May God have mercy on you.' He pointed out that although a decent girl would shudder if, on her way home from the meeting, she was spoken to by a drunken man, in Hell her only company would be that of libertines, drunkards and murderers.

This part of the address was attacked savagely by a Glasgow Unitarian minister, John Page Hopps, who said that even in this world a genuinely wicked woman who was put in prison would not expect to be shut up with drunkards, libertines and murderers. Why should such travesties of justice happen in the world to come? 'We are further behind than we hoped we were,' Hopps said, 'the religion of the nation is still the religion of brutality and fear: the dread of Christendom is

Hell; its hope is Blood; and it is left to a Unitarian—like the voice of one crying in the wilderness—to rebuke this horrible profanity and speak a word for humanity and God.'[25]

The paragraph to which Hopps referred did not appear in the London version of the address, but apart from this passage the correspondence between the two accounts is so exact that I see no reason to reject these as Moody's words. They say rather strongly what he was saying anyhow, and they probably represented a momentary illustration which Moody did not keep in a permanent form. The passage brought out the sub-Christian note in Moody's addresses to which Hopps rightly drew attention; Moody might have justified his position in terms of the traditional theology, but he would have found it much harder to justify the tone which he employed. Hopps accused Moody of enjoying the picture of the young woman lost among the drunkards and the libertines: this was his personal reaction, but one is conscious of Moody's strong will to exercise power over his hearers, his need to make them suffer, and this I take to be essential in the professional revivalist's make-up. What the incident also illustrated was that prison reformers and penal theorists like Elizabeth Fry were more effective solvents of theological orthodoxy than the Biblical critics, for what made eternal punishment incredible to so many in the long run was the change in the civilized attitude to prisons and punishment, the decay in serious belief in the value of retributive punishment.

Moody ended this address with two long stories, one of which was based on the parent-child relationship and the other on the husband-wife relationship: these relationships formed the dramatic structure of most of Moody's anecdotes. In the first story, the son had become divided from his parents. (In Moody's stories this was almost always the child's fault.) In the second, the husband was estranged from his wife. The first story was frankly sentimental, again characteristic of his method. A wicked young man, who had already broken his mother's heart, came home for what was clearly the last time. His father could not persuade him to stay, and so lay in his path across the threshold of the front of the house. The young

---

[25] *Mr. Moody's Late Sermon, Hell,* a lecture by John Page Hopps (T. Bennet, Glasgow 1875), p.5.

man only laughed, leaped over his father's body and disappeared (for ever) into the night. At the conscious level of argument Moody concluded that to enter Hell you had to trample on the Son of God; in this instance the Son of God was revealingly identified with the earthly father. This, however, was a minor aspect of the analogy, which has also to be understood in terms of such books as *The Way of All Flesh* if one is to grasp the kind of emotional response which Moody was seeking. Victorian family relationships were soaked in guilt: the guilt of filial disobedience as well as of immoral obedience, the guilt of despotism as well as the guilt of immoral exploitation. Moody brought all this confused, poignant feeling to the surface in a wave of repentance and remorse; he also prompted the thought that just as filial disobedience might become absolute, so might disobedience to God become absolute, and that God's rejection of the sinner might be as absolute as the parent's rejection of his child often seemed to be in everyday life.

This point was then taken up and elaborated in the final story, which was about the death of an unbeliever, just like the stories to be found in the sermons of Caughey and Weaver and Wilberforce. This unbeliever had almost become a Christian on several occasions but had never finally committed himself because of fear of the mockery of his friends. Once when he felt himself seriously ill he told Moody that he would repent, but when he unexpectedly recovered he again put off his repentance. Then, suddenly, he lay on his real death-bed. Moody visited him, and found the man insisting that he was bound to go to Hell—'it is too late, my damnation is sealed'. He told Moody that it was useless to pray for him and Moody said that when he did pray for him he found that it was impossible, the heavens were as brass. 'He lingered until the sun went down. His wife told me his end was terrible. All that he was heard to say were these fearful words, "The harvest is past and the summer is ended and I am not saved". These were his dying words. He lived a Christless life, he died a Christless death; we wrapped him in a Christless shroud, nailed him in a Christless coffin and bore him to a Christless grave.' The appeal followed.[26]

[26] In this case the use of fear as a motive was quite explicit.

The menace of this allegedly true story was that even in this life there might come a stage at which the disobedient child was already rejected by the Heavenly Father. The words, 'the harvest is past and the summer is ended and I am not saved', referred not only to Jeremiah 8.20, but also to a revivalist song well-known in the earlier nineteenth century. The song from which they were taken was included in *Richard Weaver's Hymnbook* (1861), in which it was numbered 20; Moody's reference suggests an American origin. The two most striking verses ran:

> Thousands now in Hell are crying
> All is lost;
> Amid eternal flames they're lying,
> All is lost.
> The summer's o'er, the harvest's past,
> The dye, the dreadful dye, is cast,
> And threatened woe is come at last,
> All is lost.
>
> They wring their hands and tear their hair, etc.,
> Their souls are filled with black despair, etc.,
> Like smoke their endless torments rise,
> They feel the worm that never dies,
> While unavailing are their cries,
> All is lost.

If the story were true as Moody told it, the victim might have been one of the cases of Calvinistic despair, like that of Spiera in Italy in the sixteenth century, a case well-known in the Anglo-Saxon Protestant tradition. Spiera was executed in Padua about 1550, believing himself to be damned because he had sinned against the Holy Spirit when he abjured Protestantism before the civic authorities. According to the theory which Moody was using the unbelieving man had 'grieved the Spirit': this explained why Moody found himself unable to pray for him, and this was why the unfortunate sufferer, no doubt mentally as well as physically ill, repeated passively that the harvest was past, in other words, that it was already too late for him to be pardoned by God. The sting of the threat of Hell in late nineteenth-century 'new Evangelical' teaching was that at any moment it might become too late to avoid this withdrawal of the interest of God, the departure of the Spirit, which meant that a final condemnation had been passed. This governed the form of Moody's concluding appeal, of which the following example was recorded at Manchester in 1874:

> He requested any who wished to be prayed for to rise. He quietly repeated the invitation. One was seen to stand in the left-hand gallery and cover his face with his hands; another in the area. Mr Moody said, There is one risen; thank God for that. Another: and another. Christians, keep on praying. Another. Jesus is passing by. You may never again have so many Christians praying for you. . . .[27]

At an earlier stage in this address Moody had said: 'You came here tonight to hear Mr Sankey sing "Jesus of Nazareth Passes By"—but bear in mind that you will not hear that song in the lost world; or, if you do, it will not be true—He does not pass that way.'[28]

In view of the enthusiasm with which Moody warned people against grieving the Spirit, and the repeated use of 'Jesus of Nazareth' during the London Mission, it is difficult to agree with, for example, W. D. McLoughlin, that the distinction between Finney and Moody was that Moody was the revivalist who emphasized the mercy of God's love (cf. *Modern Revivalism*, pp.249–50). In Moody's preaching both the Father and the Son retain an arbitrary power of rejection which the preacher used as a threat, and which did not resemble mercy. Moody wanted to avoid picturing God as actually sending a man to Hell: he therefore transferred the responsibility to the individual who rejected the revivalist's offer of salvation; but this did not conceal the fact that God had set up the system which Moody was administering, or that it culminated in merciless punishment for the impenitent in a world of the lost which Jesus did not even enter. Nor can one accept the view (ibid., p.247) that Moody taught that a man so hardened

[27] *Narrative of Messrs. Moody and Sankey's Labours in Scotland and Ireland, also in Manchester, Sheffield, and Birmingham, England* compiled from *The British Evangelist* and *The Christian* (New York 1875), p.97.

[28] *Mr Moody's Late Sermon, Hell*, a lecture by John Page Hopps (T. Bennet, Glasgow 1875), pp.4–5.

himself by persistent rejection of God that God 'could no longer help him'. The process was not so psychological; the whole point of the threat was that the individual did not know when he had passed the point after which, as Moody phrased it, God *would* not help him. This was quite apart from the Calvinistic assumption that men commonly reached a point beyond which an allegedly omnipotent and merciful deity could not assist them. This was why the threat was introduced into the closing appeal: no one in the audience could be sure, by the time Moody had finished, that if he refused to surrender on this occasion God would ever give him a second chance. The mood conjured up was not unlike that of the second century Apostolic Father, Hermas, who thought of God as merciful because, despite the salvation rules which He himself had established, He was prepared *on this occasion* (i.e. the writing of *The Shepherd*, by Hermas as intermediary), to forgive the otherwise unforgiveable sins committed after baptism. Even the Primitive Church rejected Hermas' teaching in the long run, but the revivalist dared not be too merciful.

Moody's other significant sermon of this type was 'Saved or Lost?', which the shorthand reporters heard in London at the Islington Agricultural Hall on 11 March, 1875.[29] Moody's theme, which he introduced right at the beginning, was that 'every man and woman in this meeting must either be saved or lost if the Bible is true'—a less ambitious statement than it might have looked at first sight. What was interesting was the string of illustrations which Moody used in order to drive his subject home. With the exception of a stock story about Rowland Hill and Lady Erskine, his anecdotes centred on the parent-child relationship. His stories taken together left the impression that the universe was cruel, violent and unpredictable, created by a God who must be accepted on his own terms.

Moody started with a short story about a Chicago woman who brought her child to a doctor to be told that it was blind —but that if she had brought the child three days before its sight might have been saved. What was the loss of sight compared to the loss of one's soul, Moody argued, but he had contrived to leave the feeling of arbitrariness as well: the story

[29] *London Discourses*, op. cit.

already made the point with which we are familiar, that one must be saved now, in this meeting, if one were to be sure that it was not too late. The second anecdote was about a party of Sunday School children who were taken on an outing. One little boy fell under the wheels of the train and the whole of the train passed over him.

> The train went back and the body was found so mangled that the School Superintendent had to take off his coat to tie up the mangled corpse.

The Sunday School teachers went to tell the child's parents; inevitably, this was an only child. The young man who had originally told Moody the story continued:

> I cannot tell you what I suffered when the mother came rushing out to me and said: 'Where is my boy? Where are his remains? Take me to them, that I may see them.' I told the mother that the body was so mangled that she could not identify it, and she fainted away at my feet.

The superficial lesson was the same as before—the loss of a child was awful, but it was nothing compared to the loss of one's soul. As to whose soul was in danger, Moody shifted the point of attack suddenly, suggesting that if the Sunday School scholar had not been killed by the train he might have grown up to be a drunkard. With a quick reference to the fact that he himself had a son, he went on:

> I tell you, my friend, I would rather have a train a hundred miles long run over my boy, so that I could not find a speck of his body—than have him grow up to manhood and die without God and without hope. It is a terrible thing for a man to die outside the ark.

He went straight into another illustration about a mother and child. Her son left home; he went to London; he died there, a drunkard. This time Moody's refrain probed the wound ruthlessly, as though he were unaware of how ordinary a story he had just told. He asserted that although the mother might still be mourning her son, she must do so without hope, because the Bible said that no drunkard should inherit the Kingdom of God.

Here Moody was asserting openly both the doctrine of eternal punishment and the view that the fate of the soul turned on the state it was in at the moment of death. Even though Pusey accepted the latter point, one can still hear him protesting that of course the woman in Moody's story must hope, if only because she could not be certain that in the very last flicker of consciousness there was not the first flicker of repentance, which God would willingly meet. At this point conventional labels ceased to count, for Moody, who regarded himself as an archetypal Protestant, the guardian of revelation, was preaching a sub-Christian Calvinism, while Pusey, the Anglo-Catholic, felt obliged to defend what amounted to salvation by a minimally merited grace. Now, after a moment of deliberate relief with Rowland Hill and Lady Erskine, Moody approached his climax, which depended upon another anecdote about a mother, this time with a little, dying child.

There was a consummate cruelty in this succession of stories. A modern reader of the address might interpret them as an unconscious attack on God and the government of the universe; it is significant that even in the late nineteenth century Leslie Stephen or a Russian radical would have understood this collection of savage, futile disasters in that way. Moody believed, however, and the success of his methods confirmed his belief, that most of his audience still accepted the idea of God's existence, and that he could use the horrors of life in a great city as a reflection of the power and even of the ruthlessness of God, without being in any danger of stirring up a critical resistance to the God whose service he sought to recommend. What emerges from these stories is Moody's underlying loyalty to the Calvinistic tradition of the sovereignty of the Creator. He had, as a would-be 'modern' revivalist who allegedly made no use of 'emotion' in his meetings, to claim that he did not frighten people into repentance with pictures of Hell and Damnation; he was the Brutus of professional revivalism, who bettered the statistical results of his predecessors by using plain speech in a quiet way; God, it was said, honoured his faith and his adherence to the simple Gospel. In addresses like the one which we are studying, however, he played on his hearers' residual fear of Hell, on their fear of death, and on a steadily incited fear of

God. As for emotion, Moody held back the expression of emotion until he had fully prepared its nature; in this instance, the story of the mother and her dying child had to be told first.

Told at great length, this tale of a little dying boy epitomized one side of the Evangelical tradition. His mother thought that her son was 'sweetly trusting in Christ, but one day as he drew along towards the chamber of death, she came into his room and he said, as he was looking out of the window: "Mother, what are those mountains that I see yonder?" His mother said, "Eddie, there is no mountain in sight of the house." "Don't you see them, mother?" said he, "they're so high and so dark. Eddie has got to cross those mountains. Won't you take him in your arms and carry him across those mountains?" His mother said, "Eddie, I would if I could but I cannot." ' Moody interrupted here to drive home his point: 'Now I want to say to you that there is a time coming when your mother cannot help you'—reiterating the point that there would be no mother to pray for one in Hell. Moody then went on to tell how the mother prayed with the child and how in the end the boy said, no doubt because he had grasped what would please his mother and like so many children was anxious to the last to gain her affection, that he could see the angels on the other side of the mountain. Even then his mother, the acme of Evangelical perfection, said that she could not carry him to them but that he must trust in Jesus. The last sentences sum up so much of the unnecessary agony that the Evangelical system inflicted on children in its heyday. 'At length he closed his eyes and said, "Good-bye, mama, Jesus is coming to carry me over the mountains"—and the little sufferer was gone. . . .' Little sufferer, indeed, but one crucified upon a human dilemma, 'saved or lost'.

Moody's reaction to the growing criticism of the doctrine of eternal punishment may now be summarized. He dropped from most of his addresses and from most of the songs sung by Shankey, the older kind of frank reference to devils, fire and torture. Instead, he implied that there was an element of tyranny in the government of the universe, a capacity and a willingness in God, Father, Son or Holy Spirit, to reject the human soul once and for all, even before death. The summer had ended, the harvest was past, and the obstinate sinner would never now be saved. All this was made clear in the story of the little, dying child. It was not that Moody thought of the child as really resisting a divine Spirit: there is no sign that Moody ever thought seriously about what he was saying. It was simply that the child must consciously comply with the Evangelical pattern of salvation as Moody understood it—must use the appropriate phrases with whatever idea of their meaning—or the angels on the other side of the mountain would watch his death impassively, without budging a wing, as though painted on the background of a Flemish master. Unless the child said that he was now trusting in Jesus, his death would be final, he would be rejected once and for all. Moody's Jesus did not pass through the lost world, from which the praying mother would also be eternally divided. Instead, 'all these long years Cain can remember what might have been'. There seems to have been an inner coldness and brutality in Moody; it was hardly surprising that when he made his appeal, and allowed those in front of him to express their emotion, they should have preferred his Heaven to his Hell.

Apart from the cruelty, what stood out was the individualism, and here it is necessary to fit Moody into his context. He had come to England at what, in retrospect, was a fatal time for the British Evangelical, and especially Anglican Evangelical, society. Michael Hennell, for example, in a paper called 'Evangelicals and the World, 1770–1870', has argued that whereas in 1770 the small group of Anglican Evangelicals thought of the world as belonging to God, and so initiated a tradition of trying to change it, which bore remarkable fruit in the careers of men like William Wilberforce and Lord Shaftesbury, by about 1870 the much larger Anglican Evangelical party in the Church of England increasingly saw the world as in the grip of the Devil, and consequently as something to be feared and fled; renewed emphasis on the inner life of the soul was to lead on from Moody to the holiness revivalism of Pearsall Smith, the family was exalted above all other human relations, and there was a fresh enthusiasm for missionary work among primitive peoples, which, in its turn, might also be interpreted as a flight from the problems of being religious in a sophisticated Western society in the late nineteenth century.[30] Men in this mood responded to Moody's invitation to declare themselves against the forces of evil; they felt at home in an atmosphere of embattled isolation; they could justify what was also the triumph of the pietism of the 'new evangelicalism' by pointing to the size of the American breakthrough. It may have been Moody's chief importance that at a critical moment his salvationist individualism seemed to many Anglican Evangelicals to set the seal of a divine approval on their own isolationism. All over Europe, in Catholic France, in Lutheran Germany and in Anglican England, the professional middle-class recoiled at the sight of the new democracy, urban, multitudinous, industrialized; there was a cobbling together of religious and pseudo-religious platforms from which the leaders could denounce the vulgarity, lack of standards and materialism of the new mass civilization. It would be unfair to call Moody one of the many fathers of later right-wing political extremism, but his social significance lay in the boost which he (among many others) gave to the self-dramatization of the professional classes of Europe, to their impulse to withdraw into a potentially destructive role.[31]

2. The Inquiry-Room

ONE of the chief causes of controversy in 1875 was the inquiry-room. Moody was obliged to defend its use before he even commenced his London meetings. Addressing a preparatory conference held in London in February, 1875, he said:

> People say that we are establishing the confessional. I don't think that we are. . . . We ask those who would like to be spoken to quietly and privately to step into another room. An impression

[30] In *Studies in Church History*, Vol. VIII, ed. G. J. Cuming and D. Baker (1971), pp.229-36. Dr Hennell would not necessarily agree with the implications of my summary.

[31] One must distinguish British Nonconformity here: for other historical reasons the Free Church groups remained active in Liberal Party politics until 1914; after that they moved to the right in their turn; but they were less susceptible to Moody's ethos in the 1870s as a result.

has gone out that there is great excitement in these meetings, but the fact is that we do not allow any noise. . . . Latterly, we have not taken the names of these persons—we found at Edinburgh the taking of names kept away a good many of the upper classes.[32]

His reference to the confessional has to be understood in terms of the Anglo-Catholic revivalism in London in 1869 and 1874, when after-meetings had been used to urge people to go to confession. According to the High Church *Guardian*,[33] a clergyman who described himself as 'a red-hot ritualist' attended this preparatory meeting and asked whether ritualistic advisers would be allowed to work in Moody's inquiry-rooms? This caused great emotion; Moody, knowing that large-scale success depended upon the willing co-operation of the Churches, seemed anxious not to commit himself. He said vaguely that when a man entered the inquiry-room they pointed him straight to Christ, his answer implying that he did not mind who did the pointing as long as that was the direction in which the pointing was done. He failed to satisfy all those who were present and one minister was quoted by the *Guardian* as saying that 'if an inquirer came to me that was a ritualist I would not send him to a Ritualist minister';[34] this was what most of the Evangelicals at the conference wanted Moody to say. The *Record* printed the *Christian*'s version of what happened: the *Christian* did not refer to the ritualist, but left the impression that only evangelical ministers would be permitted to work in the inquiry-rooms, together with reliable laymen if the supply of ministers ran out.[35] This looked like a final clerical protest against the laymen of the 'new evangelicalism', but in practice Moody's success made these limitations academic, and the inquiry-rooms were full of counselling laymen. In the actual state of Victorian church politics, it was unlikely that many High Church clergy would

[32] *Record*, 12 February, 1875, quoting *The Christian*. Many of the clergy who heard Moody at this time had already had experience of after-meetings of one kind and another.
[33] *Guardian*, 17 February, 1875. *The Christian* made no direct reference to the presence of the ritualist.
[34] *Guardian*, 17 February, 1875. The paper was not a friendly witness, but this report does not sound unduly biased.
[35] *Record*, 12 February, 1875.

apply for admission to the inquiry-rooms. On the other hand, nothing mattered more to all the ministers than what happened to those who claimed (or were claimed) to have been 'converted'; most evangelical ministers in 1875, of whatever denomination, would have regarded it as their duty to prevent such people from falling into the hands of the Anglo-Catholics. The knowledge that this was so did not encourage the Anglo-Catholic clergy to support Moody's meetings in their own congregations. Moody himself never had much personal control over this situation, which remained an unalterable fact throughout the 1875 campaign.

When the London meetings began, Moody used the noon-day prayer-meeting at the Exeter Hall as a platform on which to advertise his success and to defend himself against attacks. In the first week he twice had to defend the inquiry-room system. To begin with, he had to cope with critics who said that a preacher could only sow the seed of conversion and that to press people further in the inquiry-rooms was to interfere with the work of the Holy Spirit; this was partly a Calvinist objection, and partly an objection which arose from the common experience that revival 'converts' by no means all became permanent members of the religious community.[36] A day or two later Moody, when much the same point was raised, said that the revivalists must have a chance to persuade the inquirers to turn their attention away from themselves to the Word of God; it was no good just telling people to go home and pray and go to church and that everything would be all right.[37]

Adverse comments on the subject continued throughout the London meetings. In April, for instance, 'A Pastor of Twelve Years Standing' wrote to the *Record*, saying that he had entered the inquiry-room at the Islington Hall without being challenged, although he did not have one of the worker's tickets which had been issued as a way of meeting the criticism that the inquiry-rooms were not properly supervised. 'It was difficult to discover who were workers and who were inquirers,' he wrote, 'and I was accosted several times and demanded to tender account of my spiritual state, on one

[36] *Record*, 12 March, 1875.
[37] *Record*, 15 March, 1875.

occasion by a youth of considerably less than half my age.[38]
The Pastor gave the impression that there was little super-
vision or instruction as to what should be said. In the background to such letters (and this one was not contradicated in
the pages of the *Record*) was the constant struggle between
clerical and lay elements for the control of the revival itself;
the clergy disliked the preponderance of laymen in the
inquiry-rooms; the laymen had for the moment turned
inwards, identifying themselves with the evangelical sub-
culture, unwilling to acquiesce in a clerical monopoly of
talking and directing. In May, 1875, the Archbishop of
Canterbury, claiming to have made his own enquiries, strongly
criticized the inquiry-room in an open letter:

> If there is a difficulty in the clergy generally giving any official
> sanction to the details of the work, you will at once see that, in
> the case of Bishops, there are greater difficulties in the way of any
> direct sanction, which, coming from them, could not be regarded
> as other than official and authoritative, and I confess that the
> objections I originally felt still remain in full force, now that we
> have had time to examine and to learn from various quarters the
> exact nature of the movement. That addresses urging, in whatever
> homely language, the great truths of the gospel on our people's
> consciences should be delivered by laymen is no innovation
> amongst us, and I heartily rejoice that the present movement is
> conducted on so great a scale and with such apparent success. It
> is chiefly from the 'after meetings for confession of sin and for
> guidance of the conscience', as they have been described to me,
> that I am apprehensive lest evil may arise. I cannot think that the
> delicate and difficult duty of thus ministering to anxious souls
> ought to be intrusted to any who have neither been set apart by
> the Church for this especial office, not have given proof of such a
> spiritual insight as may in certain cases be held to take the place, in
> this particular, of the regular call to the cure of souls. I cannot but
> fear, from what I have heard, that the counsel given at these
> meetings must often be crude, and founded upon no knowledge
> of the real circumstances of those to whom it is addressed, while
> there is danger also lest some self-constituted advisers of others
> may do harm to themselves, seeking to be leaders, when in truth
> they have much need to be led. I learn also, that in the organiza-
> tion for addressing God publicly in prayer, a great deal too much

[38] *Record*, 16 April, 1875.

is trusted to the readiness of any one who may be present to accept, without due preparation, the grave responsibility of guiding the devotions of the multitude assembled.

These objections are quite independent of others, which I have heard urged upon good authority, against particular statements as to doctrine said to be made without sufficient guard or explanation. I am not alluding so much to any depreciation of the ordinances which Christ has established for the edification of His Church, but rather to the allegation that, in the discourses of the missionaries, there are unwise and untrue representations of the almost universal necessity of instantaneous conversion, and an ignoring of the full Scriptural teaching as to the nature of repentance. I cannot but trust that, if these allegations be true, friendly remonstrance may induce those who direct such missionary efforts hereafter, to avoid these obstacles to their real spiritual success.

It has been said also, probably with truth, that the great majority of those who have frequented these services hitherto have been the ordinary worshippers in church and chapels, and that comparatively few from the neglected masses of society have been reached. No doubt there is, among the respectable classes, much selfish and self-satisfied indifference, out of which it is well that the preacher's voice should startle them. But, I confess I rejoice to hear that the missionaries have now moved to that part of London which is especially inhabited by the neglected poor, and I trust that it will be found that their congregations are gathered from such as have been hitherto strangers to the sound of the Gospel.[39]

Not much correspondence on the subject now appears in Tait's papers, but the kind of letter which he judged credible still exists.[40] Thus John Moorhouse, writing from The Vicarage, Paddington West, said that he feared that Moody and Sankey 'will lead people to make too much of superficial emotion'. He also said that 'the great mass of godless working-people have not yet been touched by the American revivalists. At Astley's Amphitheatre I did not see a dozen persons in the vast throng belonging to that class—and I have been told by

[39] Dated 18 May, 1875. Copy in Tait's Private Papers, Lambeth. It was addressed to Cairns.

[40] J. C. Pollock, in *Moody without Sankey*, p.149, said that Tait's enquiries had apparently provided a false picture, but he gives no evidence for the assertion. As I point out elsewhere (pp.213–4), Tait's doctrinal criticism was certainly justified.

friends who have attended meetings at the Agricultural Hall that their experience is the same as mine'. But he added that 'vast numbers of the lower middle class are stirred to a life of deeper piety, of more decided godliness.'[41] This was much the balance of the Archbishop's own letter.

Another clergyman, William Cadman, whose address was Trinity Rectory, Marylebone, also said that he had not advanced beyond 'watchful and prayerful interest'. He criticized the organization:

> in connexion with Messrs Moody and Sankey's movement there are a number of exciteable and not over discreet persons who are engaged in house to house visitation, and employed in the Enquiry Rooms, and whose rashness and inexperience, or even perhaps conceit in some young persons, must be attended with danger both to doctrine and practice.[42]

Neither correspondent spoke directly about the inquiry-room, but it is also clear from the disappointed letter which Lord Cairns sent to Tait after the publication of the Archbishop's views, that Cairns had apparently never entered the inquiry-rooms himself. Not everyone felt the need to produce evidence of that kind. Tait preserved another letter, from a supporter of the revivalists, which said that the most inexperienced assistant at one of the after-meetings was a safer guide of the conscience than any ritualistic or Colensic clergyman.

Few discussions of the inquiry-room departed from this general ground. In one case, however, a book by the Rev. John Macpherson, one comes closer to what happened. Macpherson, a supporter of Moody, denied the charge that the inquiry-room was another form of the Roman Catholic confessional. There was, he replied, no priest, no confession of specific sins, and no absolution. 'The inquirer asks, What shall I do? the Christian worker explains the text, "Believe on the Lord Jesus Christ and be saved".'[43] This description of

---

[41] Tait, Private Papers, vol. 94, pp.175–8. Dated 25 March, 1875.

[42] Ibid., pp.179–80. Dated 25 March, 1875. Tait knew from the Hon. A. Kinnaird, who wrote to him 8 March, 1875 (ibid., pp.107–10), that Radcliffe was organizing visitations in London. Kinnaird added, 'You are aware that the meetings have been very crowded everywhere, that Mr Moody has always had a few tickets for Clergy and Ministers, so as to ensure their getting in, and I shall be very happy to furnish you with tickets at any time that you might like to have any' (ibid).

[43] J. Macpherson, *A Record of the Labours of D. L. Moody and I. D. Sankey* (London 1875).

what was done in the inquiry-room was meant literally, for Macpherson believed that for every problem raised there existed an appropriate text, and that it was the business of the Christian worker (and 'Christian' carried its usual sense here of 'belonging to the new evangelicalism') to find it, or perhaps to be guided to it, by the influence of the Holy Spirit. (The same approach controlled the training of the counsellors for the Billy Graham Crusade in Manchester in 1961.) This was why laymen could be employed safely, for what was needed was not ordination but a knowledge of the Bible, and not every minister knew the text of the Scriptures as well as a layman trained in the school of the Plymouth Brethren, for example. It was in the inquiry-room, as much as in Moody's addresses, that what would now be called fundamentalism was of supreme importance; for many of the inquirers this amounted to an almost magical belief in the spiritual efficacy of the texts quoted, and in the availability of texts (often held to be directly prompted by the divine Spirit) for every kind of spiritual condition. The move to the inquiry-room was a move towards a further simplicity of attitude, towards a naive trust in the *power* thought to be resident in the appropriate verses. For the moment the sub-culture had become totally enclosed, prohibiting any questioning of itself.

What this meant was revealed in an illustration given by Macpherson himself to press the point that in the inquiry-room the workers must not let their subjects off too lightly— he called it 'healing the wound slightly'. They must not let the anxious leave the building hugging their fears about their spiritual condition as a badge of merit, but having given nothing but vague promises to do better in future. One young man whom Macpherson tackled, continually returned to the statement, 'I cannot believe'. Macpherson continued:

'After a pause, during which I prayed for direction, for I was baffled, I said very solemnly, "There remains nothing to be done, it is simply this—'He that believeth not shall be damned'." Had the ground beneath the feet of the young man suddenly given way he could not have exhibited greater astonishment. All arguing was now at an end. When he had recovered himself from what seemed to be a blow from an unseen hand, he replied, "I admit it, there is nothing left but that I should be damned".

From that moment, he began, as he thinks, to believe; and certainly his subsequent course has not belied his profession. The lie here was the abuse of an important truth. Under cover of the truth that of his own power he was unable to believe, he was all the time trying to conceal the sin and danger of his unbelief. From this false refuge he was driven forth, as he now hopes, by the simple word of God, and the power of the Holy Ghost.[44]

Another inquirer was a woman who believed that she had committed the sin against the Holy Ghost, said to be un-forgiveable by God himself, and a frequent source of misery to people suffering from depression. Macpherson was unable to help her until he suggested the text, 'The blood of Jesus Christ cleanseth from *all* sin': the woman then was able to balance this new text against the one which had been harrowing her. Another woman, a minister's wife, complained that she 'could not realize Christ as a person.'[45] Macpherson said to her, 'If you were in the dark and heard the sound of a human voice would you have any difficulty or doubt in identifying the voice with a person?' 'None whatever', she answered. 'Then surely', said Macpherson, 'you have not been listening to the voice of Jesus in the Word, else you should realize the person by the voice.' And Macpherson claimed that the woman was satisfied by this dubious logic.

All this was in line with answers which Moody himself had given at a question session at the Opera House on 18 May, 1875. Asked how to deal with 'anxious inquirers', he said that he liked to deal with them with an open Bible, pointing to various passages. He discouraged discussion in the inquiry-room quite deliberately. 'Avoid discussion with them,' Moody said, 'at Edinburgh I only prayed, and would not discuss, with an infidel. I hear he has since become converted.' When he was asked how he would deal with a man who came into the inquiry-room without apparently feeling anxious, Moody replied that he would not talk to him too much about his feelings but 'I would read Scripture to him and pray with him, and leave him to Christ.'[46]

Macpherson gave one example of a case in which he ceased

[44] Macpherson, op. cit., pp.157–8.
[45] Ibid., p.172.
[46] *Methodist Recorder*, 18 May, 1875.

giving direct quotation from the Scriptures. Instead, he asked his obstinate inquirer, who had doubts about the Bible itself, was he immoral? The answer, perhaps not unreasonably, was in the negative. Was he a drunkard? Again a negative answer. Did he frequent haunts of vice, and so on? The answer was always the same. Finally, Macpherson told him that if he had pleaded guilty to all these charges he would not have been worse than he already was, because he had again and again charged God Himself with falsehood in asserting that the Bible was unreliable and untrue. This was a short way with biblical critics and the young man was appropriately amazed. 'After a pause, I added, "What do you say?" "It is too true, sir," he answered with some tenderness. "Well, then, are you prepared to go on deliberately and persistently in this fiend-like iniquity, calling God a liar?".' The young man capitulated, and Macpherson drew the moral that 'it is sometimes necessary and salutary to give the unbelieving inquirer a sudden shock.'[47]

Any judgement here is a judgement on American revivalism and its English offshoots. American revivalism appealed to a largely lower middle-class society in which Protestant Evangelicalism functioned much as religion usually does in the Western tradition, providing passage-rites, and the basis of small social groups in which men could find a personal identity. But alongside this social religious behaviour there was also an individualistic religious tradition, according to which a man should utterly reject his own personal identity and wait in patience until God by a supranatural act should choose to regenerate him. This existential crisis—whatever its real significance and relevance to society, both of which were bound to change through historical time—became the core of a Protestant theory of personal salvation; it was really a very specialized kind of religious behaviour, rarely achieved but easily imitated. (I do not mean just counterfeited, but that it was not difficult for people to convince themselves that they had done what was required.)

It was widely held in the early nineteenth century that the Evangelical Revival of the previous century had proved that it was possible to democratize this experience; Søren Kierke-

[47] Macpherson, op. cit., p.160.

gaard stood out as a clear critic of this view, and Anglo-Catholicism began as a protest against it, though the protest was to change to virtual imitation in the generation after 1860. American revivalism claimed that what happened in the inquiry-room was this traditional experience of salvation. From Moody's point of view, indeed, Tait slightly mis-understood the situation in his public criticism, for what Tait was concerned about was what he would have called the pastoral position of the inquirer who, as the Archbishop saw it, might need various kinds of help which only a trained priest could give—and the professionalization of the priest-hood had been under way, though not very efficiently, from the 1840s; whereas Moody (and Macpherson) ignored the 'pastoral' implications of the inquiry-room, because they thought of it as the scene of this salvific encounter.

When one studies the evidence offered by both Moody and Macpherson one is likely to agree with Tait's unfavourable attitude. The inquiry-room (and its later varieties in the history of American popular revivalism) revealed the nemesis of the classical Protestant spirituality—the existential dis-covery of faith in 'God' at the moment of apparently ultimate alienation from him had been reduced to a brief evening's encounter between inquirer and revivalist in which all the revivalist's energies were bent on compelling the inquirer to repeat the verbal formula, to 'accept Christ'. The aggression of men like Macpherson showed how easy they felt the process to have become: there was no good reason why the inquirer should not give way. The revivalists had developed a blind faith in the allegedly overwhelming 'religious' value of the decision which they sought to wrest from those who came to them; but one also suspects that much of the energy which they showed came from a personal need to dominate other people, to use them to confirm the revivalists' basic pre-suppositions. Tait's instinct was sound. The superficiality of the American revivalist's interpretation of what was meant by the classical Protestant idea of 'rebirth' made the methods of the inquiry-room superficial as well. A contributory factor here was the revivalist's recognition that many people (especially in working-class, as distinct from lower middle-class, audiences) showed no interest in religious behaviour which obliged them to concentrate on a sense of personal guilt; they saw no religious value in self-rejection. This helps to explain Moody's attitude to repentance. At the close of the London campaign Moody answered questions about his methods at a meeting at the Opera House. One of those present asked whether, in dealing with inquirers, the duty of repentance should not be impressed upon them before the accepting of Christ? It was a regular question to revivalists, and had been put again and again in 1859. Moody replied:

> That depends upon what you call repentance. Some say it is godly sorrow for sin, but I do not think that an unconverted man can have 'godly' sorrow. Repentance means right about face. If I preach repentance I don't get people to Christ, but if I preach Christ I do get them to repent.[48]

This was the kind of statement which Tait had in mind when he spoke of 'unwise and untrue representations of the almost universal necessity of instantaneous conversion, and an ignoring of the full Scriptural teaching as to the nature of repentance' (v.s.). Stripped of the theological forms into which the disagreement easily, but irrelevantly, fell, Tait saw the traditional religious pattern as one which could only rarely be operated on anything approaching a mass scale, and then as one which required expert handling; whereas Moody, aware to some extent of the growing indifference to the approach, sacrificed everything to finding a formula which *could* be used on a large scale. The 'delicate and difficult duty of . . . ministering to anxious souls', as Tait described it, had also been simplified for a mass operation.

[48] *Methodist Recorder*, 18 May, 1875.

6

Sacred Songs and Sankey

THIS analysis of Moody's preaching is confirmed by an examination of *Sacred Songs and Solos*, the revivalist songbook which grew from the booklet of thirty songs, which Sankey published in 1875, to a formal hymnbook which contained about twelve hundred songs. The musical best-seller of its generation in religious circles, the book still retains some popularity, chiefly in the north of England, and the style which it established remained in use by modern professional revivalists like Billy Graham well into the 1960s.

Sankey himself was thirty-three when he came to England. He had been born in western Pennsylvania, fought in the American Civil War, and became a professional religious worker in the Young Men's Christian Association. It was probably at a Y.M.C.A. Conference in 1870 that he first met Moody, who recognized his possibilities as a singer and said, as Sankey at any rate reported, 'I have been looking for you for the last eight years'. Sankey had no singing reputation at the time, and had never thought of writing either the words or the music of a song himself. He brought with him to England in 1873 a small group of songs, many of which had been written by Philip Bliss, another American revivalist, whose death in a railway accident in 1876 removed Sankey's only serious rival. The songs which Sankey sang in England had been composed in the United States between 1860 and 1872; they were unknown to his audiences for the most part, though Phillip Phillips, an itinerant American singing evangelist, may have used some of them on his tours of Britain in the 1860s. Phillips, born in 1834, had been Sankey's earliest model as a singer; he accompanied himself, as Sankey was to do, but Phillips was primarily an entertainer, who put on a two-hour one-man performance of monologues, ballads and songs. A few items from his repertoire appeared in *Sacred Songs and Solos*. 'In some way or other the Lord will provide', for example, was number 19 in the earliest collection. Phillips, however, had not been so great a success as to blunt the novelty of Sankey's methods and music. Sankey was not over humble, but he was telling the truth when he wrote of his first English services, held at York in 1873, that 'it was with some difficulty that I could get the people to sing, as they had not been accustomed to the kind of songs that I was using'.[1] Bliss' neatly polished, catchy tunes, each with its instantly memorable chorus, quite unlike the stately English hymn or the genuinely 'folk' revivalist melodies of the first half of the nineteenth century, soon made their own way and solved part of Sankey's problem; he solved the difficulty of persuading the English to sing by making a massed choir on a voluntary basis a central feature of all the major urban campaigns in which he shared. By the time that Billy Graham ran his North of England Crusade in 1960–1, the choir had outgrown the singer and the supply of new religious songs seemed to have dried up as far as revivalism went.

There lay behind Sankey, however, the new American popular music industry which had been developing steadily since the 1830s. Lowell Mason, born in Boston in 1792, did much to create this industry, which catered in a genteel way for a newly prosperous society, willing to listen to 'European' music, to patronize Handel and Haydn societies, and to buy the 'original' church music poured out by Mason and his friends and successors, among them William Bradbury, who averaged two books of music a year from 1841 to 1867, and the Root brothers, who were well known to Sankey himself. In fact, the emphasis on church music 'was by no means as churchy as might appear at first sight . . . any tune which appealed to the taste of the day, whatever its origin, was likely to be adapted as a hymn'.[2] Immense quantities of 'new' religious music were published in the nineteenth century, as revivalists and writers grasped the size of the market which had formed in the wake of the Evangelical and Catholic revivals; but the musical taste involved was essentially secular,

[1] Ira Sankey, *Autobiography* (Philadelphia 1906), p.19.
[2] G. Chase, *American Music* (New York 1955), p.156.

and soaked in sentimentality, whether in the romantic mood of 'Woodman, spare that tree', or in the religious mood of songs which were supposed to be sung by children on their death-beds.[3] The American industry profited from the Civil War, and, when it ended, turned to chapel choirs and revivalist meetings as a fresh source of profit. It proved as easy to combine the sentimental and the religious in peacetime as it had been to combine the sentimental and patriotic in wartime. Peace, however, for once lasted longer, and so the process became out of hand: long before the end of the century, the religious music market had become saturated. It is said that Fanny van Alstyne, for example, wrote about five thousand sets of words under many different signatures: Fanny Crosby, Ella Dale, Jenny V., Mrs Jennie Glen, Mrs Kate Grinley, Miss V., Miss Viola V.A., Mrs V., Viola and so forth.[4] In the later editions of *Sacred Songs and Solos* it becomes almost impossible to tell one batch of words and music, each with its inevitable chorus, from another. The chorus, however, was at least evidence of the other side of the tradition, the 'spiritual folk-songs' which George Pullen Jackson collected in the 1930s, of which the purest examples, the tune of 'Amazing Grace', for example, essentially of Southern origin, did not reach England in the 1870s. The standard of the sentimental, more Northern tradition of popular religious music declined steadily from 1875 to 1914 as it became more commercialized.

Sankey, however, came at the beginning and set a new fashion in popular religious music as far as Britain was concerned. His massed choir was the ideal instrument for making the new songs tell in big buildings like the Islington Agricultural Hall. Moody might often be hard to hear, but Sankey's music never failed to cross the gap. He really depended upon a repertoire of about thirty songs, which he sang slowly, very clearly, and with emphasis; these songs all shared certain

[3] Cf. 'I should like to die, said Willy, etc.', by Philip Bliss (*v.s.* pp.93–4). Bliss was perhaps imitating Phillips' style; but the song was quite seriously intended. Bliss was a Baptist, like W. H. Doane.

[4] Frances Crosby (b.1823) was the blind wife of a blind musician, Alexander van Alstyne. She was a Methodist, born in New York. Her first published hymns appeared in one of William Bradbury's collections, *The Golden Censer* in 1864; she was still publishing at the end of the century. Her verses were very feeble, and her immense vogue—millions of copies of her collections were sold—owed almost everything to the tunes of W. H. Doane, G. F. Root and Sankey himself.

characteristics which help to explain their and Sankey's success.

First of all, they provide evidence of the existence in the nineteenth century evangelical pietist world of a siege mentality not unlike that which was common in continental Roman Catholicism in the same period. In all the editions of *Sacred Songs and Solos* the first song was 'Ho, my comrades, see the signal', better known by the opening phrase of the chorus, 'Hold the fort, for I am coming'. Philip Bliss had written this in 1870, basing the catch-phrase on a signal given by General Sherman during an engagement in the American Civil War. The song became so well known in England, despite the fact that the historical reference had little or no emotive value, that Lord Shaftesbury was able to say at the farewell meeting for the American revivalists in 1875 that 'if Mr Sankey has done no more than teach the people of England to sing *Hold the Fort* he has conferred an inestimable blessing on the British Empire'.[5] Shaftesbury was a confused, impulsive peer, but not, one feels, an ironist.

> Ho, my comrades, see the signal
> Waving in the sky;
> Reinforcements now appearing,
> Victory is nigh.
>
> *Chorus:* Hold the fort, for I am coming,
> Jesus signals still.
> Wave the answer back to Heaven,
> 'By thy grace, we will'.

'Hold the Fort' seems to have expressed the characteristic evangelical pietist conviction that the true Church was only to be found in a remnant of faithful believers who were holding bravely on in the hope that the Second Advent would soon bring reinforcements from the sky. Its great popularity argues that the revivalist meetings had a defensive, sectarian ethos. It is significant that if one reads the sermons preached by that other example of great popular religious success in the nineteenth century, Charles Spurgeon, one finds the same emphasis. Spurgeon, who, like Moody, felt in the Calvinist tradition,

[5] For Shaftesbury, cf. the life by Professor G. F. A. Best, 1964.

gave his congregation the impression that they were an oasis of truth in a desert of secularity and corrupted Christianity: God's chief outpost in a fallen world was the massive but isolated Metropolitan Tabernacle in London.[6] God would only bless this chosen remnant, however, if it retained its own distinctness from the world outside: it was almost always the remnant's own responsibility if the work of revival did not prosper. Sankey printed Bliss's song which expressed this conviction:

> There's sin in the camp, there's treason today—
> Is it in me? Is it in me?
> There's cause in our ranks for defeat and delay—
> Is it, oh Lord, in me?[7]

A second element in the early Sankey songs was what might be called the theme of rejection, the threat that God himself sometimes rejected the impenitent sinner before he died. As we have already seen in the case of 'Jesus of Nazareth', this fitted in with Moody's own residual Calvinism, and with the revivalist's practical need to press for decisions at the close of the meeting. A parallel to 'Jesus of Nazareth' was 'In the silent, midnight watches' (number 217 in *Sacred Songs*, etc.), another American song, written by an American Episcopalian, Arthur Cleveland Coxe, who became bishop of Western New York in 1865. As a young man in the 1830s and 1840s, Coxe had poured out the heavily stylized verse which was so popular with the writers of hymn-tunes, and this song came from his *Athanasion* (1842). The last stanzas described the reception at the gate of Heaven of someone who had died impenitent:

> Then 'tis time to stand entreating
> Christ to be let in;
> At the gate of Heaven beating,
> Wailing for thy sin.
> Nay, alas, thou guilty creature,
> Hast thou then forgot?
> Jesus waited long to know thee—
> Now, he knows thee not.

[6] *The New Park Street Pulpit*, Vol. I (Sermons preached in 1855) London 1963, or any of the innumerable volumes of Spurgeon's weekly outpourings.

[7] *Sacred Songs and Solos*, 422.

More popular, perhaps, but in the same vein, was Fanny van Alstyne's 'Pass me Not', written in 1868, and issued in her *Songs of Devotion* (1870) in America.[8]

Such hymns did not dominate Sankey's Collection as such, though they dominated Moody's meetings in the 1870s. A reassuring and sentimental tone predominated in *Sacred Songs and Solos*, and it is clear from the direction in which the volume developed that the compilers thought that this was one secret of its success. Nevertheless, it is important to remember the continuing presence of the rejection-theme. The kind of theological belief to which this picture of a harsh, arbitrary God appealed may be seen in another of Sankey's early favourites, 'O Christ what burdens bowed thy head':

> Jehovah lifted up his rod;
> O Christ, it fell on Thee,
> Thou was sore stricken of thy God;
> There's not one stroke for me;
> Thy tears, thy blood, beneath it flowed,
> Thy bruising healeth me.
>
> Jehovah bade his sword awake;
> O Christ, it woke 'gainst Thee.
> Thy blood the flaming blade must slake;
> Thy heart its sheath must be.
> All for my sake, my peace to make;
> Now sleeps that sword for me.[9]

This crude interpretation of the death of Jesus was the work of a Mrs Cousin (1823–1906), the wife of a minister in the Free Church of Scotland; she published *Immanuel's Land*, a collection of 107 hymns, in 1876, and her most popular work was 'The Sands of Time are Sinking'. Sankey presumably approved of the verses quoted above, for he actually set them to music himself.

Sankey's approval is important, because the words of the hymn go to the emotional centre of popular orthodoxy. To

[8] The tune mattered more than the words. It was by W. H. Doane, a Baptist, born in Connecticut in 1832; achieved fame as a song-writing Sunday School superintendent; he turned out a thousand tunes, including that of 'Rescue the Perishing', once a music-hall joke, the words again from Fanny van Alstyne's pen.

[9] *Songs and Solos*, 44.

place the images accurately one has to compare Mrs Cousin's version with the relevant passages in the Anglo-Catholic *Lux Mundi* (1889), and in the Liberal Anglican Matthew Arnold's *God and the Bible*, which was published in the same year as the London revival of 1875. At first sight both were critical of what they understood to be the popular view of the significance of the death of Christ. The writer in *Lux Mundi* said:

> The doctrine of the Atonement, more than any of the great truths of Christianity, has been misconceived and misrepresented, and has therefore not only been rejected itself, but has sometimes been the cause of the rejection of the Christian system as a whole. . . . The truth of the wrath of God against sin and of the love of Christ by which that sin was removed, has been perverted into a belief in a divergence of will between God the Father and God the Son, as if it were the Father's will that sinners should perish, the Son's will that they should be saved; or as if the Atonement consisted in the propitiation of the wrathful God by the substituted punishment of the innocent for the guilty . . . [whereas] if the death of Christ was necessary to propitiate the wrath of the Father, it was necessary to propitiate his own wrath also; if it manifested his love, it manifested the Father's love also. . . .[10]

It is interesting to see how the author, Arthur Lyttelton, later a bishop, failed to break out from the attraction of the language about wrath and propitiation; he tried to balance tradition and sophistication, but the emotional pull of the familiar phrases was too great: it is clear that he could not have used words as unequivocal as those of Mrs Cousin, but his emotional position was not far from hers. The obscurity of his final formula, in which Christ appeared to be propitiating his own wrath by offering himself his own death as satisfaction, suggested the depth of his embarrassment.

Arnold, on the other hand, was perfectly clear:

> I heard Mr Moody preach to one of his vast audiences on a topic eternally attractive—salvation by Jesus Christ. Mr Moody's account of that salvation was exactly the old story, to which I

[10] *Lux Mundi* (14 ed. 1895), pp.225–6.

have often adverted, of the contract in the council of the Trinity. Justice puts in her claim, said Mr Moody, for punishment of guilty mankind; God admits it. Jesus intercedes, undertakes to bear their punishment, and signs an undertaking to that effect. Thousands of years pass; Jesus is on the Cross at Calvary. Justice appears, and presents to him his signed undertaking. Jesus accepts it, bows his head, and expires. Christian salvation consists in the undoubting belief in the transaction here described, and in the hearty acceptance of the release offered by it.

Never let us deny to this story power and pathos, treat with hostility ideas which have entered so deep into the life of Christianity. But the story is not true; it never really happened. These personages never did meet together, and speak, and act, in the manner related. The personages of the Christian heaven and their conversations are no more matter of fact than the personages of the Greek Olympus and their conversations. Sir Robert Phillimore seeks to tie up the Church of England to a belief in the personality of Satan, and he might as well seek to tie it up to a belief in the personality of Tisiphone. Satan and Tisiphone alike are not real persons, but shadows thrown by man's guilt and terrors. Mr Moody's audiences are the last people who will come to perceive all this; they are chiefly made up from the main body of lovers of our popular religion—the serious and steady middle-class, with its bounded horizons. To the more educated class above this, and to the more free class below it, the grave beliefs of the religious middle class in such stories as Mr Moody's story of the Covenant of Redemption are impossible now; to the religious middle-class itself they will be impossible soon. Salvation by Jesus Christ, therefore, if it has any reality, must be placed somewhere else than in a hearty consent to Mr Moody's story. Something Mr Moody and his hearers have experienced from Jesus, which does them good; but of this something they have not yet succeeded in getting the right history. . . . However honest and earnest Mr Moody may be, all we can say of a man who at the present juncture bases Christian salvation on a story like that, is that he shows a fatal want of intellectual seriousness. . . .[11]

All the evidence suggests that Arnold was right, and this in turn means that when Moody and Sankey combined Moody's emphasis on a simple substitutionary version of the atonement with Sankey songs of the Mrs Cousin variety, they were automatically limiting their appeal to a section of the Victorian

[11] *God and the Bible*, M. Arnold (London 1875), pp.xxiv–v, xxxii–iii.

middle-class. By 1875 neither the educated upper-class (to stick to Arnold's way of putting it), nor the working-class which had, as Arnold realized, now broken free from its earlier Victorian middle-class religious conditioning, was interested in stories of this kind. They disbelieved them as stories and disvalued them as myth. Even the section of the middle-classes which clung to *Sacred Songs and Solos* as its only real hymnbook for thirty years and more, did so more because it was able to transform and sentimentalize the contents by multiplying songs about a travel agent's idea of Heaven, than because of the attraction of the salvation-rejection songs about the atonement.[12]

The full impact of these facts did not strike British religious leaders until many years later. It may be found, for example, in a book like *The Army and Religion* (1919), an honest, official report on how far the British Army which had been fighting on the Western Front had been Christian. The report, based on the evidence of many chaplains and soldiers, was largely drafted by Professor Cairns of Aberdeen, with the Bishop of Winchester (E. S. Talbot) as his Anglican colleague. Cairns regretfully concluded that the dogmatic side of Christianity had never made any permanent lodging in the minds of most of the soldiers; 'they did not need it for the life they were living, and so it became atrophied and has fallen away' (p.50). The soldiers had few intellectual difficulties to raise about such ideas as the incarnation, atonement, or resurrection: they attached no significance to them in the first place, but were indifferent to them. From this point of view all the Evangelical, Revivalist and Anglo-Catholic work of the nineteenth century seemed to go for nothing as far as the majority of the male part of the population was concerned, at the time when it was most prompted by circumstances to turn to whatever gods it knew.

I do not think that this meant that the British Army in France lacked any kind of 'religious' system; the Talbot-Cairns Report was based on a purely 'Christian' definition of

---

[12] This is not to say that hymn-singing was ever a very natural activity: folk-singing, music hall songs, ballads, etc., arose much more spontaneously; the hymn, even Sankey's songs, needed a *raison-d'être* which working-class life did not provide; nowadays, the 'Red Flag' seems as artificial in socialist circles. It is significant that they were called 'songs'.

religion: what was not 'Christian' was not 'religious', and 'Christianity' was defined as though Jowett and Arnold, to keep to the English theological tradition, had never written a line. Without a proper understanding and appropriation of the dogmas of incarnation, atonement and resurrection, for example, one could not really be regarded as 'Christian'. This clinging to traditional mythological language might have justified itself if the myths had proved effective in the extreme circumstances of the war, but one thing which *The Army and Religion* betrayed was a frightened clerical suspicion that these myths were hardly touching the imagination of the soldiers at all, and that this could not simply be explained by saying that they did not 'know' the stories and the ideas based on them (though there was some talk about the appalling 'ignorance' of the troops), for they had been told them. Still less did the clerical investigators suppose that the working-classes in particular might live religiously in non-Christian terms. What this suggests is that the London revival of 1875 was probably the last major occasion in the history of English popular religion—Northern Ireland and Wales must be deliberately excluded here—when the symbolism of divine rejection at the gates of heaven could be used openly, and when the image of Christ as a supernatural redeemer, who satisfied the anger of God which otherwise threatened the whole human race, could be stated in quite so crude a form. It was significant here that where popular religion and Christianity remained on mythological terms in the late nineteenth century, they did so through the more concrete symbols of *glossolalia* and 'spiritual healing'.

Apart from the strictly 'revivalist' songs, in which the rejection-theme predominated, a number of other themes ran through Sankey's original songbook. Among them were: the reunion of families in heaven; the prodigal child; the theme of tiredness, illness and healing, with its corollary, the 'sympathizing Jesus'. These were not songs used to bring inquirers out to the front in the revival hall; they were not used to force people towards the vital moment of decision; in fact, they might be called 'edifying' rather than revivalist. They were written and used because the revivalists knew that many people came back to the meetings again and again, were even

converted again and again. There was a large revival following, for whom the great, throbbing occasions became the
essence of religious experience; a revivalist 'denomination'
developed, a loose association of people which existed as long
as the revivalists stayed in England, often collapsing as soon
as they returned to America, but easily renewed when they
came back to Europe. These themes echoed the religious
feelings and needs of this permanent audience. These were the
songs, especially those about illness, weariness and healing,
which remained popular in Protestant chapels up and down
the country for as much as sixty years after Sankey's last visit.
In the last analysis, what Moody and Sankey had to offer was
consolation, as much as conversion.

The ideal audience of these songs were all sufferers whom
the world had wronged; their children were all either dead or
ungrateful, or had wandered away into the depths of the urban
maze, forgetful of their parents—though of course their
parents remembered them and would welcome them back
home with open arms at any time. . . . So the parents (rather
than the children) needed sympathy, comfort, consolation,
strength from a source outside themselves. Above all, it seems
that they liked to go back in imagination to the days of their
own childhood, when the world was a big back kitchen with a
Yorkshire range, filled with an extended family which one
knew, and when people outside seemed no more frightening
than the chilly air of a northern morning. This picture of the
past became in its turn the basis of an almost secularized
image of heaven, a heaven brought down to earth and
identified with Home as it used to be before Father and Mother
died and the children had to go out to work and lost their
primal personalities. Many of these touches reached women
rather than men, though the emphasis on disease, weariness
and healing had their appropriateness for men as well as for
the mass of Victorian women of all classes who lived exhaust-
ing lives, were worn out by too many pregnancies, and
carried too much domestic responsibility. A few of these
songs reflected Moody's own fondness for stories about the
deaths of children, a fondness which did not arise from his
own life-history, but from experience as to what was effective.
Once again, the chosen themes had only a limited appeal to

the masculine part of the Victorian working-class, which had come to repudiate Protestantism's traditional pessimism about human nature, and rejected the assertion that the miseries of the present time were the result of God's prodding, providential action. It was this apologetic aspect of Protestantism which most affected the nineteenth-century proletariat, not the so-called Protestant work-ethic; for them work was not a matter of religion and morality, but of economic luck a good deal of the time.

The first booklet of songs issued by the American revivalists (who started by briefly using Phillip Phillips' songbook, as the only American one to hand) contained sixteen songs; the earliest I have actually seen, published by 1873, contained twenty-nine. The worst of these, two or three at most, descended to the level of music-hall morality:[13] 'Let us gather up the sunbeams lying all around our path', for example, with its refrain 'Scatter seeds of kindness for our reaping by and by', which had been written in 1867 by Mary Riley Smith (born in 1842), the wife of the Reverend Albert Smith of Rochester, New York. The song made no mention of Christianity at all, but attacked the consciences of parents directly:

> If we knew the baby fingers
> Pressed against the window-pane
> Would be cold and stiff tomorrow
> Never trouble us again—
> Would the bright eyes of our darling
> Catch the frown upon our brow?
> Would the prints of rosy fingers
> Vex us then as they do now?
>
> Ah, those little ice-cold fingers
> How they point our memories back
> To the hasty words and actions
> Strewn along our backward track:
> How those little hands remind us
> As in snowy grace they lie,
> Not to scatter thorns, but roses,
> For our reaping by and by.

[13] *Sacred Songs and Solos*, sung by Ira Sankey at Gospel Meetings (Morgan and Scott, n.d., but 1873). This was number 11.

An even purer example of the genre was number six in the 1873 collection, 'When the dewy life was fading'. In the original pamphlet, Sankey printed as an introduction a story about a woman who had struck her daughter for breaking a dish. The child died soon afterwards, saying, 'I was always in your way, mother—you had no room for little Mary—and I shall be in the angels' way'. This was versified, almost inevitably, by Fanny van Alstyne:

> Mother, in that golden region
> With its pearly gates so fair,
> Up among the happy angels.
> Is there room for Mary there?
>
> Mother, raise me for a moment,
> You'll forgive me when I say—
> You were angry when you told me
> I was always in your way;
> You were sorry in a moment,
> I could see it in your brow;
> But you'll not recall it, mother,
> You must never mind it now. . . .
>
> In the bright and golden region
> With its pearly gates so fair,
> She is singing with the angels,
> 'There is room for Mary there'.

This still remained in the 750-song edition, as number 371. The story of the dying child who either forgave or converted his parents on his death-bed had a long ancestry in evangelical magazines and pulpits, but this was not pietism, but the sentimentality which Mrs Ewing exploited to such effect in her children's stories. In revival meetings songs of this kind had the added advantage that they helped to weaken the audience's resistance to the speaker; they might awaken feelings of guilt, of loss, of remorse, or just self-pity. People ceased to be the passive, though interested panel of judges who were to vote on Moody and Sankey's various abilities. That the song was sung at all, however, suggests the survival for a long time in the revival world of an element of entertainment which Sankey inherited from Phillips; perhaps also a memory of a slightly wider audience than usually came to the Agricultural Hall at Islington.

A theme which revivalist songs exploited much more consciously for religious purposes was that of the Prodigal Son. In the early 1873 collection, this was represented by 'Come Home, Come Home, you are weary at Heart'. Yet another East Coast American woman, Ellen Gates, from Torrington, Connecticut, wrote the words; W. H. Doane supplied the tune. There were four three-line stanzas of which the third was typical:

> Come home, come home from the sorrow and shame,
> From the sin and the shame and the tempter that smiled—
> Oh prodigal child, come home, come home.

Sankey sang this with great effect in 1873–5, though the tune seems utterly banal. On his second visit, in 1882, he replaced it with 'Where is my wandering boy tonight?' (no. 303 in *Sacred Songs and Solos*). Robert Lowry provided both words and music, an American who was not only a Baptist minister, but had also been a Professor of Rhetoric in a New England Baptist theological seminary. In both songs the writers exploited the sentiment of the New Testament story about the Prodigal Son, but secularized it by allowing the audience to identify itself with the Father who longed, and suffered and forgave. The climax of Lowry's verses was:

> Go for my wandering boy tonight;
> Go search for him where you will;
> But bring him to me with all his blight
> And tell him I love him still.

The song worked on two different levels. The revivalist used it straightforwardly to point his appeal, but many of those who listened to Sankey sing it were moved because they read their own circumstances into it. In the chaos of late nineteenth-century urban life, the family came to mean far too much to some of those who made it up. It became the principal source of personal identity and stability: of individual power and affection; its break-up, which happened inevitably, seemed disastrous, especially to those who remained on the original scene. The boy who left home to work, even the girl who left to marry, could seem an enemy, ungrateful, almost wicked. The conviction that one had stayed at home and had been morally right was fortified by this side of revivalism.

Equally important was the feeling that the tight denominational framework of British Christianity, Roman Catholicism included, was showing weakness in the new urban situation; if this centrifugal force was not checked, then the social influence and political power of all the Churches would stand in jeopardy. Fear of the break-up of Anglicanism had prompted Keble's Assize Sermon in 1833; fear had driven the clergy in their opposition to *Essays and Reviews*, when they caught their first glimpse of the possible disintegration of belief. A fresh wave of anxiety ran through the British Churches in the closing quarter of the century as their statistical margin began to crumble. If Moody and Sankey could tighten the bonds of ecclesiastical loyalty, so much the better, and for that result some of the boys must be persuaded to come home. They were needed for political purposes too—to maintain the strength of the Free Church votes which were becoming so vital to the survival of the Liberal Party in the short run, and so inimical to its survival in the long run.

Even more popular than the songs about the wandering boys were the songs about Heaven. Heaven, significantly, was constantly described as 'home', as the place where the family would be reunited. Some of the images used derived from biblical pictures of the next world as a golden shore. In the 1873 collection Sankey included, 'There's a land which is fairer than day', with its candid refrain—'In the sweet by-and-by we shall meet on that beautiful shore'. Another had a chorus about 'meeting the loved ones [sic] in the dazzling city'. The names used to indicate Heaven shared a common ethos: 'the summer land of love' (Fanny van Alstyne, 604), 'Home, beautiful home' (H. R. Palmer, 599), 'the ever-green shore' (Ira Sankey, 516), 'A Home beyond the Time' (C. Dunbar, 407), and 'the highland of glory' (W. O. Cushing, 315). Fanny van Alstyne's masterpiece was perhaps 284, with its refrain:

> Roll on, dark stream, we dread not thy foam,
> The pilgrim is longing for Home, sweet Home.[14]

The frankest expression of the idea of family reunion and solidarity came perhaps in number 600:

> On that happy Easter morning
> All the graves their dead restore;
> Father, sister, child and mother meet once more.

A more general version of the same idea occurred in number 479 (the words by E. G. Taylor, the tune by George Stebbins, who wrote the tune of the previous example as well):

> Meet me there, oh meet me there,
> No bereavements we shall bear,
> There no sighings for the dead,
> There no farewell tear is shed;
> We shall, safe from all alarms,
> Clasp our loved ones in our arms.

In fact, these songs do not leave the impression that Heaven consists of white-robed choirs endlessly playing their harps and singing their songs (with 'Hold the Fort' no doubt a heavenly favourite); instead, they suggest a Heaven which is an everlasting Festival of the United Family:

> They are watching at the portal,
> They are waiting at the door,
> Waiting only for my coming,
> All the loved ones gone before (no. 352)

'All the children whose voices on earth are still, now sing in that city of gold', promised another, and so the note of golden reassurance rolled on from song to song. It is hard to believe that this massive outburst of hymns about heaven resulted from some otherwise unnoticed return to an otherworldly outlook. There was dissatisfaction with the traditional imagery; the new images, or the new effect given to old ones, secularized the earlier picture, and suggested a movement away from belief in the supernatural, not an increased

---

[14] Cf., however, no. 263, 'As the wanderer sings in a far away land, of his own sweet [*sic*] home on a beautiful strand.' The words were by Eben Eugene Rexford, born in 1848; they owed their survival perhaps to the fact that the tune was by Philip Bliss.

belief in it. The process which was at work was also parallel to the rapid disappearance of existential belief in Hell, about which no new songs seem to have been written. Another change was also taking place in the background: the *crêpe*-encrusted High Victorian funeral was slowly being humanized and, in a quite shocking change in burial customs, inhumation was gradually giving way to the idea of cremation. The cry for an eternal family reunion may have been more of a cry of pain that it seems in the sentimental clothing given it in *Sacred Songs and Solos*: pain at the failure of an idealized family life to produce an earthly paradise; pain about children's deaths, about dragging pregnancies; pain at the thought that there might be no further chances of happiness; the revivalists could not cope with what was really happening to their lower middle-class audience, they could only respond with chorus after chorus. In the meantime those outside the tradition looked with a mixture of amusement and contempt at these uninviting pictures of a Christian future life. It is not surprising that most of these songs vanished without trace from the popular mind in the First World War. Revivalism, which had sounded aggressive and even possibly relevant to the future when it used the threat of Hell, sounded anaemic and unconvincing when it reduced its appeal to the promise of an unendurable heaven. *Davon kann mann nicht sprechen, darüber muss mann schweigen.* At this extreme the claim that Moody and Sankey were keeping alive the Old Time Religion collapses as an absurdity.

Adventism and spiritual healing did not feature much in *Sacred Songs and Solos*. Pentecostalist and adventist sects grew in the last years of the nineteenth century, without competing for territory with the American revivalists. In a generalized sense, however, the healing-motif permeated the songbook. The 1873 collection included Philip Bliss's song, 'Down life's dark vale we wander', of which the third and final verse said:

> He'll know the way was dreary,
> He'll know the feet grew weary,
> He'll know that griefs oppressed me,
> Oh, how his arms will rest me.

In the larger edition, Fanny van Alstyne, in song number

276, said of Jesus that 'With a sympathizing heart He removes every care: what a balm for the weary, oh, how sweet to be there'. She was probably borrowing from a hymn written by William Hunter (an Irishman who had been taken to America in 1817 at the age of six, where he grew up to become a Methodist and Professor of Hebrew in Allegheny College), who published a hymn in his *Songs of Devotion* (1859) which began:

> The great Physician now is near,
> The sympathizing Jesus.

Hunter's hymn was actually number 49 in *Sacred Songs and Solos*. The relevance of this image of Jesus as the sympathizing physician to the kind of pietist world with which the American revivalists were concerned needs no emphasis. One other example might be given, from number 293, by G. F. Root:

> She only touched the hem of his garment
> As to His side she stole,
> Amid the crowd that gathered around Him,
> And she was whole.

It was in the Women's Meetings, the Women's Fellowships, the Ladies' Bright Hours, that such songs were popular: one has to hear them sung by little groups of ailing and elderly women in one of those dowdy 'class-rooms' at the back of a crumbling late Victorian chapel before one understands their function.

To sum up, the songs which Sankey sang in 1873–5 were not pre-eminently concerned with sin and salvation, though the threat of eternal punishment still sounded in a few of them, and the offer of safety in Christ was still made. The primary appeal of the songs was one of reassurance, and this was the characteristic note of the ten songs (one third of the 1873 edition of the songbook) of which Philip Bliss contributed either the words or the music or both. In this sense it was Bliss rather than Sankey who overcame British resistance to American revivalism in 1875. 'I am so glad that Jesus loves me', 'Free from the Law, oh, happy condition', 'Whosoever will, may come', and 'Go bury thy sorrow, the world has its share'—all sound the same note of cheerful reassurance, echoed (in the 1873 Edition) by Fanny van Alstyne's 'Safe in the arms of Jesus/Safe on his gentle breast'. As *Sacred Songs and Solos* expanded, this theme became more important and its popularity explains the large number of hymns about the reunion of families and the pleasures of a bourgeois Heaven. Sankey's own comparative unimportance in this early period is illustrated by the fact that he wrote only two tunes for this edition. One was to words written by Philip Bliss, a strange elaboration of the twenty-third Psalm with the refrain, 'There's a light in the valley for me', another instance of the reassurance theme. The other was composed for verses written by Horatius Bonar (1808–89), a Free Church of Scotland minister who had been publishing hymns and verses since 1843, but who wrote 'Yet there is Room' in 1872. This belonged to the group of rejection songs, and ended with the warning: 'Ere night that gate may close and seal thy doom: Then the last, low, long cry: No room, no room'. This was the solitary British representative in the 1873 edition; it echoed the self-consciously evangelistic Calvinism of the Free Church of Scotland, a more formative influence on Moody and Sankey than American historians have realized. The words 'ere night' meant before, and not after, death.

There is another way of looking at Sankey's musical invasion, however, and that is to compare *Sacred Songs and Solos* with the hymns printed in the *Book of the Mission*, the small paperback which the Cowley Fathers prepared for the Anglican mission to London in 1869. The *Book of the Mission* had a large black cross on the cover together with the words 'Time is short, eternity is long'. It contained only 12 hymns, a few of which, such as 'Rock of Ages', 'Jesu, lover of my soul', 'Onward Christian soldiers', and 'Hark, hark, angelic songs are swelling', had been chosen because of their familiarity. Indeed, the two books had enough in common to show how far both reflected a similar judgement of the popular mind. The Cowley hymns included 'Daily, daily sing the praises/ Of the City God hath made', which was a straightforward invocation of the beauties of Heaven, and differed only in one important way from what might have been found in Sankey's songbook: it contained no reference to the possible reunion of the family and friends of the singer, who was simply to be a member of the heavenly throng. This was also true of 'O Paradise, O Paradise', one of the best-known hymns of the Roman Catholic convert from Anglicanism, F. W. Faber: the subject was heaven and the singer was just as 'weary waiting here' as any of the singers of Sankey's solos, but he was an individual member of the Church and what he was looking forward to was Heaven itself and the presence of God, rather than to the restoration of the family. Another of Faber's hymns was printed—'We come to thee, sweet Saviour'—and this had a soft self-indulgent note not unlike what might be found in the American songs:

> We come to Thee, sweet Saviour,
> And Thou wilt not ask us why,
> We cannot live without Thee,
> And still less without Thee die.

What really established the distinction between the American and Cowley attitudes, however, was two much more doctrinally significant hymns. One of these, 'O Father, Son and Holy Ghost', came from the *Catholic Hymnal* of 1860 (no. 168), and was an example of how careless the Cowley Fathers were of offending contemporary Anglican opinion. It was printed as part of the service for the Renewal of Baptismal Vows, which had formed the climax of some of the Anglo-Catholic missions in 1869 (*v.i.*) This hymn, which was anonymous, began with a reference to infant baptism, and then continued:

> Then we were free from guilty stain,
> But sad and sinful now,
> With contrite hearts we come again
> To make our solemn vow;

While the last verse said:

> Thy Blood our only treasure is,
> The Cross our chosen part,
> The Sacrament our highest bliss,
> Our home, Thy Sacred Heart.

Here the idea of Missions and the idea of the Eucharist were firmly linked together in a way which would have been inconceivable in the American revivals. The second hymn was

'Hail the sign, the sign of Jesus'. This also differed profoundly from the Sankey songs, deliberately invoking the ideas of the Church, the Saints, and the Martyrs, and saying:

> Lo, the Cross of Christ my Master
> On my brow I trace;
> May it keep my mind unsullied,
> Doubt and fear displace.
>
> Lo, upon my lips I mark it,
> Sign of Jesus slain;
> Christian lips should never utter
> Words impure and vain.
>
> Lo, I sign the Cross of Jesus
> Meekly on my breast,
> May it guard my heart when living,
> Dying be its rest.

7

Anglo-Catholic Revivalism

1. Anglo-Catholic Missions

EVANGELICAL tradition has always celebrated Moody's attempt to revive London in 1875, but the earlier Anglo-Catholic Twelve Days Mission to London in 1869 and the follow-up Mission on a broader basis in 1874 have left little memorial. Nevertheless, the Anglican experiment, which involved one hundred and twenty London parishes, preceded Moody's services in the Islington Agricultural Hall and created a sensation at the time. Indeed, the impression which the Twelve Days Mission gave of an aggressive sacramental revival helps to explain why so much Evangelical support surrounded Moody: he came as a Protestant counter-blast to the Catholic revivalists, not as a solitary American adventurer. It was Anglicanism which deserves the credit for this first successful large-scale revival campaign in the capital; James Caughey never tried, no doubt partly because of the weakness of London Wesleyanism before 1870, while the Weaver-Radcliffe services of 1860 made a brief, unsatisfactory episode. This is not to say that Moody imitated the Anglo-Catholics, any more than the Anglo-Catholics imitated what they knew of American revival methods. The Twelve Days Mission deliberately opposed 'Protestant' ways of conducting a revival, an opposition marked in the choice of the term 'mission', which was a French Roman Catholic usage which could be traced back to the seventeenth century.

In fact, the contrast between Anglo-Catholic revivalism and Moody's methods was absolute. The American system depended upon the central pair of revivalists; in 1875 everything turned on Moody and Sankey as personalities. Anglo-Catholic revivalism, on the other hand, was based on the parish system of the Church of England, and varied in technique from one to another. In practice, this obsession with the parochial structure was the greatest fault of the approach. The Americans retained the traditional theology of revival, pleading for instantaneous conversions which at the same time were thought of as experiences of justification by faith. Anglo-Catholicism, however, approached its missions sacramentally; the revivalists began each day with a Eucharist; they constantly recalled the fact that their hearers had been baptized, whereas Moody usually referred to baptism only as a sacrament in which one should not put one's trust for salvation; the climax of the Twelve Days Mission in some parishes was a service for the renewal of baptismal vows, a novelty to most of those who took part in it and a scandal to many more who did not. For the American revivalist, the confession of sin was a general admission of personal sinfulness which excluded any mention of specific acts or thoughts—such a detailed confession was thought of as being made to God alone; but for the Anglo-Catholic one of the principal aims of the Mission was to popularize the idea of detailed confession to a priest as a preliminary to eucharistic renewal and possibly spiritual direction. The climax of the American system was a meeting in which converts stood up one after another and testified to the good that they had obtained from the revival; the Anglo-Catholic equivalent was a eucharistic celebration. A convert made through the American system became an initiate of the revivalist sub-world, the network of people, prayer-meetings, conferences and Bible Colleges which was slowly forming during the closing years of the Victorian period. The Anglo-Catholic convert found himself grafted into the Church Catholic or, more mundanely, into the life of an Anglo-Catholic parish.

The Twelve Days Mission to London was not completely the work of a single school but it did spring from a common anxiety. It was not, obviously, an anxiety about rural England, the loyalty of which the Victorian Churches took too confidently for granted. The Mission was the work of urban priests who still believed in the parish system even in its transformed urban setting; their efforts at revivalism showed their awareness that in the chaotic, expanding cities of industrial England the parish had less and less to offer as an effective religious base. The ideal still remained very much what the curate of St Peter's, Stepney, James Rowsell, had told the House of Lords *Select Committee on the Deficiency of Spiritual Provision for Populous Areas* in 1858:

> the treating of the parish, as far as possible, as a family—as gathered together round one house of God, there being an entire sympathetic communion between the clergy and their flocks, visiting and advising with them not merely in sickness but really sympathizing with them in their hours of leisure and amusement, in other words, as Our Blessed Saviour said, going in and out amongst them and, if necessary, sitting down with publicans and sinners

—words which suggest a conscious attempt to carry into the city the habits and possibilities of a small country parish.[1] This was the ideal which Bishop Blomfield and the Ecclesiastical Commissioners (who were the nearest thing to a coherent planning board which the nineteenth century Establishment possessed) earnestly pressed on their contemporaries, breaking up the large, populous urban parishes, building hundreds of new churches and aiming at an institutionally reformed Church divided into thousands of small units, each with a parson, curate, full-time paid Scripture Reader or City missionary (they cost rather less than curates, approximately £75 a year in the mid-century, and were regarded as distinctly the curate's social inferiors), and a variety of lay, voluntary workers, most of them women. In a longer perspective it is clear that the Anglican reformers of the 1830s and '40s were mistaken in supporting the extension of the parochial system in an essentially rural form to the changed conditions of the great cities.[2] Even in 1858 there were those who already suspected this, men like Thomas Fraser Stooks, secretary of the London Diocesan Church Building Society, which had been inaugurated in 1854.

Stooks clung with part of his mind to the traditional scheme. He had a simple programme: commence with a reasonable-

---

[1] *House of Lords Select Committee on the Deficiency of Spiritual Provision for Populous Areas*, 1858, Q. 1125.

[2] Cf. Olive J. Brose, *Church and Parliament, the reshaping of the Church of England, 1828–60* (1959) for further discussion. For the wider problem of Anglican organization, see K. A. Thompson, *Bureaucracy and Church Reform, 1800–1965* (1970).

sized district, put down a clergyman who would use a school building as a church in order to find the nucleus of a congregation; finally, the time would come for a building and a permanent, official formation of a parish. Faced with the fact that many of the new churches in the East End were poorly attended he defended his position desperately. He told the House of Lords Select Committee:

> it must be remembered that in most cases where new churches have been built the population has been neglected for years, and that adults, now heads of families, grew up in the earliest part of this century, which I suppose was one of the deadest times of the English Church. The consequence is that it is now extremely difficult to bring these people to church. It is only little by little that the clergy can overcome their apathy. When therefore we build new churches we cannot expect them to be filled at once [this was what Blomfield and his supporters had really thought would happen]. I think that a generation must pass before we can see that.[3]

With another part of his mind, however, Stooks admitted what his experience as a church-builder was no doubt teaching him, that 'the first thing towards the spiritual and moral improvement of the people would be to improve their physical and social condition'. He would have liked legislation to guarantee a holiday during the working week so that the poor would be freer to attend church at the weekend. He agreed that there was scarcely a school in London in 1858 that had any playground attached to it. He wanted twelve, instead of six, hundred clergymen in London, but confessed that he had no idea where to find the money to pay for them.

Twelve years later, in 1870, one of the leaders of the 1869 Mission to London, W. D. Maclagan, published an essay on 'The Church and the People',[4] which suggested that not much further progress had been made. He started from the notorious absence of workingmen from churches in the larger towns, a fact which had really been admitted since the Religious Census of 1851. He explained this withdrawal partly by the fact that

---

[3] *House of Lords Select Committee*, Q. 1286.
[4] 'The Church and the People', in *The Church and the Age*, ed. A. Weir and W. D. Maclagan (1870), pp.423–66.

the poor were driven so hard at work that it was understandable that they should want to treat Sunday as a day of relaxation—if in reality they stopped working on the Sunday, for many of the men described in Mayhew's books were compelled by poverty to work on at the weekend. If the poor wanted to pursue social or political questions they were bound to do so on Sunday. Railway excursions tempted another group, and public-houses others still. Meanwhile the Church itself had alienated the working-class by lethargy, social distinction, and careless organization:

> When we think of the aspect of an average London church about twenty years ago, or as it still may be seen in by no means the most obscure portions of the great metropolis; the cushioned pews with their exclusive occupants; the stately beadle warning off the *profanum vulgus*; the discriminating pew-opener inwardly calculating with an accuracy acquired by long experience the probabilities of a sixpence being ready to hand; and then, worst of all, the open benches ranged along the centre passage, or stowed away in the furthest corners of the church as free seats reserved for the use of the poor; when we think of this, and then imagine ourselves in the position of an honest labouring man or thriving mechanic in some of the courts or narrow streets which hem in the wealthy neighbourhood—can we, any of us, in our conscience say that we should have liked to go to church in such circumstances?[5]

What followed from Maclagan's analysis was (a) that the Church of England was seriously hampered by the financial burdens of the parish system (pew-rents survived for financial, not social, reasons), and that a much simplified organization was needed if the Church was to function efficiently; and (b) that if the industrial system was not working in the interests of the Church, the Church was not obliged to refrain from criticizing the industrial system. It did not follow that working-men would have returned to the parish church as a result of such a programme, but Maclagan's own solutions, which ranged from the formation of lay fraternities about the Eucharist to an increase in the number of the episcopate (though not, he added, the kind of political episcopate whose

[5] Ibid., p.430.

activities were the admiration of *The Times*) were hardly conceived with even one eye on the poor.

The central point of his essay, however, was the advocacy of parish missions, 'an attempt to reach and lay hold of the careless and the ungodly by efforts which could not be continuously sustained, but which from time to time may be most effectively employed'.[6] Maclagan was at least concerned about those outside the Church altogether, whereas Moody was really concerned about those who already had some place in institutionalized religion. Apart from this, the idea of the parish mission was an admission that, if the Church of England wished to continue to regard itself as the Church of the English People, it would have to go out and bring the masses (or some substantial part of them) back into the parish churches: middle-class congregations were not enough. Maclagan also assumed that 'cultural Anglicanism' and 'folk religion' were not enough for personal salvation (and G. H. Wilkinson, one of his more prominent supporters and like him destined to become a bishop, held a strong belief in the existence of the Devil). In effect, however, the use of revivalism seemed like an admission that the Establishment had neither the will nor the political influence either to provide a new structure for the Church itself or to change the industrial system. Even successful revivalism—and this the later Victorian period did not see as far as the working-classes were concerned—would not have filled the parish churches on such terms. A century later, the *Paul Report* revealed that the imbalance of clergy between town and country, which the traditional parochial system helped to maintain, had still not been corrected, and that the supply of ordinands, already inadequate in the nineteenth century, was drying up.[7]

Maclagan was not an extreme Anglo-Catholic and he deplored the way in which the public concentrated on the bizarre aspects of High Church revivalism. Nevertheless, the main leaders of the 1869 Mission to London, apart from himself, were a group of Anglo-Catholics which included R. M. Benson and S. W. O'Neill of the Cowley Fathers, as well as members of the Society of the Holy Cross such as Charles

[6] Ibid., p.442.
[7] Leslie Paul, *The Deployment and Payment of the Clergy* (1964).

Lowder, A. H. Mackonochie and W. J. E. Bennett. (Bennett, who was the incumbent of Frome, in Somerset, had had a mission there in 1868 conducted by the Cowley Fathers, and when he printed his London Mission Sermons in 1869 dedicated them to the same order.) It is also worth noting that in a statement made to the Upper House of Convocation of Canterbury in 1877, the Society of the Holy Cross explicitly claimed to have organized the Mission to London in 1869. It is true that the Society's back was to the episcopal wall at the time because of the controversy which gathered around its use of the book called *The Priest in Absolution*, a translation of a French Roman Catholic manual for confessors, and it may have hoped that at least its mission work would be counted to it for righteousness. The Society made no reference on this occasion to the part played by the Cowley Fathers. Charles Bodington, moreover, in his chaotic little book, *Devotional Life in the Nineteenth Century*, published many years later in 1905, repeated the Society's claim with approval.

The Anglo-Catholic inspiration of the 1869 Mission has been somewhat obscured by the accident that much of the information that we have about the meetings that led to it comes to us through the voluminous official biography of George Howard Wilkinson, a man who slowly changed his ecclesiastical position and whose importance in the period can easily be exaggerated.[8] This is also the point at which to mention an interesting discussion of Wilkinson by Dieter Voll under the title *Catholic Evangelicalism*, a book published in 1963.[9] Dr Voll sought to show that in the second half of the nineteenth century the Oxford Movement accepted 'evangelical tradition', forming a unique blend of the divided forces of the Church of England and offering a relevant model for the ecumenical future. Dr Voll's argument fails, I think, because he did not pay enough attention to the idiosyncratic nature of Anglo-Catholic revivalism, but assumed that any enthusiasm for aggressive preaching must be evidence for 'evangelical' attitudes; an assumption that ignored the history of Roman Catholic revivalistic missions since the seventeenth century and made the error of method of supposing that

[8] A. J. Mason, *Memoir of George Howard Wilkinson*, 2 vols. (1909).
[9] This was a translation of Voll's *Hochkirchlicher Pietismus* (Münich 1960).

'revivalism' was necessarily Protestant, when in fact it may be said to have both Protestant and Roman connotations. He also failed to discuss the missions of 1869 and 1874 in sufficient detail, and treated Wilkinson as too static and significant a figure, a mistake which was really a tribute to Wilkinson's own powerful self-regard.

Wilkinson, who rose rapidly in later years and became first, Bishop of Truro, and then, after some kind of psychological collapse, Bishop of St Andrews and Primus of the Scottish Episcopal Church, had in fact been moving towards the Anglo-Catholic point of view from about 1863, when he first read Goulburn's *Thoughts on Personal Religion*. In 1865 he first met T. T. Carter of Clewer and read his *Doctrine of Priesthood in the Church of England*; in the same year he made the acquaintance of George Body, then a curate at Wednesbury, and Canon Ashwell, who taught in Anglican theological colleges and influenced Wilkinson on subjects such as confession and absolution. By the time that Wilkinson left Bishop Auckland for London in 1868, he was completely the High Churchman, and Dr Voll hardly seems justified in calling him a Tractarian who embraced the virtues of Evangelicalism; he had given up Evangelical opinions for the most part by 1868. That Anglo-Catholics should be interested in revivalism in the sense of replacing the traditionally rather static Anglican attitude towards society with one more dynamic was not surprising: the second generation of the movement, which may be identified with H. P. Liddon, for example, was not deeply affected by Biblical criticism or by theological liberalism, but was horrified both by the indifference of urban populations to the celebration of the Eucharist, and by the numbers of poor people who did not attend services at all. The movement did not draw on Evangelical sources for its revivalistic technique, however, but turned to French Catholic precedents, in which preaching had always been as prominent as it was in Protestantism. There was in Roman Catholicism a contrast between the low emotional key of normal worship and the orgy of emotionalism to which the same congregation might be exposed when the periodic mission was preached. This ambivalent attitude to preaching now took root in Anglicanism for at least a generation, though Anglicanism did not prove very receptive to a revival of Romantic preaching. Some form of Anglo-Catholic aggression was inevitable because the movement could not rely on pre-existing sympathy for its aims; most people knew nothing of the traditions which Anglo-Catholics wanted to restore, and many reacted with hostility to what they saw or heard. The new priests had to explain and had to proselytize, or the movement would have collapsed.

The Anglo-Catholic missions were not, therefore, an exercise in ecclesiastical compromise. One can see the methods already developing in the *Suggestions for a Mission Week* which Wilkinson and a few others drafted to serve as a basis for the Mission which they wanted to hold in Wilkinson's parish of Bishop Auckland in 1865. Mason's statement, in his biography of Wilkinson, that this was 'to all appearance, the earliest effort of the kind in the Church of England', was certainly wrong.[10] R. M. Benson had taken part in a parish mission at Bedminster in Bristol which was certainly not 'evangelical', in 1862; in Benson's manuscript notebook, which is kept at Cowley, this is described as 'the first of our modern missions'; Lowder and Rivington took part with Benson, and all three were present at the final meeting to arrange the 1869 Mission to London.

Even in 1864 one of the '*Suggestions*' stated that 'the Methodist idea of a revival should be in every way avoided; the word should be avoided and another adopted—e.g., 'A Mission Week'.[11] The plan of this 1865 Mission was that the nine clergy engaged should meet each morning for Holy Communion at 8 o'clock: 'several of the parishioners were also present, and the number of communicants was never less than 20, and on two occasions exceeded 50'.[12] The clergy spent the morning first in joint study of the Bible and then in private meditation. In the evenings special services were held in two centres, followed by after-meetings at which notice was given that anyone who wanted further advice should approach the clergy. At the end of the nine days Mission, a meeting was held, at which

[10] Mason, op. cit., Vol. I, pp.126-7.
[11] Ibid., p.125.
[12] Ibid., p.131.

the teaching of the week was repeated, and it was clearly set forth, that there was no need of any human being intervening between a soul and its Saviour. All therefore who felt that they had learned the way of salvation, and were able for themselves to seek the Saviour, were next desired to retire. It was clearly explained that the names of those who remained would be taken, and that they would be regarded as asking for help and guidance from their Ministers, as having been taught by God to see their own sin, and as earnestly anxious to be reconciled to Him against whom they had offended. After this explanation several retired, and at least 80 persons humbly and thankfully gave in their names.[13]

This long drawn-out process was not what the nineteenth-century Methodists or Anglican Evangelicals meant by revivalism. The professional revivalist always pressed for immediate decision. The gap between Anglicans of this school and the revivalism of the Evangelical tradition may be seen in Canon G. E. Mason's description of Robert Aitken's after-meetings:

It was quite impossible to attend these meetings without being impressed, and conceiving a deep respect for the venerable and enthusiastic leader. On the other hand, some of his assistants, who in their extempore prayers mistook loud tones of voice for spiritual force and fervour, imperative conjunctions and vehement gesticulations for the same, were distinctly repellent. I remember on another occasion hearing Mr Aitken preach in a London church a very striking sermon on the visit of the Queen of Sheba to Solomon. We then repaired to the schoolroom. I retired to the corner of the infants' gallery, where I thought I should be safe. But the hope was vain. It was not long before I found Mr Aitken was advancing along the row, and at last my turn came. It was no good my saying that I hoped and trusted that I was in a state of salvation, or that I was reading for Orders, I was required to say that I was saved, and to repeat the words, 'My Saviour', as the sign of my personal assurance. He knelt beside me, he shook me, he clapped me on the shoulder. 'Speak to me,' he said, 'as if I were your father.' All eyes were turned towards me, until at least he uttered some kind of hope or blessing, and left me, obstinate still. I could not honestly have repeated after him the words he pressed upon me. It would have been untrue. It would have meant one thing to him and another to me. To him it would have meant that

[13] Ibid., p.133.

I had undergone certain experiences which I had not undergone, and that I possessed a 'Wesleyan' assurance. I was grateful to him for his anxiety, but I could not fall into his groove.[14]

As this quotation suggests, there is no serious evidence for Dr Voll's idea that Robert Aitken, a would-be charismatic leader who failed to find a following, fathered a 'Catholic Evangelical' movement of which Wilkinson and Maclagan were part; he had nothing to do with the London Mission of 1869. There was only a superficial resemblance between his methods and those which Wilkinson described as having been used in the case of the inquirers at the Bishop Auckland mission:

We have seen them all, some several times. Some were in great anxiety. I never saw such a deep sense of the burden of sin, except in those who had lived immoral lives, whereas these were with scarcely an exception amongst our most respectable people. Nearly all who were deeply in earnest found peace, after much teaching about the Saviour's work and much prayer. At one time nearly every room in the Parsonage had some one in it who had no place to pray at home, but who was seeking with many tears.[15]

This comes from the account which Wilkinson wrote for his parish. The Bishop of Durham, Baring, who was also Wilkinson's parishioner, withheld his sanction from the mission, saying that anything it might accomplish could be more legitimately secured on the old lines of faithful preaching and house to house visiting. Baring, who dismissed Wilkinson by saying that he drew more women than men to his communion services, also intervened when Wilkinson wanted to oblige his confirmation candidates to pledge themselves to attend Communion regularly after confirmation. Baring prohibited this on the ground that the pledges were both useless and illegal.[16]

Wilkinson was not deflected. He moved to London and in 1868 he took part in missions in Maclagan's parish of Enfield;

---

[14] Quoted by Charles Bodington, in *Devotional Life in the Nineteenth Century* (1905), pp.86–7. Cf. the discussion of the inquiry-room in chapter 5.

[15] Mason, op. cit., p.135.

[16] Baring disliked Wilkinson's increasing Anglo-Catholicism and probably suspected the instability which showed itself in later life.

in January 1869 he assisted at another in Staffordshire at Willenhall, where Charles Bodington was incumbent.[17] In July, 1869, he held a small conference on mission technique at his London house, when he and Maclagan predominated.[18] This Conference marked the decisive break with the methods of revivalists like Caughey, Finney and Robert Aitken, who had set out to draw people into the inquiry-room, where they could be subjected to intense personal pressure. In 1860, for instance, when the lay revivalists Radcliffe and Weaver were refused the use of Exeter Hall, they worked the Surrey Theatre for three months on Sunday evenings. After they had spoken and Weaver had sung,

> Mr Radcliffe concluded by asking any present who had been aroused by anxiety for their souls to remain after the departure of the congregation. Another hymn was sung to as lively an air as before, and the majority of the people left, but some hundreds remained and Mr Radcliffe and his helpers went among them. Groups were seen here and there, and in one or two cases the anxiety was expressed by weeping.[19]

The helpers, laymen in this case, urged them to 'surrender themselves to Christ': the evidence of surrender was expected to appear as an ecstatic feeling of joyous freedom, analogous to the Wesleyan idea of 'assurance' which Canon Mason used to interpret Robert Aitken's attitude.

Most of those who attended Wilkinson's Conference had seen this emotional reaction at first hand. The Willenhall mission had been organized to produce this result.

> Wilkinson only preached twice, and took part in the prayer-meetings after the sermons, but he made and received a deep impression. After the first of these sermons, which was on Ahab (a favourite subject of his) he found himself guided to a man at the bottom of the church. Wilkinson told him to pray. 'But,' the man answered, 'I never prayed in my life and don't know how to

[17] Others at Enfield were Hay Aitken (the son of Robert Aitken), Walsham How (later Bishop of Wakefield), and George Herbert of Vauxhall, a strong Anglo-Catholic who had almost annual missions in his parish from 1865.

[18] The others were J. H. Moore, who had been a curate at West Hartlepool; C. H. Cope, who had come south with Wilkinson to assist him; and Malcolmson of Deptford.

[19] *Guardian*, 12 December, 1860.

do it.' 'Then kneel down,' he said, 'and tell God that you do not know how to pray and ask Him to show you how.' The man did so, and before long Wilkinson had to come back from dealing with some other souls and ask him to restrain himself, as the man was confessing all his sins in a loud voice and in deadly earnest.[20]

Mason's account suggested that Wilkinson was satisfied with this experience but the record of the Conference implies the opposite.

When the Conference discussed evangelism, it was agreed that after-meetings were the key, but there were two views as to how to run them. On the one hand, as at Willenhall,

> the clergy and some laymen, during singing or prayer, dispersed themselves through the room and addressed each individual as to his religious condition, such inquiries often leading to separate prayer being offered up aloud with, or by, the individual addressed.[21]

On the other hand, the Conference produced criticism of this system. It was said that the noise and confusion was liable to hinder the calm work of the Holy Spirit and produce excitement likely to be injurious; some who needed help might be missed. A third criticism was certainly present in Wilkinson's mind. At Willenhall laymen as well as ministers had helped enquirers, and sincere Anglo-Catholics were doubtful about the wisdom of using laymen in this way. This is not to say that Anglo-Catholics made no use of the laity: in 1869, for example, women from the recently formed religious communities helped in the West End midnight meetings for prostitutes; but here they acted in a limited and clearly subordinate role.

Such a reaction followed logically from the Anglo-Catholic emphasis on the priesthood. After about 1850 the movement was firmly committed to the image of the priest as the spiritual director of the people of his parish, but it was also recognized that the laity were neither accustomed nor anxious to unburden their inner selves to the new priests. This resembled the course of Wesleyan history, for John Wesley similarly

[20] Mason, op. cit., Vol. I, p.227.
[21] Ibid., p.229.

longed to know the contents of men's minds, and hoped to do so through the class-meeting, in which a good Wesleyan was supposed to reveal his condition willingly to others; but the system broke down more quickly than Methodist historians admit, as the Wesleyan laity recovered from the hysteria of the early revival and ceased to rely on the discretion of those who heard their confessions. In 1843, John Keble complained to Coleridge of the distance between him and his people:

> How blindly I go about the parish, not knowing what men are really doing; and when I do make my discoveries, they disclose a fearful state of things; and even when there is some seriousness, of respect and confidence towards the Priest as such there is none.[22]

Wilkinson, and others of the second generation of Anglo-Catholics valued revivalism as a way of breaking down the barrier between parishioners and their priest, and putting the laymen in a dependent position in which they as individuals confessed their sin and asked for help. This side of Anglo-Catholicism attracted Wilkinson; he had as strong an impulse to control the lives of others as he had inability to cope with his own over-scrupulous, easily depressed, rather vain personality. In 1891, when he was fifty-eight, Wilkinson resigned the see of Truro because of a period of deep depression in which he felt that God had abandoned him altogether; he recovered after two years, and was restored to the episcopate, in Scotland, however. His temperament did not alter: 'towards the end of his life he often spoke of death, and of the almost intolerable sense of sin which preceded its approach in some souls'.[23]

Wilkinson, therefore, did not want to use the after-meeting to convert people: he wanted to use it as a way of introducing into a parish religious control of the individual by the priest. At Bishop Auckland, after a short address intended to deepen impressions already made, those who said that they required 'guidance' were asked to arrange a private interview with one

[22] See W. J. A. M. Beek, *John Keble's Literary and Religious Contribution to the Oxford Movement* (Nijmegen, 1959) for this subject.
[23] Mason, op. cit., Vol. II, p.243. He died in 1907. Much of what he took to be religious experience was probably the outcome of acute states of clinical depression.

of the clergymen taking part, 'and a first meeting for this purpose was all that was arranged at the public meeting'.[24] In his report on the St Peter's, Windmill Street, share in the later London Mission, Wilkinson used much the same terms under the heading: 'Personal interviews, means taken to secure'. He said that

> the people had for a year been trained to come to the Vestry in cases of awakening. Frequent invitations (for appointments) in Church. Appointments at after-meetings by Visitors and Clergy when the soul was impressed—not leaving the impression to be effaced on the morrow, but fixing the time and obtaining the promise to go to the Vestry at a fixed time next day.[25]

Here Wilkinson avoided the use of the word 'confession', which had become notorious in the London Mission itself. The implications of what he said become clearer in the light of two other passages in the records of the first Mission Conference:

> Souls are not to be neglected after conversion. . . . It is important so to bear in mind the natural evil of the heart as not to leave an awakened soul to itself, till the Holy Spirit has either guided it to peace or in some degree settled it. Many of the clergy awaken a soul (by God's help)—and perhaps speak once or twice to it in private, and then leave it. I think this is very dangerous, and ignores the power and malice of the Devil.

Wilkinson seems to have relied on the power of the Devil as one way of maintaining his own mental balance; his belief in the Devil enabled him to attribute some part of what he regarded as his own inner corruption to an outside agency.

> Neither are souls to be made dependent on the priest, but their union with Jesus through the Spirit in the humble use of the means of grace is to be kindly cherished.[26]

Wilkinson thought of the process which began at the after-meeting as entailing the unremitting spiritual direction of the awakened person by the parish priest. This was the funda-

[24] Mason, op. cit., Vol. I, p.229.
[25] Ibid., Vol. I, p.237.
[26] Ibid., Vol. I, p.230.

mental difference between his position and that of the Evangelicals; his aim was to build up that peculiar kind of religious intimacy between priest and people which became the hallmark of the true Anglo-Catholic parish. His language also reflected the need to rebut the standard criticism of the Confessional in later Victorian England, summed up by the northern Dean who said that the Confessional made men women and women worms; there was to be, in theory, no dependence on the priest. By the time of the second Mission to London in 1874, Wilkinson had reached the point where he was ready to defend publicly a limited use of aural confession.

Here the influence of his associates in the 1869 Mission was important. The second of these Mission Conferences was held on 23 September, 1869, at Cowley, Oxford, at the headquarters of R. M. Benson's order, the Society of St John the Evangelist, founded as recently as 1866, the first Anglican order for men since the Reformation, and specifically intended to supply the Established Church with mission priests in the French style.[27] Benson was bound to appeal to Wilkinson. When on one occasion an Evangelical asked him, 'Have you found peace?', Benson replied, 'No, war.' It was an answer which chimed with Wilkinson's own experience, though he could not treat his own pessimism with the skill of the neo-Jansenist monk. Most of those at the Conference belonged to the Order—Benson himself, Prescott, Grafton and O'Neill; or were members of the Society of the Holy Cross which had been started in 1855 by Charles Lowder, Newton Smith and A. Poole.[28] Lowder was present, as was A. H. Mackonochie, Master of the Society, another troubled spirit; L. Rivington, C. Parnell, George Herbert and Charles Bodington all belonged to the same group. Wilkinson was accompanied by J. H. Moore, Furse, who had taken part in one of the Enfield missions, George Body, and possibly by one of his clergy, W. B. Smith. Maclagan was not present; Hay Aitken's absence underlines the weakness of Dr Voll's thesis.

[27] There is no good life of Benson; for the order, cf. A. M. Allchin, *The Silent Rebellion* (1958); M. Hill, *The Religious Order* (1974). Allchin ignores the use of French models, Hill over-values the sociological insights of Weber.

[28] There is still no real history of the Anglo-Catholic movement; too much time has been spent on the personalities of the first decade, and on Newman especially; cf. J. Embry, *The Catholic Movement and the Society of the Holy Cross* (1931).

Wilkinson's interest in missions was that of a priest anxious to increase his spiritual control over his parish; psychologically, he was closer to Keble and Benson than to the younger Anglo-Catholics, whose immersion in urban life had to some extent freed them from the self-absorption of the Tractarian tradition. Charles Lowder had gone to St Barnabas, Pimlico, in 1851; Mackonochie to St George's in the East in 1858, whence he shifted to the new parish of St Alban's, Holborn, in 1862; Arthur Stanton joined him there at the same time. They all shared a knowledge of the apparent impotence of the Christian version of the Western religious tradition in the cities.[29] Maclagan wrote:

> To some, it may appear as if the work was almost hopeless. Let anyone go and see for himself the condition of the people in some of the districts of the Metropolis. Let him walk through some of the narrower streets, or even the crowded thoroughfares, of Lambeth, of Shoreditch, of Bethnal Green. Let him look at the men and women whom he meets, and always with this one thought present in his mind—'These are immortal souls, children of one Heavenly Father, and many of them, perhaps most of them, living without God and without hope. What will become of them? What can be done for them?' Let anyone face these thoughts and grapple with them, remembering too that these souls are but thousands among tens of thousands, and only in one great city among many; and can we wonder if sometimes the answer to these inquiries comes to the heart speaking less of hope than of despair.[30]

The sincerity of the reaction does not guarantee the rightness of the Anglo-Catholic decision to use the parish mission. That choice assumed that the future of the Church of England ought to be on a parochial basis, whereas by 1870 considerable evidence existed to show that neither the men nor the money nor the lay support could be found for such a policy. Another

[29] Here again the history is lacking, but one must distinguish between the rural priests of the earlier period and their successors: the earlier group wanted to make their parishes replicas of the ideal Church of England, the vision of which nagged them constantly, but their problem was small-scale, and they did not feel themselves to be in either a cultural or numerical minority; the ascetic, earnest image they fostered made them more remote from their parishioners than some eighteenth-century priests had been. It was not the movement of Anglo-Catholic priests into cities which mattered, so much as what being in the cities did to the Anglo-Catholic priests.

[30] Maclagan, op. cit., pp.431–2.

clue to the Anglo-Catholic choice of the parish mission—and probably the vital one—can be found in the early life of Charles Lowder. Years before, in 1854, Lowder, in his thirties, ran into trouble during a vigorously contested election to the office of churchwarden in the parish of St Paul's, Knights-bridge.

> To the crypt at St Barnabas there is an underground passage from the choristers' vestry, where the boys occasionally lurked and larked. Among these was at this time a cousin of Charles Lowder, a Christ's Hospital boy, who was on a visit from the College. He was inflamed by the sight of 'Vote for Westerton'—the 'Protestant' candidate—carried on a board, sandwich-wise, through the streets near St Barnabas. He and the other boys conceived a fierce desire to do battle with the innocent bearer of the obnoxious placard, and he entreated his cousin to allow them to throw something at the man. Charles bade him not throw dirt or stones, but gave the boys sixpence to buy rotten eggs. They were not slow in using them, carrying the war into Ebury Street, and the bespattered 'sandwich' man complained to his employers, who speedily invoked the aid of the law against the assailants. Charles was interrogated, and took all the blame of inciting the boys to bedaub the inscription. Before the police magistrate he repeated publicly the admission of the indiscretion. . . . The newspapers, of course, made large capital of the occurrence, proclaiming a Puseyite conspiracy to put down Protestant churchwardens by force.[31]

Bishop Blomfield intervened and suspended him from his curacy for six weeks. During his suspension he went abroad, and spent some days at the Petit Seminaire at Yvetot, in the diocese of Rouen, where he seems to have taken up in the library the *Life of St Vincent de Paul*. Long afterwards he wrote of 'the deep impression made on his mind by the sad condition of the French Church and nation in the sixteenth century and by the wonderful influence of the institutions founded by St Vincent',[32] and he added, significantly in view of what had been said above:

> The spiritual condition of the masses of our people, the appalling

---

[31] *Charles Lowder*, by The Author of *St Teresa* (1882), pp.56–7.
[32] Ibid., pp.64–5.

vices which prevail in our large towns, and especially in the teeming districts of the metropolis, the increasing tendency of the people to mass together, multiplying and intensifying the evil, and the unsatisfactory character of the attempts hitherto made to meet it, were enough to make men gladly profit by the experience of those who had successfully struggled against similar difficulties.[33]

Anglo-Catholics like Lowder were not in the mood to adapt Evangelicalism to their own purposes. They were much more easily impressed by Roman Catholic models, and St Vincent de Paul was no minor figure in the history of the Roman Church. He first conceived the plan of his congregation of Mission Priests in 1617, began to hold missions himself in the French countryside in 1618, and first elaborated his Rule in 1626. Lowder, by the time that he returned from France, was already scheming to form a similar order; the immediate result was the Society of the Holy Cross, which dated from 1855. Of this he wrote that

its objects were to defend and strengthen the spiritual life of the clergy, to defend the faith of the Church, and to carry on and aid mission work both at home and abroad. The members of this society meeting together as they did in prayer and conference were deeply impressed by the evils existing in the Church, and saw also, in the remedies adopted by St Paul, the hope of lessening them. They all felt that the ordinary parochial equipment of rector and curate, or perhaps a solitary incumbent, provided for thousands of perishing souls, was most sadly inadequate; that in the presence of such utter destitution it was simply childish to act as if the Church were recognized as the mother of the people. She must assume a missionary character, and by religious association and a new adaptation of Catholic practice to the altered circumstances of the nineteenth century and the peculiar wants of the English character, endeavour, with fresh life and energy, to stem the prevailing tide of sin and indifference.[34]

The Roman Catholic origin of the mission system was well understood at the time. As the Rev J. Edwards, of Prestbury, wrote to the *Guardian* in 1869 about the use of the service for the renewal of baptismal vows during the London Mission:

[33] Ibid., p.65.
[34] Ibid., pp.74-5.

the candle-bearing I am not disposed to defend, as we did not where I was adopt this edifying system; but I may be permitted to say that Blunt is certainly wrong in supposing that this ceremony is 'an invention of Ritualism', or 'without any precedent in the modern Church to justify it.' It is one of the many edifying customs for which the Catholic revival among ourselves is indebted to the modern Roman Church, and so found its fit place as the concluding service of a Mission which, in its main idea, as well as in all its chief features, derived from the same source.[35]

Lowder wrote to the Bishop of London in 1857 that 'evidently something more elastic and energetic is wanting than the old parochial system; are we to fall back upon Wesleyanism or on the old Catholic teaching of the Church?' It is evident that a clear distinction existed in his mind between 'Wesleyanism' and 'Catholicism'; he meant more especially the contrast between the disciplined use of the Catholic order of mission priests committed to sacramental principles, and what he took to be the disorderly activity of unauthorized preachers who undervalued the sacramental system. He started by creating a permanent mission station at St George's in the East in 1856; for a time in 1857 he had four clergy and a small sisterhood working with him there, and this was the community which Mackonochie joined in 1858; though not fully monastic the group lived according to a Rule which left little time for anything but prayer and hard work. Lowder failed, however, to expand his St George's Mission into a larger brotherhood capable of taking on missionary work elsewhere in London; it was not until 1862 that the first special Parochial Mission was given at Bedminster. On this evidence, Lowder's Society of the Holy Cross claimed in 1877 to have originated at St George's the first Anglican Home Mission; to have inaugurated at Bedminster the first parochial mission: this was held to be the first because of the difference between its methods and those which Anglican Evangelicalism had practised (at Wednesbury, for example) under the leadership of Twigg; and to have held the first spiritual retreat for the clergy, for which the Society gave the date 1856, though a more correct date might have been 1858—it is again a question of method.

[35] *Guardian*, 15 December, 1869.

It was R. M. Benson who carried on and completed what Lowder had begun. Benson was the sixteenth member of the Society of the Holy Cross, he conducted its first retreat proper at Chislehurst (1858), he was a Vicar of the Society, and took part in the Bedminster Mission (1862). When he formed the Society of St John the Evangelist (popularly called the Cowley Fathers—they were, and are, based at Cowley, in Oxford) he meant it to be a society of mission priests; its vigorous share in the London Missions of 1869 and 1874 was in line with Lowder's aims as well as Benson's. The personal link between the two men was very close; when Lowder almost collapsed under the strain of running the St George's Mission single-handed in 1857, it was Benson who helped him and who did not leave the Mission until Lowder had recovered his health. Thus, while it may be true to say that a sermon preached by John Keble in 1863 was one of the factors which prompted Benson to start his Order, it is truer to say that the Cowley community grew out of the Society of the Holy Cross, and that for years before 1863 Benson had been in touch through Lowder with the fact as well as the idea of a group of priests living together according to a severe rule in order to discharge the missionary responsibility of the Church. He was quite familiar with St George's, where the monastic hours were said, the Eucharist was celebrated daily, the group lived with great simplicity, and—with about one exception in twenty years—all remained unmarried. Nor is it surprising that Benson took less interest in parochial missions as time went on: he was fifty in 1874.

Lowder and Benson were repeating in their own way not only the experience of St Vincent de Paul in the seventeenth century, but the wave of similar missions in France under the Restoration, when the French mission orders struggled to recover for the Roman Church the loyalty of the countryside which had been lost in the long years of the Revolution and Empire. Ernest Sévrin has described these efforts in detail.[36] Lowder and others almost certainly knew of these nineteenth-century campaigns. On the other hand there is little evidence that the Passionist and Rosminian missionaries who worked in England more especially after 1848 had any direct effect on

[36] *Les Missions Religieuses en France sous la Restauration*, E. Sévrin, Vol. 1 (Paris, 1948).

the Anglo-Catholic missions, though they often worked among the Irish poor in London.[37] Dr Gilley describes the climax of the Passionist mission to Rotherhithe in 1861, when

> the impact of the events of the mission—Solemn Benediction and Papal Blessing and the confirmation of a hundred and sixty adults and children—was reinforced by indulgences offered for kissing a ten-foot cross on a high brick platform, with the scourges hanging from the arms, the sacred monogram nailed above the red thorn crown, and the lance and sponge affixed to the pole.[38]

Lowder would have recognized this combination of romantic and hell-fire preaching with an underlying sacramental framework. Both the Passionists and the Rosminians preached about death, hell and judgement with the sort of simple clarity which James Joyce illustrated in *Portrait of the Artist as a Young Man*.[39] One of the best-known Passionists was Joseph Furniss, whose tract *Sight of Hell*, was notorious.[40] There was no question here of some hypothetical 'Catholic Evangelicalism'; Catholic mission preachers preached about Hell because they believed in it.[41] Revivalism was a product of orthodoxy, orthodoxy about the 'signs' appropriate to 'conversion', orthodoxy about the fate of the finally impenitent. Evangelicals believed that the London poor stood in danger of hell-fire despite their baptism; Anglo-Catholics believed that they stood in danger partly as having been baptized. There is no doubt what Benson believed:

[37] For the Catholic missions, cf. Conrad Charles, 'The Origins of the Parish Mission in England and the Early Passionist Apostolate', *Journal of Ecclesiastical History*, xv (1964), pp.72–4.

[38] Sheridan Gilley, 'Catholic Faith of the Irish Slums, London 1840–70', in *The Victorian City*, ed. H. J. Dyos and M. Wolff (1973), Vol. 2, p.839.

[39] See James Docherty, *Modern Philology*, lxi (1963), pp.110–19, for discussion of the use Joyce made of F. Pinamonti's *Hell Opened to Christians to caution them from entering into It*, a seventeenth-century work available in England throughout the nineteenth century.

[40] For Joseph Furniss, cf. G. Rowell, *Hell and the Victorians* (1974), pp.171–3.

[41] Once launched, abstractions like 'Catholic Evangelicalism' can be eliminated only with difficulty; M. Hill, e.g., in *The Religious Order* (1974), a sociological study of nineteenth-century Anglican monasticism much influenced by Weberian terminology, endorses Dieter Voll's statement that 'we see the renaissance of the monastic ideal as a symptom of Catholic Evangelicalism in the Anglican Church', (Hill, op. cit., p.238). Neither Hill nor Voll see that the missions, on which they depend for the 'evangelicalism', had perfectly straightforward Roman Catholic ancestry. It is curious how hard some writers on early nineteenth-century Anglicanism find it to realize that both Roman and Anglo-Catholics could try to convert people without any 'Evangelical' inspiration.

Mr Benson dwelt on the soul in its departure, describing in heart-stirring words the awful time when it must appear before God in whose image it was created, the fiends who tempted it, the sins manifesting themselves as its accusers, and no hope remaining unless it had been cleansed in the blood of Christ. The preacher solemnly warned his hearers that everyone must come to that awful time. In the (ninth) sermon he spoke of the soul attaining its end. A time would come, when if it had lived for itself, it might go in vain to the throne of God to have its memory cleansed from the tormenting remembrance of the evil which it had done in the body, and which must ever cling to it, for the answer would be, 'He that is filthy, let him be filthy still'. On the other hand, if it could, amid many imperfections, remember some acts of true penitence, contrition and satisfaction, it might hear the words, 'let him that is holy be holy still' spoken of itself, and might enjoy the bliss of knowing that it had in some measure, however small, corresponded to the love of God, and attained the end for which it was created.[42]

2. *1869 London Mission*

Much of this experience already lay in the background of the Conference which met at Cowley in September, 1869, to plan the London Mission, which followed in the November. The Cowley Fathers and the members of the Society of the Holy Cross dominated a discussion which specifically dealt with Confession: how to bring people to it; how to prepare them for it; its desirability; penances. No record of the details of the meeting survived, but what happened during the actual Mission showed that there had been no objection to Confession as a principal feature. As a result of the Conference a letter was sent to most of the London clergy:

> Knowing the power of union, we have agreed to join together in making a special attack upon sin and Satan, by devoting twelve days preceding the season of Advent . . . to earnest prayer for the conversion of sinners. . . . No uniformity of method in the different churches will be attempted. Each Parish Priest must judge the needs and capabilities of his own people, and arrange his services accordingly. Our union consists in making simultaneously

[42] *Guardian*, 1 December, 1869. Here again, there was nothing Evangelical in Benson's description of the agonized soul after death recalling 'some acts of true penitence', etc.

this special supplication to God and appeal to man, and in our remembering in prayer, not only each one his own needs, but also each one the needs of his brethren. We venture to recommend, however, that, wherever the circumstances may be favourable, there should be, if possible, a frequent, if not daily, Celebration of the Eucharist, and that the course of sermons might in some instances, be advantageously preached not by different preachers but by the same preacher throughout.[43]

And so, within the limitations of the parochial system, there was a 'mission to London': it lasted from 14 November to 25 November, 1869, with O'Neill acting as secretary. In central and west London, about sixty-four parishes with some degree of Anglo-Catholic sympathy took part; another forty-eight parishes, most of them in East London, took part after the Mission had started, mostly confining their activity to preaching services of the traditional evangelical sort.[44] At the halfway stage *The Times* reported that a meeting of the missioners had claimed that attendances were good, reaching about 35,000 people a day.

The style of the Anglo-Catholic missions is best exemplified by the programme followed at some of the churches. At St Paul's, Knightsbridge, for instance, one of the missioners was the veteran Anglo-Catholic, W. J. E. Bennett of Frome in Somerset. On 15 November, 1869, *The Times* published an angry letter from a Charles Westerton of Knightsbridge protesting against the list of what he called 'performances' which were to be given at St Paul's during the Mission. There was to be Holy Communion daily at 7 a.m., 8.30 a.m. and 9.15 a.m.; Matins at 8 a.m.; a Litany of Penitence and the Catechising of Children at 11 a.m.; Evensong was to be at 5 p.m., together with an instruction class for women; the mission service proper with sermon at 8 p.m. with an instruction class for men. In addition, Bennett was to be available for confession every day from noon to 4 p.m., and a Canon Jenkins would hear confessions from 5 p.m. to 8 p.m. At

---

[43] The letter was issued with the approval of the bishops of London, Winchester and Rochester: as such, it was a declaration of intent, not a call to mission, as far as the 'Catholics' were concerned.

[44] *The Times*, 20 November, 1869. On 16 November, 1869, Maclagan answered this complaint, saying that not all the missioners would take the same pattern, but that harmony of purpose prevailed over differences in detail.

All Saints, Margaret Street, the senior priest was R. M. Benson himself: he was to attend in the vestry daily from noon to 1 p.m., from 2 p.m. to 4 p.m., from 5 p.m. to 6 p.m., and also after the service in the evening, to see anyone who wanted either to confess or to be helped more generally. At St Alban's, Holborn, where Mackonochie and Stanton normally officiated, the Mission preachers were O'Neill and Charles Bodington. Throughout the Mission the Eucharist was celebrated there four times in the early morning; there was a Litany at 1.30 p.m. and 4 p.m., a Choral Evensong at 5 p.m. and the mission sermon at 8 p.m. *The Times* commented on St Alban's that

> there is no disguise about the subject of confession . . . there can be no doubt in the minds of those who have attended these Mission services that Confession is no longer a moot point or a matter of discussion, but part and parcel of the religious revival, and differing only in very slight degree from the practice of the Roman Catholic Church.[45]

Another important contribution by the Cowley Fathers was the *Book of the Mission*. No copy of this seems to have survived, even at Cowley, but it probably began with an Evening Service, which started with the Lord's Prayer; had lessons at discretion; suggested Psalms 51 and 120 and ended at the Third Collect, the first collect being that of the Twenty-First Sunday after Trinity. The Book also contained the service for the renewal of baptismal vows which was used at St Alban's, Holborn, St Philip's, Clerkenwell, All Saints, Kensington, and Holy Trinity, Shoreditch; this was made up of extracts from the Commination and from the services for Baptism and Confirmation. The Book ended with instructions on Confession.[46] At a meeting held at Sion College after the Mission it was said that nearly 18,000 copies of the *Book of the Mission* had been sold, as well as 10,000 copies of an abridged edition; 6,000 copies of a *Guide to the Mission Services* had also been dis-

[45] *The Times*, 23 November, 1869. A writer to the *Guardian*, 24 November, 1869, had visited St Michael's, Shoreditch—'where prudence seems to have been cast to the winds'—and where Nihill was doing the Via Crucis; St Barnabas, Pimlico, and St Augustine's, Haggerston, where he heard E. A. Hillyard give a long, colloquial address, in defence of auricular confession.

[46] *v.i.*, p.266, for the *Record*'s view of the *Book of the Mission*.

posed of, but the purchasers here presumably overlapped with those already mentioned.

The ubiquitous clerical reporter, Maurice Davies, visited St Alban's, Holborn, and composed one of his amusing, Broad Church articles about what he heard and saw.

... For the first time I found the form of service followed out as it stands in the little penny books with the big crosses outside. It was very doleful. The Penitential Psalms were chanted slowly to the most unmitigated Gregorians, and the prayers monotoned very low down in the gamut. One cannot help wondering whether a little cheerful music written in round notes on five lines would not suit these simple people as well as the dreadful squareheaded notes on four lines. Why must we go back to imperfect musical notation when we want to sing about religion? The hymns, however, were more lively, and 'There is a fountain', followed by its refrain, 'I do believe, I will believe', put one in mind of the meeting-house. In fact, the whole affair is a wonderful congeries of the Roman and Ranter elements grafted on the stock of the Church of England as by law established. By all means let us be eclectic. We cannot afford to neglect any means for 'evangelising the masses', as the phrase goes. The sermon of the Rev. 'Father' O'Neill was on the Sacrament of Penance. Think of that and weep, ye orthodox, who teach your little children to answer the question, 'How many Sacraments?': 'Two only'. The Rev. 'Father' preached on the Sacrament of Penance. He was a little stiff and unnatural, labouring under a conscious effort to popularize an unpopular and unpalatable subject. It failed utterly, because it was unnatural, and the congregation, not large at the beginning, dribbled away perceptibly on the women's side. . . . I kept looking back around and about me with real curiosity, but I could not see the faintest trace of enthusiasm, or anything suggestive of a revival service. In fact, to my mind, the characteristic of the service was listlessness; of the sermon—effort—and effort unsuccessful in attaining its real end. In plain words, the whole affair at St Alban's on Monday night hung fire. . . .[47]

Davies was a professional (ordained) journalist; he lacked the 'seriousness' which usually inhibited Victorian descriptions of such occasions; but he could be fair to what seemed to him sincere. In fact, he preferred Anglo-Catholics to Evangelicals,

[47] *Orthodox London*, by C. Maurice Davies, 2nd ed. (1876), pp.151–2.

on whom he was often severe. It is significant that he, as an experienced observer, thought that the use of chorus hymns was 'eclectic' only; he was clear that the 'ranter' element had nothing to do with the sermon, or with the aim of the service. G. W. E. Russell, a more partisan observer, quoted part of Davies' account in his history of St Alban's but said that by the end of the Mission O'Neill's passionate evangelism had broken down the resistance of his audience. The Mission at St Alban's ended with the service for the renewal of baptismal vows, of which Russell quoted another description:

At eight o'clock St Alban's Church was crowded, the whole of the centre part of the church being railed off for penitents, one side for men and one side for women. . . . The scene was very striking; the body of the building was a blaze of light, while the chancel was very nearly dark. Father O'Neill, addressing the penitents, said: 'This is indeed a happy time; you are in the presence of God, and stand like wise virgins with their lamps trimmed'. He said then very slowly and solemnly: 'Do you here in the presence of God and of this congregation renew the solemn promise and vow that was made in your name at your Baptism?' To this there was the loud and startling response of 'I do', and so ended the London Mission of 1869.[48]

The *Guardian* contained another picture of this final service.

O'Neill said he would explain the service. First the candles would be blessed in the same way that vessels and all vestments were blessed before they were used. A candle would be given to each one who was about to renew his vows. This candle he would have lighted and what was not consumed of it might be taken home. . . . The questions which would be put would be taken from the Prayer Book, and he trusted that all would give their answers in a bold and manly way, so that the Church might be glorified and the Devil might tremble. The candles were then blessed at the 'altar'; but how this ceremony was performed was not seen by anyone who was not in the Chancel.

It is clear from Russell's account that the Chancel was almost in darkness compared with the remainder of the Church.

[48] G. W. E. Russell, *St Alban, The Martyr, Holborn, A History of Fifty Years* (1913), p.89. Russell wrote the official life of Charles Stanton in 1917. M. Reynolds, *Martyr of Ritualism* (1965), has nothing to add in terms of Mackonochie, as far as missions go.

In a minute or two afterward these were lighted (they were thin wax ones of about a foot long) and each of the penitents, to the number of nearly five hundred men and women, held one of them while a penitential hymn was sung. . . .

O'Neill then asked them:

'Do you here in the presence of God and of this congregation renew the solemn vows and promises that were made in your name at baptism'. . . . After this part of the ceremony Mr O'Neill went to the Altar and was vested in a splendidly embroidered cope. He was joined by the Revs Mackonochie, Walker, Hows and Willington, several members of the Society of St John the Evangelist, and a large number of choristers—and the procession accompanied by banners moved round the church, the five hundred men and boys, women and children, following in their train. . . . When the clerical part of the procession had reached the Chancel and the penitents had regained their places, the Blessing was pronounced, and the candles having been as if by one single breath blown out, the congregation dispersed.

Here the French Catholic influence on Anglo-Catholic piety and revivalism came out strongly. O'Neill compared his penitents to the wise virgins with their lamps trimmed because each was holding a lighted candle as was the custom in the Roman service which he was imitating. Sévrin (v.s.) described several ceremonies characteristic of the French missions of the Restoration: French Catholics took part in day-long processions bearing the reserved sacrament; whole parishes consecrated themselves elaborately to the Virgin Mary. These, together with the gathering in the local cemetery where the preacher gave an address on mortality by the side of a freshly dug grave, were hardly possible in Victorian England; nor was the planting of a Parish Cross to commemorate the Mission itself. Anglo-Catholic missions lacked the social and political support which made such gestures credible in France in the 1820s (however, most of the crosses were torn down again in the Revolution of 1830, and Republicans planted Trees of Liberty in reply). The service for the renewal of baptismal vows was the most convenient French ceremony to reproduce in England; it could take place inside a church-building, and it offered a logical and symbolical climax to the parish mission itself. Moreover, it emphasized the sacramental essence of revivalism as Anglo-Catholics understood it.

The sacramental approach to Christianity was fundamental to this second generation of Anglo-Catholics. Historians have often alleged that there was no real continuity between Tractarianism and so-called Ritualism, but Ritualism was an inevitable development of Tractarian piety. The original university Tractarians had stressed the doctrine of the real presence of Christ in the eucharistic elements; in the second generation, men like Arthur Stanton carried this dogmatic truth into the worship of the local parish church. They wanted, one might say, to objectify the presence of Christ before they attempted to be possessed by it subjectively. For Anglo-Catholic priests in the mid-nineteenth century, that is, the real presence (not simply the idea of the real presence) of Christ in the Eucharist meant the reassertion of the immediate knowableness of God in a post-Enlightenment society; here on the altar of the simplest parish church the presence of God might be encountered sacramentally, and not only at the end of some mysterious pilgrimage into another world.

Similarly, the Confessional objectified forgiveness. The Tractarians found Evangelical piety too subjective, and therefore too defenceless in an increasingly 'liberal' climate, if 'liberal' be defined as 'rationalist' in Newman's manner. The uncritical Evangelical demand for 'repentance' and for some kind of subjective sense of having been forgiven fell far short of the cathartic, objective experience which the younger Anglo-Catholics were already pursuing in the 1840s. W. J. Butler, for example, wrote to John Keble in December, 1845:

If we are to be a Church, surely our clergy must be holy. And I know personally a very large number who, partly from defective superintendence, partly from natural badness, passed the whole time of school and college in a most reckless and unholy way. Then perhaps in a year, without any sort of askesis, but merely the repentance of a heart not knowing its own sinfulness and yet not wholly devilish, they were ordained. Many of these, my own personal friends, are now repenting bitterly; their sins are lying like a heavy load upon them, and torturing them indescribably.

They long to go to confess and to go through some form of prescribed penance.[49]

Butler wanted Keble to hear his confession, but it was Pusey who acted for him. In March, 1846, having made a general confession to Pusey, Butler told Keble that now that it was becoming customary for men to make a general confession, it was becoming a serious question what they were to do in the future.

> As far as I know, though many are desirous to make a confession and to continue it as a habit through life, the thing is all but impossible.[50]

Men who had, as they believed, purified themselves by divine assistance for their priesthood through the use of what to them was sacramental confession, were likely to try to spread the practice in their parishes, and to insist on the spiritual value of the joint objectification of forgiveness and of the presence of Christ. The adoration of the reserved sacrament was logically present already in the 1840s.

This sacramental presence was then carried a stage further by another member of the Society of the Holy Cross, Orbey Shipley, who argued that Evangelical Protestantism had failed to talk England into Christianity, that the poorer and less educated classes were left unmoved by the complicated theological presuppositions and peculiar language of the Evangelical preachers, whom Charles Simeon had fixed in what seemed, and often still seems, an unbreakable mould. What would attract the masses and penetrate their minds more easily was the use of symbol, colour, processions, music, drama—a pattern which the sacramental system justified theologically. The sacraments of the Church, which the Ritualists did not limit to those of Baptism and the Lord's Supper, offered the proper basis, not only for a symbolical presentation of Christianity which was to communicate where language had failed, but which would also communicate the reality of what was symbolized, for the Anglo-Catholics

---

[49] *Life and Letters of W. J. Butler*, Anon. (1898), p.33. Butler was one of the pioneers of women's orders in the Anglican Church.
[50] Ibid., p.35.

believed that the symbols of bread and wine made available not only the idea of God, but the presence of God. The poor in the new industrial centres were starved of religious symbols and therefore of religious experience. Orbey Shipley was quite clear about the essential difference between Evangelical and Anglo-Catholic. Where Evangelicals had talked to the poor about the Spirit, Anglo-Catholics should bring them the real presence of Christ in the Eucharist. Where the Evangelical offered them a subjective kind of self-forgiveness for their sins, Anglo-Catholics should offer them the objectivized forgiveness of priestly absolution in the Confessional. Where the Evangelical talked only about Sin in general, Anglo-Catholics should not hesitate to point to particular sins.

There was nothing surprising, therefore, in the prominence given to the Confessional in the Anglo-Catholic centres of the 1869 Mission to London. The Evangelical reaction may be found in the pages of the *Record*. On 15 November, 1869, in its first discussion of the Mission, the *Record* concentrated on *The Book of the Mission*, singling out the section on confession as 'especially marked by priestcraft. What, for example, could be more enslaving than this: "3. Take care to be plain and simple; and if you find it difficult, ask the priest to help you. 4. If you doubt whether anything you have done is sinful, ask the priest".' The *Record* duly noted that the form of confession suggested advised the penitent to confess 'to you my Father', and to use the formula: 'I am truly sorry for these and all my other sins, which I cannot now remember, and I pray God to pardon me, and you, my Father, to give me penance, counsel and absolution.' On 22 November, 1869, the *Record* said that at Christ Church, Clapham, where there was so much incense 'that it was impossible to distinguish the features of a person who sat a few pews off', the Rev. Provost Fortescue of Perth exhorted those who were to take part in the service for the renewal of baptismal vows to confess themselves first. A leading article on 22 November, said of the Mission that 'the attempt seems to be one which grafts the earnestness of revival preaching on the sacerdotal errors of Romanism, and associates the call to repentance with the deadly poison of the Confessional'. A final leader on the Mission (29 November, 1869), said that in as much as the Anglo-Catholic campaign had advanced the practice of the Confessional it had been a ghastly failure.[51]

The Confessional stood out in the preaching of the more striking Anglo-Catholics. The best example was George Body, who took the main preaching-services at All Saints, Margaret Street. *The Times* reported that he said 'plainly that he has no power in himself of absolving from sin; and pointing to the image of Our Blessed Saviour over the altar he says that it is to Him and to Him only that the sinner must look for forgiveness and peace. He also says afterwards, "If you come to me, I don't ask you, if against your conscience, to confess your sins to me" '.[52] Maurice Davies brought out strongly the effect of one of his evening sermons:

> Mr Body preached on the Magdalene at the house of Simon, though he was so nearly voiceless as to be obliged to forego his Bible-class. His subject naturally led him to speak much of the social evil, *par excellence*, and he was just enough to address his sharpest remarks to the men's side of the congregation. He told a somewhat sensational story of a poor creature from the streets who the evening before had been attracted to St Alban's simply by seeing the large cross at the head of Mission's bill outside, and went in to ascertain its meaning. The 'priest' saw her and spoke to her; the result being that she left her course of life, and 'that night, instead of sleeping in a haunt of sin, slept in a house of penitence'. He truly said, if no other result than this case came from the Mission—supposing this to be permanent—that Mission had not been in vain. After the sermon the men were again invited to stop for confession. 'Do stop now? Won't you stop?' But, alas, they didn't stop. It was rather too much for our English reserve just yet to expect one or two individuals to come out from that congregation and undergo the unaccustomed ordeal of confession. I do not think the preacher expected it; for he was so very urgent in his invitation. He said he had no difficulty with the women but that he wanted the stronger sex. I fear it will require a great deal of Mission work before any of the stronger sex, really deserving the name, will be up to confession point.[53]

Davies' closing comment illustrates the normal English

[51] Again the curious conjunction of revivalist earnestness and Roman doctrine, as though the two elements had never been joined before: the writer in the *Record* obviously knew nothing about Roman Catholic missions.

[52] *The Times*, 19 November, 1869.

[53] Davies, op. cit., p.150.

reaction to the idea of confession at this time. Speaking in the House of Lords in 1873, Lord Salisbury said that confession diminished a nation's virility. George Body's appeal to confession, however, was the equivalent of the American revivalist's appeal for conversion: proof of the genuineness of repentance was to be seen in a man's willingness to go to the priest, unsupported by the excitement of a great occasion, to kneel and tell him exactly what one had done wrong, and to receive through him the declaration of God's forgiveness which, given and accepted in terms of authority, would need no further guarantee in the form of subjective religious experience. This owed nothing to the older Evangelicalism; in fact, the appeal to the Confessional expressed a deep dissatisfaction with the apparent subjectivism of traditional Protestant revivalism. Moreover, the consequence of such confession must be a further willingness to communicate, to live as part of the Church as Anglo-Catholicism conceived it. And whereas the American revivalist taught his hearers not to regard 'conversion' as an event to be repeated at regular intervals (but rather as an event which ought to have happened once and for all), the Anglo-Catholic penitent was taught to regard regular confession as a normal part of a healthy Christian spiritual life. 'Conversion' formed part of the Evangelical's past; confession remained integral to the Anglo-Catholic's future. This idea was summed up and projected forward in the service for the renewal of baptismal vows. Like the Roman Catholics on whose example they drew, the Anglo-Catholics measured the success of a mission by the increase in the number of those using the Confessional and the Eucharist which it produced.

The most that the *Record* wanted to approve was the 'earnestness' of the preaching. Body's vivid style drew much comment, but the pictorial, even sensational style followed directly from Orbey Shipley's argument about communicating the Gospel and owed little to Charles Simeon. Indeed, the comment which Body aroused depended on the sharp contrast between the style of the younger Ritualists and the kind of preaching which had characterized the Tractarians. Maurice Davies wrote:

It was amusing to notice how the former generation of so-called Puseyites, represented by such men as Messrs Liddell and Bennett, was completely distanced by the modern Ritualists. They cannot get out of their old habits of rigidity and formalism, which these young Titans have thrown to the winds. The sermon [i.e. Bennett's at Knightsbridge] was exceedingly dry, and not preached, but read from a manuscript. In fact, both time and place lifted it out of the category of Mission sermons. It was a Belgravian discourse *pur et simple*, and even made distinct reference to the sins of the London season.[54]

F. D. Maurice, on the other hand, seems to have regretted the sobriety of former days. He was glad that he was in Cambridge during the Mission, he said, because he would not have liked to have thrown cold water on it, 'yet I could not have joined it without adopting a style of preaching that appeals more to the sense than the spirit'.[55] As for the *Guardian*, with High Church rigour in its printer's ink, the leader writer said that much of the preaching had been exaggerated, even 'erotic' in style—which referred partly to the sermons about prostitution and sexual offences in general. 'It is notorious that warm feelings of no religious character have been excited by these tumultuous and sensational performances', he said, drawing a parallel with the 'Methodist revivals' in Cornwall, Wales and the United States.[56]

The centre of much of this criticism was George Body, who was still only twenty-nine; journalists called him everything from the 'English Boanerges' to the 'English Hyacinthe'.[57] He spoke very quickly in a powerful voice with a great deal of action—Davies described him speaking in the middle of the chancel at All Saints, Margaret Street, ignoring the chair that had been set for him, running up and down and sometimes falling on his knees. The description contains an echo of the

---

[54] Ibid., pp.149–50.

[55] *Life*, by his son (1884), Vol. II, p.596. Maurice, however, rarely agreed with anything other people did. He might have accepted the Mission's parochial basis, but was bound to reject its dependence on Anglo-Catholicism.

[56] *Guardian*, 24 November, 1869, commenting on the Mission as a whole.

[57] Père Hyacinthe was actually Charles Loyson, born in Orléans in 1827. It was on 20 September, 1869, that he issued his Manifesto calling for far-reaching reform of the Roman Catholic Church. He was then a Carmelite, but in 1872 he married in London; Dean Stanley attended the wedding. He moved to Switzerland, where he founded the Christian Catholic Church of Switzerland.

pulpit manners of Spurgeon in full flow. At his final meeting
he had his audience in tears, and no wonder, for he used the
kind of illustration which Moody also found effective, and
which one finds also in the mouth of Richard Weaver in 1859
—it was the stock-in-trade of Victorian religious sentimentality: 'the mother was pointed to the arms of her dead
baby-boy beckoning her forward, or the young man urged by
the love of a lost mother'.[58] He was less skilful than the
equally unconventional Arthur Stanton, whom *The Times*
reported as having distributed handbills all round his parish
calling people to flee from the wrath to come; he processed
through the district in the evening, nosing into the alleys and
backstreets, saying extempore prayers and litanies in order to
gather an audience. Stanton's biographer quotes him as telling
another clergyman that he always threw the Book of Common
Prayer out of the window at the start of a Mission. Preaching
at St Columba's, Kingsland Road, he said:

> It is a cold night, a very cold night. The bitter north wind is
> blowing and the stars are shining outside. Hark. Don't you hear
> someone outside in the cold, knocking at your hearts and saying,
> 'let me in, let me in'. Will you not take him in and warm him with
> the fire of your love? Salvation is waiting for you, will you not
> open and take him in? Now if you will, will you not open and
> take it in? Now if you will, you can refuse to see him, but a day
> will come when you will see him face to face, and he will say,
> 'Do you remember that cold night in St Columba's Church when
> I came to you and you refused to see me? Now, depart from
> before my face for ever.'[59]

At the end of this service a woman suddenly shouted out,
'I want to pray'. Stanton said, 'If you want to pray, pray'. She
did. Stanton said afterwards that while it was true that St
Paul had said that women ought to be silent in the Church, yet
if this particular woman thought that she was moved to pray
it was better that she should. This kind of elasticity in the
Anglo-Catholic missioners surprised some observers: *The
Times* said that their plain speech was interspersed with
friendly and chatty remarks which a rigid High Churchman

[58] Davies, op. cit., p.154.
[59] *Life*, by G. W. E. Russell (1917), p.110.

would think almost profane.[60] Stanton also borrowed hymns from revival hymnbooks, using, for example, 'Shall we gather at the river/When the surges cease to roll'. His methods seemed shocking to many Anglicans at the time. For them the essence of Anglicanism was what they might have called 'maintaining a standard' in worship, preaching and so forth. They left it to the Dissenters to fill their chapels by popular methods. Success, indeed, had always been a little common, even suspect, not only to Keble's High Anglican traditions but also to the Islington Evangelicals, who also regarded persecution as a mark of the true Church. This mood became less dominant as the century progressed; the very fact that Anglican leaders came to feel that the Establishment needed a visible popular religious movement of its own in order to justify its claim to be the Church of the English people was evidence of a weakening of the tradition, for it would not have occurred to John Keble that national apostasy lessened the authority of the Established Church, at any rate as established by God. As it was, E. W. Benson, one of Tait's more irrelevant successors as Archbishop of Canterbury, negotiated with the Salvation Army in the hope of drawing William Booth into the service of Anglicanism; when this failed he sanctioned the formation of the Church Army as a direct imitation of, and competitor with, Booth's organization. Stanton did not look so far afield; his anxiety was to make contact, to make his congregation feel at home in the parish church. He accepted, as Mackonochie never did, the existence of a religious 'style' in the urban poor. He tolerated the New Year Watchnight service for which Mackonochie could find no good Catholic precedent and which he dismissed as superstition; his motive was again to make contact.[61]

3. 1874 and after: the Confessional

The Anglican Mission of 1869 is evidence that one must not restrict the idea of Victorian revivalism to the Americans and their imitators. The Church of England, through its parish

---

[60] *The Times*, 23 November, 1869.

[61] Cf. 'Feelings and Festivals', by the present writer, in *The Victorian City*, ed. H. J. Dyos and M. Wolff (1973), Vol. II, pp.855-72.

priests, had tried to evangelize London twice, in 1869 and 1874, before Moody and Sankey arrived there at all. In fact, preparation for the second Anglican Mission to London began formally in May, 1873, when the three bishops who had juris-diction in the metropolitan area invited their clergy to take part in it, at least by intercession, if not by special services. Moody and Sankey, by comparison, did not land at Liverpool until 17 June, 1873; they did not reach Edinburgh, the scene of their first significant public impact, until 23 November, 1873. On 4 November, 1873, however, the bishops of London, Rochester and Winchester had addressed a mass meeting of their London clergy in St Paul's Cathedral on the need for the Anglican mission, and a conference on aims and methods had completed these episcopal exhortations. When the Anglican mission actually started, on 8 February, 1874, Moody was still in Scotland, opening his Glasgow campaign, in which he repeated and confirmed his triumph in Edinburgh.

In adopting the Second Mission, the bishops were evidently trying to ensure that the extremer Anglo-Catholics would be less noticeable in a more widely-based effort. The Mission, which once again operated on a parish level, lacked a centraliz-ing personality, and could hardly have had one in the divided state of Anglicanism at that time. It lasted for ten days, until 18 February, 1874, and distinctly belonged to the past by the time that the Dublin correspondent of *The Times* first brought Moody and Sankey to London breakfast tables in the Novem-ber of the same year. Moody did not commence his London meetings in the Islington Agricultural Hall until 9 March, 1875.

If some commentators saw the Anglican evangelism of the 1860s, culminating in that of 1869, as a reaction to the Evangelical revivalism which had spread to a limited extent from Ireland in 1859–60, no similar connexion could be traced here. In reality, it was the advantage which the Anglo-Catholics gained in 1869 in once again making the doctrine and practice of Confession the central talking point of the Mission which went a long way to explain the enthusiasm with which the Evangelical Pietist sub-culture supported the Americans. The dogmatic system of Anglo-Catholicism, and the novelty of its consequences, had enabled the movement to take the initiative even in revivalism. Moody and Sankey were called upon to reverse the swing and to encourage Evangelicals in their fight for survival. And here it was perhaps Sankey who mattered, rather than Moody. Moody preached what revivalists had been preaching for years; his colloquial style, his American accent apart, had little novelty in the wake of Spurgeon. Sankey's music, however, was new; it was the key to the Americans' success, the product of a genuinely popular lower middle-class culture which made the Confessional seem after all esoteric and too sophisticated. Moody without Sankey, and Moody without the pressure which an aggressive Anglo-Catholicism had set up in the English Churches, would have made only a minor impact on England, as distinct from Ireland and Scotland, in the early 1870s.

How deeply revivalism and the confessional had become intertwined becomes obvious if one looks at the historical context of the second London Mission. In May, 1873, when preparations for the Mission had already commenced, the more extreme Anglo-Catholics submitted to Convocation through the Archbishop of Canterbury a petition signed by 483 priests on possible changes in the Book of Common Prayer. The proposed new clause which attracted most attention read:

> that in view of the widespread and increasing use of Sacramental Confession, your Venerable House may consider the advisability of providing for the education, selection and licensing of duly qualified confessors in accordance with the provisions of Canon Law.[62]

Pusey thought this 'that ill-advised petition', and produced, in December, 1873, in conjunction with men of the older Tractarian outlook, the kind of declaration which he thought that the petitioners ought to have presented. Only Mackonochie of the younger Ritualists was asked to sign this more conservative version. Apart from the question of timing, Pusey complained that 'the younger men mostly maintain confession to be necessary for the forgiveness of sins'[63], a proposition which he did not accept in this simple form. The

[62] *Chronicle of Convocation*, 9 May, 1873.
[63] H. P. Liddon, *Life of E. B. Pusey* (1893), Vol. IV, p.266.

gap between the generations had widened but remained hard
to define. Pusey regarded Lowder, for example, as a ritualist
who stressed what was not really important: 'I do not know,
e.g., that censing persons and things has anything to do with
setting forth the Real Presence. Yet Lowder . . . said that he
insisted upon censing persons and things, as being as important as anything'.[64] In the biography of Lowder, however,
it was argued that 'he was not a ritualist at all in the modern
sense of the word, after the gushing, effeminate, sentimental
manner of young shop-boys, or those who simply ape the
ways of Rome'.[65]

The petition had no result beyond controversy: virtually all
the English Bishops agreed with Tait, the Archbishop of
Canterbury, that neither the sacramental view of confession
nor the practice of habitual confession was Anglican. An
official episcopal statement to this effect was published in July,
1873, which said that an Anglican priest was not authorized to
teach that habitual confession to a priest, or being subject to
what was called the direction of a priest, was a condition of
attaining to the highest spiritual life. Pusey and the more
conservative Anglo-Catholics issued a dissenting statement of
their own in December, 1873; they wanted to guard a position
which they felt the rashness of the Ritualists to be endangering.
This declaration said that no priest ought to require private
confession as a condition of receiving Holy Communion—
that was a point at which Pusey felt able to draw a clear distinction between what he believed to be the Anglican position
and the practice of the Church of Rome; on the other hand,
the statement also said that in the course of a lifetime an
individual might frequently feel that he needed to confess
before communicating, which amounted to the admission that
Pusey wanted habitual confession to be established on a
voluntary basis, a distinction too fine for general episcopal
acceptance in the 1870s. And it was the more extreme Anglo-
Catholics who made the running as far as the London Missions
were concerned. The Bishops made sure that the Mission of
February 1874 included every type of Victorian Anglican, in
the hope of smothering the impact of a second wave of sacra-

[64] Ibid., p.280.
[65] *Charles Lowder*, op. cit,, p.284.

mental revivalism. The climax of the controversy over the Confessional was delayed until 1877 when the confessor's manual, *The Priest in Absolution*, which belonged to the Society of the Holy Cross, was denounced in the House of Lords; the bitterness of the Evangelicals and the confidence of the Ritualists must both be traced back in some degree to the London Missions of 1869 and 1874.

Further evidence of this occurred on the eve of the second Mission, when several hundred people signed a petition drawn up by Lords Exeter, Darnley, Harrowby, Lawrence and Cadogan which protested against any idea of the Mission being used to extend the practice of Confession. The Bishops replied in an open letter to *The Times* in which they hinted that *they* hoped that the Mission would not be used for such purposes either, but that there was not much that they could do to prevent it; they also said that they objected to any proposal to add variety to the Mission services by inviting Nonconformist or lay preachers to occupy Anglican pulpits. The Bishop of London received a separate protest from an anti-confessional meeting held in Chelsea; he replied that he strongly disapproved of the doctrine and practice of sacramental and auricular confession, but that 'as a doctrine, it is impervious to authority'.[66]

The Bishops had done their best. They had taken responsibility for the Mission; they had made clear that they regarded the Ritualists' form of revivalism as non-Anglican; those immediately responsible had addressed the preparatory meeting in St Paul's, in November, 1873. The Bishops of London and Rochester also appeared for the first of five special sermons preached at St Paul's on the first day of the Mission: they heard Walsham How, himself later to become Bishop of Wakefield and in no way a controversial figure, but they left before either George Body or R. M. Benson spoke.[67]

[66] *The Times*, 7 February, 1874.
[67] Maurice Davies' summary of Benson's address is interesting. 'In sharp, ringing voice Father Benson said we must, as mission priests, keep before our eyes the sight of Jesus at the right hand of God. The throne of God is the centre of all His Church's action, wherever an apostolic ministry is labouring in His name. Let us realize this gaze of the soul on Jesus as the source of our power. Ours is no mere Jewish ministry, but a ministry of resurrection life. . . . Think what it is to be the representative of Christ among benighted people. This demands for us to separate ourselves from all that is not of Him. We come hither as the prophet came to Nineveh. He went on the strength of

In doing so, they missed the sensation of the meeting. Haslam, who spoke as the representative of the more revivalistic Evangelicals, went out of his way to attack Anglo-Catholicism. He asserted that the sinner needed no mediator between himself and Christ, which was meant as a hit at private confession. He continued, 'There is one distinguishing mark which separates our Church from the Church of Rome—that it denies that Christ is on our altars and declares that He is present only in our hearts'—a direct assertion that Anglicanism rejected any doctrine of the Real Presence in favour of what is usually called Virtualism. At this point a considerable number of High Church clergy rose and left their seats, offended at this open assault on their doctrine of Holy Communion, and as they felt, on the Church of England itself; they did not return until Haslam had finished speaking.[68] No doubt Haslam felt obliged to 'testify', as did some of his audience; but the incident underlines the reality of the difference between the beliefs of the Evangelicals and those of the Anglo-Catholics, and that there is nothing to be gained by asserting that they were really saying the same thing in different ways. It is difficult to accept the view of Professor Horton Davies, for example, which has become something of an orthodoxy in an ecumenical climate, and which he summarized in this way:

It has been customary to define the relationship between the Evangelical and Tractarian parties as an antithetical one and, indeed, the later so-called 'Ritualistic Controversy' (which was, in fact, a controversy about ceremonial) was sufficiently embittered to lend colour to this view. On the other hand, ceremonialism was

---

his three days burial and came forth in the strength of his resurrection life and struck Nineveh dumb. So in the power of a like burial we go forth (one could not help suspecting a side reference to the monastic in these words). . . . We stand here as the angels of the resurrection, as ourselves partakers of the death of Christ, and having passed into his resurrection. The sermon, redolent of the very "highest thought", was intently listened to by a congregation which was evidently to a great degree sympathetic to the preacher' (Davies, op. cit., pp.384–5). How, later a bishop, was High Church-sentimental; Chapman (of the Lock Hospital) Evangelical, as was W. Haslam. Body and Benson had much in common theologically, but Body's popular rhetoric did not really compare with Benson's thoroughly medieval style.

[68] Davies omitted the incident from his account. There was a reproachful story in the *Guardian*, 11 February, 1874; the journal defended the Mission in a leader on 18 February, 1874. At another point, when the *Veni Creator* was sung during the service at St Paul's, the High Church party knelt but the rest of the clergy, including the Bishops, remained standing.

a later development of Tractarianism, and not expressive of its early genius, at least as discoverable in the first Tractarian leaders, who had a very minor and subsidiary interest in ceremonial matters. . . . The view will be maintained that ultimately the Oxford Movement is not so much an antithesis or opposition to the Evangelical wing as it is a supplementing of it with elements of thought and practice that were lost or forgotten.[69]

This is the interpretation to which Dieter Voll (*v.s.*) tried to give further support in his discussion of revivalism. What both writers neglected, however, was that in the last resort Pusey was always obliged to fight *for* the Ritualists rather than against them, and this was because Lowder and Stanton were not men to whom the real genius of the Oxford Movement was alien, and who had therefore substituted a superficial passion for ceremonial, as though censing persons and things, to quote the example given earlier, really went to the heart of one's religious faith; both men were deeply committed to the doctrine of the Real Presence and to the idea of spiritual direction; they were not, quite properly, to be intimidated by the suggestion that the genius of early Tractarianism had established once and for all the limits of change in High Anglican doctrine; indeed, they probably realized that neither Keble nor Pusey possessed the theological power to lay down such limits in the first place, while Newman, if *he* had been genius of the Movement, could hardly be quoted against them in the long run. The claim of the old generation that they had the authority to halt the development of Tractarianism was a political one; it depended on Pusey's judgement of what was negotiable. One ought not to chop off the history of Anglo-Catholicism at the point at which Ritualism appears; the deep disagreement between Evangelical and Ritualist, which cannot simply be reduced to questions of ceremonial, may be inconvenient to a late twentieth-century ecumenical interpretation of nineteenth century British church history, but this is not sufficient reason for smothering it.

Despite this atmosphere of controversy the extreme Anglo-Catholic missions again concentrated on a call for confession and the renewal of baptismal vows. On this occasion Maurice

[69] Davies, H., *Worship and Theology in England, 1690–1850* (1961), p.244.

Davies picked out as his example W. J. Knox Little, who was the mission preacher at St Thomas, Regent Street. This building had been better known in the past as Archbishop Tenison's Chapel, something which had never pretended to be anything but a 'preaching-shop'. Now, however,

> its walls and ceilings are flatted red, white and blue in a way which brings its native ugliness into prominence. . . . But the sacrarium and altar redeem, or are meant to redeem, everything, and cover a multitude of sins. The holy table was vested in black on Saturday night, and eight tapers were standing on it, divided by the central cross, and flanked with two huge bougies at the north and south ends. . . . Station pictures of no very high order of art decorated the walls; and altogether staid old Tenison's Chapel was in a very advanced condition indeed. . . .[70]

Knox Little made a fervid and impetuous call to confession:

> Confession was an act of the Incarnate leading the soul to God. To hold back, if God calls, was most dangerous to the spiritual life. If there were secrets in the souls, and God gave the chance of speaking them out and getting absolution, then to hold back was the most terrible danger, and involved the most terrible responsibilities. Don't hold back, he kept repeating—when the end of the Mission had come, then would be the time for making resolutions. If God has said, in the course of it, 'Confess', then don't hold back. In the name of your Creator, don't hold back. If you do, the blood of Christ has been shed in vain. That was the one question. Have I had that message in the mission? If so, am I holding back: if that were the case, he would say, go home and fall on your knees, and say, 'I will hold back no longer'. Hold back, and that truth will haunt you in the shape of that word that man spoke to you at the Mission. If we accept it, all the world may argue, men may ridicule or persecute, public opinion may scoff, but it would not matter to us.[71]

Little was then about thirty-five years old, an Irishman who had taken a third class in the Cambridge Classical Tripos and worked as a schoolmaster before entering the Anglican ministry; in 1881 Gladstone nominated him to a canonry at Worcester. In 1877 he published *Meditations on the Three Hours*

[70] Davies, Maurice, op. cit., p.391.
[71] Ibid., pp.392–3.

Agony of our Blessed Redeemer; he also wrote novels, like *The Child of Stafferton* (1889). In the controversy of 1877 he issued a fierce defence of the practice of confession, the *Priest in Absolution*, based on a sermon preached at St Alban's, Manchester. There was no question of Little blending Evangelical with Tractarian in the London Mission. Neither Finney nor Moody, Richard Weaver nor Robert Aitken would have finished with an appeal of this kind, which was nevertheless entirely in accordance with the Roman Catholic idea of a Mission based on the Sacraments. Little was openly defying the Bishops, who had said that it was non-Anglican for a man to set out to persuade members of his congregation to confess; confession, if it did arise, should do so spontaneously, without any kind of leading from the priest. For Little to tell his hearers that the message of the Mission was that God wanted them to confess was to provoke the kind of comment which Maurice Davies made: 'Of course, the question remained—Was the doctrine unEnglish or not?'[72]

The importance of the Confessional was also shown in the fate of G. H. Wilkinson himself, who had moved from St Peter's, Windmill Street, to the rather more upper-class St Peter's, Eaton Square, where he supported the Mission warmly but gave the lead to Charles Bodington. The constant influence of the Anglo-Catholics on Wilkinson is illustrated by a letter which he wrote to Charles Bodington a long time afterwards, in 1897:

> Among many blessings which I owe you few are greater than the wish you expressed after your St Peter's Mission that I should begin daily celebration. It was indeed a blessed help in many dark and difficult hours, and my experience there made me begin it as soon as the cathedral at Truro was consecrated.[73]

Wilkinson ran into trouble in the course of the Mission because of a sermon which he was said to have preached on the same subject of confession. The Bishop of London mentioned the matter discreetly in the course of a letter to Wilkinson (25 February, 1874), and the popular version of the story said that 'when the gas was lowered the clergy went about and urged

[72] Ibid., p.393.
[73] Mason, op. cit., Vol. I, p.308.

the people who remained to go to Confession'.[74] A broad hint was dropped to Wilkinson that 'in the highest quarters—I mean at Windsor—your attitude on this matter is misunderstood.' Wilkinson had preached at Windsor in 1871 when his sermon on the follies of the fashionable life had drawn from the Queen the comment, 'What has all this to do with me?'[75]

Wilkinson seems to have done his best at first to shift responsibility for the incident on to Charles Bodington, from whom he obtained a letter with which he sought to placate one of his more formidable parishioners, Lord Chelmsford, now elderly, but a former Lord Chancellor. Bodington, who was in any case entitled to say that Wilkinson must have known the kind of mission which he would hold, would go no further than stating that 'no pressure was to the best of my knowledge put upon any of them to bring them to confession'.[76] He added that the missioners were bound to suppose that people who stayed for the after-meeting did so for a purpose, and that he and the remainder of the clergy—there were about fifteen of them altogether—had gone from pew to pew to find out what they wanted. They did not intend 'to urge all who remained to go to confession'. The other clergy made similar statements to Chelmsford (in Victorian Anglicanism a peer in good standing was worth at least a bishop in ecclesiastical chess) who was not, however, satisfied. He had apparently heard Bodington himself, and noted that Bodington only claimed not to have urged *all* to go to confession. His verdict was:

To this I must say, that after such a general invitation as Mr Bodington gave, followed up by a particular application from pew to pew, I cannot understand what was intended except to encourage persons to open any grief which might be pressing upon their souls, which, by whatever name it might be called, is admitted by Mr Bodington himself to be an invitation to an act of private confession and absolution. After carefully considering the tenor of these letters I cannot bring to my mind any other conclusion than the painful one that private confession followed by absolution, if not suggested, or pressed, or enforced, as a duty,

[74] Ibid., pp.308–9.
[75] Ibid., p.310.
[76] Ibid., p.313.

has been invited and encouraged, and, I may add, recommended as a practice.[77]

As of course it had: the most that Wilkinson and Bodington could deny, or really wanted to deny, was that they were teaching the strict Roman Catholic rule that confession and absolution were necessary before communion; their difficulties partly arose because Evangelicals would hardly admit that any other teaching about the Confessional was possible. As to the wilder accusations which had been made, it should be noted that the lowering of the lights, and even the total extinction of light, was a mission technique not unpopular in Italian Roman Catholic circles. However, when the Salvation Army became prominent a few years later, a similar story circulated about the audience 'creeping to Jesus' after the gaslight was put out.

Wilkinson, who had not come out of this very well, wisely decided to commit himself once and for all. On 15 March, 1874, he preached on Confession, and on the following Sunday on Absolution. In these sermons he attempted to show why a fresh enthusiasm for the Confessional had revealed itself in the Church of England. Some men, he said, were drawn to confession in order to humble themselves; they felt the good opinion of other people unbearable (this sounds like Wilkinson talking about himself) and desired for once to be real. (Confession, in fact, might be a substitute for a more public act of neurotic self-humiliation). Some wanted to anticipate the shame of the Last Judgement; others wanted sympathy and help. He went on:

If I know—as I do know—that many are unable to quiet their own consciences; that some are disquieted as to whether their repentance is real, and others are disturbed as to whether their sins are washed away in the Precious Blood; if I am desired, whenever I give notice of Holy Communion, to invite any who cannot quiet their own conscience to come to me; if, in the case of the dying, I am bound, not merely to offer this help, but to *move* the sick man to make a special confession if he feels his conscience troubled by any weighty matter; if I believe from my heart—as I do believe—that my Church is a true branch of the

[77] Ibid., pp.313–14.

true Church . . . am I not obliged in certain cases to permit confession; nay, sometimes, to *move* my brother to unburden his soul.[78]

This psychological approach was unusual in late nineteenth-century controversy: the battle about confession had been fought largely in terms of authority and precedent, the alleged intentions of the sixteenth-century Reformers and the nature of the Established Church. Wilkinson took the same strong psychological ground in his defence of absolution—he insisted that he had known people who for years had been unable to believe that their past was forgiven and forgotten, but whose lives had been transformed by an act of private absolution. He was evidently offering the right explanation of the popularity of a system to which he himself had only slowly been converted. He still used the system openly in what was his last major evangelistic effort, the Mission to Leeds Parish Church in 1875. This was one of a number of missions held in big cities after the London Mission of 1874; besides Leeds and Manchester (*v.i.*), they were held in Doncaster, Hull, Lincoln, Nottingham and Sheffield. About twenty outside clergymen assisted in the Leeds Mission; at the concluding service about 500 people received memorial cards as signs that they had received particular benefit from it. Wilkinson gave a series of addresses: Sin; The Discovery of Sin; The Confession of Sin; The Atonement; The Price Paid; The Love of Atonement; Beholding the Lamb; Self-Surrender; The Sacramental and Obedient Life.

He took great pains to connect his message with the familiar words of our Church services; showing, for example, how closely all he taught followed the line of the Confession and Absolution in Matins and Evensong. Then came the teaching about Absolution, and the direct counsel to any who found their minds burdened, and could get no relief, to use the most valuable means, in entering on the new life, the Church's medicine of Confession. He guarded his words by the counsel of the Prayer Book; and I know that he heard many confessions at that Mission.[79]

[78] Ibid., pp.315-16.
[79] Ibid., R. G. Wynne, quoted in Mason, op. cit., Vol. I, p.334.

Soon after, however, for whatever personal reasons, he abandoned his role as one of Anglicanism's leading revival preachers.

One has the impression that in the later nineteenth century the Anglo-Catholics inherited the burden of the guilt of a section of the religious middle-class which the Evangelicals had borne in the earlier part of the century. From this point of view Moody's revival campaigns were always a little old-fashioned, at least as far as Anglicanism was concerned. Moody hoped to 'convert' the broad fringe of church- and chapel-going people who had no vivid religious experience, who knew the vocabulary of sin, guilt, wrath, blood, repentance, forgiveness, and so on but who had never undergone for themselves the pattern of behaviour which revival tradition associated with these words. Despite what he sometimes said, Moody knew that his audience came from inside the existing Churches, and many middle-class people in those Churches in the 1870s and 1880s no longer felt drawn or convinced by the Evangelical Pietist solutions of the problem of defining and attaining personal religious experience. They had absorbed enough of the normal Christian attitude to feel themselves dissatisfied with their behaviour as Christians. They made little of Moody's appeal to them to 'have faith' in order to find 'forgiveness'. In such cases, the act of humbling themselves in the priest's presence, of telling him something of the detail of their weakness, of receiving his spoken absolution as also coming from God, seemed intensely rewarding.

There were obviously other factors. The new approach had a temporary novelty. Nothing like this had been done formally in England by Protestants for centuries, and the Roman Catholic associations of the Confessional gave some people the kind of thrill they might have expected to obtain from attending a Black Mass. As for the priest himself, by reintroducing the Confessional he hoped to retrieve some of the professional status which he had been losing during the century. The authority of the confessional, the expertise of spiritual direction, were to be set against the greatly increased professional prestige of other walks of life: the doctor, the surgeon, the teacher, the scientist and so on. It is not altogether accidental that the drive to popularize the use of the

Confessional came in the period 1869–75, when it was clear that the parson was about to lose the privileged position in popular education that he had retained so long.

The Confessional was also useful as a defining instrument. Recent sociologists of religion have concentrated, perhaps too much, on religious sects, attracted no doubt by the comparative ease with which the small, separated religious group can be described both theologically and socially. When applied to the nineteenth century, this technique may give a misleading impression of the religious field as a whole, for it leaves one with, on the one hand, a collection of sects, some of them analysed elaborately, and on the other hand, a group of large denominations, which have not really been analysed on the same scale. Since neither Anglican Evangelicalism nor Anglo-Catholicism became separate bodies in the simple sense but continued throughout the century to operate within the limits of the Establishment, they are not regarded as sects, and the kind of typology which Dr Bryan Wilson[80] and others have proposed for the sect as commonly understood has not been extended to include them. Modern Anglican historians are not anxious to emphasize the tensions which existed in the Victorian Church of England; they treat both of the extreme groups as though they were complementary movements of the 'Anglican' spirit. It is more useful, however, to drop the rigid idea of a 'sect' which has crept into common practice, and which makes rather more than is necessary of the fact of absolute organizational independence; no doubt all small and independent religious groups have their smallness and independence in common, but the result of employing these as criteria is to lump together bodies which have not much else in common, while failing to attach sufficient importance to the role of Evangelicalism and Anglo-Catholicism because they apparently did not set up separate organizations at all. Each resembled a 'sect' at least as much as it resembled a movement within a 'Church'. Part of the function of the Confessional was that its use drew a firm boundary round the Anglo-Catholic 'sect', marking off the priests who heard confessions from those who would not do so, and the congregations in which confession was possible from those in which it was impossible. The

[80] Cf. for example, Bryan Wilson, *Religious Sects* (1971).

original Tractarian emphasis on episcopacy had only served the first generation as a serious rallying cry, for the Bishops proved unwilling to support Anglo-Catholicism, and called many Ritualistic practices non-Anglican; it was hard to advocate episcopacy against the Bishops; the Confessional, on the other hand, was an innovation which all could unite in demanding from them. To the extent that Anglo-Catholicism was in any case a movement of the clergy in search of an improved status, a clash with the episcopate was always probable. The hearing of confessions was something which the clergy could do whether the Bishops liked it or not; it represented the Clergy's claim to an independent right to reconstruct 'Anglicanism'; in the form which this proposed reconstruction took, the idea of the Confessional represented independence as much as reform. Finally, there was the further advantage that confession was a symbol which the Evangelicals were extremely unlikely to imitate, and the same was true of the Broad Churchmen, whose theoretical tolerance vanished when they were asked to accept the introduction of the custom.

The importance of the symbol was made evident again in an address given by Charles Lowder on the eve of the Mission to Manchester which Bishop Fraser organized from 27 January to 7 February, 1877. This is not a history of Anglican evangelism as such and therefore no detailed account of this Mission is required here; once the Bishops had taken up the idea of general Missions to urban areas they gradually emasculated the practice by insisting on 'comprehensiveness'. The Manchester Mission ran into controversy, however, because of the excitement which the ill-fated Public Worship Regulation Act, which had come into operation in July, 1875, was stirring up at the same time. The Act had been a desperate attempt by Archbishop Tait, who genuinely regarded Ritualism as an illegitimate extension of the meaning of 'Anglicanism', to restore some kind of common discipline within the Church of England. As Dr P. T. Marsh has written:

the Act was a fiasco. It was bound to be so because it relied ultimately on force either in the form of inhibition and deprivation or through imprisonment. As ever in a contest with determined religious conviction, force backfired on those who employed it. In this case force was particularly dangerous because employed, not by the State against the Church, but within the Church by one of its parties supported by the State against another. The Act was meant to prevent a widening of this internal division and of the division between Church and country by restraining ritualism. Instead the Act brought out the tenacity of ritualism, won new sympathy for its advocates, deprived its opponents of popular favour, and allowed them to be frustrated through the bishops' vetoes and the Act's own intricacies.[81]

The date of the Manchester Mission followed closely on the imprisonment, in January, 1877, of the Rev. Arthur Tooth, of St James, Hatcham, in the diocese of Rochester, technically for contempt of court, but actually as a result of a prosecution brought under the Public Worship Regulation Act. The Missioner whom the Dean of Manchester Cathedral, B. M. Cowie, had invited to work at the Cathedral itself was Knox Little, who had openly supported Tooth, who was a member of the Society of the Holy Cross, and a friend of Arthur Stanton. Charles Bodington, who also took part in the Mission, had been proceeded against on similar grounds in August, 1876, at St Andrew's, Wolverhampton, had evaded his pursuers on technical points, but was to suffer a fresh prosecution in March, 1877. The missioner at Knox Little's church was George Body; while at St John the Baptist, Hulme, was another priest familiar with episcopal discipline, Mackonochie himself. A public meeting was held at the Cathedral to protest against Little's appointment, on the various grounds that he himself violated ecclesiastical law, belonged to the English Church Union, which was Anglo-Catholic, and supported Tooth.[82]

As a counterblast the Dean of Manchester called in Charles Lowder, who gave a lecture in the Manchester Memorial Hall, with the Dean himself in the chair, the night before the Mission was due to go into action.[83] Lowder took as his subject 'The

[81] P. T. Marsh, *The Victorian Church in Decline* (1969), This was the first serious study of Archbishop Tait.
[82] *Manchester Guardian*, 17 January, 1877.
[83] Ibid., 27 January, 1877.

Mission Work of the Church of England', and made no bones of concentrating on the idea of confession. He made no attempt to conciliate, an attitude for which Tooth's imprisonment was no doubt responsible. He said that men should be encouraged in their sorrow for sin

> to receive consolation from those whom Christ had sent forth with his commission, and with the commission which was given to every priest at his ordination. . . . He knew nothing more touching than hearing the confession of a hard-working man. They were told that confession was not manly; that it was all very well for women. . . . He knew nothing more manly than for a hard-working man to kneel down before his God and before his priest and pour forth his troubles and woes.

He argued that other Churches had their equivalent of the system; he believed that the Wesleyan who went to his class-meeting with the intention of obtaining grace and help from God received that help. And making a point related to the housing conditions of much of Manchester, he defended ritual in the Anglo-Catholic style on the ground that it made an effective contrast with the 'desolateness and slovenliness of many of the homes of the people'. This address provoked the Rector of St Paul's, Brunswick Street, the Rev. E. Hewlett, into announcing that, although at his meetings during the Mission opportunities would be given for personal interviews with the ministers, 'the confession of sin to the clergyman is neither invited nor desired. The Church of England knows nothing, and her faithful clergy know nothing, of auricular confession'.[84] Hewlett said that he was sure that in most parishes the teaching of the Mission would be of the simplest and purest Evangelical kind. It was not so long, of course, since Moody had visited Manchester; here was the same firm contrast between the Evangelical confession that one was in a sinful condition and must rely on God for deliverance, and the Anglo-Catholic anxiety to bring the penitent to the confession of specific sins and the acceptance of some form of spiritual direction.

This exchange had a bearing on another side of the Manchester Mission. Canon Crane had written to the Licensed

[84] *Manchester Courier*, 29 January, 1877.

Victuallers' Association asking if in the parish of St George public-houses could be closed at 7.30 p.m. during the Mission. It was hardly surprising that the secretary of the Association should reply with a refusal, but he also went on to tell the Canon that revivals were a mistake; they did more harm than good. They were, he said, a reflection on honest, hard-working clergymen. As for those parsons who could not support the plain scriptural teachings of the Established Church, they should leave it. The *Manchester Guardian* commented that

> the parsons are all very well as allies so long as they assist the publicans in electing a parliament which is free from crochets about early closing . . . but the relations between the two bodies assume a new character when one of them is found proposing what amounts to a declaration that the other is a moral and social nuisance.[85]

The Licensed Victuallers' letter was much in the style of an Evangelical attack on the Mission, delivered on 26 January, just before its commencement, by the Rev. Dr Edward Verity, Vicar of Herbergham. He said that

> as to the attempt on the part of the Puseyites to get up so-called 'missions' in England (a Christian country) . . . it is an insult to the inhabitants and parochial clergy. . . . Evangelical clergy should stand aloof from all such Jesuitical movements, whether in London, Leeds, or Manchester.

The Anglo-Catholics, he said, simply wanted to accustom people to their practices, to the use of painting, music and flowers in lieu of religion; they wanted to persuade honest Protestants to 'put faith in confessionals, priests and idol-wafers'.[86]

One cannot leave the Manchester Mission without reference to the activities of Bishop Fraser, himself a Broad Churchman. He spent part of the Mission speaking to the theatrical profession. At the Theatre Royal, the front of the stage was enclosed by a scene, so that the Bishop standing in the fore-

[85] *Manchester Guardian*, 31 January, 1877.
[86] *Manchester Courier*, 26 January, 1877. The *Courier* was, of course, the Conservative organ in Manchester.

ground appeared to be speaking in a Gothic chamber. The stalls were reserved for the leading artists and chorus; the pit for the other members of the companies; the meeting began with 'Oh, come to me, ye weary', sung by the Chorus, and closed with 'Rock of Ages'. The Bishop made a second appearance, this time at the Prince's Theatre.[87]

4. Conclusion

Various conclusions may be drawn from this material. First of all, that nineteenth-century revivalism was not just a product of the American and Evangelical traditions, but that Anglo-Catholic revivalism developed independently, drawing its theory and methods largely from Roman Catholic sources. From a psychological point of view this Anglo-Catholic revivalism grew naturally from the changing urban situation of the period, and from the older Tractarianism; a generation of younger men, led by Lowder and Mackonochie, were eager to spread their sacramental view of the Church at the parish level but were conscious of the hostility of the environment, both socially and religiously speaking. They did not try to blend Evangelical and Anglo-Catholic approaches; they deliberately repudiated the 'Protestant' tradition of revival in favour of a Roman Catholic tradition of mission.[88] In this way Ritualism emerges, not as something unnatural to Tractarianism (as though the potentialities of the original movement were summed up for ever in the personalities of Keble, Newman and Pusey, of whom only the first was a parish priest, and he in the most non-urban of contexts), nor as a dissipation of its early Gothic doctrinal grandeur in an unworthy obsession with ecclesiastical millinery, but as an intelligent attempt to embody Tractarian dogma in visible, liturgical acts, not only in order to communicate more easily with poor and under-educated people, but also in order to

---

[87] *Manchester Guardian*, 3 February, 1877. The *Guardian* played the actual mission down, by and large.

[88] As late as 1908, when Paul Bull, of the Community of the Resurrection, published *The Missioner's Handbook*, his list of 'Books useful for Mission Preachers' began with Bishop Gore's *Epistle to the Romans*, and then continued with *Le Prêtre*, by J. Berthier (Lyon n.d.); *Manuel de Missionaire*, by A. Nampon (Lyon, n.d.); and Jouve, *Le Missionaire de la Campagne*, 4 vols (Paris, n.d.). These were the books specially recommended.

enable the Anglican religious middle-class to identify themselves through these practices with the 'sect' as such. In this
period the increasing secularization of the dominant forms of
British culture was pushing the Church of England into a
defensive role as one part of a sub-dominant religious culture,
whose very existence was still concealed from many observers
by the extent to which Anglicanism and Dissent seemed
totally separate in their aims and interests, while Anglo-
Catholicism and Evangelicalism seemed likely to tear the
Establishment apart before very long.[89] Nevertheless, the
urban clergy were aware of the secularizing process by the
1870s. They reacted against it: Victorian revivalism sought in
the last quarter of the century to halt this shrinking of the
influence of the Church. Here Evangelical revivalism largely
failed, partly because its methods depended upon the prior
existence in the population of precisely those 'protestant' ideas
and emotions which were vanishing. Anglo-Catholicism had
the advantage that its methods meant that converts to the
system would be doing something novel; its sacramental
attitude, moreover, established a clear pattern of withdrawal
from the ethos of the dominant culture. At the same time, by
its willingness to express an interest in 'music, painting and
flowers'—to which drama can also be added—Anglo-
Catholicism showed a stronger desire than did Evangelicalism
to make possible a reformulation of a dominant culture based
on Christianity. This attitude reflected the social composition
of Anglo-Catholicism, and while it was a forlorn hope, at
least the gesture permitted some contact with sophisticated
culture outside the Church. To this extent, Anglo-Catholicism
was less 'sectarian' than Evangelicalism.

It is important to realize that, insofar as the Anglo-Catholic
missions were advocating auricular confession, they were
resisting the dominant culture and asserting that the Church
could make absolute demands for submission on the individual, in his private as well as in his public life; part of the
secularizing impulse always consisted of a denial that any
institution had the authority to interfere with the individual

---

[89] 'The Role of Religion in the Cultural Structure of the Later Victorian City',
Transactions of the Royal Historical Society, 5th Series, Vol. 23 (1973), pp.153–75, by the
present writer.

in his private capacity. This element in the battle around auricular confession became obvious in the controversy over *The Priest in Absolution*, a manual for confessors which was prepared for the Society of the Holy Cross by the Rev. J. C. Chambers, Vicar of St Mary's, Soho, between 1866 and 1870, had circulated privately but was suddenly brought to public attention by Lord Redesdale in the summer of 1877 (when Chambers himself had been dead for three years). The details of the controversy do not matter here, but the content of the manual is relevant. Inevitably, it was partly concerned with sex:

Adults: 'with whom they had to do: whether more than once with the same person: when it took place, with the view of learning what occasions of sin might be avoided: how often the sin was consummated, and how often it was interrupted before consummated. In regard to married persons, the priest is bound ordinarily to inquire, when he finds it necessary, of wives, if they have rendered the benevolence, and that only in the most modest way he can, and not inquire further, unless he be asked questions himself. Wives should be asked whether they have not caused their husbands to blaspheme by not rendering the benevolence. Wives often by refusing the latter are damned, and cause the damnation of their husbands by driving them to thousands of iniquities. The question should be veiled in discreet language: "Do you obey your husband in what belongs to the married state?" '[90]

Michael Reynolds' comment on this, in his study of Mackonochie, *Martyr of Ritualism* (1965), was that he could not 'detect a vestige of the salacity of which the Victorians complained. It is the ineptitude of the writer's approach to human problems, his insistence on seeing everything in terms of sin, which the modern reader is likely to find distasteful and distressing. . . . The clash was between two schools of puritanism'.[91] There is truth in this, but I think that Reynolds exaggerated the significance of the contemporary attack on the book as obscene. This attack was convenient because according to the conventions of the period it was difficult to answer. The real issue, however, was that of the authority of the priest

[90] M. Reynolds, *Martyr to Ritualism* (1965), pp.217–18.
[91] Ibid.

over the layman. Pusey, in his own belated manual on confession, *Advice for Those who Exercise the Ministry of Reconciliation*, the introduction to which was dated 1877, said stormily that

> plainly there are provinces, religious, moral, practical, spiritual, upon which we, the clergy . . . can give more competent opinions to the people committed to our charge, than they can form for themselves. Else there would be no occasion for the office of pastor. One wonders, sometimes, what those, who speak against sacerdotalism, really conceive the office of the clergy to be? To read prayers (intercessors under the great Intercessor according even to the old sign, 'The Parson prays for all', they would hardly allow us to be), to preach sermons (which any or all should criticise, or pronounce not to be the Gospel), to teach little children (which is of course a high office), or to be a respectable class of Police officers, to teach the poor obedience to the law or non-interference with the rich; and the performance of certain religious acts which, although really sacerdotal, they do not acknowledge to be so—these are certainly no large dimensions of the sacerdotal office, but what more they would leave us, I know not. It would be well if they would ask themselves.[92]

This was what really mattered, however: whether the priest had the right to ask certain things, and whether, having asked them, he had any special competence to deal with the situations which he might have exposed. The layman had no prior confidence in the ability of the priest to advise him as to what was sin and what was not sin in matters of personal conduct; the manuals which Chambers and Pusey published failed to convince the majority that the Anglo-Catholic priest possessed the power to 'give more competent opinions' than his parishioners could work out for themselves. The nineteenth-century struggle to raise the social and professional status of the clergy failed.

Finally, while Anglo-Catholic revivalism undoubtedly served the purpose of accustoming people to Anglo-Catholic ritual and sacramental principles, thus making the position of the movement more secure in the Church of England, it was also true that the first Mission to London in 1869, and the

[92] E. B. Pusey, *Advice for Those who Exercise the Ministry of Reconciliation* (1893), Preface, signed 1877, p.clx.

Ritualist share in the Second Mission of 1874, stimulated Evangelical support for Moody and Sankey. Moody's successes balanced the successes of the Anglican London Missions and led on to the further outburst of Evangelical energy in the Holiness revivalism of Pearsall Smith and the Keswick movement. In Leeds in 1875 and Manchester in 1877, Anglo-Catholics and Evangelicals deliberately pitted their strength against one another in a contest for public support. Revivalism thus became for a short time a prominent feature of the power struggle in the Church of England. For such a battle Anglo-Catholic revivalism was better prepared theologically than its American equivalent. The Anglican missioners exalted the sacraments, whereas the Americans were often tempted to criticize both the idea of the Church and the sacramental understanding of Christianity, as part of their standard contrast between formality and the religion of the heart. Anglo-Catholic missions related easily to a single conception of the Church of England, towards which converts were directed; the American revivalist, on the other hand, suffered from the difficulty that although he was nominally seeking converts for the various denominations which provided him with money and voluntary assistance, in fact he wanted to knit his converts to a revivalist sub-culture, another 'undeclared sect' (like Anglo-Catholicism and Evangelicalism) or para-denominational network. And while the Anglo-Catholic offered his converts the Eucharist as a continuing centre of the Christian life, together with an austere conception of Christian holiness still rooted in the ascetic tradition which the process of secularization was obliterating, the American revivalist was tempted to make the centre of the continuing Christian life the next revival meeting. The Keswick doctrine of holiness, moreover, was too crude theologically to survive criticism.

After about 1880 Anglo-Catholic revivalism declined. There was no place for it in *Lux Mundi*. There was another mission to London—to West London at any rate—in 1885, but this attracted much less attention than its predecessors. The third generation of Anglo-Catholics was more relaxed than the second, and more concerned with social problems than with revivalism. The frontiers of Anglo-Catholicism had been established; as an 'undeclared sect' operating within the

Church of England the movement inevitably found limits set by the resistance of other groups; an effort to expand more widely would have had to be based on secession, and this was financially as well as socially impossible. Missions, while not abandoned altogether, became a subordinate part of the machinery. The monastic orders survived but failed to grow; they were caught up in the general development of twentieth-century Christianity which was to involve Roman, as well as Anglican, orders in an increasing shortage of vocations. The weaknesses of revivalism of any kind had become apparent before 1914. Moody's returns to England after the 1870s excited less and less attention; he had failed to give the Evangelicals predominance in the Church of England, and it was not the least of his failures. Ritualist revivalism, on the other hand, had helped to make the Church of England safe for Anglo-Catholicism, and it was perhaps the most important result which revivalism helped to bring about in the whole of the nineteenth century.

8

Holiness Revivalism

1. The Urban Fragmentation of Nineteenth-century Protestantism

AMERICAN influence on nineteenth-century English popular religion was by no means limited to revivalism as either Finney or Moody practised it. From about 1825 to the end of the century, a small but important Holiness Movement developed on the outskirts of nineteenth-century Protestantism. This movement spread from the United States to England and involved the types of revivalism associated with the American James Caughey, Phoebe Palmer (and her husband), Robert Pearsall Smith (and his wife) and Asa Mahan, as well as the marching brass bands of the Salvation Army and the more stationary, annual tents of the Keswick meeting in the Lake District.

These Holiness groups formed part of a more general fragmentation of the urban thrust of Protestantism, a fragmentation which had already begun in the early nineteenth century. It took three principal forms: Adventist, Healing and Holiness. Early nineteenth-century Adventism was simply the belief that the Second Coming of Christ was literally and historically imminent; later, the failure of many ingenious prophecies of the exact date led to more subtle pictures of what a Second Advent might be, or even, according to some experts, Swedenborgians, for example, had already been. The healing sects—and we have already noticed the role which disease and healing took in the Sankey songbooks—all offered an escape from pain, disease and, on occasion, death. Sometimes Healing was also thought of as visible evidence of the power of the divine Spirit, a kind of supplementary proof of the existence of God. Other members of Healing sects were too sophisticated to believe in this kind of direct action by the Holy Spirit; for them healing was obtained through the mastery of an exotic Gnosis. Holiness sects varied in a similar way. For some, Holiness was obtainable in the same way as justification: on the spot, through faith. For others, purification came as the result of a slow growth in understanding, an attitude which would have been as reasonable as it sounds if what had to be understood had not been the writings of Mary Baker Eddy, for example.

As an intellectual fashion of any substance, Adventism belonged to the Evangelical Pietist world of the early nineteenth century, a world in which sense and nonsense were not always very effectively distinguished. George Eliot damned it intellectually for ever in her ruthless analysis of the evangelical Dr Cumming:

> Dr Cumming's delight in shadowing forth the man of sin, in prognosticating the battle of Gog and Magog, and in advertising the pre-millennial advent, is simply the transformation of political passions on to a so-called religious platform; it is the anticipation of the triumph of 'our party', accomplished by our principal men being 'sent for' into the clouds.

The best-known British group of this kind,[1] the Plymouth Brethren, emerged from Anglican Evangelicalism in the late 1820s; from 1859 onwards the Brethren interested themselves keenly in all revival movements.

After about 1860, Adventism lost this passing grip on comparatively sophisticated circles and the centre of the Adventist world shifted to the United States where the Seventh Day Adventists had been gathered by William Miller between 1833–44, and then decisively reformed by Mary Ellen White.[2] It was only towards the close of the nineteenth century that the Seventh Day Adventists, and their powerful offshoot, the Watchtower Movement, began to set up fresh

---

[1] There were other Adventist groups in England. Southcottian meetings of one kind or another spanned the century; for instance, Joanna herself died in 1814; John Wroe of Ashton-under-Lyme and Wakefield in 1863; James White of the Flying Roll in 1885. (For James White, see *The Sixth Trumpeter*, the story of Jezreel and his Tower, by P. G. Rogers, London 1963). These were all small groups, often very local in their membership; but there is no suggestion that Britain had to draw on the United States for Adventist adventures. On the whole, the theme was worked up in Anglican circles in the early part of the century; rejected as unsatisfactory by the middle of it; and only brought back on a noticeable scale by the Americans at the very end of the century.

[2] There were Millerites in England, however. It was among surviving Millerite congregations in the Midlands that Dr John Thomas, the founder of Christadelphianism, was best received on his visit to England from America in 1848.

churches in England. By that time the survival of Adventism as an independent sectarian theme depended upon the implausible assertion that the Advent had already taken place.

As a secondary theme, however, Adventism could be combined with both Healing and Holiness to form a single sect-pattern: this was essentially the case with Pentecostalism. In the nineteenth century, however, America also exported at least one sect in which the interest in disease and healing predominated by itself. This is less surprising if one considers the importance of the disease-motif in Sankey's *Sacred Songs and Solos*, itself a creation of the second half of the century. The First Christian Science Church was formed in 1879 and the movement officially invaded Britain in 1897, when Mrs Baker Eddy sent Mrs Julia Field-King to England. It is significant that on the Continent, a much less successful body of a similar kind centred round a Belgian called Louis Antoine (1846–1910), who seems to have worked out a parallel brand of gnosticism for himself. A French scholar has neatly summed up the relation between the two groups:

> Evidemment, on froisserait singulièrement les disciples de Mme Baker Eddy si on leur disait que la Christian Science est un Antoinisme pour dames distinguées, et L'Antoinisme une Science Christian pour milieu populaire.[3]

Even as late as 1920 it was still possible for Alexander Freytag (1870–1947) to lead a considerable continental breakaway from the Jehovah's Witnesses on the basis of a combination of the Healing and Holiness themes. For his movement, Les Amis de l'Homme, as for the Christian Scientists, healing, or the recognition of health, depended upon a change of mental attitude in the supposed sufferer, and so was quite different from the kind of healing associated with the early twentieth-century Pentecostalist groups, in which healing resulted from the miraculous intervention of the power of the Holy Spirit, preferably in the course of a public meeting. Sects of the Christian Scientist type might be called perfectionist as well, because the achievement of their goal for the individual included the disappearance of all apparent evil as far as he was concerned.

[3] *L'Offensive des Sectes*, by H. Chéry (Paris 1959), p.256.

In the second half of the nineteenth century, however, the Holiness theme mattered more than either Adventism or Healing. Both James Caughey and Phoebe Palmer had claimed that thousands were sanctified in the course of their local revivals, but neither concentrated wide public attention on the subject. Mrs Palmer, however, certainly passed on to the Booths the characteristic form of the Salvation Army's Holiness teaching, which was a vital factor in its success in the 1870s. The turning-point in the rise of Holiness revivalism, however, was the visit to England of Robert Pearsall Smith in 1873. Smith was yet another American, and he made Holiness revivalism part of the experience of the pietistic middle-class. From Smith's Brighton Holiness Conference in 1875 sprang the Keswick Movement, which was to institutionalize Holiness revivalism in the bigger Protestant churches while the Salvation Army was institutionalizing it outside them. Despite appearances, and claims to the contrary, the Keswick Movement was a kind of sect. It did not set up the kind of totally independent structure which one sees in the Salvation Army; instead, like other varieties of Victorian religion, it devised its own kind of sect structure, which permeated the existing denominations and was parasitic on them.

When the problem of nineteenth-century sect-formation is looked at as a whole, it becomes clear that the genesis of most, if not all, of these Victorian sects required at least leadership, and commonly membership as well, drawn from the older religious bodies. Most of the original Plymouth Brethren, for example, came from the Church of England. Victorian Anglican Evangelicalism, which was another example of a sect not quite without a name but without a totally independent structure, relied to some extent on families which had left the Society of Friends for the Establishment. In its formative generation the Salvation Army owed much to the older Methodist groups and to the sympathy of Anglican Evangelicals. Pentecostalism had an equally mixed background: of its early leaders T. B. Barratt was a Methodist minister who had been working in Norway, Alexander Boddy was the evangelical Anglican incumbent of All Saints, Sunderland, where he enjoyed the mild oversight of an evangelical Bishop, Handley Moule, who had closely identified himself with the milder second phase of the Holiness movement based on Keswick. When the Pentecostal Missionary Union was formed in 1909 it was largely based, as far as structure was concerned, on the model of the China Inland Mission, the instrument used by Anglican Evangelicalism for missionary work in the Far East. The American revivalists played an important part in this process, for Moody, Pearsall Smith, Torrey and others assisted as centres of attraction to draw people together from different denominations. It was Moody's first visits, those of 1873 and 1882, which thoroughly mixed up Anglican Evangelicals with others of the same ethos; without Pearsall Smith's personal impact the Keswick Movement would probably never have existed.

This mixture of influences comes out strongly in the case of Reader Harris. He was justified in 1884 after reading *Union with Christ*, by the Anglican Henry Moule. Like many other pietist laymen Harris was impatient with the institutional churches; in 1885 he started his own Church, Speke Hall, at Battersea. He had also joined in the Moody and Sankey meetings in London in 1884 and could be found at Salvation Army meetings in the early, more open stages of the movement. Two other, minor American revivalists, F. D. Sanford and G. D. Watson, spoke at the Speke Hall in 1889; they convinced Harris of the truth of the Holiness teaching, and he himself received the 'sanctifying fullness of the Holy Spirit'. In 1890 he was present at the Star Hall Holiness Convention in Manchester; he had now to decide whether to open new Halls, or whether to join an existing group. He decided to go on independently, and in 1891 founded the Pentecostal League of Prayer, whose aims were 'the filling of the Holy Spirit for all believers; revival in the Churches; the spread of Scriptural Holiness', defined as complete cleansing. There was no question yet of *glossolalia* and healing. At the League's first Annual Meeting, at Exeter Hall in 1892, G. D. Watson was one of the speakers and Frank Crossley, the Manchester businessman and owner of the Star Hall, another.

This process of sect-formation must have meant serious losses in membership for some of the older groups. In the *Daily News* survey of London religious life in 1903 the Salvation Army, after a generation of well-publicized activity, was recorded as having attendances in the whole of the London area of 38,896, about 22,000 of these being within the London area proper. This actually showed a decline from the *British Weekly*'s survey of London church attendance in 1886, when the total attendance at Salvation Army services was said to have been 53,591.[4] The Army owned about 150 places of worship, with an average total attendance of 260. The Brethren, the next most successful of the sectarian groups at the time, though normally ignored by historians, who prefer the more colourful Salvationists, were reported as having a total attendance of 31,065; of these nearly 17,000 were in London proper. The Brethren had more places of worship than the Army, 236, and this meant an average total attendance of about 130. At first sight these are small figures; the total attendance of the Wesleyan Methodists came to 122,000, itself a total well below that of the Congregationalists, 159,000, and that of the Baptists, 161,000. But the *Daily News* added two other figures to those outside the regular denominations. One is that of a group of large independent Evangelical Missions, whose total attendance came to about 21,000; the other was what the Survey simply called 'other services', for which the total rose as high as 76,000. When these various figures were added together, one finishes with a total attendance of fringe Protestants of about 167,000, a figure higher than that of any of the big Nonconformist denominations, which were evidently unable to check the growth of this evangelical dissidence.

The 'other services' took place in 422 Halls: for purposes of comparison, one may note that the Baptists had 443 churches, the Congregationalists 345, and the Wesleyan Methodists 254. These Halls were not very carefully distinguished in the Survey. Some of them belonged to the London City Mission; there were many small Railway Missions, Holiness Missions, Temperance Halls, a Prohibition Church and Spiritual Societies. The investigators found a Christian Science Church in Chelsea with a total attendance of

---

[4] The *Daily News* survey was published as *The Religious Life of London*, edited by Richard Mudie-Smith, London, 1904. The figures given here were probably more accurate than those printed in the *British Weekly* in 1886. Comparison of the two sources suggests a definite decline in the strength of the London churches in the last quarter of the nineteenth century.

553, and a Pentecostal Hall (Speke Hall in Battersea) with a total of 557. There were three tiny Mormon congregations in Enfield, Finsbury and West Ham; a Seventh Day Adventist Church existed in Westminster. Very many of the halls, however, reduced their titles to the kind of bare postal identification which expressed the last stage of the Puritan objection to naming churches after saints: thus three successive entries for Hammersmith ran: '30, Bulwer Street, Wood Lane; Lockhart Hall, King Street West; Bethany, 57, Railway Arches'. The combined total Sunday attendance of these three meetings came to 142.

The resulting picture is one of fantastically diversified would-be evangelization, and there can be no doubt that the prestige of the American professional revivalists was one of the chief factors which persuaded so many men and women to devote the best part of their lives to the unsuccessful obscurity of these Gospel Halls. What is also striking is the degree of alienation from the older denominations which this elaborate pattern implies. This alienation from older ecclesiastical structures goes a long way to explain the late nineteenth-century popularity of American revivalism. Both revivalism, and the formation of new sects may be interpreted as the product of a movement of protest within the older structures of British Protestantism, including the Church of England. This dissatisfaction was partly doctrinal, partly structural. In the latter case, what predominated was the rejection of the traditional, full-time ministry of the Churches. The Brethren always denied the possibility of the Church's existence in the present dispensation, and in a group of former Anglicans this was doubly significant. Anglican Evangelical laymen like Lord Shaftesbury and Sir Algernon Blackwood[5] commented on the tension which existed between the Evangelical clergy, who distrusted lay initiative, and Anglican laymen anxious to evangelize. The Salvation Army adopted a secular sounding military hierarchy which was the antithesis in dress, language and technique of the dark-clothed popular preachers or robed Anglican celebrants. Christian Scientist practitioners functioned as a kind of anti-ministry.

[5] *Life*, ed. by his wife, London 1896. A civil servant, converted in 1856, his enthusiasm created constant difficulties in 1859–60 with London parish priests.

Even within the older Churches, similar tendencies showed themselves. In Wesleyan Methodism, for instance, Thomas Champness,[6] a minister whose successful journalism made him almost independent of connectional discipline, started to employ his own paid lay evangelists as early as 1885; their purpose was to save British villages from the threat of Anglo-Catholicism. 'I am much impressed', he wrote, 'about the villages. If they are to be saved from the priest, we must combine as we have never done. Ministers alone cannot do it'.[7] As late as the 1880s Wesleyan leaders were still more concerned about the countryside than the town. 'We cannot afford to lose the agricultural labourer from Methodism', Champness said.[8]

By 1889–90, however, he had turned his attention overseas as well, with the extraordinary result that he sent his 'Joyful News Evangelists' to compete with his own denomination's missionaries in China and India. He described the professional minister as a 'costly tool': where he found the right man he wanted 'to employ him, not as a minister, to administer Sacraments, to meet classes, but to bring men to Christ. . . . I would have you bear in mind that these men will cost £200 less than a minister each'.[9] It was character, not learning, he said, that made a successful missionary.

In fact, Champness had to admit that his 'lay missionaries did not work well with the Wesleyan Missionary Society; this was partly because the *Joyful News* Agents did not specialize in medicine or education, but were simply would-be revivalists who competed with the ministers in China and India just as their equivalents did at home. Even their cheapness became an embarrassment in 1890, when Champness became involved in the Wesleyan Missionary Controversy, which started because Hugh Price Hughes' personal journal, the *Methodist Times*, published articles which alleged that Wesleyan missionaries in India were living in comparative luxury while failing to convert the Indian population. The presence of *Joyful News*

---

[6] Eliza Champness, *The Life-Story* (1906). He was born in 1832 and died in 1905. His weekly paper, *Joyful News*, began to appear in 1883. Challenges to the tightly organized Wesleyan circuit system became increasingly common after 1860.

[7] Loc. cit., p.223.

[8] Ibid., p.230.

[9] Ibid., p.254.

agents in India at this time helped the campaign against the missionaries. The Wesleyan Mission House defended itself successfully, though more recent history has implied that some of the criticisms made in the late nineteenth century—and extended to most Western missionaries—were justifiable, in as much as the typical European or American missionary set up a social, economic and psychological barrier between himself and even his converts.

At home, at any rate, Champness believed that if one cut out the long and expensive training of the professional minister one would have not only a cheaper but a better man. He pointed to the Salvation Army, which seemed immensely successful to contemporaries, and whose agents looked like laymen to the average Free Churchman. 'What is the reason,' he said, 'why so many of our good men have gone into the Salvation Army? Some of the best men General Booth has, we ought to have had.' He meant that Booth was prepared to accept for full-time evangelistic work men who were not likely to be accepted for training as full-time ministers in the Wesleyan Methodist and other Free Churches; their rejection, he claimed, was the result of the over-intellectualism, snobbery and indifference to the working-classes of the ministerial caste.

An Anglican parallel to Champness' anti-clericalism and personal denominationalism was John Kensit[10] and the teams of Wycliffite Preachers which he sent out in 1898 'to expose sacerdotalism in the National Church'. Kensit had established his City Protestant Book Depot in Paternoster Row in London in 1885, the same year in which Champness began his evangelistic campaigns. This was the origin of the Protestant Truth Society. He died in a riot in Liverpool in 1902, after which his son, also John Kensit, became the leader of the movement. Both Champness and the younger Kensit set up their own training colleges; these were a kind of anti-theological college, in which the students were protected from the evils which would come from a normal ministerial education. They had the precedent of Charles Haddon Spurgeon, whose reaction

[10] For Kensit, cf. *John Kensit, Reformer and Martyr*, a Popular Life by the Rev. J. C. Wilcox, B.A., Vicar of Shepcombe, Gloucestershire, and Chaplain to the Wycliffite Preachers, London 1902. Of course, Kensit's anticlericalism was stirred up by the advance of Anglo-Catholicism in the last quarter of the nineteenth century, but the hostility to the clergy was already there.

to the effect of Biblical Criticism on the Baptist ministry had been to set up a college for training pastors himself. Moody's success in 1873–5 and again in 1882–4 raised the prestige of unordained preachers and evangelists of all kinds. Like Moody, neither Champness nor Kensit made a formal breach with older religious institutions, but both acted in ways which made clear their distrust of them.

This raises three questions: why, for example, did a new group of religious movements (sects) appear in the course of the nineteenth century? How was their appearance related to the visits of the American revivalists? What was the role of the Holiness revival movement in all this?

The problem of sect-formation has interested sociologists of religion in recent years. They have largely rejected the older view that such bodies formed in response to economic distress in certain sections of the population. Dr Bryan Wilson, in *Sects and Society* (1961), for example, stressed the importance of what he called cultural disinheritance and social isolation, the way in which the process of social change stranded certain groups and challenged the accepted self-estimate of others. There is no doubt that cultural disinheritance and social isolation affected many people in Victorian society, but these were broad enough generalizations to have explained large increases in the membership of certain sects, whereas in fact Victorian sects attracted only small numbers of people. Part of the explanation of this was probably that the large denominations, including the Church of England, were only superficially homogenous. Away from what central or official headquarters they possessed, the denominations existed as local churches, which varied in many ways, in belief as well as in social composition, even within the same denomination. For some local churches the denominational structure barely impinged. This diversity enabled the bigger ecclesiastical bodies to cope just as successfully as the smaller ones with the kind of people influenced by the sociological factors which Dr Wilson mentions. People seeking compensation for economic and social deprivation could find it as easily in one of the larger as in one of the smaller bodies; from this point of view, indeed, there were no sects, only Churches which had failed; while the Churches, of course, were sects which had made good. In a later essay (see the *Archives de la Sociologie des Religions*, 1963), Dr Wilson proposed a sevenfold typology of sects, based on the way in which they reacted to society; but the definitions which he gives would apply equally well to aspects of the larger religious bodies. Even the most obvious common element in the outlook of these smaller religious groups—that they expressed an anxiety to withdraw to a greater or lesser extent from society in general—could also be predicated of the major Victorian Churches, all of which were characterized by a degree of refusal to share the common cultural life. Without this impulse to dissent from the secular reality Christianity cannot preserve any serious identity.

Granted, however, that 'sect' is not a very useful category, it is true that in the Victorian period a number of new religious groups were started, all of which saw themselves as Churches and hoped to expand rapidly, but failed to do so. One is still left with the question as to why men chose one sect and not another, and as to why most men chose none of them. Dr Wilson thinks that we cannot explain why a man chose to become a member of an Adventist group, for example, either in terms of what the Adventists taught or in terms of what the theologian would call 'faith': 'faith', as Wilson understands it, is the function of religious adherence at its most general and so cannot be used to explain why a man believes in the imminence of the Second Advent in particular. It is natural that a sociologist should minimize the role of doctrine, but I would suggest that the teachings of a group may partly explain its failure to find recruits in its primary creative phase, a stage in which its doctrines play a much more significant role than they do two generations later, when the membership of the body has become much more hereditary, so that the original doctrinal emphases fall into desuetude, because the members are no longer pressed to maintain their separate identity over against other religious bodies, but aspire instead to assert the movement's status as a respectable Protestant evangelical denomination. (This is the general history of Pentecostalism during the past seventy-five years.) In the primary period, however, when the doctrinal element was well to the fore, the average man found it impossible to take seriously either the imminence of the Second Advent or the desirability of speaking with tongues. He did not want to compensate for his cultural disinheritance by proclaiming his adherence to the pattern of religious explanation put forward by the Jehovah's Witnesses.

Dr Wilson himself suggests the force of this argument when he appeals to 'differentiated social and psychological dispositions' to explain why men chose a particular sect, so that 'sects' 'recruit those for whom they can fulfil more specific social functions'.[11] Such an argument, however, brings us back to the individual Adventist rather than to generalizations about his total environment, cultural or economic, and to the individual Adventist as the subject of psychological description, or explanation. For example, one of Dr Wilson's explanations of the attractiveness of the Pentecostalist sect, Elim, involves this kind of argument:

> In a sense the group takes over the individual neuroses and institutionalizes them . . . its function offers very obvious analogies with group psychotherapy, in which the minister is the leader . . . the basis of the organization is one of sharing a guilty feeling, sharing a deep-laid sense of sin. . . . There is a type of group free-association and a group-transference—the individual unloads his insecurity feelings into a situation where all recognize his frailty, and do not condemn him for it. To the individual participant he unloads his burdens on Jesus—
>
> > Rolled away, rolled away,
> > And the burden of my heart rolled away—
>
> is the chorus which is sung over and over again.[12]

In a passage like this Wilson seems to have returned to the idea of faith in practice, after first restating it in psychological terms which will permit him to assert that it is not faith he is describing. The Adventist, however, is not obliged to accept Wilson's very acute observations as a complete account of what takes place in such an experience. In any case, what Wilson describes would apply to nineteenth century revival meetings held in the major as well as the smaller groups; it could apply to the 'coming-out' of the penitents at one of

[11] Wilson, B., *Sects and Society*, 1961, p.354.
[12] Ibid., p.346.

Moody's meetings. And once one reaches these psychological categories, it becomes difficult to describe the in any case limited attraction of the smaller religious bodies in terms of the social and cultural environment of the new member; one may as well suppose that what the sect teaches and practises (especially in its worship, whether revivalistic or regulated by some kind of Book of Offices) is what offers specific satisfactions to a particular individual with his own psychological make-up. This may not be what Wilson means by 'social function'. He rightly emphasizes the fact that the smaller religious institutions provide aspirations and status for their members, as of course they do, although here what one has to explain is why people should seek this particular kind of social status at the high price of membership of the sect: other kinds of social status are in fact available. One has also to distinguish the member who satisfies the group's own criterion of a 'religious' person, and the member who seems to have lost (or never have had) 'religious' reasons for belonging to the group but who still behaves as a member in external ways, giving time, money, and the appropriate answers to any sociological questionnaires which may come his way. It is the case of the 'religious' member which matters, and one cannot help feeling that the 'religious' content of the group, what it teaches and practises, accounts very largely for his adherence.

This brings us back to the question why new religious groups like the Adventist and Pentecostalists formed in the nineteenth century. Here the important clue lies in the nature of their membership. There is good evidence to show that in the nineteenth century the original members of these groups were people whose lives had always revolved around religious organizations; they had been what one may call religion-centred. This implies that the simplest theory of the growth of these bodies in the Victorian period is that they witnessed to a subtle decline in the religious satisfactions, including conscious religious 'experience', which people could obtain from belonging to the older religious bodies. The 'sects', that is, and the revivalism which so often formed their basic technique, were not a function of what the Churches were trying to do for people outside their normal scope, or even a by-product of groups socially and economically deprived in late nineteenth-century society, but rather the product of a process which had been going on inside the churches from the start of the century. Between 1830 and 1900 the concept of valid religious experience was increasingly challenged; yet at the same time the decline of other sorts of religious authority—the Bible and the institutional Church for example—made religious experience more than ever the last stage of any serious defence of the reality of Christianity itself. The decline in the number of Victorian worshippers (a fact from the 1880s) had two chief causes. The non-religious factors which had brought people into the churches lost some of their potency; while those who still attended church or chapel began to question more and more whether what they heard and did there had any fundamentally religious content for them. It was the growth of liberal Christianity, the disappearance of a familiar orthodoxy, which had much to do with the growth of the new bodies, though an exception must be made for the doctrine of eternal punishment, which many of the new groups found it necessary to repudiate despite their claims to orthodoxy. The business of the sects, at their various social levels, and taking into account differing levels of intelligence and credulity, was to deal in religious experience: 'here', it was claimed (by any particular sect) 'if nowhere else, you will both *feel* and *know* that God is present and acting. In the great institutional churches God is dead, but among us He is alive and powerful'.

This need to find a ground of valid religious experience explains, of course, the Anglo-Catholic emphasis on 'the Real Presence' in the Eucharist, an emphasis which culminated in the twentieth century in the kind of church in which one might find displayed on the closed doors of a chapel, where the Eucharistic elements were reserved, a card with the words, 'God is here. Let no one enter except for prayer'.[13] At the opposite liturgical extreme, the great attraction of the first generation of Brethren was the way in which they presented

---

[13] 'Not long ago I was in a church in which there was displayed on the closed doors of a chapel, where the sacred elements were kept, a card, with the written words, "God is here. Let no one enter except for prayer". The conception of the Divine Presence suggested by that card is neither Primitive nor Catholic. I submit that the cult of the Reserved Sacrament is the outcome of a particular line of development in the Church, and that such divines as Augustine, Jerome, John of Damascus, Ratramnus, Ridley, Laud, Waterland and Westcott represent a wholly different tradition of thought'— *Reservation*, Report of a Conference held at Farnham Castle on 24–27 October, 1925

the Lord's Supper as a simple democratic event; the group felt that they were taking part in a small domestic meal, an interpretation of the rite quite forgotten in the English religious tradition at this time, and so likely to arouse unusually strong feelings of actuality: this was what the Lord and the Apostles had done, and in following their example closely one achieved a more vivid sense of the divine immanence. The original members of both movements were drawn from the educated minority of Anglicans; they were mostly people for whom the central experience of the eighteenth-century Evangelical Revival, justification by faith, had become a sterile repetition of only too well-known formulae. In comparison with what for the moment seemed an old-fashioned, subjective kind of piety, the Communion Service glowed with apparent objectivity. It is probable that the introduction of revivalistic methods into the Anglo-Catholic system in the late 1860s meant that the first impulse and satisfactions of the movement had weakened, and that this involved a temporary swing back to methods more characteristic of the Evangelical world. On the other hand, Anglo-Catholic revivalism was able to offer the sacramental life of the mission, including aural confession, as a means of obtaining objective contact with God, and it is all the more significant of the cold climate of late Victorianism that this method of evangelism should have largely failed.

Nineteenth-century Adventism served very similar purposes. The visible return of Christ literally 'on the clouds of Heaven' offered the possibility of just the kind of visible phenomena which most easily satisfied the demand for more convincing religious experience. The Second Advent, whether in 1836 (Bengel's date, spread in England by John Wesley's *Notes on the New Testament*) or in 1843-4 (dates arrived at by William Miller in the U.S.A.) would simultaneously prove the existence of God and flatten the rationalist theologians whose arguments were otherwise difficult to counter. The failure of

(London 1926), p.11. The speaker was Dr A. J. Tait. The Conference included men of all shades of clerical opinion in the Church of England. In fact, of course, what one senses behind such a placard is not the weight of a particular theological tradition but the presence of a familiar anxiety—how, despite all the philosophers, can one *prove objectively* the existence of God. I have often heard preachers assert quite dogmatically from the pulpit that the Real Presence is a *fact*.

these—and other—eschatological calculations gradually depressed the level at which Adventism remained intellectually credible, and the attempt to revive the movement by asserting that the Advent had already taken place did not restore its appeal to sophisticated people. In the later nineteenth century, Adventism tended to fall into the background of sectarian teaching and was subordinated to other themes, such as Healing and Holiness.

In the last quarter of the century rationalism, Biblical criticism, Darwinism and a host of other factors affected the 'religious society' deeply. The growth, at the same time, of a Roman-Catholic healing shrine like that at Lourdes shows how widespread was the desire for evidence of God's visible activity in the present. Pentecostalism operated at much the same level, offering both cases of divine healing and what was called 'speaking with tongues'. In these cases divine intervention took the form of making the victim speak in some unknown tongue which it normally required another equally inspired interpreter to translate. Why the divine Spirit should act in such a roundabout manner has never been satisfactorily explained. But the Pentecostalist could point to these activities as signs of the power and presence of his God. A residual Adventism coloured the pattern, for Pentecostalists believed that the *glossolalia* and healings were scriptural announcements of the End of All Things.

2. Holiness Revivalism and Phoebe Palmer

The Holiness Movement of the 1870s appealed over a wider social area. In the Salvation Army, as we shall see, the attraction was relatively uncomplicated. The Army's 'holiness meetings' revealed a strong surviving urban nostalgia for the methods and excitements of earlier Methodism, not least in its Primitive Methodist form; the undisciplined emotion of the social pursuit of sanctification was its own sufficient guarantee of the divine presence.

The Keswick movement was a more subtle affair. One has the impression that the original meetings at Brighton in 1875 'for the deepening of the spiritual life' called together an astonishing variety of Evangelical men and women, many of them in early middle age or older, all of them somehow dissatisfied with the Evangelical tradition in which they had developed and looking for a fresh kind of religious experience which would reassure them about Christianity. Marianne Farningham, for instance, a Baptist journalist who edited the *Sunday School Times* from 1881 to the end of the century, said in her autobiography, published in 1907:

> Never after did I find it possible to be afraid of everlasting punishment, so assured was I that love would find some other way. A great hope rose within me that there might be unread meanings in some of the words of the Lord Jesus, which as yet we had never fully understood. In any case, I lost a burden at Brighton which has never since been laid upon me, and I am profoundly thankful for the joyousness which then entered into my personal experience.[14]

This was only one reaction to the Brighton meetings and it was not even a typical one as far as its reference to eternal punishment was concerned. It underlines, however, the fact that the Holiness movement succeeded at its more sophisticated level because its revivalistic methods seemed to release and soothe the anxieties which had been building up in the evangelical world since the 1830s. The term 'holiness' must therefore be treated with some caution. In the case of the Salvationists, it stood for an act of will which took place in circumstances of great emotional excitement; at Keswick the term involved relaxation rather than effort, and the Wordsworthian background of the Lake District contrasted powerfully with the anonymous barracks in which the Victorian poor were huddled. In neither case did 'holiness' mean quite what the layman would have expected.

In England, Holiness revivalism was always associated with American professionals. James Caughey had worked on this theme in the 1840s and the published results of his preaching always included a return of the sanctified. On 21 March, 1847, for example, he preached in the Bethel (Primitive Methodist)

---

[14] *A Working Woman's Life*, an autobiography (London 1907), p.150. Born in 1834 in West Kent, Marianne Farningham's real name was Hearn, and she wrote religious verse for such periodicals as *The Christian World*, with which she was associated from its beginnings in 1857. Farningham was the name of her birthplace. Her importance may be measured perhaps, by the fact that within ten years of starting, 1867, *The Christian World* claimed to have a weekly circulation of 100,000.

Chapel near Sheffield on behalf of the General Baptist Sunday Schools. He was reported (*The Wesleyan*, 24 March, 1847) to have justified 111, of whom 1 was a Baptist, 2 were Anglicans, 2 belonged to the Methodist New Connexion, 3 were Primitives and 20 Wesleyans. The 'sanctified' amounted to 37, of whom 34 were Wesleyans, 2 Primitives and 1 was a member of the Methodist New Connexion. When Caughey was attacked by the Wesleyan Conference in 1847 and forbidden the use of Wesleyan premises, one of his defenders replied by giving a table of Caughey's alleged results in the British Isles up to that point:

	Justified	Sanctified
Dublin	700	100
Limerick	130	30
Cork	300	50
Bandon	70	20
Liverpool	1,300	400
Leeds	1,600	1,000
Hull	2,300	900
Sheffield	3,352	1,448
Huddersfield	1,879	755
York	1,314	727
Birmingham	2,800	1,400
Nottingham	1,412	553
Lincoln	368	283
Boston	260	140
Sunderland	711	227
Gateshead	80	46
Scarborough	134	66
Chesterfield	599	137
Doncaster	356	170
Macclesfield	260	140
Wakefield	200	130
Various visits to London, Belper, and other places at a moderate computation	1,500	500
	21,625	9,222[15]

[15] *A Brief Memoir of the Labours and a Vindication of the Character and Call of the Rev James Caughey*, etc. by A Wesleyan Methodist, London, 1847. These figures are given on pp.40–1.

If these two figures were added together, nearly 31,000 people had been affected by Caughey's revivalism, but in fact there was some duplication of names. The figure for Sunderland, for instance, in the list given above is 711 justified and 227 sanctified. In another pamphlet issued in 1847 in the Caughey controversy another of his apologists, *A Wesleyan Leader*, gave the same totals for Sunderland but broke them up as follows:

	Justified	Sanctified
Members of society	360	219
Backsliders	37	3
From the world	314	5
	711	227

He added that if 38 were cut off for people whose names had been entered twice, that is, in two columns, the number was 900.[16] Duplication does not affect the fact that Caughey could claim that more than 9,000 people had been sanctified under his preaching.

When he returned to England in the late 1850s, Caughey still published his results in the same detail. He preached at Rotherham, for instance, from 11 November, 1858 to 11 January, 1859. The statistics were: pardoned (that is, justified), 354—'nearly all out of the world', backsliders 56, and sanctified 110. In a neighbouring chapel he had added an undifferentiated total of 391, and it is interesting to note that in the two places no fewer than 520 had signed the teetotal pledge.

Caughey's interest in sanctification undoubtedly reflected the first stirrings of the Holiness Movement in American Methodism. The Tuesday Meeting for the Promotion of Holiness had been started among New York women in 1835; Phoebe Palmer herself was 'sanctified' in 1837, and the famous meeting, held usually at the Palmer's house in New York, was thrown open to men in 1839. In the same year Timothy

---

[16] *A Dialogue on the 'Whole Case' of the Rev. James Caughey*, by A Wesleyan Leader, printed in Sheffield in 1847, p.8. This was a 12-page pamphlet. *The Whole Case Stated*, by a Wesleyan Methodist, was another item in the controversy. Caughey's preaching of Holiness does not seem to have become an important factor in the controversy about him, which followed the normal lines of revivalist-controversy: did he convert anybody, were his converts, if made, permanent, did he use undue emotional pressure, was he subject to the authority of the Wesleyan Conference, etc.?

Merritt, who had published a little treatise on Christian Perfection in 1825, founded a monthly periodical, the *Guide to Christian Perfection*, later renamed the *Guide to Holiness*, to stimulate interest in the doctrine. The historian of the doctrine of Christian Perfection in American Methodism, John L. Peters, has said that 'as early as 1840 the work of Bangs,[17] Merritt and the Palmers began to show results. In 1841 the *Methodist Quarterly Review* observed the "work of holiness among us" and was thankful for the instances of the "clear, sober, and Scriptural profession of that blessed state among our people".'[18] Moreover, C. J. Finney adopted a new emphasis on perfectionism after 1836, questioning the quality of converts produced by his previous efforts at revivalism. He was convinced, he said, that revivals would become more and more superficial and finally cease unless something effectual was done to elevate the standard of holiness in the church.[19] By the mid-1830s the revivalistic élan which had excited the American churches since the beginning of the century had almost burned itself out.[20] Other radicalisms, summed up in the programme of Garrison's *Liberator*, which demanded the emancipation of women quite as loudly as it demanded the emancipation of the negro, competed for youthful enthusiasm. The Holiness Movement was to some, including Finney himself, a way to keep the old fires burning, to others a cautious retreat from the dangers of social and

[17] Nathan Bangs was one of the most powerful of nineteenth century American Methodists. He was in effect editor of most of its publications, a historian of the denomination between 1829–40, and a definer of its doctrinal position. He supported Phoebe Palmer at almost every point, not least on the highly controversial view that no one could remain sanctified who did not openly testify to his sanctification. His influence partly explains hers.

[18] J. L. Peters, *Christian Perfection and American Methodism* (New York 1956), pp.114–115.

[19] See W. G. McLoughlin, *Modern Revivalism* (New York 1959), p.148. McLoughlin's indifference to non-Presbyterian revivalism comes out at this point, for he makes no mention of Phoebe Palmer in his book at all, and discusses Finney's conversion to perfectionism very briefly, as evidence of his doubts of the value of his revivalistic past. Perfectionism, on the other hand, became the foundation of a quite new outburst of revivalism under Palmer, as well as Caughey, whose name is also missing from McLoughlin's index. Finney held the same view of perfection, as being normally the product of an instantaneous experience, as did the two Methodists; he hardly belonged to the gradualist school which, in American Methodism itself, attacked these methods and the Holiness Camp-Meetings which developed from them.

[20] For this point see W. Cross, *The Burned-Over District* (1950). Cross describes all the varieties of revivalism, utopianism, millennianism, and social radicalism which interacted with one another in the East in this period.

political involvement. Personal vices, besetting sins like drinking or smoking, were the favourite targets of the holiness orator. Even here, the patterns of the time overlap, for Phoebe Palmer's influence and revivalist preaching showed a freedom from masculine control which irritated more than American Methodist bishops, and caused criticisms of her behaviour when she visited England.

There was little indication of a similar British interest in the doctrine of Holiness between 1830 and 1840; and yet, when Caughey began to preach along these lines in the 1840s to audiences which were largely Methodist, he had undoubted response. Part of the explanation was that in the course of its institutionalization after John Wesley's death in 1791, Wesleyan Methodism went through a crisis of respectability which lasted until the 1860s. American revivalism, and the doctrine of Holiness, which the Wesleyans inherited from Wesley, both became involved in a domestic struggle about the nature of Wesleyan Methodism. Both parties in the conflict wished to appear loyal to the past, and so those who opposed institutionalization compared American revivalism with the Wesleyan evangelism of the eighteenth century; the organizers of Wesleyanism as a regular denomination, however, men like Jabez Bunting, saw no resemblance between Caughey and John Wesley or George Whitefield.

In the case of the doctrine of Christian perfection, the difference might be summed up in a comparison between the way in which two Wesleyan theological writers, Adam Clarke and Richard Watson, expounded it. As an ageing man in the 1820s, Adam Clarke became a hero of the men who opposed change in the structure of the Wesleyan societies; Richard Watson was Clarke's younger, successful rival, and his theological text-book[21] moulded the minds of hundreds of Wesleyan preachers in the mid-nineteenth century. Both were old-fashioned by the German standards of their day, and it is fascinating to think that they both died at about the same time as Schleiermacher.[22] Neither wrote much about the subject of Christian Holiness, but they managed to disagree on it. Adam Clarke, emphasizing one side of John Wesley's teaching,

[21] *Works of the Rev. R. Watson*, XI vols., London, 1834.
[22] Clarke died in 1832, Watson early in 1833, and Schleiermacher in 1834.

was all for complete Christian perfection as a gift which God bestowed instantaneously in terms of human faith. This approach naturally commended itself to revivalists, who saw themselves as drawing people forward until they underwent this sudden transformation. Richard Watson did not deny the possibility of this instantaneous act of God, but preferred to think of complete holiness as a kind of spiritual maturity for which time and gradual development were needed. This was another side of John Wesley's own teaching,[23] and it appealed to men cautious about Holiness revivalism. Richard Watson's views were those of the dominant party in British Methodism in the 1830s and 1840s, but Adam Clarke's attitude naturally suited the anti-institutionalists, and in fact most of Caughey's support was to come from people who dreaded any change which would tend to make Wesleyan Methodism a Church rather than an evangelizing society. Clarke and Caughey were both Wesleyans in as much as they accepted the possibility of a man being wholly sanctified long before he died. Without this idea, which was rejected by all Protestant evangelicals in the main stream of the Reformation, holiness revivalism was theologically absurd. There must be the necessary ground for a concluding offer of instantaneous sanctification. The remarkable achievement of Mrs Palmer and Pearsall Smith was that they convinced some Anglican Evangelicals, nurtured in suspicion of all forms of perfectionism, that they might legitimately seek immediate freedom from sin for themselves in what became the Keswick movement of the 1880s.

The development of the Holiness movement after 1850 was to be found in this extension of the social respectability of instantaneous change. Caughey, Phoebe Palmer, Booth and Smith all repudiated the assertion that 'holiness' resulted only from a slow process of change, in which a man quietly set out with divine assistance to practise the virtues and avoid the

[23] Cf. J. L. Peters, op. cit., on this whole question. On balance, I feel that John Wesley encouraged the 'instantaneous' interpretation of sanctification. In the *Arminian Magazine*, which he issued from 1778, John Wesley published a series of autobiographies written by his itinerants. A number of these illustrated the 'instantaneous' point of view. The best example is that of Alexander Mather, which Wesley (in 1780) deliberately praised. 'What I had experienced in my own soul was an instantaneous deliverance from all those wrong tempers and affections which I had long and sensibly groaned under; an entire disengagement from every creature, with an entire devotedness to God. . . .' *The Lives of the Early Methodist Preachers*, edited by Thomas Jackson, Vol. I, p.278 (2nd ed., London 1846).

vices; or from the sort of asceticism which attached moral superiority to abstinence from money, sex and individual initiative. 'Holiness' was instead something which God 'gave' and gave suddenly; Phoebe Palmer called it a state of soul.[24] A proper analogy would be the sudden illumination with which a struggling mathematician finds himself able to solve a type of problem hitherto impossible for him. This new 'state' did not necessitate a violent change of personal habits; the kind of ethical behaviour associated with 'holiness' in the revivalist theology was that of classical Evangelical Pietism—no cards, no novels, no theatres, nothing, in fact, which would stimulate the imagination and give rise to what were seen as 'temptations', especially the temptation to break away from the pietist society. Indeed, for all these revivalists 'holiness' might be described (though they themselves used different language) as the discovery of power to resist specific personal temptations; as a result of the sanctifying experience, one was enabled—the verb is the one normally used, and is significant —to refuse to associate with non-pietists, to overcome the desire to read novels or to knit frivolously on the Sabbath, to live, in other words, as one had expected to be able to live when one was first converted and became a member of the Evangelical Pietist Society. In itself, the gift of 'holiness' narrowed and intensified the individual character, and this was because the kind of man or woman who pursued 'holiness' in the revivalist school did so in order to find a way of fulfilling the demands of the traditionally limiting Evangelical ethic.

The only ethical addition which the American revivalists made to the content of 'holiness' was the doctrine of teetotalism, for whose growth in England they had more responsibility than is usually recognized.[25] Here the change in habits was very marked. When Henry Venn Elliott (whose mother was a daughter of the Evangelical patriarch Henry Venn of Huddersfield, and whose father built St Mary's Church to be an Evangelical thorn in the flesh of Brighton) obtained a Trinity Fellowship in 1816 he sent to his sisters some verses translated from Sophocles and 'seven dozen of

---

[24] P. Palmer, *Entire Devotion*, p.22.

[25] For teetotalism, cf. B. Harrison, *Drink and the Victorians* (1971); the first properly critical history of the movement.

Trinity audit ale to his father as "the first-fruits of his Fellow-ship".' Two generations later such an action would have been unthinkable in the Evangelical world. Caughey's interest in the subject has already been noted; Mrs Palmer found her insistence on teetotalism her main difficulty in holding revivals in Wesleyan churches.

The issue arose in December, 1860, for instance, at Banbury, where five hundred had already been justified and scores had been sanctified. Then one afternoon when Phoebe Palmer was speaking to a man at the altar rail in the chapel, 'I caught the fumes of his breath, which told too plainly that he was addicted to the intoxicating cup'. She asked him to promise to take the pledge but he would not. And so, although he had answered in the affirmative when she asked him if he now felt he had found his Saviour, she told him that 'his right-hand sin would probably sink his spirit into deathless burnings'. Her heart, she said, grew sad and sick. At the evening meeting, although she herself felt rather better, 'instead of scores rushing forward to the altar and vestry as in all the previous meetings, it was some time before even one came'. It was, she says, also some time before she remembered her alcoholic penitent, whose refusal to became a teetotaller she now used to explain why the revival had suddenly stopped. She now also discovered that there was a brewer in the local Wesleyan society and that the members drank. She summoned the Society and put it to them that the Lord had checked the revival so as to show them that drinking was evil; a few responded and took the temperance pledge. Most, however, including the brewer, did not. And there the revival ended. Mrs Palmer had played her personality as a trump card, and failed.[26]

It is obviously impossible to say what really happened at Banbury. On Mrs Palmer's own understanding of the ways of Providence, it might have been argued that her ruthless treatment of her penitent had provoked divine intervention, and was the real cause of the collapse of the Revival. At a more mundane level, it is possible that her action at the altar rail had either awakened sympathy for the offender in the local

[26] Phoebe Palmer, *Four Years in the Old World*, comprising the Travels, etc., of Dr and Mrs Palmer (New York 1866), p.379.

Society, or had led them to demonstrate their opposition to her teetotal point of view. Wesleyan Methodism was still at this time officially uncommitted to the teetotal crusade. On the other hand, Phoebe Palmer may have seized on the incident because the revival was already slackening: it would serve either to stimulate fresh interest or to justify an immediate withdrawal. Writing her account for an American public, Mrs Palmer did not paint a very amiable picture of Wesleyan Methodism in England; she neatly disposed of her apparent failure by blaming it on the Wesleyan brewer, whose very existence also showed the superiority of American Methodism, in which, she boasted, brewers were impossible. Whatever the truth of the incident, however, Phoebe was making teetotalism a part of her definition of faith, and abstinence a sacrifice essential to the reception of the gift of 'holiness'. This was a development novel in the history of British Evangelical Pietism, and it is hardly surprising that at first many Evangelicals declined to succumb to Mrs Palmer's pressure. Mrs Palmer, however, connected the ideas of 'holiness', 'power' and 'Teetotalism' tightly together. In Sunderland, for example, in November, 1859, she told a Temperance lecturer who had two drinking sons that now he had been sanctified 'he would have an increase of *power*, and might confidently expect the speedy conversion of his children', a conversion which would, of course, mean their becoming abstinent. It happened, she reported, as she had promised.[27] And one explanation of what looks like her overconfidence in the affair at Banbury may be found in her account of how in September, 1860, she had driven from the local Wesleyan Society at Poole in Dorset 'the most noted maltster in the town' on the ground that she could not revive a church which tolerated a brewer on its membership roll.[28]

As to the mechanics of all this, Mrs Palmer's was undoubtedly the dominant influence. The best summary of her point of view is to be found in *The Way of Holiness*[29] (a reprint

[27] *Four Years*, etc., p.128.

[28] Ibid., pp.327-8. In England, she said, 'for a minister or member to sign the temperance pledge is decidedly unpopular'.

[29] *The Way of Holiness*, with notes by the way, by Mrs Phoebe Palmer. First English edition reprinted from the 34th American edition. With preface by the Rev. Thomas Collins, London 1856. Collins was a Wesleyan minister.

of the thirty-fourth American edition), published for the first time in England in 1856, three years before she crossed the Atlantic. That she had something unusual to offer was evident on the first page, on which she promised 'a shorter way' of coming into holiness. She could put it like this because if by 'holiness' you meant, not the achievement of a Christian version of maturity, but the acquisition of the power to resist specific temptations, then it was conceivable that there might be a short cut to the goal.

Theoretically, the Wesleyan Methodist tradition (at any rate as Adam Clarke had transmitted it) had always offered this short cut: faith provided the ground and 'holiness' was the instantaneous divine gift. Something had gone wrong with the Wesleyan Methodist tradition, however; men struggled to approach the divine source of the power of holiness but they still found themselves yielding to temptations, and they did not seem able to attain the kind of subjective experience which they could interpret as evidence that 'holiness' had been given them. In fact, as Phoebe Palmer shrewdly diagnosed, they became 'more solicitous about feeling than faith; requiring feeling, the fruit of faith, previous to having exercised faith' (p.19); they wanted a subjective shock which they could identify with the reception of the gift. In effect the current Wesleyan approach demanded (or seemed to demand) tremendous effort without apparent result; people felt that 'holiness' was an attainment beyond their reach.

It was on the basis of this apparent lack of result that Phoebe Palmer established her system; the weak point of the older technique became the strong point of hers. Why expect ecstacy, she asked her readers, or spiritual transformations so violent as to be physically perceptible?[30] One had to offer oneself entirely to God (Mrs Palmer usually talked about 'consecrating' oneself on the 'altar of Christ'); to make a deliberate covenant with God to that effect; and then relax, taking one's 'holiness' on trust. She gave an example: 'Oh Lord, I call heaven and earth to witness that I now lay my body, soul and

[30] 'Will you come, dear disciple of Jesus, and venture even *now* to lay your all upon this blessed altar? He will not spurn you away. No; "His side an open fountain is"; "His nature and His name is love". Surely you will now begin to say "O Love, thou bottomless abyss, etc." Rest here. Remember, "The just shall live by faith", not ecstasies. . . .' *Entire Devotion*, p.42.

spirit, with all their redeemable powers, upon Thine altar, to be for ever Thine. 'Tis done. Thou has promised to receive me. Thou canst not be unfaithful. Thou dost receive me now. From this time forth I am Thine, wholly Thine' (*The Way of Holiness*, p.19).

Mrs Palmer's language was reminiscent of that in the Wesleyan Order of Service 'for those who wish to enter into or renew a Covenant with God', where the actual Covenant begins, 'I am no longer my own, but Thine', and concludes, 'And now, Oh glorious and blessed God, Father, Son and Holy Spirit, Thou art mine and I am Thine. So be it. And the Covenant which I have made on earth, let it be ratified in Heaven'. One has the impression that in the case of the Covenant Service, Wesley's pragmatism defeated his theological common sense; the Presbyterian atmosphere of the Covenant never suited Methodism. Mrs Palmer seems to have developed the Wesleyan doctrine of Holiness in what might be called a Calvinist manner, emphasizing the objective side of the process. Her attitude reminds one of the early nineteenth-century Anglican Evangelicals, which makes it less surprising that in the long run her teaching, when known through other sources, should have proved popular in that world, as at Keswick.

The 'shorter way' came precisely at this stage of relaxation, which Mrs Palmer called the 'rest of faith', a phrase, based on the Epistle to the Hebrews, chapter 4, verse 3, which was often used in the early days of Keswick. Mrs Palmer said that once one had laid one's all upon the altar one 'laid oneself under the most solemn obligation to believe that the sacrifice became the Lord's property; and by virtue of the altar (Christ) on which the offering was laid, became "holy" and "acceptable".' Her biblical explanation of this theory also shows how directly she drew on Adam Clarke.

> Holiness is a state of soul in which all the powers of the body and mind are consciously given up to God; and the witness of holiness is that testimony which the Holy Spirit bears with our spirit that the offering is accepted through Christ. *The work is accomplished the moment we lay our all upon the altar* [italics mine]. Under the old Covenant dispensation, it was ordained by God that whatsoever touched the altar should be holy. 'Seven days thou shalt

make an atonement for the altar and sanctify it; and it shall be an altar most holy; whatsoever toucheth the altar shall be holy' (Exod. xxix.37). And in allusion to this Our Saviour says 'The altar that sanctifieth the gift', (Matt. xxxiii.19). As explanatory of this subject Dr Clarke says, 'This may be understood as implying that whatsoever was laid on the altar became the Lord's property, and must be wholly devoted to sacred purposes'. Under the new Covenant dispensation the Apostle to the Hebrews says, 'We have an altar, whereof they have no right to eat which serve the tabernacle' (Heb. xiii.10). Dr Clarke again says, 'The Christian altar is the Christian sacrifice, which is Jesus Christ, with all the benefits of his passion and death' (*Entire Devotion to God*, pp. 40–1).

This ambiguous doctrine sometimes went home with tremendous force. Mrs Palmer cited the case of a woman at Sunderland in 1859 who cried out in the course of one of the meetings, 'What a fool, what a fool I have been all my days. I have been giving, giving and giving myself to God, but never believing that he received me'.[31] In other words, Mrs Palmer sometimes succeeded because she enabled people to release energy which they had damned up in fruitless conflict; paradoxically, this often meant that they now fulfilled the demands of the very Evangelical pietism which had frustrated them before, finding their religious certainty in the performance of such obligations, instead of continuing their search for a more direct experience of divine power.

It is easy to see why Phoebe Palmer's critics accused her of teaching: 'believe that you have it (holiness) and you have it'.[32] She could write very casually at times. For example, in *Entire Devotion*, she described how she had shown a seeker after holiness 'that the blessing was received through faith— that, after I had made an entire consecration of myself to the Lord, I was bound to believe that He, faithful to His promise, accepted the sacrifice, and sanctified it for His service'.[33] Of

[31] *Four Years in the Old World*, p.125, in a letter of 14 November, 1859.

[32] Mrs Palmer denied that there was any real ambiguity. If one is wholly consecrated to God, if one is wholly God's, then one is holy, for what more can God require? Cf. *The Way of Holiness*, pp.12–15. But Mrs Palmer held an altogether simpler view of the human personality than is possible today, and therefore regarded entire consecration as possible. Pragmatically, moreover, many of her sanctified friends lived with much less internal friction.

[33] *Entire Devotion*, p.184.

course, Mrs Palmer emphasized the word 'entire', and of course her critics emphasized the words 'bound to believe'. It is interesting to find James Caughey, in a sermon published in England in 1857,[34] warning his hearers against the idea, 'believe that you have it, and you have it'. He told them:

> Many have stumbled here, I do not wonder at it. And now suffer me to implore all you who are in the habit, in these meetings, of instructing seekers of full salvation, to avoid such teachings and phrases as you would the plague. They have done more to bring the doctrine of sanctification by faith into disrepute than all else put together, the inconsistent lives of those who profess it excepted. There is no foundation for such sentiments in the Word of God, nor in reason or common sense.[35]

But just how difficult it was for the Holiness Revivalists to avoid the language which Phoebe Palmer used, and which her admirers exaggerated, could be seen if one read a little further in Caughey's sermon. For his positive statement went like this:

> Desire, pray, believe. If there happen to be any defect in your consecration, or in renunciation of sin, or any idol lurking in the secret place of your heart, your sanctifying Lord will reveal even this unto you. But keep on desiring, praying, renouncing, consecrating, as you can, and obstinately believing all the while. Never attempt to believe you have what you know and feel you have not. But do attempt, and with all your might, to believe that you do receive it, and he who has power to do it will cut the work short in righteousness, and save you to the uttermost.[36]

Caughey, in other words, though attempting, as always, to strike out his own line, was not really disagreeing with Phoebe Palmer. This is the place to make a simple comparison between Palmer and Caughey. On the basis of the figures which Phoebe Palmer gave in *Four Years in the Old World*, figures which she was not likely to have minimized, it looks as

---

[34] *Earnest Christianity Illustrated, Etc.*, ed. by James Unwin of Sheffield, London 1857. The sermon was called 'The Besetting Sin detected and Slain'. Unwin presents his sermons as though Caughey preached them during the Huddersfield Revival of January, 1845. No doubt Caughey resembled other famous revivalists, who rarely changed their successful sermons.

[35] Ibid., pp.198–9.

[36] *Earnest Christianity Illustrated*, p.202.

though Caughey was much the more successful. Caughey's figures were 21,625 justified and 9,222 sanctified in the revivals of the 1840s. Mrs Palmer's total is more difficult to arrive at, but it was about 17,634 in the first category, and at least 2,287 sanctified, or about 20,000 as against nearly 31,000. I suspect, however, that Mrs Palmer failed to break up her totals correctly in describing the earlier, more successful part of her tour, and that her totals should read more like about 15,000 justified, and 5,000 sanctified. It is interesting to divide her results into years:

	Justified	Sanctified
1859 (from September)	7,656	200
1860	4,500	1,400
1861	2,263	317
1862	859	156
1863 (to September)	2,356	214

In 1859 the figure for sanctified is certainly too low. In 1861 the total was brought up by a visit to Liverpool, where the Palmers operated outside the Wesleyan sector, in the Pannell evangelical chapels, which were independent. The final year, 1863, produced good results at Birmingham, Manchester and Nottingham; the big drop in 1862 was certainly due in part to the ruling of the 1862 Wesleyan Conference that the Palmers should not be allowed to work on Wesleyan premises: the better results in 1863 were due to the readiness of the Palmers to work in anti-Wesleyan circles. The figures for sanctification in 1861–3, however, have to be taken seriously, and mean that, as a Holiness revivalist, Phoebe Palmer did not succeed to anything like the extent that Caughey did. Her role was rather, in England, at any rate, to maintain the continuity of the holiness tradition, and to determine the form in which Holiness teaching reached the 1870s. Her part in the spread of teetotalism ought not to be ignored, however. A few of her figures were broken down in the Caughey style: she also went to Rochdale in 1861, but not to Baillie Street, where Caughey worked, but to the Wesleyan Methodist Chapel, and recorded 541 seekers; 374 justified, 157 sanctified; of these 62 were described as Rochdale Wesleyans, 82 as Wesleyans from elsewhere; 230 were allegedly 'from the world'.

3. The Salvation Army and Phoebe Palmer

More important, however, because of its long-term consequences, was Mrs Palmer's effect on William and Catherine
Booth, the founders of the Salvation Army. Their earliest
known contact with Phoebe Palmer took place in December,
1859, when William Booth, then a minister of the Methodist
New Connexion, was stationed at Gateshead, and the Palmers
were holding revival services in Newcastle on Tyne. A local
Independent minister, Arthur Augustus Rees, published a
violent pamphlet in which he denied, on scriptural grounds,
the right of a woman to preach. Mrs Booth wrote:

> It was delivered in the form of an address to his congregation,
> would you believe that a congregation half composed of ladies
> would sit and hear such self-deprecatory nonsense? They really
> don't deserve to be taken up cudgels for.[37]

Nevertheless, she published an answer to Rees in which she
roundly defended Mrs Palmer's rights.

> Whether the Church will allow women to speak in her assemblies
> can only be a question of time; common sense, public opinion,
> the blessed result of female agency will force her to give us an
> honest and impartial rendering of the solitary text on which she
> grounds her prohibitions.[38]

She was therefore, bound to be interested in what Phoebe
Palmer had to say, quite apart from the fact that the Booths,
like the Palmers, were revivalists by instinct, rather than
settled ministers, and were feeling their way towards the same
kind of partnership as existed between the two Americans.[39]

---

[37] F. de L. Booth-Tucker, *The Life of Catherine Booth, the Mother of the Salvation Army.*
First edition, 1892. This is a quotation from the third edition (London 1924), p.177.
Catherine Booth, by Catherine Bramwell Booth (1970), adds almost nothing to the
earlier life.

[38] Ibid., p.178. The N.T. passage referred to is, 1 Cor. 14: 34-5.

[39] The man and wife team was perhaps an almost inevitable concomitant of the
struggle for female equality in practice. In the 1860s American revivalism still retained
its radical streak, its anxiety to be ahead of the pew, doctrinally, technically and
generally. By the end of the century this impulse had spent itself, and revivalism became
more of a defensive occupation; as such, it no longer attracted the able woman, still
battling for emancipation. It is clear that Mrs Booth's ability and leadership drew a
number of young middle-class women to her in the 1878-85 period, because she
symbolized their own sense of revolt. Recent American writers have claimed that

Although the Salvation Army's public image as a Holiness Movement belongs to the 1870s, after Pearsall Smith had visited England, the Booths claimed to have been sanctified long before, in 1861. Mrs Booth's letters give a detailed account of her experience, and make it quite clear that she and her husband had completely accepted Phoebe Palmer's doctrine of holiness. This seems to be entirely ignored by modern historians of the Salvation Army, and the passage is therefore worth quoting in full.

I struggled through the day until a little after six in the evening, when William joined me in prayer. We had a blessed season. While he was saying, 'Lord, we open our hearts to receive Thee', that word was spoken to my soul: 'Behold I stand at the door and knock. If any man hear my voice and open unto me, I will come in and sup with him'. I felt sure He had long been knocking, and Oh, how I yearned to receive Him as a perfect Saviour. But Oh, the inveterate habit of unbelief. How wonderful that God should have borne so long with me. When we got up from our knees I lay on the sofa, exhausted with the excitement and effort of the day. William said, 'Don't you lay all on the altar.' I replied, 'I am sure I do.' Then he said, 'And isn't the altar holy?' I replied in the language of the Holy Ghost, 'The Altar is most holy, and whatsoever toucheth it is holy.' Then he said, 'Are you not Holy?' I replied with my heart full of emotion and some faith, 'Oh, I think I am.' Immediately, the word was given to me to confirm my faith, 'Now are ye clean through the word which I have spoken unto you.' And I took hold—true, with a trembling hand, and not unmolested by the Tempter, but I held fast the beginning of my confidence, and it grew stronger; and from that moment I have dared to reckon myself dead indeed unto sin, and alive unto God through Jesus Christ my Lord.

I did not feel much rapturous joy, but perfect peace, the sweet rest which Jesus promised to the heavy laden, I have understood the Apostle's meaning when he says, 'We who believe do enter into rest.' This is a just description of my state at present. Not that I am not tempted, but I am allowed to know the Devil when he approaches me, and I look to my deliverer, Jesus, and He still gives me rest. Two or three very trying things occurred on

---

perfectionist revivalism from the 1840s onwards played a large part in the growth of egalitarian feminism: see, 'Your Daughters Shall Prophesy: Feminism in the Age of Finney', by Nancy Hardesty (unpublished Ph.D., Chicago 1976).

Saturday, which at another time would have excited impatience, but I was kept by the power of God through faith unto full salvation.[40] And in another letter written a little earlier, she said that 'since that hour . . . although I have been tempted, I have not taken back the sacrifice from the altar, but have been enabled calmly to contemplate it as done.'[41]

The links between this passage and Mrs Palmer are overwhelmingly strong. The three questions which William Booth asked his wife summarized exactly Phoebe's characteristic thesis, that one is obliged to believe that one is sanctified once one has laid one's all upon the holy altar. Mrs Booth's insistence that she was now enjoying 'rest' rather than 'rapture' is equally characteristic of Mrs Palmer, and the quotation from the Apostle which Mrs Booth now understood more fully was the very passage from the Epistle to the Hebrews which Mrs Palmer used as a proof text to establish her doctrine. The reference to not taking back the sacrifice from the altar is also in Phoebe's vein. Once one grasps the kind of shorthand which was being used, Mrs Booth's letter ceases to be a simple account of a subjective experience, the story of how the Booths discovered holiness for themselves, and becomes instead a description of an exercise in Phoebe Palmer's spiritual discipline. Mrs Booth was well aware of this when she wrote her letter; her biographer, on the other hand, was probably unaware of the significance of the language which she used. When later writers have paid any attention to the Booths' holiness teaching they seem to have assumed that it was a personal embroidery of John Wesley's teaching; but in fact what the Booths adopted in 1861 was the revivalist holiness doctrine which Mrs Palmer brought with her from the United States. Mrs Palmer, however, although for long one of the most prominent American exponents of this revised Methodist teaching, obtained no entrée into Anglican Evangelical circles in the 1860s and so was largely forgotten after her return to America in 1863. But when the Booths, following the trend of evangelical fashion, turned back to the idea of holiness in the early 1870s, it was to Mrs Palmer's writings that they clearly referred; the Salvation Army press

[40] F. de L. Booth-Tucker, op. cit., pp.208–9.
[41] Ibid., p.206.

republished her devotional works for many years. She was not mentioned by name as a source, however, in the official documents of the Army, and this partly explains why historians of the Army have neglected her important influence.

This did not mean that the Booths placed a great emphasis on holiness revivalism in the 1860s. The Articles of William Booth's Christian Revival Society, drawn up in 1865, referred to the subject only in an abbreviated way. 'We believe that repentance towards God, faith in our Lord Jesus Christ, and regeneration by the Holy Ghost are necessary to salvation.' Throughout the 1860s, having broken with the (Methodist) institutional Church, Booth struggled unsuccessfully to find a place as a professional and independent revivalist in the American tradition. Later biographies portray him as advancing inevitably towards his destiny; in reality, his final emergence as a public figure was by no means inevitable. He had set himself up as an independent revivalist at exactly the wrong moment: there was little demand for the professionals in the 1860s, and Booth showed no particular ability to overcome this handicap. He was extremely ambitious, however, and desperation drove him back in the direction of institutionalization. The first conference of The Christian Mission (1870), the next stage in his institutional pilgrimage, accepted a more precise statement about holiness, one which was to appear, with certain additions, in the foundation deed of the Salvation Army itself (1878). This statement said:

> We believe that it is the privilege of all believers to be 'wholly sanctified' and that 'their whole spirit and body' may 'be preserved blameless unto the coming of the Lord Jesus' (1 Thessalonians v.23).

It was the general growth of the holiness movement in the evangelical pietist world which brought success to Booth, rather than he who commanded it. The rules of The Christian Mission, issued in 1870, included one, number twenty-eight, which referred to 'meetings for promoting holiness' which were to be held weekly, on Fridays for preference. It is commonly said that the first Salvation Army holiness meetings were held in 1877–8, but these meetings only continued the earlier custom. In her life of Bramwell Booth (William's son), her father, Catherine Bramwell Booth quotes from a letter which Bramwell wrote to Railton (17 October, 1874) and says that this contains the earliest reference that she could find in Bramwell's correspondence to the establishment of holiness meetings as a regular part of the Mission's programme; she seems unaware of the reference in the original rules.

According to this letter William Booth had just been sanctified himself; there was no reference to his earlier experience of sanctification in 1861. Bramwell wrote:

> He [William Booth] is strongly inclined, to make an effort at the country on the question; so far as I can see the present plan is to establish a weekly Holiness prayer meeting in London. . . . He wants to know what you think. I think, and I am on the spot, that it is a very good idea. I think the London meeting would be very good.[42]

Granted that the Booths had experienced sanctification in 1861, and that holiness meetings had formed part of the programme proposed for the Christian Mission in 1870, this amounted to the third occasion on which William Booth had tried to capture attention by using the holiness theme. Even now, he owed his comparative breakthrough to the excitement which yet another American revivalist, Pearsall Smith, stirred up around the holiness teaching in the wider Anglican and Free Church pietist society. The leaders of the Christian Mission followed the shifts of this middle-class religious feeling with close attention. The Brighton Holiness Convention took place in 1875: for the moment holiness both as doctrine and experience absorbed the pietist world. At the Christian Mission Conference of 1876, Railton, the ablest of the early officers of the Army, proposed and carried a resolution which was intended as an explanation of what the Christian Mission meant by its older statement on the doctrine of holiness. The resolution obviously resulted from the pressure of the movement which Smith had inaugurated at Brighton. Railton moved:

---

[42] C. B. Booth, *Bramwell Booth* (London 1933), p.141. The book offered a passionate apologia for William's son and successor as General, whose deposition from the Generalship in his old age had deeply wounded his daughter.

We believe that after conversion there remain in the heart of a believer inclinations of evil or roots of bitterness which, unless overpowered by divine grace, produce actual sin, but that these evil tendencies can be entirely taken away by the Spirit of God, and the whole heart thus cleansed from everything contrary to the will of God, or entirely sanctified, will then produce the fruits of the Spirit only. And we believe that persons thus entirely sanctified may by the power of God be kept unblameable and unreprovable before him.[43]

The words of this resolution must be compared with number 482 in the *Salvation Army Song Book*, published in 1878:

> Jesus, a word, a look from Thee,
> Can search my heart and make it clean;
> Purge out the inbred leprosy,
> And save me from the roots of sin—
>
> Lord, if Thou Wilt, I do believe,
> Thou dost the saving grace impart;
> Thou dost this instant now receive
> And cleanse and purify my heart.

These lines were originally written by Charles Wesley, the eighteenth-century Methodist hymnwriter; they represent the tradition on which both Adam Clarke and Phoebe Palmer drew. Whether they are classically orthodox is another question: the knowledge of teaching like this helps to explain the underlying suspicion of Wesleyan Methodism in some quarters, even in the later nineteenth century.

Railton's resolution, in any case, was an uncompromising reassertion of the doctrine of entire sanctification in this life; it became a part of the actual text of the eleven points of doctrine contained in the Army's official handbook, remaining so until 1927; in the edition published in that year it became an indented paragraph in the text; in the edition of 1935 it became a footnote. However, although Railton's resolution acquired great prominence, it was not included in the Deed Poll of the Salvation Army of 1878; too much should not be

---

[43] *The History of the Salvation Army*, by Robert Sandall, London 1947, Vol. I, appendix. F. Sandall did not comment: writers on the Army always seem to leave the subject undiscussed.

made of this, however, because until 1958 the 'definition' was automatically printed as part of the so-called Articles of War.[44]

Not much is known about the circumstances in which Railton's resolution was moved, but it is clear that Pearsall Smith's renewed emphasis on Holiness had reacted on the Christian Mission, and that the enthusiasm of some of the leaders for Holiness revivalism played a powerful part in the emergence of the Salvation Army, in which the doctrine was given great prominence for at least ten years after 1877. This did not happen without some internal opposition. William Booth had taken absolute control of the Christian Mission in the January of 1877 and its last Conference as such was held in the following July. In his main speech to the Conference Booth made three points. He was anxious to reform the Hallelujah Bands, and the singing of the Army; his third point was the centrality of the Holiness teaching.

Holiness to the Lord is to us a fundamental truth; it stands to the forefront of our doctrines. We write it on our banners. It is in no shape or form an open debatable question as to whether God can sanctify wholly, whether Jesus does save his people from their sins. In the estimation of the Christian Mission that is settled for ever, and any evangelist who did not hold and proclaim the ability of Jesus Christ to save his people to the uttermost from sin and sinning I should consider out of place among us.[45]

Railton also attended this conference and defended his definition against the opposition which had emerged in the ranks of the Mission. He said that holiness implied 'full deliverance from all known sin; the consecration of every known power and possession to God and his work; constant and uniform obedience to all the requirements of God'. It was possible, he said, to attain a state in which one could live out these implications fully. 'It is still a condition of conflict and suffering, of danger, but without sin. Love is the fulfilling of the law, and with a heart full of love to God and everybody else, the soul has no consciousness of sins'. Railton was careful to add that the sanctified would not be without mental and physical imperfection. 'We still suffer as a consequence of the Fall from disease, and are liable to mistakes and errors.' There

[44] Cf. R. Sandall, *History of The Salvation Army* (1950), Vol. II, p.53.
[45] Robert Sandall, op. cit., Vol. I, p.209.

was still temptation, and the possibility of falling back into a sinful condition. 'The angels in Heaven who kept not their first estate and Adam, who unquestionably was sinless in Paradise, fell. . . .'[46] These were normal Wesleyan qualifications to the definition of perfection, but the qualifications have to be set against the explicit promise that the condition of the sanctified, though not without conflict, suffering and danger, was *without sin*. Railton was not a pale reflection of the mind of William Booth; his conception of the Army was so austere that he wanted the uniform to look as unattractive as possible and thought that the brass bands of the later 1870s were a step back from the days when there were just one or two individual instruments.

Begbie, in his life of William Booth, was inclined to suggest that the General did no more than tolerate the holiness meetings, but this judgement was probably influenced by the fact that to Begbie, writing more than thirty years later, the Holiness episode looked little more than a distraction from the proper business of the Army; it clashed with the later, more familiar picture of the Army as a body dedicated to social evangelism and soup kitchens. Begbie may not have known about the earlier Holiness meetings; he gives the impression that they were introduced as late as 1877; and this led Professor Inglis, for example, to suggest that perhaps William Booth was purifying his troops for their war with the Devil, using the holiness meetings as a way of creating an army of saints.[47] The evidence suggests, however, that the Christian Mission had held meetings of this kind at least as early as 1874, and that the fresh enthusiasm generated by Pearsall Smith's campaign among the religious middle-class prompted an attempt to save the Mission, which seemed to be declining again in 1876–7, by a drive along the same lines. The Holiness meetings served the purpose of a stimulus; they also attracted wide attention, evoking the hostile attitude which worked psychologically to the advantage of the Army. The meetings reached a peak of intensity in 1878–9 when Bramwell Booth, then just over twenty years of age, began to hold what he called 'All Nights of Prayer'; these combined holiness and

[46] *The Christian Mission Magazine*, Vol. IX (1877), p.193.
[47] K. S. Inglis, *Churches and the Working-Classes in Victorian England* (1965), p.180.

prayer meetings, and were designed, said Catherine Bramwell Booth, 'to help anyone seeking deeper spiritual experience'. What they were really like at this time may be judged from one or two descriptions written down at the time by Bramwell Booth himself. He described one to his father:

> I preached last night at Sunderland. . . . After this we had an All Night of Prayer. . . . It was a remarkable night. All the officers did well. Coombes and Lock charming, and Agar almost as good as she should be. Of course, we went straight on in the Holiness line. There were thirteen pipes, with several tobacco pouches, a scarf pin and a lump of twist, two or three cigars, two snuff boxes, ten feathers, a string of flowers and a brooch, voluntarily surrendered amidst a scene of sobbing and shouting rarely surpassed. . . .[48]

This incident suggests a pathetically literal application of Phoebe Palmer's doctrine that all should be laid on the altar, but she was guilty of the same kind of exaggeration herself when she made teetotalism a precondition of sanctity. The description also helps one to understand why the Holiness meetings were popular; men and women felt that they could understand and even pursue holiness if holiness was presented to them largely in terms of sacrifices of this kind; they were bombarded with the assurance that, if only they could surrender completely, some amazing spiritual experience would happen to them. This assurance they translated in their own terms, and another scrap of Bramwell Booth's correspondence, a note written to Railton, probably in 1879, shows what this often meant.

> I shall see you tomorrow some time and so need not write at length. The night (All Night of Prayer) was one of the most utterly wild I ever was at. Until this I have never seen either jumping or somersaulting to any extent, but at 2.30 this morning. . . .[49]

The history of religion furnished plenty of precedent for this kind of behaviour; it is rather more difficult to credit what Bramwell Booth told Begbie about these meetings.

[48] Catherine Bramwell Booth, op. cit., p.93.
[49] Ibid., p.109.

He described how men and women would suddenly fall flat on the ground and remain in a swoon or trance for many hours, rising at last so transformed by joy that they could do nothing but shout and sing in an agony of bliss. He tells us that beyond all question he saw instances of levitation—people lifted from their feet and moving forward through the air. . . .[50]

Bramwell compared all this to 'something of the same force which manifested itself on the day of Pentecost.[51] and the idea is significant, for it was along this line of interpretation that Pentecostalism was to emerge from the Holiness movement. In the 1870s however, the Salvationists were reactionary, they represented the older American tradition of revivalism; their shouting and jumping recalled the Second Great Awakening in America, the vivid physical excitement of the early Primitive Methodists, and the similar phenomena associated with the Irish revival meetings of 1859. Moody and Sankey had repudiated such signs of the Spirit's working in 1873, and so helped to cut themselves off from the lower social levels of the British religious sub-culture. This, rather than the para-Christian working-class, formed the Army's constituency, and here the holiness meetings succeeded because they stirred up memories of the past, appealing to people who felt that the Primitive Methodists had gone the way of the Wesleyan Methodists, had lost their primal fire, and drifted into urban respectability. They appealed to others who measured revival by the Ireland of 1859 and remained unimpressed by the conscious restraint of Moody. The return of intense economic misery in the 1870s made it more likely that the submerged tenth of the religious society would seek release in excitement; official Christianity did not provide a place for dancing as a natural religious and social activity. These uninhibited out-bursts had died down by the time that Thomas Huxley began to attack what he called 'corybantic Christianity' in 1890.

Thomas Huxley had a vision of the Army as a totalitarian political group; later political experience has given this vision a touch of reality, but as a contemporaneous criticism of William Booth and his followers it was absurd. Huxley took Booth's personal government of the Army too seriously; he

[50] H. Begbie, op. cit., p.410.
[51] Ibid.

334

had no idea that the new organization marked the end rather than the beginning of a revivalistic tradition. The Army's apparent success alarmed him because he shared the widespread middle-class fear of the developing power of the working-classes; this led him into absurd prophecies of a day in the future when Booth would only have to give the word of command to his massed legions and England would be at his feet. It is interesting that a normally sensible man should be so easily thrown off balance by a military metaphor and a brass band uniform; he took the 'General' and his 'war' almost as seriously, and much more literally, than the Booths themselves. The Army had little religious influence on the working-class of the 1890s and no political influence at all. Huxley did not grasp that the Booths used middle-class fears of a working-class revolution as a lever to prise money and support from the middle-class. Under Booth's direction the Army supported the social *status quo* and rejected 'Christian Socialism'. *Darkest England* appeared when the original religious basis of the Army was proving too weak to sustain the initial success, but the programme which Booth there advocated was economically conservative and quite unconnected with the political realities of the period.

The Salvationist Holiness tradition did not die out as rapidly as had the memory of Phoebe Palmer. When the *Doctrines and Discipline of the Salvation Army*, a manual intended for the use of those training Army officers, was published in 1881, it contained 133 pages, of which 60–91, or not much less than a quarter, came under the heading of Sanctification.[52] Although neither Keswick nor Phoebe Palmer were mentioned by name, this section set out what was in fact a summary of Phoebe Palmer's doctrine.

The conditions of entire sanctification were defined as conviction—admitting that one needed to become holy—renunciation, consecration and faith. Renunciation meant the giving up of all known evil, which was what Bramwell Booth's penitents were doing when they solemnly laid on the table their tobacco pouches and feathers. It included one point

---

[52] *The Doctrines and Discipline of the Salvation Army*, prepared for the Training Homes by the General (London 1881). A small red book which looked at first glance like a copy of the Queen's regulations.

characteristic of the Nonconformity of the period. The question was asked 'Should you tell a man seeking the blessing that he should give up his pipe and his glass?' The Regulations said yes, 'because in this age, especially in the Army, few, if any, can smoke or drink without feeling both to be wasteful. injurious and unclean habits, and if they feel them such, or have even a question about their lawfulness, the indulgence must be given up at once, for he that doubteth is condemned.'[53] Twenty years before, however, Phoebe Palmer had been denouncing Wesleyan congregations for permitting brewers to retain their society membership.

Out of renunciation flowed consecration, the kind of self-offering which Mrs Palmer had in mind. Once it was effected, sanctification followed. The *Doctrines and Discipline* used Mrs Palmer's vocabulary with great precision.

> When it is done, when all is laid on the altar—body, soul, spirit, goods, reputation, *all, all, all*—then the fire descends and burns up all the dross and defilement and fills the soul with burning zeal and love and power.[54]

The *Doctrines* even attempted to deal with the problem which Phoebe Palmer's teaching had always raised. The question was put, 'Is it fair to tell a man seeking purity that if he believes that the cleansing work is done—then it is done?' Naturally, Booth repudiated this idea in its obvious form, but added that if someone really believed that God would purify him, then, 'in the moment that faith is exercised'[55] the transformation would take place—which was exactly what Phoebe Palmer had said herself. Her name might have vanished from the records, but her soul was marching on.

Nor was this only a matter of what was printed in the *Doctrines and Discipline*, as can be seen from *The Salvation War*,

[53] Begbie, op. cit., p.454, quotes another list of articles surrendered at this time: 'All got down after Mr Ballington said a few words; then came the glory; such a rush out; then a fight and a struggle. Out came seven feathers, three pipes, three pairs of ear-rings, three brooches, two other fine things, one grand pin, one Albert chain, one tobacco pouch, two pieces of twist, one twenty four and half inches long. . . .' When one remembers the comparative poverty of most of the people concerned, it is at once a practical and a pathetic view of holiness.

[54] Ibid., pp.79–80.

[55] Ibid., p.82.

1882, under the Generalship of William Booth.[56] This book of
more than 200 pages, was an account of the Army's experience
in 1882, and it included the story of how the Salvationists took
over the famous London public house, the Eagle. A day of
processions and riotings ended in a service inside the old
licensed premises.

> After the sisters had had their ten minutes, the band played while
> the offering was being made, after which the drum was set up as a
> penitent form, and an appeal was made for those who were
> seeking salvation, or the blessing of a clean heart, to come
> forward. There were four seekers, and after a short but blessed
> season spent in prayer and intercession, three were able to testify
> to a full salvation, and the other that God, for Christ's sake, had
> pardoned his sins. . . . After the drum had done duty as a mercy-
> seat it was used as a target for those who had a free-will offering
> to give the Lord. . . .[57]

This event was one of the most celebrated in the Army's
annals, so that its culmination in a service in which three men
were sanctified was specially significant.

How much not only the Salvation Army but also Robert
Pearsall Smith owed to Phoebe Palmer is obvious when one
looks at the Holiness hymns in the Salvation Army's hymnbook, *Songs of the Salvation Army*, which was published in 1878.
The volume contained 532 songs, together with an Appendix,
'Miscellaneous', containing another 101. The principal Holiness section ran from 445 to 484, and there were 35 more in
the Appendix, making about 75 out of 633. This fat section on
Holiness was an obvious difference between the Army book
and *Sacred Songs and Solos*. The difference is even more obvious
when one looks at *Holiness Hymns*,[58] a small paperback put out
at one penny a copy over William Booth's name in 1880; this

---

[56] *The Salvation War, 1882, under the Generalship of William Booth* (London, n.d. but
probably late 1882). The book gives an elaborate account of some of the persecutions
undergone by the Army during the year, describes work overseas, and includes long
statements about the money given to the Army during the year, and about Army
property.

[57] Op. cit., p.91.

[58] *Holiness Hymns* selected from the various songbooks of the Salvation Army, and
especially adapted for use at Holiness Meetings and All Nights of Prayer. By William
Booth, London 1880. The theology of the book depended on Mrs Palmer; so far as
hymns are concerned, the immediate source seems to have been the group which
surrounded R. P. Smith; this increased the American influence on the book, because the
Smiths used American hymns with which they were already familiar.

carried 101 hymns, all the most characteristic of which did not appear in the contemporaneous Sankey.

Perhaps the strongest example of the continuity of the Holiness tradition was this:

> Come Holy Ghost, all-sacred fire.
> Come, fill Thy earthly temples now;
> Emptied of every base desire,
> Reign thou within, and only Thou.
>
> Thy sovereign right, Thy Gracious claim,
> To every thought, to every power;
> Our lives—to glorify Thy name,
> We yield thee in this sacred hour.
>
> Fill every chamber of the soul;
> Fill all our thoughts, our passions fill;
> Till under Thy supreme control
> Submissive rests our cheerful will.
>
> 'Tis done. Thou dost this moment come;
> My longing soul is all Thine own;
> My heart is Thy abiding home;
> Henceforth I live for Thee alone.—
>
> The altar sanctifies the gift;
> The blood insures the boon divine;
> My outstretched hands to heaven I lift,
> And claim the Father's promise mine.[59]

Here was a straightforward summary of Phoebe Palmer's teaching, but although it was printed in the Salvation Army songbook, it was written by the Rev. F. Bottome, a Derbyshire man who had emigrated to the United States and become a minister of the American Methodist Episcopalian Church in 1850. He helped Robert Pearsall Smith to compile his *Gospel Hymns*, published in London in 1872, and this hymn had been included in the book. Two more of Bottome's hymns, 'Full Salvation, full salvation'[60] and 'O bliss of the purified, bliss of

---

[59] This was number 46 in the Appendix to *Salvation Army Songs*.

[60] 'Full Salvation, full salvation' was number 33 in *Salvation Army Songs*; in the 1936 revision of the *Keswick Hymn-Book* it was retained as number 167. Bottome was born in 1823.

the free' were printed in *Holiness Hymns* and in the *Salvation Army Songs*. American Methodism has never been identified as a formative influence on the Salvation Army, but in fact links were close.

Even more elaborately typical of the Palmer teaching was number 32 of *Holiness Hymns*:

> Come, now before thy Maker,
> And own Him Lord of All,
> Lay all upon the altar;
> 'Be holy', hear His call.
>
> Thy friends and time and talents;
> Thy body, spirit, soul,
> Now bring, nor be reluctant,
> If small, 'tis thy whole.
>
> For Jesus is the altar,
> He sanctifies the gift;
> Oh come, and do not falter,
> Bring all and let Him sift.
>
> Trust Jesus now to clean thee,
> From all thine 'inbred sin',
> Of 'carnal mind' to rid thee,
> Make thee pure within.
>
> Still rest thee on thy Master,
> Nor from His yoke depart;
> Take nothing off the altar,
> And He will keep thy heart.

Another of these Holiness hymns is important because it illustrates the true context of the famous Army motto 'Blood and Fire', a phrase which must always have puzzled the uninitiated:

> My body, soul and spirit
> Jesus, I give to Thee,
> A consecrated offering,
> Thine evermore to be,
> *Chorus:* My all is on the altar,
>   I'm waiting for the fire.

Oh let the fire descending
Just now upon my soul
Consume my humble offering,
And cleanse and make me whole.
    Chorus: My all is on the altar,
          I'm waiting for the fire.

I'm Thine, O blessed Jesus,
Washed by Thy precious Blood,
Now seal me in Thy Spirit,
A sacrifice to God.
    Chorus: My all is on the altar,
          I'm waiting for the fire.[61]

The 'blood' meant justification or 'conversion'; the 'fire' descended on the convert and sanctified him by destroying once and for all the roots of his sinful personality. Even the Army's most famous slogan was a Holiness slogan.

4. *The Brighton Convention and Keswick, 1875*

That hymn is also important, however, because it was one of the direct links between the Salvation Army and the Brighton Convention of 1875. On the evening of the fourth day of the Convention, for instance, Theodore Monod finished his address at the Dome with tremendous emphasis on the idea of God as a consuming fire, and they sang 'My all is on the altar' as the concluding hymn.[62] They sang it again at Robert Pearsall Smith's meeting at the opening of the sixth day, the turning-point for the success of the Convention. This hymn was retained in the 1936 revision of the *Keswick Hymn Book*, but by that time significant changes had taken place. The second verse, with its passionate invocation of an almost Old Testament fire, had disappeared; an alternative chorus was printed which also dispensed with any reference to 'fire'; and the last verse had been altered in a way which destroyed the original sense; the imploring 'Now seal me', with its sug-

[61] *Holiness Hymns*, op. cit., number 4.
[62] *Record of the Convention for the Promotion of Spiritual Holiness* held at Brighton, 29 May to 7 June, 1875 (Brighton and London 1875) no author stated, p.100. Monod, French Reformed pastor, was born in Paris in 1836, but studied for the ministry at Western Theological Seminary, Allegheny, Pennsylvania, before returning to Paris, where he worked from 1860.

gestion of sanctification to come had been replaced by the much tamer 'Sealed by the Holy Spirit', a confident, or even complacent, assumption of sanctification which had already taken place.[63]

The year 1875 was the peak year of the American revivalist invasion of Britain and the Brighton Convention for the Promotion of Scriptural Holiness was sanctification's highest moment in 1875. As many as five thousand people were fed on the principal days. The ghosts of the Royal Pavilion must have been staggered when they saw their old quarters used for holiness inquiry meetings. Continental Evangelicals recruited by Robert Pearsall Smith on a whirlwind tour of Europe— the most important of them was Theodore Monod from Paris —mingled with their British counterparts. Dwight Moody sent encouraging telegrams from London which were read out to enthusiastic audiences. Anything might have happened, in the Evangelical world at any rate, if Robert Pearsall Smith, the American businessman turned revivalist who was promoting all this, had not gone the way of many perfectionist teachers before him. The ghosts of the Royal Pavilion had their revenge; his fall from grace was sexual, irreparable and swift. He had returned to the United States before most of his admirers knew what had taken place, but he made a permanent imprint on the British revivalist tradition.

Brighton and its aftermath left the Evangelical world both delighted and divided. The founders of the Keswick Convention, most of whom were Anglicans, dedicated themselves to methods of spreading scriptural holiness which depended less on striking personalities; they substituted the Wordsworthian Lakes for Regency Brighton. The most rugged and conservative of all Anglican Evangelical personalities, however, J. C. Ryle, attacked the Palmer-Smith-Keswick Holiness teaching with all his might. And, almost without being aware of it, Robert Pearsall Smith had given the Salvation Army a much needed stimulant for growth.

[63] *The Keswick Hymn Book*, number 23, where it is attributed to Mrs James. The alternative chorus goes: My all is on the altar;
                                Lord, I am all thy own;
                                Oh, may my faith ne'er falter,
                                Lord, keep me Thine alone.
This is much feebler.

The Brighton Convention was so important in the tragic history of the nineteenth-century Evangelicalism that it is worth describing in some detail.[64] The original invitation promised to those who attended 'a life of maintained communion and victory in a degree hitherto unlooked for'— revealing words—as a result of 'an entire surrender to and trust in the Lord'.[65] Once again, as with Phoebe Palmer, the bait was the offer of the short cut. Mrs Pearsall Smith made this clear in the first high pressure speech of the Convention. The secret of Holiness, she said, lay in belief in Christ's power to change the individual. Her example was the favourite one of the period, a drunkard. He knew that he was about to break the pledge, so he went to a friend who understood the Higher Life and asked her if there was a kind of salvation which would prevent him from drinking again. The friend said, yes, if he asked Jesus. They knelt and prayed together—and he never became drunk again. Mrs Smith assured her hearers that she could quote many cases of 'spiritual diseases of all sorts healed

[64] See *An Account of the Ten Days Convention for the Promotion of Scriptural Holiness* held at Brighton, 29 May to 7 June, 1875. Published by F. E. Longley, at his Depot for the English and American Literature of the Higher Christian Life, 39 Warwick Lane, London. Paperback, eighteenpence, p.3.

[65] *Record of the Convention for the Promotion of Scriptural Holiness* held at Brighton, 29 May to 7 June, 1875 (Brighton and London 1875), p.6. This was the other, and more official record of the meetings, the earlier part of which had been revised by Pearsall Smith himself. The Brighton invitation also included a long list of practical instructions, which make their own comment on the kind of pietism which was at work here:

1 Come in a receptive spirit, submit your whole being to the teaching of the Holy Spirit. God speaks by His word; be willing to lay aside all preconceived opinions.
2 Heartily renounce all known evil, and even doubtful things not of faith.
3 Come waiting on the Lord. Expect confidently blessings on your own soul individually.
4 Make the Bible your chief, if not your only reading.
5 Avoid conversation in your lodgings which shall divert your soul from the object of the meeting. Especially avoid controversy. If any differ with you pray with them.
6 Eat moderately, dress simply, retire to rest early.
7 Let your first waking act each morning be to remind yourself
    (i) that *your* every sin is washed away by the blood of Christ;
    (ii) that you are wholly His by purchase and by deliberate self-surrender;
    (iii) that there is no cloud or even shadow between your soul and God;
    (iv) that the Word assumes the hourly keeping of the life and work thus committed to Him. Let this morning act be the continuing attitude of the soul all day. If interrupted by momentary failure let instant confession restore full communion.

If all these instructions were faithfully carried out Pearsall Smith's work was done already.

completely in answer to faith, by the mighty power of God.'[66]
She ended:

> Pray: 'Oh Thou great Physician, I believe Thou art able and
> willing to heal me, and I am willing to be healed, and I commit
> my case to Thee now.' And then say, Jesus saves me now;
> Jesus saves me now. And keep on saying it. Do not rise from
> your knees and begin at once to wonder what is your condition,
> and why you do not have a different state of mind. You are going
> to give yourself to the Lord. Then do not worry yourself about
> that miserable self anymore. Take a little rest about it. . . .[67]

One can see the listening faces, with their mixture of hope and
doubt. It is not surprising that, when she spoke on the second
day of the Convention, she was able to say that she had received a note from some who were present which said that
they had 'for a long time been giving themselves to the Lord,
but nothing had come of it'. 'The eighteenth and nineteenth
verses of the twenty-sixth chapter of Deuteronomy tell us
what comes of it'—she replied—'for the result of not believing
that God had taken them to be His peculiar people was that
they took themselves out of His hands.'[68]
This insistence on the individual's responsibility for his
own sanctification was reinforced by Pearsall Smith himself in
a short and powerful speech in which he said:

> If there are any present who are doubtful as to whether or not
> they have brought their all to Christ, who have any lurking
> uncertainty, any twilight, under the shade of which they do not
> know whether some things are God's or their own—if there are
> any such I beseech you at once to give yourself wholly to God.
> A complete consecration is an easy life of rest and ease to the soul,
> and a partial consecration is the very opposite—a hard and
> difficult life. . . .[69]

The reference to 'ease' was reckless enough; his practical
advice was disingenous:

> May I now entreat you to go quietly home, and the moment you

[66] Ibid., p.33.
[67] Ibid., p.34.
[68] Ibid., pp.56–7.
[69] Ibid., p.58.

see anything contrary to God, deal with it suddenly. When you lay your heads on your pillows will you not say 'All for Jesus' and you will thus in a great measure remove the obstacles which have prevented your full communion with Jesus. . . .[70]

The saving words—'in a great measure'—were as good as dishonest; the whole tenor of what he said denied the need for such a qualification; but it was there to safeguard him against criticism.

In these early days of the Convention the speakers concentrated on the need and the possibility of absolute consecration in Phoebe Palmer's sense, and on the completeness of the self-mastery which flowed from it. Thus on the third day Mrs Pearsall Smith spoke at length about a woman who tried to be a Christian but who could not keep her temper when shut up with her own family: this was the kind of self-contradiction which so many evangelicals found at the heart of their personal piety, and the illustration must have gripped many of her audience. The woman was advised to read the Epistle to the Romans, chapter six: 'Reckon yourself dead to sin'; she made up her mind to obey this command and to reckon herself *on the authority of God's word* 'dead to sin', that is, so far as she understood the words, no longer able, or perhaps suffered by the Holy Spirit, to sin—by which she meant losing her temper in private with her family.[71] When she came down to breakfast the following morning she found that her problem was solved, that she was not losing her temper, that she had achieved the 'rest of faith'. It is noticeable that the process involved just that attitude of absolute acceptance of the supernatural authority of the word of the Bible which was becoming more and more difficult for Europeans to sustain. At the height of the Convention, Theodore Monod told a story about a certain Pastor Haeter, a German Protestant, who, in his youth, while studying theology, had become greatly bewildered, and even thought of abandoning Christianity.

In his difficulty he went and consulted Professor Emmerich, who

[70] Ibid., p.61.

[71] Cf. Longley, op. cit., p.30, where Pearsall Smith is quoted as saying that 'ladies think they may be cross with their maids sometimes; careful Marthas think they may be cross to their servants sometimes.' This type of domestic comparison suggests the kind of social background which Smith wanted to imply.

told him, 'Read your Bible *like a* peasant'. The advice saved him, and I recommend all present to follow it.[72]

Nothing could be more revealing of the kind of strain which the late nineteenth-century middle-class pietist was feeling or of the role which the Brighton Convention played in the life of so many. If these experiments in the religious control of everyday behaviour worked, then they also confirmed the traditional view of the Bible's authority; if the experiments failed, it was always possible to argue that this was because the Christians concerned had rejected the peasant's humble acceptance of the meaning of the Scriptures.

Once the possibility of absolute consecration was established, and its amazing consequence made clear, the language of the two Americans became more openly that of Phoebe Palmer. On the fourth day of the Convention, Pearsall Smith described how he first accepted the holiness doctrine.

'I remember when the possibility of living a life, not only *beneath* the will of God, but *in* the will of God, first dawned upon me, as a friend, looking into my eyes, said "By God's grace I have given my all to Jesus. I have laid my all upon the altar; and I feel that he has received and accepted my unworthy gift".'[73]

Smith put tremendous emotional pressure on his audience, telling them that he was convinced that from now on the Church would regard anything else than 'continuous victory over sin' in the same way as a lack of personal assurance of forgiveness had been regarded in the past—in the Evangelical pietist world, at any rate. Sanctification, he more than implied, would become as normal as justification, and by sanctification he more than implied 'continuous victory over sin'. It is fascinating to think of a vast gathering of evangelical pietists, many of them with long experience as religious teachers and leaders, bemused by the personality of the speaker and the needs of their own lives into accepting a view of human nature which flatly contradicted the evangelical pessimism in which most of them had been reared, and the doctrine of faith in which they had been trained. Pearsall Smith was also

[72] *The Brighton Convention,* etc., p.141.
[73] Ibid., p.99.

reflecting the Quaker background of his wife, for this kind of
bold proclamation of universal holiness recalls the language of
George Fox as he infuriated his gaolers by gently admitting
that he was perfected.

The climax of the Convention came on the sixth day. The
editor of the Convention history writes:

> Many had probably come to Brighton expecting to find joy, but
> instead they had had to face conflict such as they had never known
> before. Then with deep searching *the sacrifice had been laid* on the
> altar, and now though all might feel emancipated from the burden
> which laid them low, there seemed to rise a tremulous expectation.

On the evening of the previous day Webb-Peploe, one of the
Anglicans prominent in the movement, and later a founder of
the Keswick Convention, had said that the time 'has come, if
there is to be any blessing, those who have been attending the
meetings ought to begin to experience it'.[74] One can only be
thankful that such a perfectly frank 'trigger speech' was so
loyally recorded. This conscious use of a series of meetings to
heighten the psychological tension of a group of people to the
point when it has to find release in an outburst of speech and
action is of the essence, if not *the* essence, of revivalism, and
explains why I have called this a Holiness revivalist movement. This technique involved checking the old tumultuous
excitement which had characterized the frontier camp-
meetings of the early nineteenth century, and which last
appeared in Britain in the holiness meetings of the Salvation
Army; when Moody and others claimed that there was no
emotion at their meetings they were thinking of this earlier,
undisciplined behaviour; emotion still dominated their
methods. It was the business of the revivalists to quicken that
expectation until it became an uncontrollable longing to
release the built-up tension in some kind of public affirmation.

Pearsall Smith's morning address was masterful in the sense
of aiming directly at mastery over his hearers. He was a far
finer speaker than Dwight Moody, as indeed he needed to be,
for a high proportion of his audience had had long experience
at revivalism themselves. It was as an expert addressing
experts, a preacher grappling with professional evangelists

[74] Ibid., p.135.

that he begged them now to present their bodies as a living sacrifice to the Lord.

> Now, just as definitely as ever an Israelite brought his gift and laid it on the altar, we desire you not so much to bring your gifts but yourselves, the entireness of your being, a living sacrifice (in contrast to the old, dead sacrifices) offering all the energies of your nature, your will, your affections, your intellect, upon God's altar. Have you done this? Or having done it has anything withdrawn it from that altar?

Here was the familiar Palmerian emphasis upon keeping the gift on the altar which seemed at times to make Holiness as much an effort of the will as ever it had seemed to be in the past.

> As the parent must have complete obedience from his children, so God will not give us unclouded communion with Him, except there is entire obedience at every point. . . . Get this point yielded and your faces will shine.[75]

He besought them to consecrate themselves fully:

> We do not come here to talk about the thing but to do it, and to live afterwards in the realization that it is an accomplished fact, a real transaction between us and God. When God asks you for your whole heart and you give it to Him, does He accept it? *When your gift is laid upon the altar, does the altar sanctify the gift? There is but one answer.*[76]

Such language could only be understood by people who had been trained in Phoebe Palmer's doctrine, and knew already what the correct answer was. But by now the crisis was over, the blessing was being received, and the remainder of the Convention was taken up in the effort to consolidate what had been done.

Pearsall Smith held meetings, for example, at which he

[75] Ibid., p.169.

[76] Longley, op. cit., p.97: Pearsall Smith quoted as saying 'I think there are thousands here in whom there is no allowed sin, no unholy ambition, making a free acknowledgement that they are still infinitely far from what they would be'. The second half of the sentence makes the whole almost a nonsense statement; but in fact the qualifications represented Smith's desperate attempt to keep on terms with the professional theologians: he meant to say that the meetings had produced thousands in whom there was no conscious awareness of doing something wrong.

answered ministers' questions;[77] the questions showed how instinctively the evangelical pietist translated 'holiness' in terms of his inherited moral attitudes. Was it consistent for one who loved the Lord to drive in a cab on the Sabbath? Possibly Smith had his doubts, for he evaded any definite answer, while assuring the meeting that he was very jealous of the Lord's Day. On other subjects, however, Pearsall Smith was more specific. When a layman said that he was sure that he could not enjoy this life of peace in the world of business, he replied that in that case one could only retire from business.[78] And on teetotalism he shared Phoebe Palmer's opinion. To the question 'Should not every Christian, in these days when strong drink is doing so much damage to the cause of Christ, abandon its use?' he answered without hesitation, 'A thousand times *Yes*'. Smith added, 'As, however, they would have no prejudice here concerning the use of liquor, but would regard it as a matter between each man and his God, he asked them to kneel down and request that God would communicate His mind regarding it to them'.[79] Not all the European or Anglican ministers present would have been teetotallers in 1875. Some of Smith's answers were very dogmatic, and explain why J. C. Ryle, for instance, said that the Holiness movement did not use the term 'sin' in a way that he (Ryle) did. To one, 'Are we to look for instantaneous victory after trusting', Smith said that he could give only one answer; 'According to your faith it is unto you'.[80] This left the easy explanation of unbelief if holiness did not appear. In answer to another question, 'What is the cause of failure in a trusting Christian?', he said firmly that 'Falling is a want of faith'.[81] An earlier answer recalled Phoebe Palmer's teaching that the holy person proclaimed his holiness. 'I have never known any who retained this blessing in the Lord shrink on every suitable occasion from saying what the Lord had done for them'.[82] There was also Phoebe's threat that the blessing vanished if it were concealed.

[77] Cf. Longley, who compared these question sessions with Moody's 'question drawer'.
[78] *The Brighton Convention*, etc., p.289.
[79] Ibid., p.113.
[80] Ibid., p.209.
[81] Ibid., p.210.
[82] Ibid., p.172.

The final evening of the Convention commenced with joint Communion Services in the Corn Exchange and the Dome. In the Dome, Dr Prochnow of Berlin presided; he was a Lutheran who had worked for the Anglican Church Missionary Society in the Himalayas. In the Corn Exchange, M. Rappard of Chrischrona presided, Monod and Smith sitting silently at hand. All the Scriptural words of administration were read, and then the foreign pastors and 'some English pastors' communicated; having done so they distributed the elements throughout the 'waiting thousands'.[83]

Pearsall Smith's final meeting—it was final in more senses than one—followed straight on. In this address he returned to the point of one of his wife's earlier speeches, that according to the Epistle to the Romans (chapter 6) we ought to believe that we are dead to sin.

> If you are the person that believeth you can reckon yourself dead unto sin. In the face of all your past and present experience consider yourself dead. If you have an angry temper say, 'Well, by God's grace I reckon myself dead to that', and you will find it true, that as you thus reckon yourselves it becomes a reality.[84]

At the close of this exhortation the hymn 'One more day's work for Jesus, One less of life for me', was sung, and then

> amid profound silence, one and another rose in different parts of the densely crowded room and quoted passages of scripture expressive of their full trust in God, and the joy they experienced in consequence. Most of the utterances were in English, but many of the foreign pastors spoke in their native tongues. At the suggestion of Mr Smith those who had obtained this blessing rose and sang the verses beginning 'I have entered the valley of blessing so sweet'. Then the meeting was again hushed in silent prayer till the words of 'Not a sound invades the stillness' were sung in subdued tones. The Benediction was pronounced by a French pastor and the large gathering separated in silence, Mr Smith having strongly requested that tonight no earthly discourse might dissipate the halo of the divine presence which had been spread over them.[85]

[83] Ibid., p.334.
[84] Ibid., p.337.
[85] Ibid., p.338.

Such was the conclusion of a convention which marked the highest point of Evangelical efforts to solve the problem of being Christian in the late Victorian world. Brighton had called together the cream of the evangelical sub-culture, lay and clerical, men and women who felt a bitter contrast between their own commitment to traditional Protestant orthodoxy and their relative social and religious ineffectiveness, whether at home, or in the religious world; in the streets and courts of Victorian cities in which they worked tirelessly for others; in the Churches—where either Anglo-Catholicism or religious liberalism always seemed the party in power, or in the secular society beyond all these. It was no wonder that eschatological longings, familiar in the Evangelical world ever since the French Revolution,[86] should reappear strongly in the last quarter of the century. Neither Evangelicalism nor Revivalism had ever escaped from their local and rural origins and adjusted to the new industrial society. Historians sometimes write as though the Victorian period saw the collapse of an integrated society which had reached a state of balance at some time in the previous century.[87] A different interpretation of events is possible, however, which would start from the assertion that it is in the early nineteenth century that the local individual really begins to face the full pressure of a national community upon itself, a pressure which has steadily increased. The late nineteenth-century Evangelical often wanted to escape from the crunching grip of a secularizing society; he did not want to change his mental furniture or alter the ways in which he expressed his religious sensibility. When he sat in the Dome at Brighton and listened to Pearsall Smith, it seemed to him that here at last was someone who could conjure power, directly effective spiritual power, out of the Old Religion, who could reduce to nothing Darwinism, Biblical Criticism, the dark forces of lower-class unbelief and the nagging torments of evangelical doubt. The strain of the

---

[86] For a brilliant account of how the French Revolution led to a new interest in the seventeenth-century prophecies of Pierre Jurieu, who had foretold a revolution in France at the end of the 1780s which would overthrow the Roman Catholic Church and usher in the ruin of the Papacy, see M. Vereté, *The Restoration of the Jews in English Protestant Thought, 1790–1840*, '*Middle Eastern Studies*' (1972). I am grateful to Dr. John Walsh of Jesus College, Oxford, for this reference.

[87] E.g. A. MacIntyre, *Secularisation and Moral Change* (1967).

century made the Protestant Evangelical as willing to deceive himself about Brighton as the French Roman Catholic with a similar background was willing to deceive himself about the visions of Lourdes or La Salette. Both needed the reassurance which for the moment words and conventional religious habits could not always give. They wanted to *see* their miracles, and although Hannah Smith's healing stories were usually moral and not physical, and always seemed to take place off-stage, the Evangelicals at Brighton felt for the most part that a new source of practical power was being offered to them. How long they remained satisfied depended upon the individual, but it was not to be long before *glossolalia* and physical healings were reported on the fringes of the Holiness world. These claims to have assisted at 'speaking with tongues' were very important because they represented the ultimate in the reduction of the inward and spiritual to the external and measureable. It is probable that these 'experiences' worked socially: a small, inward-looking, anxious group of people, their personalities only expressible through religious forms (although often weak in religious substance), would generate this kind of 'religious' activity by a kind of collective spontaneity.

From the Evangelical point of view, Pearsall Smith's enforced retirement was probably fortunate, for his personal approach had divided the Evangelical world. No doubt a sense of the socially inappropriate, a lingering disapproval of American revivalists, a dislike of over-active laymen, all played a part. It was Smith's theological naïveté, however, that mattered more than all these factors, and would have done so even if he had remained a Holiness leader. This naïveté made it easy for J. C. Ryle, the self-appointed conscience of Anglican Evangelicalism, to drive home his belief that any alliance with the Americans involved disloyalty to the seventeenth-century Calvinist authors in whom he saw the best side of the Anglican tradition. Ryle made a perfect example of the kind of late Victorian Christian to whom Smith had nothing to offer; he was psychologically satisfied with the system of traditional Protestant orthodoxy; he constantly studied the Bible through the minds of men who had died long before the nineteenth century and who naturally had no notion of Victorian religious problems; he lived for years in the depths of Suffolk, an outstanding example of that army of Victorian clergy whose outlook on the world was a rural landscape; he did not even find the country entirely to his taste, for he belonged to the group of ascetic Evangelicals who laid their sporting guns on the altar of sacrifice; the archaizing strain was strong, for he was actually the son of a Liverpool business-man. He reminds one of the conservatives whom Trollope describes, men who knew that affairs had been degenerating steadily since the beginning of the century, and who could not understand why. Like many of his friends he had a sharp feel-ing of persecution: only a few years before the Brighton Convention he had dismissed the disestablishment of the Anglican Church in Ireland as

> a deadly blow at a scriptural branch of the Church of Christ and a clear concession to Popery. . . . I advise English Churchmen to set their house in order. Our turn will come next. Truly, we live in 'perilous times'.

Ryle was a man of certainties, belonging to the generation of Evangelicals of whom F. D. Maurice said that in all their attitudes they started from sin and not from God. In fact, Ryle's most famous book, entitled *Holiness*, and meant as a counterblast to Pearsall Smith's teaching, began with a chapter headed starkly 'SIN', and the vividly non-Mauricean assertion that 'the plain truth is that a right knowledge of sin lies at the root of all saving Christianity.'[88] Ryle's complaint against Pearsall Smith was that the American had no sound ideas on sin at all; by Ryle's standards, Smith did not know what the word meant.

Ryle made his position clear in a pamphlet published before the Brighton Convention actually met.

> 'I cannot support it,' he said. 'Some Christians seem to be able to get good out of any meeting, however strange the teaching may be, just as Samson sucked honey out of the carcase of a dead lion. I trust it may be so with many at Brighton, who go in their simplicity and see no evil. To my eyes the movement seems only calculated to increase the divisions of Evangelical Christians and to do no real good to souls.'[89]

[88] J. C. Ryle, *Holiness* (1952), p.1.
[89] *A Letter on Mr Pearsall Smith's Brighton Convention by the Rev. John C. Ryle*, dated 25 May, 1875, published from Stradbroke Vicarage, p.4.

This was Ryle's summing up; his opening had been just as sweeping.

> I frankly confess that I cannot understand the distinctive theology which is the foundation of the Brighton Convention. This may be, perhaps, the natural dullness and stupidity which attend advancing years. But one thing I do know. I can thoroughly understand the theology of Moody and Sankey, and go along with it entirely. . . . But I cannot take in many statements which have been put forward on various occasions by many of the supporters of the Brighton Convention . . . the difference between Moody's theology and that of the 'Oxford Conference' is the difference between sunshine and fog. Was it not in a fog that the great steamship *Schiller* lately made shipwreck?[90]

Ryle probably understood quite clearly why the new Holiness teaching looked obscure on paper. Just because he was personally satisfied with traditional puritanism he seized on, exposed to view and rejected the Palmerian offer of the short-cut. No doubt Pearsall Smith was right in saying that 'we ought not to expect defeat in the pursuit of holiness': 'But will the new teachers tell us that the believer is not to expect *conflict* in the pursuit of holiness between the time of his conversion and his death?' If so, they must cope with Ryle's favourite authorities, Hooker and Baxter, Rutherford and M'Cheyne. When Saint Paul said that the good that he would he did not, but that the evil that he would not, that he did, he was describing his own experience as a *Christian*, not as an unconverted Jew; moreover, he was offering 'a literal, perfect, accurate, correct photograph of the experience of every true saint of God': whatever else 'holiness' might mean in terms of this world, it did not mean freedom to fulfil the moral law. It was no accident, Ryle added, that the daily services of the Book of Common Prayer included a Confession of Sin; the Ninth of the Anglican Articles said that original sin, 'this infection of nature', remained 'in them that are regenerated'; the Fifteenth, in expounding the sinlessness of Christ himself, added that the rest of mankind, 'although baptized, and born again in Christ, yet offend in many things; and if we say we have no sin we deceive ourselves. . . .' Unless they had been

[90] Ibid., p.1.

cruelly misrepresented, Ryle concluded, it was difficult to reconcile the teaching of Holiness advocates with the authorized standards of the Church of England.

Smith was unhappy with this kind of criticism. He had tried to avoid conflict with Saint Paul himself by suggesting that what the Apostle recorded in the seventh chapter of the Epistle to the Romans was some disastrous personal backsliding; his inability to fulfil the divine law was the outcome of a temporary loss of faith and so the powerlessness which he described was not to be regarded as the normative state of the Christian. In *Holiness Through Faith* Smith had written that the Christian was cleansed 'not only from the stain of sin, or the punishment of sin, but from sin itself'. It is true that he immediately tried to qualify the effect of what he had said, but his qualifications gave the impression of a man who was afraid of what he wanted to believe. To Ryle's Anglicanism he naturally had no answer at all. His own holiness beliefs, like Phoebe Palmer's, were a by-product of an American world suffering from the strains on American society which were produced but were not healed by the Civil War. Their teaching expressed a desire to escape from those strains, to contract out of a social situation which had divided their own religious groups. The mood was so all-pervasive that at its closest approximation to reality it culminated in a view of holiness as a kind of frictionless domesticity, a dream of America full of happy families, wrapped up in themselves and their personal religion. In fact, Mrs Palmer's theology represented an important stage in the transformation of the original form of American Protestantism, which had sought to mould a rural nation in its own image, far from the wiles of a corrupting Europe, into modern American Protestantism, which has largely remoulded itself in the image of an industrialized nation, not so very unlike Europe after all.

In Ryle, however, Smith encountered one of the few English Evangelicals whose style recalled the very America from which he was dissociating himself; Ryle was bound to remind Smith of the inevitability of conflict; as inevitably, Smith was bound to twist and turn in his anxiety to evade images which were in any case all too familiar. One explanation of his personal breakdown might be on this level, for his version of *normal* Christian experience defied reality too completely to survive. Indeed, there was always something unsatisfactory about the holiness revivalists. An atmosphere of slightly dubious vulgarity hung about James Caughey; the Palmers' reaction to the threat of the American Civil War had been to leave America and sit out the conflict in England, clinging to what Donald Dayton has called a 'parlour' version of holiness.[91] As for Pearsall Smith himself, his indiscretion with one of his female followers was less remarkable than the reaction of the controlling group of Evangelicals, which included William Cowper-Temple (later Lord Mount Temple), Lord Radstock and Stevenson Blackwood. They extracted from him a written confession that he had talked in antinomian terms with his arm round the shoulders of a young woman; they used this to compel the Smiths to return to America in July, 1875; Smith's career as a revivalist was finished, and he lost his faith altogether before the end of his life. The English Evangelicals concealed—the word seems perfectly fair—what had happened in 1875:[92] there was vague talk of illness, but no admission of the truth, despite the rumours of adultery which circulated. For a holiness movement such behaviour seems too secular altogether; no doubt, social, as much as religious feeling was involved; Smith's banishment was the equivalent of Moody's rebuff at Eton. The Anglican Evangelical milieu was austere in its concept of religious experience and had been won over to revivalism chiefly through the pressure of nineteenth-century Evangelical decline. The Keswick Convention, which emerged from the perfectionist débâcle in 1875, was not revivalist, and it survived into the twentieth century by gradually substituting for the language which Phoebe Palmer had taught the Smiths a much vaguer vocabulary about the Christian's chances of finding perfection in an Evangelical sub-culture. Short-cuts to holiness have a way of turning out to have been a wrong turning.

[91] See his important paper, 'The Holiness Heritage between Calvinism and Wesleyanism', given at the Oxford Institute of Methodist Theology, held at Lincoln College, Oxford, in July, 1977.

[92] J. C. Pollock, *The Keswick Story* (1964), gave the first official account of what actually happened. His final comment was informative: 'that he was removed before the first Keswick Convention was afterwards recognized as "the over-ruling Providence of God" '; Pollock, however, thought that the movement's leaders would have been wiser to admit the truth.

9

Conclusion: The Political and Religious Significance of the Revivalist Tradition

TECHNIQUES of persuasion, menace and group intoxication have characterized Revivalism throughout its history. The dominating, appealing, frightening or reassuring central personality, the revivalist himself, has always been there, from Caughey to William Booth, from Father Ignatius to Billy Graham. Succeeding leaders have modified the dissenting conservatism of the religious and political outlook involved, but have never altered the mixture radically. The revivalists always allegedly stood for a religious tradition said to be in danger, for a Holy Book in which, it was claimed, almost no one else truly believed; for the rejected, regenerated layman against the powerful but un-converted cleric. Revivalists usually adopted those attitudes or practices which the religious establishment of the day wanted to ignore or stifle, from teetotalism in the 1840s to speaking with tongues in the twentieth century.

All revivalist groups believed that men could be moved to sudden, radical change in their style of behaviour, whether this meant joining the religious sub-culture for the first time, or identifying oneself with previously rejected attitudes or habits; the patterns recommended varied all the way from Keswick to the Cowley Fathers. The model revivalist convert of the later nineteenth century would have enjoyed a brief life of evil in his late teens, have come out (or stayed behind) and have 'found Christ' (or renewed his baptismal vows), either at one of Moody and Sankey's meetings, perhaps the famous one at the old Guildhall in Cambridge in 1882, or at an urban Anglo-Catholic parochial mission. He would then have testified to his former friends, have given up shooting, drink (or sex), the theatre (can one imagine R. M. Benson going to the theatre?), and any inclination towards the Church of Rome (if now an evangelical), or Protestantism (as defined in High Anglican circles). Ideally, the process did not even finish there. Divinely called, he would enter either a monastic order or a missionary society and set out for Central Africa, or India or China, with little training or knowledge of local languages (the divine Spirit was sometimes expected to provide direct tuition), and without any encouragement to respect the culture to which he went. The importance of the consequent missions has always been exaggerated in Western Christian writing, but a proper assessment of their significance had better be left to African, Indian and Chinese historians. Certainly, the bold campaign to overthrow the religions of the rest of the world failed. As far as the convert was concerned, what had happened was that his dissenting conservatism, an underlying, non-religious stance which had much to do with his original conversion, had led him first to withdraw from the mainstream of English culture into the English religious sub-culture, and then to move away from that into a more primitive social context, or at least what he interpreted as a more primitive social context.

At one extreme, then, Revivalism became, in the late Victorian period, an aspect of that anti-modernist, anti-materialist, anti-democratic and often anti-intellectual movement which had secular as well as religious forms, and which might in religious terms be labelled the cult of 'Christ against Western culture'. Even the so-called 'Christian Socialist' tradition, which might seem an exception in its Anglo-Catholic form, drifted, in the hands of men like B. F. Westcott, towards the same kind of negative radicalism, the radicalism of the right in political language. The Western missionary running his mission station and mission compound may not always have been denying in practice either Western middle-class material standards, or the Western drive for power of all kinds—but he *thought* that he was, and in this sense the mission-station was related to the wave of community-experiment which was to return to England from the United States of America in the 1960s, sometimes on a religious basis, sometimes not.

It is along lines like this that one has to work out the

political significance of nineteenth-century Revivalism. The relevant political question was: what was wrong with a society in which a section of the middle-classes, more or less well-educated, spent their emotional life on Keswick, for example, and a cult of pseudo-perfectionism? Both Moody and Mrs General Booth raised money for their organizations in the 1880s by promising to prevent the spread of 'agitation' in the urban working masses, employed and unemployed. There is no evidence that they kept their promises any more effectively than did the teams of hired strike-breakers which appeared briefly in Edwardian England as a logical but politically ludicrous answer to businessmen's anxieties about the growth of trade union 'power'. Organized Nonconformity was less revivalist, more decidedly political, and if professional revivalists helped to keep the Free Churches going between 1860 and 1914 (and they did a little to maintain the cohesion of the membership, if nothing else), they made a contribution to the history of the Liberal Party for which many of its far from Nonconformist leaders probably never wanted to thank them. The urban revival campaigns, which the newly-formed national Free Church Council launched in the first decade of the twentieth century, were as much political as religious, for with the Liberal Party, as they thought, within their grasp, the Nonconformist leaders needed to increase, if possible, the vote which they appeared to control. The collapse of the Liberal Party after 1914 suggests the extent to which revivalism failed to achieve much political influence; Anglican Evangelicalism, of course, contracted out of politics quite consciously in the course of the 1870s; the professional revivalists aided, rather than limited, this development. It would be unfair, as I have already said when discussing Moody's preaching, to call him one of the fathers of later right-wing extremism, but what political significance he had lay right of centre, and what mattered here was not so much the being socially conservative, as being psychologically kin to the irrational and violent strains which are only one, but often a very powerful, element in right-wing attitudes. It was politically, in other words, and not theologically, that Moody's premillennialism mattered; he belonged, from about 1872 at the latest, to the far-out wing of American Protestantism which held that the general conditions of human society would deteriorate steadily until the Second Coming. This attitude reduced political action to a police operation, and set a premium on fresh disasters, especially as the premillennialists usually convinced themselves that the Second Advent was now imminent. The books of addresses which Moody published in England were reticent on the subject, but they were all tinged with the same social pessimism: if you became converted, you would not really care what happened to stocks and bonds, to employment, to the future of society in general. There has been no essential change in revivalists' ideas on this subject—Billy Graham, for example, when preaching in Manchester in 1961, usually linked together denunciations of private and public immorality and threats of possible atomic destruction, and this in turn led rapidly to the implication that the Second Coming of Christ could not be far off. Indeed, Graham's style at that time corresponded more to Moody's preaching in America in the 1880s and '90s, than to his English addresses of 1873–5 and 1882. Graham openly allied himself to the Republican Party and to the ill-fated Nixon administration, which collapsed morally in 1974; he had been regarded as something of a court chaplain in Nixon's closing years of power. Once again, however, as in the case of the British Liberal Party in the Edwardian period, events belied the claim that Revivalism had played an important moralizing role in politics. In the alliance between the politicians and the revivalists, the latter were the gainers, not the politicians. But when the politicians fell, the preachers normally kept their feet, if not exactly their previous standing.

Historians have taken the revivalist less seriously than they should have done in his political capacity, but have more often criticized him for an alleged failure to revive the Victorian working-class. The gap which the revivalist consciously tried to fill, however, lay inside rather than outside the 'churches'; the gap between the 'churches' and the working-classes was another matter—at the crucial point in 1876 no one was making striking claims about success at that social level. As far back as 1859 it had become clear that the revivalist technique was irrelevant to the average working-man. He had little 'use' for institutionalized Christianity, and there was something in the 'Journeyman Engineer' Thomas Wright's forceful phrase, that the working-man regarded himself as 'the Ishmael of Modern Society' (in *Our New Masters*, 1873, p.17). Ishmaels did not take kindly to established religious institutions, and even the Salvation Army, which set out in the 1870s with a very deliberate intention of converting poor people, did not consider what kind of a religious system the poor wanted, but assumed that one could still impose a very primitive form of Protestant evangelicalism as long as one modified the techniques of presentation—adapting the proletarian cult of the brass band to revivalist purposes, for instance.

The revivalists missed what most Victorian observers missed (Charles Booth being perhaps the most obvious exception), and what modern writers like Professor K. S. Inglis (in *Churches and the Working Classes in Victorian England*, 1964), have also missed, that the working-man who rejected the revivalist system, according to which he was a sinner under the wrath of God, and in need of forgiveness which could be obtained only through penitence and faith in the death of Jesus Christ, nevertheless often lived in terms of a simpler religious system of his own. He accepted, for example, the idea that certain 'rituals' were needed for the 'blessing' of life, or perhaps for the prevention of disaster. The idea had seemed natural in a rural community, and, even in the new urban industrialized society, the worker might still prefer to have his daughters married in church and their babies baptized; but he did not suppose that one had either to belong to a 'Church', or to believe in particular Christian dogma, to justify such actions. Still less did he think that one needed to attend revivalist preaching, stay behind for the meeting in the inquiry-room, accuse oneself of sin, and become 'converted'. Apart from rituals intended to mark the chief events of life, what he valued most in 'religion' was its capacity (or otherwise) to give meaning and order to existence; the revivalists, however, showed no skill in the use of what may be called the 'explanatory' side of religion, but often, as in Moody's case, made the chaos of life seem more chaotic, more ruthless, more irrational. Both the Anglo-Catholic and the American revivalists guessed that new 'rituals' might attract some of the working-classes; but they had both to invent them and to convince people of their value. The Harvest Festival for urban chapels was one instance of this kind; the American mass meeting, with special music and the invariably answered appeal, was another. But although these new rituals might have a basis in theology or antiquarianism or businesslike pragmatism, they lacked the life which only a more spontaneous social generation could have given them. Ritual, to be successful, must develop spontaneously. Industry depends upon machinery which by its very nature needs no supernatural assistance; ritual was likely to atrophy in the nineteenth-century town, not because of some 'anti-religious' ethos in the place, but because ritual can only flourish where it serves an accepted social purpose.

The working-man, moreover, took little interest in a theological tradition, which not only told him that he could not do the good that he might want to do, but also said that only faith (together with, on occasion, the Sacraments) could save him from the consequence of this inability. He doubted the existence of any link between Christian profession and ethical behaviour, and it was the morality that he cared about. Thus Thomas Powell, a working-class witness before the Royal Commission on Elementary Education in 1887, said that 'there are a great many things which are presumed to be belonging to religion which are altogether unnecessary to religion; there are a great many dogmas welded in'. Thomas Smyth, a plasterer from Chelsea, told the same Commission that he favoured the new Board Schools because 'there is not any particular form of dogma taught'; he thought that the teachers should be able to 'inculcate the morality without the aid of religious teaching at all', where 'religious teaching' meant the use of ecclesiastical authority and dogma. This was representative opinion in working-class urban circles by the late 1880s: non-religious moral instruction became the ideal of many labour leaders, and if one adds the demand for ecclesiastical rituals like baptism and marriage, which many working-class people still valued as passage-rites without attaching much in the way of dogmatic or ethical importance to them, one has the essence of a working-class religious system which had almost entirely parted company with official Christianity. Neither Moody nor Booth could make, or be expected to have made, much impression on people who did not seriously consider themselves to be without any 'religion'; who simply rejected the notion that in order to be 'religious' one had to be 'born again'; and whose conception of 'morality' gave the revivalists no scope because it was aristocratic, not bourgeois-evangelical; the trade union programme, for instance, was based on ideas of 'natural law' and 'natural justice', not on the concept of Sin.

The working-class attitude to religious institutions was ambiguous, in as much as working-class people took advantage of the existing Churches to provide themselves with rituals for events like birth, death and marriage, but frankly refused to support the Churches at other times. They might well have enjoyed a religious system in which the priest was a superior kind of witch-doctor, but, when a superior kind of religious system told them that the priest was not a witch-doctor, they rejected both priest and witch-doctor together. Victorian working-men formed new political institutions, the trade union, for example, but showed little enthusiasm for new religious institutions—neither the Salvation Army nor the Labour Church movement prospered after an initial period. Neither Anglo-Catholic nor Evangelical Revivalism had any profound understanding of the political outlook of the proletariat; in the same way, the Christian Socialism of the 1880s, exemplified in Westcott's Christian Social Union, although it had advanced to the extent of granting the men's right to form trade unions, did so with the proviso that well-run unions never came out on strike. A revivalism which could find so little meaning in the institutions which the working-class itself produced, was unlikely to recommend traditional religious institutions. Moody must have found this even more difficult, for he only believed in the institutions which he himself set up, the Northfield Conferences in Massachusetts and the Chicago Moody Bible Institute of his later life; but these were American projects which hardly affected the English scene at all.

In England, therefore, revivalism failed to alter either the religion or the politics of the poor; religion might have been the opium of the poor, but they were not addicted to it.

Revivalism had more effect within the borders of the Christian sub-culture, where it fastened on the gap which had been widening in England since the eighteenth century between the professional priesthood and that section of the evangelical laity which devoted its emotional and intellectual life to religious activity but did not want to accept clerical leadership without question. Throughout the nineteenth century, the revivalists appealed to these people for support. Americans like Finney and Caughey never hesitated to attack the ordained ministry, to which they themselves belonged in theory, as second-rate; Weaver flaunted his lack of ordination as a guarantee of superior power; Moody presented himself as an ordinary man who simply happened to be able to do the work of converting people better than the priesthood. Women evangelists like Phoebe Palmer and Mrs General Booth inevitably challenged the masculine monopoly of both the pulpit and the priesthood.

In England the clue to the situation lay in the history of the denominations. In Anglicanism, for instance, the Evangelical clergy, frightened by the expansion of the Methodist bodies, viewed with suspicion even as late as 1859–60 any Anglican layman who wanted to preach, unless he was prepared to take the humble role of the Scripture Reader, whose rules allowed him to explain the Biblical passages he read but certainly not to preach on them, and whose social status was inferior to that of the meanest curate. In nineteenth-century Methodism a sharp struggle for power between the Wesleyan ministers and their laity ended in the withdrawal of a large section from the original body, and the formation, between 1797 and 1857, of a group of sects in which the power of the ordained ministry was severely restricted. As a result, Wesleyan Methodism, the parent group, took little interest in the professional revivalists, who were warmly welcomed on the other hand by the predominantly anti-clerical Methodist Free Church. There, as in many local Baptist and Congregational churches, the pastor himself adopted an anti-ministerialist style which he himself would often have called 'anti-sacerdotal'. Ministers of this type dropped the title 'reverend' and wore no distinctive ministerial dress. Even in the Church of England the growing strength of the Anglo-Catholic party sometimes led the

Evangelicals to adopt what were virtually anti-ministerial positions. This enabled the revivalist to pick up allies from the ministry as well as from the laity. As the power and separate style of the traditional ordained ministry declined, however, as it did even in Anglo-Catholic parishes, later nineteenth-century revivalists were freed to move to a central stance. The move was natural because the revivalist found the laity more useful than the clergy. Indeed, if the specifically Christian mythology was handed on in Britain between 1870 and 1914, it was not the routine clergy who were chiefly responsible; the new Board Schools were the places where, once again, and however feebly, the basic Christian stories were taught to working-class children.

This brings us to the final aspect of nineteenth-century revivalism on which we have to comment, its attempt to generate experiences which would be accepted as 'religious' by popular Protestantism, or by Anglo-Catholicism. The latter was a special case, for the parish mission of the 1860–80 period, true to its French Roman Catholic model, aimed at persuading people to return to the life of the institutional Church, to renew their baptismal vows in a special service at the climax of the mission, to go to confession (this was the most disputed innovation as far as other Anglicans were concerned), and to become regular communicants. 'Religious experience', that is, was identified less with the revivalism of the mission itself than with the sacramental life of the parish to which they theoretically pointed. If this sort of revivalism failed, it was because there was no great demand in Anglican parishes for a 'Catholic' type of religious behaviour. Traditionally, of course, if one wanted to behave 'religiously' in this style one left the Church of England for the Church of Rome, and the movement in that direction of so many of the first Tractarians, men like Faber, Manning, Newman and Ward, only confirmed the tradition. The sudden shift of so many able men in a single generation (a process which did not continue) surprised people, but did not change the fundamental relation between the two denominations. It was not likely, therefore, that Anglo-Catholic revivalist mission shock tactics would stimulate more than a minority, and in the history of Victorian religious moods these missions were strictly subordinate to the Anglo-Catholic campaign for a eucharistic revival. By 1900 it was evident that the rise of the Anglo-Catholic movement had modified but not radically altered the balance of power in the Church of England. The mission-system, that is, was no more successful in transforming the Established Church in England than it was in rechristianizing rural France.

On the Protestant side of the revivalist tradition, one has to remember that often the emotions felt in revivalist meetings only created or reinforced states of mind—teetotalism, for instance, and masculine attitudes to parenthood, as well as general nostalgia for an idealized 'domestic' past—which had no necessary 'religious' status, though they were often associated with religion in the Victorian age. Directly and indirectly, fatherhood stood for power and motherhood for vulnerability in Moody's vocabulary; unmarried mothers, of course, stood only for masculine wickedness, they had little or no symbolical or other reality in themselves. Teetotalism was used to define the group, to which 'drinkers' simply did not belong. Moody's certainty about social roles must have attracted some people; others came because they felt a strong need to impose definitions of these roles on others.

Whether there was a specifically 'religious' experience involved in revivalism was at the heart of the contemporary discussion about the inquiry-room method. Moody claimed that individuals passed through the classical Protestant sequence of conviction of sin, repentance, and assurance of divine forgiveness on these occasions, but those who criticized the mass revival system often did so on the ground that one should not systematize the sequence and compress it into a single evening, that to do so was to minimize the ethical and theological content of the event in order to highlight a petty drama of the will. Such critics did not say that it was impossible for a man to change, or find that he had changed, his whole life-style in a single act of choice; such transformations were familiar in a secular context; but they doubted that one could organize and multiply such effects in a predictable fashion night after night in the Islington Agricultural Hall. And so if revivalism seemed to work, if night after night the revivalist's appeal for people to 'come forward' succeeded, there must be a simpler, non-Augustinian explanation; perhaps an explanation that was not 'religious' at all.

In this sense, the apparent triumph of the method, the climactic moment when the appeal was made, when a brief pause ensued, and when a flood of response started, was also its moment of weakness. It was for the sake of this experience that people returned to the meetings night after night; not in order to be 'saved' themselves, but for the sake of the moment of tension and deliverance in which it seemed incredible that any one should respond, and then incredible that so many should have responded. There were those who went in order to provide that response, and those who went in order to see the response provided. This was what everything led up to, the celebration of a sub-culture. There is no surviving detailed description of Moody on the appeal, and one may therefore take as an example an appeal made by Billy Graham in Manchester in 1961. The source of the account is in notes taken by the present writer; the meeting took place on 3 June, 1961; the official attendance at Maine Road was 38,500; the number of enquirers was given later as about 1,800.

> What do I have to do, Billy? Repent. I am willing to give up my sins, that's repentance. Receive Christ. . . . Why come forward? If you don't confess *me* before men. . . . Why do you want to be so quiet and personal? I want you to come. Get up, hundreds, maybe thousands. There may never be another night like this for you—Monday night may be too late. . . . Come right now— every head bowed—I want there to be prayer. Then I'm going to ask you to come. Get up out of your seats.

Here Graham repeated directions about how to descend from the stands of the Manchester City Football Ground and reach the playing-area on to which enquirers filed to stand before Graham, who was elevated well above them on a platform.

> Christ came all the way from Heaven, you can come a few steps. You come, we're going to wait for you. Get up right now, quickly. Whole families ought to come, get up and come right now.

At this stage there was a pause, to allow the first group of enquirers to sort themselves out. Then came the second appeal.

'The little child sitting by you asking you to come; you'd better come right now. Come to the rails if the red carpet is full.'

At this point Graham paused again and the massed choir which was ranged behind him sang 'Just as I am without one plea, Save that thy blood was shed for me'. Then the third appeal began.

> There will never be another chance like this . . . the battle in the heart of the man in the stands. . . . I think we ought to wait another moment for you. . . . Pray for the struggler in the stands. . . . You get up and come, we'll wait a few seconds more.

In fact, there was more singing and a fourth appeal, similar in content to the others, before the closure, which came without drama; the drama had already taken place.

Graham did not then come down and join the throng of inquirers, but left the task of advising them to his 'counsellors', the exact equivalent of the people who had done a similar job in Moody's inquiry-rooms. Once the final wave had broken and washed to the feet of the waiting revivalist, the ritual was over. *Missa est*. The professional revivalist had always made it clear that nothing which the ritual left behind should be allowed to call in question its declared success; Moody had prevented the issuing of official statistics about 'converts'. The ritual was a divine self-testimony which could not be assessed by isolating some of the people in the crowd and analysing their descriptions of their experience of what had happened. The individual was always available and so was his story of his experience. The specific 'religious' content of the mass revival meeting lay at the climax of the appeal, when the assembly divided into those who testified and those who testified to the testimony.

It was a strange conclusion. American revivalism began as a method of obtaining (at least in appearance) the external signs of conviction, repentance and rebirth which would justify the admission of the children of church-members into church-membership; and it was still true in the 1960s that a high percentage of the enquirers in the Graham meetings came from children and adolescents. Nevertheless, by the 1960s, what was being demanded of the audience, at any rate as far as England was concerned, was a much more Durkheimian kind of act, in which a self-consciously religious sub-culture came together and sought to generate from its own solidarity a sense of the transcendent. As so often in the history of the Protestantism which Kierkegaard knew so well, a religion of fear and trembling had transformed itself into a religion of consolation and reassurance.

Index